MERGERS, ACQUISITIONS,

AND OTHER CHANGES OF CORPORATE CONTROL

SECOND EDITION

ESSENTIALS OF
CANADIAN LAW

MERGERS, AQUISITIONS,

AND OTHER CHANGES OF CORPORATE CONTROL

SECOND EDITION

CHRISTOPHER C. NICHOLLS

Faculty of Law, University of Western Ontario

IRWIN
LAW

Published in 2012 by

Irwin Law Inc.
14 Duncan Street
Suite 206
Toronto, ON
M5H 3G8

www.irwinlaw.com

ISBN: 978-1-55221-237-0
e-book ISBN: 978-1-55221-238-7

Library and Archives Canada Cataloguing in Publication

Nicholls, Christopher C.

    Mergers, acquisitions, and other changes of corporate control / Christopher C.
Nicholls.—2nd ed.

(Essentials of Canadian law)
Includes bibliographical references and index.
Issued also in electronic format.
ISBN 978-1-55221-237-0

    1. Consolidation and merger of corporations—Law and legislation—Canada.
I. Title. II. Series: Essentials of Canadian law

KE1462.N52 2012   346.71'06626   C2012-900586-X
KF1477.N52 2012

The publisher acknowledges the financial support of the Government of Canada
through the Canada Book Fund for its publishing activities.

We acknowledge the assistance of the OMDC Book Fund, an initiative of
Ontario Media Development Corporation.

Printed and bound in Canada.

1 2 3 4 5 16 15 14 13 12

SUMMARY
TABLE OF CONTENTS

DETAILED TABLE OF CONTENTS

PREFACE TO THE SECOND EDITION

The bearded fellow at the front of the classroom that morning had been invited by our professor to deliver a guest lecture. (Inviting a "guest lecturer," as I would discover years later, is perhaps the most artful form of shirking known to the university teacher.)

When this gentleman wasn't waiting tables at the local Mother Tucker's, he apparently directed stage plays for a living. He was a fount of practical wisdom. "The purpose of the first rehearsal," I heard him declaim above the chorus of yawns, "is simply to get the company to the second rehearsal."

The meaning of this curious comment was quite lost on me in that lecture hall several decades ago. But I now understand the sentiment perfectly. And so I have come to believe that the purpose of a first edition of a law book is chiefly to get one to the second edition.

I have often read prefaces to second editions of legal texts in which the authors have haughtily explained that their "thinking has evolved" since the first edition. This incomparable expression appears to mean no more than this: that the author has spotted all the howling errors he made the first time around. It is easier on the ego, of course, to insist that one has climbed to a higher intellectual plateau than to admit that one has turned up a pile of embarrassing mistakes. Admitting mistakes seems to suggest that one is not infallible, which is bad, or that one is prone to change one's mind, which is worse. Openly changing one's mind, observation suggests, is altogether to be avoided if one is running for public office or writing a second edition. For my part, however, I am attracted to the famous rejoinder ascribed to John Maynard Keynes. Accused that he had reversed himself on some point, Keynes is said to have responded, "When the facts change, I change my mind. What do you do, sir?"[1]

I believe this second edition to be an improvement over the first, but I am quick to concede that it is not infallible. This is not of the slightest concern to me. Like most lawyers, I don't believe in infallibility. I believe in courts of appeal.

The first edition of this book was published five years ago. And as Winston Churchill once observed, "five years is a lot."[2]

Back then, in the early months of 2007, M & A markets were still buoyant. Concerns about the U.S. subprime mortgage market had certainly begun to surface,[3] but the magnitude of the financial debacle that was about to grip the world still seemed beyond the contemplation of most investors and commentators. The ill-fated Lehman Brothers firm, for example, was still enjoying considerable success. Its status as a mergers and acquisitions adviser had been on a two-year rise,[4] and, although it was known to be exposed to the subprime mortgage sector, it still appeared to be performing well financially. A 15 March 2007 story in the New York Times, for example, quoted a senior Lehman executive's assurances "that Lehman's subprime business accounted for 3 percent of total revenue, and that the company's positions were 'well protected' against subprime trouble through hedges."[5]

Since then, we have suffered through the "credit crunch," which became the "financial crisis," and then the "economic crisis," and the Great Recession. In many ways we are now living in a very different, darker financial world than we were half a decade ago.

But this book is not about the international financial crisis. It is about the legal world of mergers and acquisitions. That world has also

---

1   That Keynes was prone to reverse his views was a frequent criticism levelled against him by his intellectual opponents. However, this famous quotation is, alas, almost surely apocryphal. Nicholas Wapshott, for example, reports that there is no "evidence that Keynes made this remark." See Nicholas Wapshott, *Keynes Hayek: The Clash that Defined Modern Economics* (New York: W.W. Norton & Co., 2011) at 312, n8.

2   Winston S. Churchill, *A History of the English Speaking Peoples, Vol 1: The Birth of Britain* (New York: Bantam, 1956) at 34.

3   See, for example, Gretchen Morgenson, "Crisis Looms in Market for Mortgages" *New York Times* (11 March 2007) A1.

4   A significant part of Lehman's success had been attributed to George Young, whose resignation from Lehman Brothers was reported in February 2007. See, for example, Andrew Ross Sorkin, "Top-Producing Banker Resigns Abruptly at Lehman Brothers" *New York Times* (12 February 2007).

5   Associated Press, "Trading Activity and Expansion Abroad Drive Profit Up 5.6% at Lehman" *New York Times* (15 March 2007).

changed a great deal in the past five years. The liquidity "tap" mentioned in the Preface to the First Edition was turned off and tightened. The financial landscape changed, and the legal and regulatory landscape has also developed. This second edition discusses the implications of a host of M & A legal and regulatory changes since 2007, including Multilateral Instrument 62-104 and the parallel Ontario securities law developments, groundbreaking court decisions including the Supreme Court of Canada's judgment in *BCE Inc. v. 1976 Debentureholders*, the British Columbia Court of Appeal's decision in *Icahn Partners LP v. Lions Gate Entertainment* and major Delaware opinions such as *Air Products and Chemicals, Inc. v. Airgas, Inc.* and *Lyondell Chemical Company v. Ryan*, as well as many securities commission decisions including *Re Neo Materials Technologies, Baffinland Iron Mines Corp., Canadian Hydro Developers, Re Pulse Data Inc., Re VenGrowth Funds,* and *Re Patheon Inc.*

Finally, emulating the verbal economy of the short form prospectus system, I hereby incorporate by reference all of the thanks and acknowledgements set out in the preface to the first edition. I would like to add thanks to Alisa Posesorski at Irwin Law for her excellent work on the manuscript. And I must also reiterate special thanks to my wife, Andrea, who has helped me in many more ways than words can express, and our children Rob, Diana, and Tori—three remarkable people whose wisdom and good humour is a constant inspiration.

C.C.N.
London, Ontario
January, 2012

PREFACE TO
THE FIRST EDITION

In January 2007, participants at the World Economic Forum in Davos, Switzerland met for a session entitled, "The M & A Landscape: Developing the 2007 Heatmap."[1] The notice for the session trotted out one of the dazzling M & A numbers of the past year: the volume of worldwide acquisitions in 2006 had reached a record-breaking $3.8 trillion. The Davos cognoscenti reportedly predicted continued high deal levels for 2007, with especially lively activity expected in the American media and entertainment industry, and in the financial services and energy sectors in many other parts of the world.[2]

It is the best of times for M & A lawyers and deal makers. Even the image of M & A protagonists is a little glossier today than it was during an earlier merger wave in the 1980s. As it has frequently been observed, yesterday's corporate raiders have become today's shareholder activists.

Seasoned Wall Street and Bay Street veterans know, of course, that all good things must eventually come to an end. Economics demands it, and history proves it. In 2001, a previous merger wave that lifted everyone's boats (and helped pay for a number of new ones) rapidly, and rather painfully, receded. The wreck of Enron and the spate of corporate scandals that followed ruined careers, destroyed fortunes and, for a time, even diverted the attention of the leader of the free world from an otherwise unrelenting "war on terror" precipitated by the horrific events of September 11. Business was bad, and many lawyers and

---

1   See www.weforum.org/en/events/AnnualMeeting2007/Programme/index. htm?id=18904.
2   Andrew Ross Sorkin, ed. "Forecast From Davos: More Media Deals Ahead" *New York Times* (19 February 2007) online at dealbook.blogs.nytimes. com/2007/02/06.

investment bankers could be spotted nervously polishing up their re-
sumes—an exercise, it may be said, for which they had a considerable
amount of free time available.

But all is right with the M & A world again; for now at any rate.
Perhaps when the history of today's merger mania comes to be written, it will bear the title, "It's about the liquidity, stupid." In one way or
another, the loose easy cash that has been sloshing around the world's
markets could hardly fail to make waves—in this case M & A waves.
We can therefore only hope that the tap will not be turned off until
everyone has had a chance to drink.

The mergers and acquisitions book market has, not surprisingly,
followed the upswing in M & A deal flow. A quick keyword check of
"Mergers Acquisitions" at my local book store, for instance, revealed 179
titles—many published within the last year or two.

But the particular impetus for this book occurred before the current bandwagon had reached cruising speed. While on sabbatical leave
at the University of Cambridge's Centre for Corporate and Commercial
Law in 2003–4, I was approached by Mr. Tshepo Mongalo on behalf of
the South African Department of Trade and Industry (DTI). DTI was
pursuing a company law reform project and was interested in having
corporate law experts from several jurisdictions prepare short papers
on various aspects of corporate law as part of a legislative benchmark-
ing exercise. I was pleased to contribute by writing a short piece on
Canadian mergers and acquisitions law.

Drafting that little paper led me to wonder if Canadian lawyers and
law students might not find some value in a more extended discussion
of some M & A legal issues, a discussion which would include not only
an overview of the subject that one hopes would be of interest to new-
comers, but would also raise a few of the scholarly debates on the topic
within a Canadian context.

Later that same academic year, I was invited to attend a special
roundtable on private equity deal-making organized by Edward Rock
and Michael Wachter of the University of Pennsylvania's Institute for
Law and Economics. The roundtable proved to be an informative and
thought-provoking event held in the elegant surroundings of Claridge's
Hotel in London. It was impossible to attend that session and not realize how important private equity had become, and how clear it was
that private equity would surely emerge as a major force in the M & A
market in the coming years. And so, as the M & A market began to heat
up, I became even more convinced that it might be worth setting aside
some time to write a lengthier treatment on the subject than the modest essay I had originally contributed to the South African DTI.

It also occurred to me that M & A was no longer a subject strictly of interest to bankers and lawyers. The implications of mergers in the global context, particularly the prospect of foreign takeovers of domestic firms, had caught the attention of many ordinary Canadians outside of financial and legal circles. Much has been said, written, and prophesied about the feared "hollowing out" of corporate Canada. Two recent studies have tried to ease Canadians' fears on the matter, suggesting that the supposed threat to Canada represented by the wave of international industrial consolidation has been exaggerated (one of those studies is mentioned in a brief note in chapter 2). But many remain unconvinced. On the very day that I write this, a column has appeared in the *Globe and Mail* challenging the sanguine conclusion of those very studies.[3]

So much for the genesis. Now, a revelation; or at least a warning. This book is a little idiosyncratic I'm afraid, not only in its content but even in its orthography. For example, as Canadian lawyers know, most Canadian securities statutes spell the word "take-over" with a hyphen. I have tended to avoid using the hyphen except when the statutory provisions themselves are being directly quoted. George Bernard Shaw famously eschewed use of the apostrophe in his work, an eccentricity that his outstanding contribution to English literature had surely earned him. Alas, I can point to no similar achievements (literary or otherwise) upon which I may presume to claim a similar licence to prefer my spelling of a word over that of our legislators; and so, unable to assert a right, I merely beg an indulgence.

It may seem presumptuous to members of the practising bar that a book on such a practical topic has been written by someone who has not been actively engaged in the private practice of law for a number of years. I can only plead that my heart and at least one of my feet have never really abandoned the financial district. It is fashionable for academics to describe their research interests as lying "at the intersection" of two or more related disciplines. I am fond of saying that my research interests lie at the intersection of King and Bay Streets. But one's interest in a legal subject and one's time to write about it do not always coincide when one is engaged in full time practice.

I owe a number of people my thanks. First, I must mention Jeff Miller at Irwin Law whom I have enjoyed working with on this, and on an earlier book that I wrote with Jeff MacIntosh on securities law.

---

3   Eric Reguly, "Pay No Attention to the Rosy Hype—Our Companies are Disappearing" *Globe and Mail* (2 March 2007) B2.

A good part of this book was sketched out at Osgoode Hall Law School in the fall of 2005. Dean Patrick Monahan had kindly invited me to visit Osgoode Hall that fall as the Falconbridge Visiting Professor in Commercial Law. I was surprised and greatly honoured by the invitation, and thoroughly enjoyed my all-too-short time there, teaching, writing, and getting to know students and faculty. I am very grateful to Dean Monahan, and to all the people at Osgoode who made my visit there so enjoyable, including, among so many others, Peer Zumbansen, Neil Brooks, Tom Johnson, Poonam Puri, and Mary Condon (I should mention that I was sorry to have missed seeing my friend Ben Geva who was himself visiting at another institution during that term).

When I began this book, I was a member of the Dalhousie Law School faculty. I enjoyed the distinct privilege of teaching at that wonderful institution for nine years and was especially honoured to have been the first holder of the Purdy Crawford Chair in Business Law. I am very grateful to Purdy Crawford, not only for the outstanding contribution he has made to Canadian business and legal education, but also for all the help and support he provided to me during my time at Dalhousie. I also want to thank all of my former colleagues there, especially Dawn Russell, who served as Dean during most of my years in Halifax, Phillip Saunders, the current Dean, and all of the outstanding people who made Dalhousie such an intellectually stimulating and personally rewarding place to work, including: Mike Deturbide, Archie Kaiser, Teresa Scassa, Mohamed Khimji, and so very many others. In 2006, I was coaxed by Western Dean Ian Holloway to return to Ontario to join the Faculty of Law at the University of Western Ontario, a faculty that, uniquely among all Canadian law schools, has chosen to make its focus "business law in the global environment." I was intrigued and eager to participate in Western's "business law school" mission; but it was still a very difficult decision, indeed, to say farewell to Nova Scotia and to Dalhousie.

Of course, as always, I must reserve my deepest thanks for my family: my wife, Andrea, and my children, Rob, Diana, and Tori. They tolerate a great deal when I am working on extended projects like this one. But no matter how long I may spend in the library or at the computer terminal, they should never entertain the slightest doubt that they are first in my heart, and first in my thoughts.

C.C.N.
London, Ontario
March, 2007

LIST OF STATUTES, REGULATIONS, SECURITIES INSTRUMENTS, RULES, POLICIES, AND ABBREVIATIONS

Statutes (Federal and Provincial)

Air Canada Public Participation Act, R.S.C. 1985, c. 35 (4th Supp.)

An Act for the Prevention and Suppression of Combinations Formed in Restraint of Trade (U.K.), 1889, 52 Vic., c. 41

Bill 176, *An Act to Amend the Securities Act* (Ontario), 2nd Sess., 32nd Parliament, Ontario, 1982

Bulk Sales Act (Newfoundland and Labrador), R.S.N.L. 1990, c. B-11

Bulk Sales Act (Ontario), R.S.O. 1990, c. B.14

Business Corporations Act (Alberta), R.S.A. 2000, c. B-9 [ABCA]

Business Corporations Act (British Columbia), S.B.C. 2002, c. 57 [BCBCA]

Business Corporations Act (New Brunswick), S.N.B. 1981, c. B-9.1 [NBBCA]

Business Corporations Act (Northwest Territories), S.N.W.T. 1996, c 19 [NWBCA]

Business Corporations Act (Nunavut), S.N.W.T. (Nu) 1996, c. 19 [NuBCA]

Business Corporations Act (Ontario), R.S.O. 1970, c. 53

Business Corporations Act (Ontario), R.S.O. 1990, c. B.16 [OBCA]

Business Corporations Act (Quebec), R.S.Q. c. S-31.1

Business Corporations Act (Saskatchewan), R.S.S. 1978, c B-10 [SBCA]

Business Corporations Act (Yukon), R.S.Y. 2002, c. 20 [YBCA]

Canada Business Corporations Act, R.S.C. 1985, c. C-44 [CBCA]

Canada Business Corporations Act, S.C. 1974–75–76, c. 33

Regulations (Federal and Provincial)

Canada Business Corporations Regulations, 2001, S.O.R./2001-512
General Regulation made under the Securities Act (Ontario), R.R.O. 1990, Reg.
   1015
Investment Canada Regulations, S.O.R./85-611
Notifiable Transactions Regulations, S.O.R./87-348

Statutes (United States)

Clayton Act, 15 U.S.C. § 12
Defense Production Act of 1950, 50 U.S.C. App. 2061
General Corporation Law (Delaware), Delaware Code, Title 8, Chapter 1
Hart-Scott-Rodino Antitrust Improvements Act of 1976, 15 U.S.C. § 18a
New Jersey Business Corporation Act, New Jersey Statutes, Title 14A
Sarbanes-Oxley Act of 2002, PL 107-204, 116 Stat 745 (2002)
Securities Exchange Act of 1934, 15 U.S.C. § 78a

Securities Instruments, Rules, Policies, and Notices

CSA Staff Notice 62-304 (2005), 28 OSCB 7305
CSA Staff Notice 62-305 (2009), 32 OSCB 10449
Multilateral Instrument 61-101 (2008), 31 OSCB 1321 [MI 61-101]
Multilateral Instrument 62-104, BC Reg 21/2008 as am [MI 62-104]
National Instrument 44-101 (2005), 28 OSCB 10385, as am
National Instrument 44-102 (2000), 23 OSCB (Supp) 565, as am
National Instrument 44-103 (2000), 23 OSCB (Supp) 1013, as am
National Instrument 45-106 (2009) 32 OSCB (Supp-5) 1, as am
National Instrument 62-103 (2000), 23 OSCB 1372, as am
National Policy 62-202 (1997), 20 OSCB 3525 [NP 62-202]
National Policy 62-203 (2008), 31 OSCB 1319 [NP 62-203]
OSC Policy 3-37, [1977] OSCB 253
OSC Policy 9.1 (1982), 4 OSCB 538e
OSC Rule 61-501 (2008), 31 OSCB 1321
OSC Rule 61-801 (2008), 31 OSCB 1365
OSC Rule 62-501 (2002), 25 OSCB 5356
OSC Rule 62-504 (2007), 30 OSCB Supp-6 at 1
OSC Staff Notice 54-701 (2011), 34 OSCB 404
OSC Staff Notice 62-702 (2001), 24 OSCB 2405
Proposed Companion Policy 62-104CP (2006), 29 OSCB 3587 [Proposed 62-
   104CP]
Proposed Multilateral Instrument 61-101 (2006), 29 OSCB 6813 [Proposed
   MI 61-101]
Proposed National Instrument 62-104 (2006), 29 OSCB 3546 [Proposed NI
   62-104]

CHAPTER 1

OVERVIEW

A. INTRODUCTION

There is no *Mergers and Acquisitions Act* to be found in the Revised Statutes of Canada or in any provincial or territorial statute books either. "M & A" is not a discrete branch of law at all. Rather, M & A law refers to a loosely related collection of legal principles and rules—drawn mainly from corporate law and securities regulation, as well as from tax, anti-trust, and a handful of other areas. This pastiche of rules and principles touches upon various legal aspects of the process by which companies combine, or by which businesses (or the shares of corporations that own business assets) are bought and sold. These rules prescribe and protect the rights and interests of people who are affected by these important transactions. It is that eclectic collection of laws, policies, and principles that is the subject matter of this book.

B. GROWTH OF THE FIRM

Like children and garden weeds, corporations are inclined to grow. Unlike children and garden weeds, business firms are propelled to grow not by forces of nature but by forces of worldly ambition. Businesses strive to "grow" their profits, to "grow" their revenues, and to "grow" their market share. All this growing, corporate managers hope, will "grow" the value of their firm's shares too. Some businesspeople claim that continuous growth is essential. Running a business, apparently, is like riding a bicycle: if you don't keep moving forward, you will collapse. The need for perpetual expansion is thought to be, at least in the eyes of these metaphorical cyclists, a dramatic "Grow or die" proposition.

There are plenty of sound reasons for promoting corporate growth. Larger businesses often enjoy advantages over their smaller rivals. Larger firms can achieve economies of scale: the fixed costs needed to produce a single widget may be no greater than the fixed costs needed to make a thousand of them. Larger firms can also achieve economies of scope: it may be cheaper to market widgets alongside a complementary product—gadgets, for example. And larger firms have more resources to invest in expensive things, such as state-of-the-art technology as well as research and development. Investments of this sort help large firms to innovate, continuously improve, and therefore keep pace with their ablest competitors.

Greater resources (in other words, more money) also allow larger firms to invest more in "branding." (Branding was once a way of marking herds of docile sheep as your own. It appears to perform an analogous function for today's business corporations.) Branding is evidently an exercise of increasing importance. Any branding consultant will tell you so. Ours is a noisy world crowded with aggressive marketers touting competitors' products and services, a world where one must struggle to ensure that one's story is heard, understood, and, with a bit of luck, at least partly believed.

Larger firms may find it easier, too, to attract and retain top-notch employees. Recent events notwithstanding, larger businesses are regarded as more stable and often more prestigious than smaller enterprises. They are typically able to pay higher wages than smaller firms in the same industry precisely because greater investment in capital leads to higher levels of per-employee productivity. And bigger firms may offer more attractive equity-based compensation packages (shares and share options) because shares of large public corporations enjoy more liquid trading markets. Larger firms also have greater bargaining leverage with their suppliers; they are often able to negotiate greater price concessions than their smaller competitors, making it possible for them to pass on lower prices to consumers. U.S. retail giant Wal-Mart, for example, has frequently been credited with using its negotiating strength to obtain favourable terms of this kind.

C. ORGANIC (INTERNAL) GROWTH AND GROWTH BY ACQUISITION OR MERGER

There are two ways for businesses to expand. They can grow "organically" or they can grow through acquisition or merger. A large firm will enjoy the benefits that come from being large whether it has grown "organically" or has, instead, merged with or acquired the business of another firm to achieve size. So, although the advantages enjoyed by large firms are a critical *component* of mergers and acquisitions, identifying these advantages does not, without more, account for the prevalence of mergers and acquisitions. It is no secret *why* businesses may want to grow. The trick is to understand why they choose to grow in one way rather than another.

1) Organic or Internal Growth

Organic or internal growth refers to the gradual process of expanding the business's own resources step by step. A retail business would be said to grow organically, for example, if it chose to build one or more new stores, or enlarged its existing locations to increase same-store sales. Organic growth can sometimes be slow. Perhaps too slow in industries where there is fierce competition.

2) Growth by Acquisition (or Merger)

Growth by acquisition or by merger is much faster than organic growth. A retail business that takes over existing store locations previously operated by other companies, for example, can enter new markets much more quickly than its organically growing competitors. Organic growth may also run into hurdles as businesses tiptoe across national or even regional borders, or venture into new lines of products or services. It is often much more efficient to buy proven expertise and experience than to try to generate your own, especially if smaller rivals are finding themselves constrained by their lack of scale and resources. As the business press sometimes puts it, a cagey acquisition can provide "turnkey" access into a new market.[1] Specific market conditions

---

1   The term *turnkey* is taken from the commercial property context: a business or office building is said to be subject to a turnkey arrangement if everything is ready for the buyer (or lessor) to walk in and immediately begin operating, with no other set up required. In such a case, the buyer (or lessor) needs to do nothing more than "turn the key" to begin using the premises.

may also influence firms to pursue acquisitions. In recent years, for example, rising international demand for commodities and raw materials has prompted many firms to acquire other companies that supply needed raw materials "in order to boost output of new materials or block competitors from gaining control of them."[2]

3) Terminology: *Merger* vs. *Acquisition*

The distinction between the terms *merger* and *acquisition* is principally a matter of commercial convention rather than legal precision. Canadian corporate statutes, unlike many of their American counterparts, do not use the term *merger* at all. However, it is generally understood that a merger involves the combination of two or more corporations. In Canada, a combination of this kind usually involves an amalgamation under applicable corporate law. An acquisition involves a purchase by one firm of the business assets or the shares of another firm. The two sorts of structures may be combined in a single transaction. For example, one corporation might first purchase the outstanding shares of a second corporation (an acquisition), then the two corporations might subsequently choose to amalgamate (a merger). Frequently in this book, unless the context requires otherwise, the word *acquisition* will be used to refer to any transaction in which one corporation comes to control all or part of the business of another, regardless of whether the method for achieving that outcome involves a purchase of assets, a purchase of shares, or a legal fusion of the two entities.

D. RATIONALE FOR GROWTH BY ACQUISITION OR MERGER

Business deal makers point to a number of advantages to pursuing mergers or acquisitions. Three of the most frequently cited explanations are: *synergy*, locating a *bargain-priced target*, and *tax efficiencies*. Other merger goals suggested in the past, such as the pursuit of diversification, have largely been discredited.

---

2   See Timothy Aeppel, "A Hot Commodities Market Spurs Buying Spree by Manufacturers" *Wall Street Journal* (14 August 2006) A7.

1) Synergy

In general terms, synergy (or hoped-for synergy) is the basis for most recent corporate acquisitions or mergers—the belief, in other words, that the value of two firms after they have combined will exceed the sum of their values as individual stand-alone firms before the merger. The source of synergistic value may be found in cost reductions or revenue enhancements that are realized when the merging companies integrate their businesses.

There are two principal types of business integration: horizontal integration—the combining of two or more businesses in the same industry; and vertical integration—the combining, for example, of one business that supplies goods or services to another. Whether synergies are realized mainly on the cost or mainly on the revenue side may well depend on whether a merger is undertaken with a view to horizontal or vertical integration. Cost reductions may flow from improved economies of scale achieved in horizontal mergers, or economies of scope in horizontal or vertical mergers. Combining similar administrative functions is one obvious way to reduce overhead costs and may also help two businesses run more efficiently as a single enterprise. Revenue enhancements are particularly associated with combining businesses that boast complementary strengths. One firm with a strong product distribution network, for example, may profitably be combined with a second firm that boasts superior manufacturing facilities, but is hampered by less developed means of selling and distributing products. Firms with a strong presence in one geographical market may profitably be combined with similar firms operating successfully in other markets. Expertise in one field may be levered to create value in a different, related field, and so on. While critics sometimes argue that the promised benefits of synergies are frequently exaggerated in the run-up to a proposed merger, it is clear that synergies can certainly be an important source of value for parties to a carefully researched business merger.

2) Identifying Underpriced Acquisition Targets

If the shares of a target company are trading at a price that does not accurately reflect the value of the company's assets (or, at least, the estimated value of those assets assuming they were under the control of the acquiring company's managers), then purchasing those shares would be a smart business decision for the same reason that snapping up any underpriced asset is prudent. Clearly, those who believe that capital markets are always and everywhere efficient will be wary of the claim that shares of any widely traded company are not reflective of their "true" or intrinsic value (absent any hoped-for synergies should the target firm be combined with an acquiror). Still, markets cannot operate with perfect efficiency as long as there are information gaps and asymmetries. In the real world, then, we might well expect to see prices from time to time deviating from the level at which an omniscient valuator might set them. Further, as discussed in Chapter 7, one of the influential ideas in modern corporate governance theory—the disciplining effect of the "market for corporate control"—suggests that one might well observe underpriced shares in cases where a target company's managers are underperforming.[3]

3) Tax

Tax-motivated mergers essentially involve a diversion of value from the public purse to the firms participating in the merger (or their shareholders), rather than a net increase in societal wealth. It would be unusual in the case of large publicly traded corporations for tax advantages (such as, for example, the ability to use large accumulated tax losses) to be the sole or even the primary driver of a merger transaction. Nevertheless, tax considerations are often important factors in determining the after-tax cost of transactions initially pursued for other reasons (for example, strategic synergistic reasons).

---

3   But some caution is warranted here as well. Legendary investor Warren Buffett famously lampooned corporations with acquisitive aspirations and a willingness to pay generous takeover premiums to acquire target companies, their confidence buoyed by unwavering belief in their own superior management savvy. He wrote: "In the past, I've observed that many acquisition-hungry managers were apparently mesmerized by their childhood reading of the story about the frog-kissing princess. Remembering her success, they pay dearly for the right to kiss corporate toads, expecting wondrous transfigurations. Initially, disappointing results only deepen their desire to round up new toads." Warren E. Buffett, from the 1992 Letter to Shareholders of Berkshire Hathaway Inc. (1 March 1993), online: www.berkshirehathaway.com/letters/1992.html. A frequently quoted earlier, extended version of Mr. Buffett's "frog-kissing" analogy appeared in his 1981 Letter to Shareholders of Berkshire Hathaway Inc. (26 February 1982), online: www.berkshirehathaway.com/letters/1981.html. A more formal exploration of the theory that takeovers may occur because of the overestimation of target companies is Richard Roll's rightly famous 1986 article, "The Hubris Hypothesis of Corporate Takeover" (1986) 59 Journal of Business 197.

4) Diversification/Risk Management

At one time, it was not unheard of for firms to justify proposed mergers on the basis of "diversification." The diversification argument had some intuitive appeal. If a Canadian company manufactures only patio furniture, then its sales will be weak in the winter months and, indeed, may drop in the summer months too if the weather is unseasonably cool or rainy. If that company merges with another firm that manufactures, say, ski equipment, then the sales of ski equipment in the winter will help offset the weaker patio furniture sales in the colder months. In fact, in years where the winter is exceptionally long and severe (and the summer exceptionally short and mild) improved ski equipment sales may help compensate for weaker than expected patio furniture sales.

Although the diversification argument is intuitively appealing, it is fundamentally flawed. Assuming that both the patio furniture company and the ski equipment company have outstanding shares that trade in public markets, investors who believe there are advantages to diversifying may simply purchase for themselves shares in both specialized companies. There is not necessarily a need for diversification to occur *at the firm level*. In fact, there are good reasons to believe that diversification at the firm level will be inefficient. Diversification works precisely because the returns on shares of companies carrying on distinctly different businesses are not positively correlated. Accordingly, the greater the opportunities for diversification, the less likely it is that opportunities for synergies will exist. Put more simply, expertise in managing a ski equipment firm does not necessarily imply much expertise in managing a patio furniture firm. (Each firm, management consultants would remind us, would be departing from its "core competency.") So combining two fundamentally different businesses may result in inefficiencies and dissynergies—the value of the combined businesses may, in fact, be lower than the sum of their individual values before the merger.[4] Accordingly, diversification would be a sensible justification for mergers only if there were some credible reason to believe that diversification at the firm level could somehow be achieved more efficiently than diversification within the portfolio of individual investors.

---

4   The simple example of the patio furniture/ski equipment store ignores, for the sake of illustration, a number of real-world considerations. For example, a patio store will need to maintain a store location throughout the year—whether it is open for business or not. This could lead to burdensome financing costs, and potentially serious cash flow problems that may not be recovered through eventual sales of furniture. Diversification in this instance, then, may be seen as a way to mitigate the risks of financial distress and may, in the real world, make good economic sense.

However, although the specific risk management benefits of diversification as a justification for horizontal mergers have been discredited, there is increasing evidence that risk management goals generally may account for many vertical mergers and, as Garfinkel and Hankins[5] have recently argued, may even have a key role to play in the development of merger waves.[6]

Regrettably, there also are a few less noble reasons for corporate leaders to want their firms to be larger than their rivals. It is no secret, for example, that compensation levels and perquisites for senior executives tend to be more generous in larger firms.

E. MERGERS AND ACQUISITIONS ACTIVITY IN CANADA AND INTERNATIONALLY

1) Increasing M & A Activity

At the time of publication of the first edition of this book, in the spring of 2007, Canadian M & A activity was booming, following several years of softness in the Canadian M & A market. According to a *Globe and Mail* report in October 2006, there had been 1,963 M & A deals in Canada in the third quarter of the year, amounting to $168.8 billion in total value and representing "the hottest takeover market this country has ever seen."[7] In the second quarter of 2007, according to Crosbie and Company Inc. ("Crosbie"), the number of announced M & A deals in Canada was 416, with a total dollar value of well over $100 billion.[8]

While this buying spree was underway, cracks were beginning to form in the U.S. subprime mortgage market that would in the ensuing two years lead to the most serious international financial crisis in the

---

5   Jon A. Garfinkel & Kristine Watson Hankins, "The Role of Risk Management in Mergers and Merger Waves"(2011) 101 Journal of Financial Economics 515.

6   It has long been noted that merger activity appears to come in waves. See, for example, Patrick A. Gaughan, *Mergers, Acquisitions and Corporate Restructurings* (New York: John Wiley & Sons, 1996).

7   Andrew Willis & Boyd Erman, "Foreign M & A Advisers Dominate Canada's Hot Takeover Market" *Globe and Mail* (11 October 2006) B1.

8   Crosbie and Company Inc., *M & A Quarterly Report – Q2/2010*, online: www.crosbieco.com/pdf/ma/MA_Q210.pdf. In an earlier report published in 2007, the M & A data for that quarter appeared to be even higher, with a reported 520 M & A deal announcements having a total dollar value of $202 billion. See Crosbie and Company Inc., *M & A Quarterly Report – Q2/2007* at 1, online: www.crosbieco.com/pdf/ma/MA_Q207.pdf.

post-war period.[9] By the first quarter of 2009, the number of announced deals had fallen to 174, with a total dollar value of less than $50 billion.[10] Although the number of announced deals increased in the ensuing quarters, the total dollar values of announced deals for each quarter remained lower—often materially lower—than $50 billion.[11] There are recent signs, however, that life is returning to the North American M & A market. In late November 2010, it was reported that the level of Canadian M & A activity in the third quarter of 2010 had reached its highest level in three years, with some 268 deals announced, representing total dollar value of $48 billion.[12] The upward trend continued through the fourth quarter. Crosbie reported that some 328 deals were announced in the fourth quarter of 2010, with a total value of some $56 billion.[13] Although deal volumes were lower in the first quarter of 2011, both in terms of number of transactions (228) and dollar value ($38 billion),[14] by the second quarter deal activity appeared to be rising once more with 836 announced transactions with a total value of $57 billion,[15] most of which were strategic acquisitions (66%) rather than private equity deals.[16] In the third quarter, Crosbie reported a total of 251 announced M & A transactions with a total dollar value of $45.5 billion.[17]

These recent figures are significantly lower than the figures reported for the peak year, 2000, when Canadian M & A activity topped U.S. $220 billion, and when global activity was almost U.S. $3.5 trillion. However, there are several reasons to believe that the North American market will continue to be robust in the near future:

• *Low-cost funding:* Interest rates continue to be low, making it relatively easy for firms to borrow money to fund acquisitions.

---

9   The literature on the recent financial crisis is immense. For a Canadian perspective on those unsettling events, see Christopher C. Nicholls, *Financial Institutions: The Regulatory Framework* (Markham, ON: LexisNexis, 2008) c. 12.

10   Crosbie and Company Inc., *M & A Quarterly Report – Q2/2010*, above note 8.

11   *Ibid.*

12   John Shmuel, "Canadian M & A Strongest in Three Years" *Financial Post* (24 November 2010).

13   See Crosbie and Company Inc., *Quarterly M & A Report – Q1/2011*, online: www.crosbieco.com/pdf/ma/MA_Q111.pdf.

14   *Ibid.*

15   See PwC, *Canadian Deals Quarterly*, online: www.pwc.com/en_CA/ca/deals/publications/canadian-quarterly-2011-08-en.pdf.

16   *Ibid.*

17   See Crosbie and Company, Inc., *Quarterly M & A Report - Q3/2011*, online: www.crosbieco.com/pdf/ma/MA_Q311.pdf.

- *Stronger balance sheets:* The significant deleveraging of firms (i.e., reduction of firm debt and issuing of new equity) that followed the financial crisis has left many firms with healthy balance sheets, and with many holding large war chests of cash.
- *Strong Canadian dollar:* The rise in the Canadian dollar, particularly compared with the U.S. dollar, could facilitate an increasing number of cross-border acquisitions by Canadian firms. Indeed, Crosbie notes that, prior to 2009, the value of cross-border deals involving foreign acquirors and Canadian targets generally exceeded the value of cross-border deals involving Canadian buyers; but since 2009 that pattern has reversed.[18]
- *Low market valuations:* Weaknesses in many stock markets worldwide may be seen by prospective acquirors to represent buying opportunities.
- *International pressure:* Continuing international competition among firms has pressured businesses in many sectors worldwide to restructure or to consolidate. The rapid growth of emerging market economies and the expansion of sovereign wealth funds suggest that many Canadian firms could become takeover targets but also that Canadian firms may increasingly look for acquisition opportunities themselves in countries where growth rates and returns may be more attractive than those available domestically.
- *Role in private equity firms and other financial buyers:* The emergence and growth of what are sometimes called "financial buyers"— namely, firms (venture capital or private equity "buyout" firms such as KKR and Blackstone) that are in the business not of producing goods or services, but of acquiring companies—have in recent years made available additional pools of capital for buyout transactions. For these buyers, "enterprise value" is the key issue, rather than considerations of synergies or strategic fit. Private equity firms have also increasingly been able to pool their resources in "consortium" or "club deals" that enable them to acquire target corporations of considerable size. That practice, as discussed below, has led to some complaints and lawsuits by investors[19] and even attracted the attention of the U.S. Department of Justice. The growth in the size of such firms, and the implications of such growth for the M & A market,

---

18   Above note 7.

19   See, for example, David Glovin & Sree Vidya Bhaktavatsalam, "U.S. Buyout Firms Hit With Shareholder Lawsuit" *Globe and Mail* (16 November 2006) B22, reporting that many major U.S. buyout firms had been sued by investors who alleged that the firms conspired to lower prices paid in major corporate buyouts.

has been chronicled in the financial press.[20] Although the role of such financial buyers will surely be eclipsed by strategic buyers in the aftermath of the recent financial crisis, these firms nevertheless remain important players in the M & A market.

- *Canada as a "small country":* As a relatively small country in global terms, it is difficult for the Canadian market to support a large number of competing firms in every industry. Accordingly, it would not be surprising to see consolidation among firms that primarily serve domestic markets and have not historically been subject to significant foreign competition. By the same token, as trade barriers fall internationally, Canadian firms may find themselves subject to competition from (larger) foreign firms that enjoy economies of scale, which enable them to compete more effectively. In turn, Canadian firms that want to expand into foreign markets may find that such expansion is best achieved through merger.

2) Private Equity Firms and Other "Financial Buyers"

It is customary to discuss mergers and acquisitions in terms of one industrial company buying (or merging with) another. It is through acquisitions of this traditional (or strategic) sort that one expects to discover those much-talked-about economies of scale, scope, and perhaps density.[21] But there is another important kind of M & A transaction that involves "financial buyers" such as private equity or venture capital firms. Private equity firms raise funds from investors and use those funds to acquire corporations. They do not intend to run those corporations indefinitely. They plan, instead, to implement some value-enhancing improvements, then profit from a subsequent sale (through a public offering of its shares or otherwise) of the corporation or of its principal assets or divisions. The financial press has reported that private equity firms have also taken fairly aggressive steps to extract cash from acquired businesses even before heading for the exit. The cash payments have come in the form of high dividends (funded by corporate borrowing), as well as management and other professional fees.[22] Extracting cash in this way is an example how those who control public corporations can enjoy "private benefits of control," a topic dis-

---

20   See, for example, Jason Singer & Henry Sender, "Growing Funds Fuel Buyout Boom" *Wall Street Journal* (26 October 2006) C1.
21   See, for example, Margaret Sanderson & Michael Trebilcock, "Merger Review in Regulated Industries" 42 Can. Bus. L.J. 157 at 160-62.
22   See Greg Ip & Henny Sender, "In Today's Buyouts, Payday For Firms is Never Far Away" *Wall Street Journal* (25 July 2006) A1.

cussed in Chapter 6. At this point, it is only necessary to point out that the growing influence of financial buyers has a number of important implications for the development of Canadian mergers and acquisitions law and practice.

Indeed, the flip side of this phenomenon—the existence of "financial *sellers*"—may also be quite important. As hedge funds and private equity funds with substantial positions in public corporations seek to exit from their investments, they are more likely to favour receiving cash rather than securities in another corporation. Accordingly, the significant presence of such funds in the marketplace may have an impact on the number of cash takeover bids, rather than securities exchange bids. The existence of financial (as opposed to strategic) buyers has been claimed, by some, to exacerbate the already growing tendency of North American corporations to focus upon short-term shareholder gains[23] rather than longer-term prospects. These claims, however, must not be accepted uncritically. The suggestion that the capital markets cannot or do not price the value of long-term investment into a corporation's current share price is highly contestable. And the fear of some managers that their performance may be judged wanting and their companies taken over could well stem from a recognition of sub-par performance rather than sincere distaste for financial opportunism.

F.   THEORETICAL EXPLANATIONS OF MERGERS

Businesspeople are unlikely to describe their decision to merge in theoretical terms. They are more likely, in fact, to roll their eyes and speak with exasperated sarcasm about such explanations, or simply decline to speak of them at all. But the validity of an economic theory of mergers cannot be judged by the approbation of those practitioners who participate in merger transactions any more than the accuracy of a mathematical calculation of acceleration due to gravity can be judged by the "gut instinct" of the average paratrooper—no matter how many more real world "jumps" he or she may have made than the desk-bound physicist or mathematician. Indeed, the overconfidence inspired by

---

23   The argument that American business corporations have become overly fixated on producing short-term gains at the expense of long-term growth has been frequently repeated. See, for example, *Overcoming Short-Termism: A Call for a More Responsible Approach to Investment and Business Management* (Washington, DC: Aspen Institute, 2009).

"real world" experience can very often impede, rather than improve, understanding of complex issues.

There are, at the broadest level, two general theoretical approaches to understanding corporate mergers—those associated with "progressive" scholars, on the one hand, and those associated with neo-classical economics, on the other. "Progressive" approaches to the law of business organizations, including the law touching upon the merger of such entities, tend to emphasize the value of human co-operation and trust, while the neo-classical views emphasize the important role of competition, contracting, and "private ordering." Those who favour a system that emphasizes co-operation over competition frequently seek to portray the co-operative urge as the more noble and virtuous, as though, somehow, the competitive instinct reveals the darker, evil side of human nature, something barring humanity from achieving its fullest level of development. Such a view is, however, surely mistaken. The competitive urge does not invariably undermine the co-operative impulse; on the contrary, it can greatly enhance it, as team sport competition rather plainly illustrates. Yet the expansion of major firms in countries with market based economic systems has raised interesting economic questions as the early work of Ronald Coase, one of the founders of modern law and economics, reveals.

In 1937, Coase, who would later receive the Nobel Prize in Economics,[24] wrote an important and lucid article framing the central economic question raised by business mergers within a market economy. If market transactions were the most efficient way of allocating resources, then why, Coase asked, do large firms develop? Such firms, after all, seem to exist precisely to *avoid* market transactions in the allocation of their own internal resources. To frame the question rather differently, why do the strongest opponents of centralized "command and control" economies nevertheless appear quite content to build and lead very large centralized "command and control" business firms? Coase's suggested answer to this curious puzzle lay in the existence of "transaction costs." Thus, Coase argued, "a firm will tend to expand until the

---

24   Coase received the Sveriges Riksbank Prize in Economic Sciences in Memory of Alfred Nobel in 1991 "for his discoveries and clarification of the significance of transaction costs and property rights for the institutional structure and functioning of the economy." See "The Sveriges Riksbank Prize in Economic Sciences in Memory of Alfred Nobel 1991," online: www.nobelprize.org/nobel_prizes/economics/laureates/1991/. This prize is popularly known as the "Nobel Prize in Economics" although, as a technical matter, a prize for economic sciences was not originally provided for in Alfred Nobel's 1895 will, but was, instead, established by Sweden's central bank (Sveriges Riksbank) in 1968.

costs of organising an extra transaction within the firm become equal to the costs of carrying out the same transaction by means of an exchange on the open market or the costs of organising in another firm."[25]

Both progressive and neo-classical views of the firm share the recognition that the firm encourages "firm-specific" investment in human or other capital. And there is little doubt that firm-specific investment has implications for opportunistic behaviour both on the part of the firm and on the part of individuals providing inputs to the firm. One might, in fact, view the development of firm-specific investment as the product of a desire to encourage *dependence* on the one hand, with the competing desire to maintain *independence* or *autonomy* pulling in the opposite organizational direction.

No attempt can be made here to review the complex economic and theoretical literature surrounding mergers and acquisitions. From a legal and regulatory policy perspective, the simplest way to distil the theoretical perspectives on mergers and acquisitions is to ask whether it is generally in the interests of society to readily facilitate such transactions or to discourage them, or whether, instead, we should perhaps remain largely indifferent to them. On the one hand, we recognize that societal wealth is increased when resources can move to their most highly valued use. A more efficient business manager can afford to pay an apparent premium for assets precisely because he or she expects to be able to generate more value from them than the previous owners. And that value increases the size of the economic "pie" for all of us.

Defenders of the hostile takeover wave of the 1980s thus argued that the acquisitions of that era—though sometimes the subject of popular disapproval[26]—were, in fact, of great benefit to the

---

25   Ronald H. Coase, "The Nature of the Firm" (1937) 4 Economica 386 at 395.

26   Consider, for example, two popular Hollywood films from the 1980s—*Wall Street* (20th Century Fox, 1987) and *Pretty Woman* (Buena Vista Pictures, 1990). In the first, Michael Douglas portrayed a heartless and unscrupulous "bust-up artist" who defiantly declared that "Greed . . . is good" and set his sights on acquiring an American airline company in order to sell its assets to foreign interests (and therefore put virtuous and hard-working Americans—including "poor but honest" union worker Martin Sheen—out of work). In the second, Richard Gere portrayed a more sympathetic bust-up artist whose cold heart was eventually melted by the simple humanity of a golden-hearted prostitute played by Julia Roberts. His epiphanic redemption was evidenced by his "noble" decision to help a struggling public company remain in the control of its founding family, rather than

"brutally" buy it, in order to heartlessly sell off its assets to others. (Never mind that the purchase would, presumably, be made from more-than-willing shareholders, and at a premium to the depressed market value the firm had suffered while in the hands of its marginally competent controlling shareholder/

economy.[27] Conversely, opponents of corporate expansion have argued vehemently against corporate mergers and takeovers, sometimes citing studies which challenge the notion that takeovers invariably enhance economic value,[28] and sometimes simply falling back upon polemical arguments reminiscent of Louis Brandeis' pre–World War I warnings against the "curse of bigness."[29] More moderate commentators have tried to assess the economics of business combinations—for example, from anti-competition and agency-cost perspectives—neither dogmatically condemning nor indiscriminately applauding each and every corporate merger or acquisition.

The purpose of this book is primarily to introduce the existing legal framework surrounding mergers and acquisitions, and so no attempt will be made to survey the considerable body of academic literature in which theoretical approaches to mergers and acquisitions are explored. But some of the insights from that literature will frequently be referred to. From a legal perspective, of course, the economic justifications for corporate mergers and acquisitions, especially hostile takeovers, are linked to the perceived need for regulation of such transactions, and the structure of any such regulation. One critical component of the law of mergers and acquisitions relates to the fiduciary duties of directors and senior officers of corporations that are engaged in such transactions.

---

managers. And conveniently ignore, too, that any sale of assets would surely be to willing buyers who might put those assets to more productive use than their previous owners creating new and more sustainable jobs.) These films are offered only as two of the more salient examples of the demonization of hostile acquisitions that won popular appeal during the late eighties and early nineties.

27   As economist Michael Jensen, a strong defender of the economic benefits of takeovers, put it, "I know of no area in economics today where the divergence between popular belief and the evidence from scholarly research is so great." See Michael C. Jensen, "Corporate Control and the Politics of Finance" in Donald H. Chew, Jr., ed., *The New Corporate Finance: Where Theory Meets Practice* (New York: McGraw-Hill, 1993) 620 at 622.

28   See, for example, Anup Agrawal, Jeffrey F. Jaffe, & Gershon N. Mandelker, "The Post-Merger Performance of Acquiring Firms: A Re-examination of an Anomaly" (1992) 47 J. of Fin. 1605. The issue of post-merger performance has been the subject of considerable economic research. One of the most widely-cited earlier papers on the topic is Paul M. Healy, Krishna G. Palepu, & Richard S. Ruback, "Does Corporate Performance Improve After Mergers?" (1992) 31 J. Fin. Econ. 135.

29   See Louis D. Brandeis, ed., *Other People's Money and How the Bankers Use It*, with an introduction by Melvin I. Urofsky (New York: Bedford Books, 1995). Brandeis's work first appeared in book form in 1914. The book was, for the most part, a collection of articles written by Brandeis for *Harper's Weekly*. Chapter 8 of the book was entitled "A Curse of Bigness."

The delineation of those duties falls to our courts and occasionally to our securities regulators; and so economic theories and empirical data concerning the value and effect of takeovers and other corporate control transactions provide useful tools with which to critique judicial decision-making in this area.

G. THE LEGAL AND REGULATORY ENVIRONMENT FOR BUSINESS ACQUISITIONS

1) Introduction

The process by which one firm acquires or otherwise combines its resources with another is subject to a wide array of legal requirements. These legal requirements have evolved to protect interests that are disparate and sometimes competing. They include the concerns of taxing authorities, small shareholders of large public corporations, vulnerable employees, self-appointed guardians of the natural environment, consumers justifiably worried about potential exploitation by monopolists or oligopolists, and nationalists wary about the waning domestic control of key industries including, perhaps, national security worries.[30] So it is that parties to a prospective corporate acquisition in Canada would need to be mindful, among other things, of the following:

- anti-competition (sometimes called "anti-trust") laws;
- foreign investment laws;
- taxation laws;
- environmental laws;
- labour and employment laws;
- pension regulation;
- securities regulation; and
- privacy laws.

   This book is concerned primarily with the law as it specifically affects the *process* of merger, acquisition, or takeover itself, rather than the tax implications of such transactions or the effects a merger or acquisition might have on such things as industry competition, labour relationships, the natural environment, and so on. Therefore, although there will be a brief canvass in Chapter 2 of a few of the basic *Competition Act*

---

30   See the discussion on national security issues and the *Investment Canada Act* in Chapter 2.

and *Investment Canada Act* rules, the remainder of the book will focus on the corporate and securities laws aspects of mergers and acquisitions.

2) Methods of Business Combination

a) Four Basic Methods
There are four[31] basic methods by which one firm may acquire the business operations of another:

* asset purchase;
* amalgamation;
* arrangement; and
* takeover bid.

The courts have made clear that parties are quite free to choose whichever structure they deem most appropriate, provided they comply with all applicable legal requirements.[32] The legal and regulatory considerations relevant to a transaction will depend significantly on which one (or perhaps which combination of one or more) of these acquisition methods is chosen by the parties.

b) Asset vs. Share Transaction
Of the four preceding acquisition methods, three constitute major share transactions. To proceed, they require the involvement of shareholders at some stage; and to succeed they must have the assent of a significant number of those shareholders. That assent might take the form of a positive shareholder vote, approving a proposed corporate transaction (such as an amalgamation or arrangement) or it might take the form of outright sale by holders of their shares (as in the case of a takeover bid).

The first acquisition method listed (asset purchase) does not necessarily require the assent of shareholders of the buying and selling corporations involved. The directors and the managers of each firm may be able to conclude an asset deal acting within their powers to manage the business and affairs of the corporation. However, there are at least two instances in which the approval of shareholders must be obtained to complete an asset purchase transaction. First, if the assets to be sold constitute "all or substantially all" of the property of the selling cor-

---

31 One might add to this list, in the interests of completeness, capital reorganizations. However, capital reorganizations are not a common method of effecting control transactions in Canada.

32 See *Stern v. Imasco Ltd.* (1999), 1 B.L.R. 198 at 213 and 216; *McEwen v. Goldcorp Inc.*, 2006 CanLII 35985 at para. 46 (Ont. S.C.J.) [*McEwen*].

poration, Canadian corporate statutes typically require that the sale must be approved by a resolution passed by at least two-thirds of the shareholders voting on the resolution.[33] Second, if the purchase price for the acquired assets is to be satisfied not by a cash payment by the purchaser, but rather by the issue of a substantial number of shares of the purchasing company's own stock, then stock exchange rules may require that the shareholders of the purchaser approve this substantial share issuance.[34] For example, the basic rule for corporations listed on the Toronto Stock Exchange is that share issuances that exceed 25 percent of the outstanding voting shares of a listed company require shareholder approval. At one time, where such issuances were undertaken in connection with a purchase of another public corporation, the TSX rules provided an exemption, subject to the discretionary authority of the TSX to require shareholder approval. The application of that rule, and the exercise of the TSX's discretionary authority, became the subject of controversy and regulatory scrutiny in *Re HudBay Minerals Inc.*,[35] a case discussed further in Chapter 8. The TSX rules were subsequently changed, and as of 24 November 2009, all issuances of TSX-listed companies (other than investment funds, in certain circumstances) that exceed 25 percent of the outstanding voting shares will require shareholder approval.[36]

c) "Friendly" (Negotiated) vs. "Hostile" (Unsolicited) Transactions

The majority of major business acquisitions in Canada (and elsewhere) are negotiated transactions in which both the acquiring and the acquired companies are active and willing participants. Weston and Weaver, for example, indicate that in each of the years in the fifteen year period from 1985–2000, hostile takeovers, as a percentage of total takeover activity, measured in dollars, rarely exceeded 10 percent worldwide in any given year, and usually constituted considerably less

---

33   See, for example, *Canada Business Corporations Act*, R.S.C. 1985, c. C-44, s. 189(3).

34   See, for example, *Toronto Stock Exchange Company Manual*, ss. 611(c) & (d) [*TSX Company Manual*]. It is possible, however, for the Exchange to approve a major share issuance without the requirement for shareholder approval. See, for example, *McEwen*, above note 32, aff'd 2006 CanLII 37415 (Ont. Div. Ct.), where a proposed issuance by a public company of shares comprising approximately 67 percent of its issued and outstanding shares was accepted by the Toronto Stock Exchange, without a requirement for a shareholder vote. See also *New York Stock Exchange Listed Company Manual*, sec. 312.03(c), online: www.nyse.com.

35   (2009), 32 OSCB 3733.

36   *TSX Company Manual*, s. 611(c).

than 10 percent.[37] However, from time to time, an acquiring firm will seek to acquire the shares of a target company against the wishes of the target firm's management and directors. Transactions of this sort are often described as "hostile" or "unsolicited" takeovers.

The Canadian statutory and regulatory infrastructure is, for the most part, the same for both friendly and hostile deals. The principal difference, from a legal perspective, is that friendly transactions raise various issues of complex contractual design and negotiation, whereas hostile deals demand careful consideration of directors' and officers' duties and what might be described as campaign strategies.

i)   Negotiated Transactions

a.   Basic Agreement Structure

Asset or share purchase agreements can be lengthy documents filled with a heavily negotiated array of terms. At the most basic level, however, such agreements typically include the following sets of provisions:

- *The basic sale terms:* The seller's promise to sell, the buyer's promise to buy, the allocation of the purchase price (if relevant), and so on, are the fundamental terms.
- *Extensive representations, warranties, indemnities, and perhaps covenants given by the seller:* These provisions identify and delimit the assets and the liabilities of the seller relevant to the transaction—typically by reference to detailed disclosure in attached appendices or schedules to the agreement—and also include representations with respect to the seller and the seller's right and capacity to complete the transaction.
- *More modest representations and warranties given by the buyer:* The buyer's principal obligation is to pay the purchase price at the time of closing; so the representations and warranties required of the buyer are, predictably, far more limited than those typically provided by the seller. Essentially, the buyer must represent and warrant that it has the necessary authority and approvals to complete the transaction, and that doing so will not run afoul of some legal or

---

37   J. Fred Weston & Samuel C. Weaver, *Mergers and Acquisitions* (New York: McGraw-Hill, 2001) at 114. There were three anomalous years in that fifteen year period: 1985 (when hostile takeovers constituted 14.3 percent of deals worldwide); 1988 (17.9 percent of deals worldwide); and 1999 (15.1 percent of deals worldwide.) More recent data compiled by FactSet Research Systems indicates that, from 2004 to 2011, of the total of 2,622 announced public deals, some 390 or 14.9 percent were unsolicited or hostile. See "Unfriendly M&A Deal Activity through 2011," online: www.factsetmergers.com. Hostile bids are discussed further in Chapter 7.

regulatory restriction or constitute a material breach of some other contractual provision by which the buyer is bound.

- *Conditions:* The agreement will typically include conditions that must be satisfied by each party before the transaction may be completed. Often, the agreement will specify that particular conditions are included expressly for the benefit of one party and, accordingly, that that party may, if it wishes, waive one or more of those conditions and complete the transaction even if the conditions have not been satisfied.

- *General ("boilerplate") provisions:* Such agreements would typically include general provisions common to many commercial contracts including a "governing law" clause, a "further assurances" clause, a provision indicating where notices are to be sent to each party, an "entire agreement" clause and so on.

Recently, the M & A Market Trends Subcommittee of the American Bar Association undertook an enlightening study of the frequency with which certain deal terms were included in M & A transactions. In December 2010 the Canadian version of that study was released: the Canadian Private Target M & A Deal Points Study.[38]

b.   "Material Adverse Effect"/"Material Adverse Change"

No attempt can, or will, be made here to consider in any way the details of the array of contractual provisions canvassed above. It is worth noting, however, that one particular clause frequently found in negotiated business acquisition agreements—a "material adverse effect" or "material adverse change" clause—has been the subject of recent judicial pronouncements in the United States that have attracted the attention of American and Canadian legal practitioners. In the current uncertain financial environment, where deal certainty is more fragile than at any time in the recent past, the details of such provisions have become especially significant. A Delaware judge has colourfully described material adverse effect clauses as "strange animals, sui generis among their contract clause brethren."[39]

The purpose of a material adverse effect clause is to protect the buyer in the event that some unexpected incident that impairs the value of the business being purchased occurs between the date on which the acquisition agreement is signed and the date on which the transaction actually closes. Typically, a material adverse change or material adverse effect clause would, if triggered, give the purchaser the right to walk

---

38   See online: apps.americanbar.org/buslaw/blt/content/2011/02/0001a.pdf.

39   *Hexion Speciality Chemicals, Inc. v. Huntsman Corp.*, 965 A.2d 715 (Del. Ch. 2008).

away from the deal. In practice, it is likely that such clauses are more often used by purchasers to negotiate a pre-closing reduction in the purchase price.

At first glance, the inclusion of a material adverse effect clause in a purchase agreement may seem quite obvious and fair: of course, if the asset one has agreed to buy has suffered a dramatic loss in its value, the buyer should not be expected to pay full price. But the logic of the material adverse effect clause is perhaps not quite so obvious as that in the case of a purchase of an operating business. Recall, first of all, that acquisition agreements typically include covenants given by the seller relating to the conduct of the business between the date of the agreement and the date of closing. In other words, any deterioration in the value of the business that was the result of the existing managers' failure to operate the business in the ordinary course, would enable the buyer to pursue appropriate remedies even without a material adverse effect clause. If the assets of the business have been physically destroyed while under the control of the seller then certainly the buyer should not be obliged to complete the transaction. But typically the purchase agreement would include separate representations and warranties relating to material damage or destruction. Accordingly, the material adverse effect clause must, presumably, relate to deterioration in value that results from matters over which the managers do not have control and which may relate to something other than physical destruction of assets. But if that is so, it is not entirely clear why buyers should expect to be able to walk away from a deal (or demand a lower price) in such cases. When an individual enters into an agreement to purchase a house, for example, the purchaser fully understands that, at closing, the purchaser must pay the agreed-upon price even if the real estate market has softened in the meantime and the house (though still in the same physical condition) is no longer worth what the buyer had contracted to pay. We recognize, in other words, that the purchaser's investment decision is made at the time an enforceable contract is entered into, and do not expect the seller to stand as a guarantor or insurer of enduring robust market conditions.

Should business purchase agreements be different? Perhaps the comparison with residential housing purchases is unfair. A fall in housing prices would presumably reflect general economic conditions, and material adverse effect clauses frequently exclude changes that result from general economic conditions, natural disasters, or conditions generally affecting the seller's industry. But not all such clauses are qualified in this way.[40] Even when they are, there is still some uncertainty as to the extent to which the material adverse effect clause is needed to address matters not covered by the sellers' covenant to conduct the business diligently in the ordinary course from the signing of the agreement until the closing date.

Gilson and Schwartz have offered some explanations for these clauses in the American context.[41] One possibility they suggest (although ultimately reject) is that the material adverse effect clause is necessary to induce purchasers to enter into agreements in the first place in light of the so-called fiduciary out cases in which courts have held that selling corporations are not only permitted, but may be required, to walk away from a sale agreement if a superior proposal emerges after the sale agreement has been signed. (The concept of fiduciary out is discussed further in Chapter 7.) As Gilson and Schwartz note, the effect of these cases is to provide sellers with a free put option (that is, they can compel the purchaser to buy the business if no better offer is received in the meantime, yet essentially remain free to sell to any higher bidder that does emerge). The resulting uncertainty, Gilson and Schwartz note, would be a significant deterrent to potential purchasers; they could be forced to overpay if the value of the business falls, yet may lose the deal altogether if the value of the business rises. Accordingly, to offset this otherwise one-sided relationship, and so encourage purchasers to negotiate agreements to begin with, sellers must be prepared to include material adverse effect clauses in acquisition agreements. Gilson and Schwartz's second (and their preferred) explanation for the prevalence of such clauses is that they encourage the target company to make what they dub "synergy investments" in the post-signing, pre-closing period.

Of greater interest to legal practitioners than theoretical models of material adverse effect clauses are the recent court decisions that have interpreted them. Three Delaware cases in particular (one applying New York law) have attracted attention. In the first, *IBP, Inc. v. Tyson Foods, Inc.*[42] the Delaware Court of Chancery granted to a seller a remedy of specific performance, compelling the completion of a merger agreement on the basis, among other things, that the target business had not suffered a "material adverse effect" ("MAE") that would entitle the buyer to terminate the agreement. There had certainly been a significant fall

---

40   The clause considered by the court in one of the leading Delaware cases, for example, contained no qualifications of this kind. See *IBP, Inc. v. Tyson Foods, Inc*, below note 42.

41   Ronald Gilson & Alan Schwartz, "Understanding MACs: Moral Hazard in Acquisitions" (2005) 21 J.L. Econ. & Org. 330.

42   A.2d 14 (Del. Ch. 2001) [*Tyson*].

in earnings in the seller's first quarter, but the court considered that "[the MAE] provision is best read as a backstop protecting the acquiror from the occurrence of unknown events that substantially threaten the overall earnings potential of the target in a durationally significant manner. A short-term hiccup in earnings should not suffice; rather the Material Adverse Effect should be material when viewed from the longer-term perspective of a reasonable acquiror."[43] The court's reasoning turned, importantly, on the precise wording of the MAE clause in question, in recognition of the extent to which merger agreements are carefully, and heavily, negotiated.

The second Delaware MAE case that has drawn considerable attention from the practising bar is *Frontier Oil Corporation v. Holly Corporation*.[44] In 2003, Frontier and Holly had entered into a merger agreement. Just before the merger agreement was finalized, Frontier provided Holly's counsel with, among other things, a newspaper article indicating that Erin Brockovich was planning major toxic tort litigation against various parties including a wholly owned subsidiary of Frontier. Following negotiation, the merger agreement was amended in a number of respects. Those amendments included a revision to the definition of material adverse effect to read:

> with respect to Holly or Frontier shall mean a material adverse effect with respect to (A) the business, assets and liabilities (taken together), *results of operations*, condition *(financial or otherwise) or prospects* of a party and its Subsidiaries on a consolidated basis.[45]

It appeared that Holly (and indeed Frontier) anticipated that if the feared Brockovich firm lawsuit materialized, Frontier could presumably avail itself of a "corporate separateness defence" since it was a subsidiary of Frontier, and not Frontier itself, that was the target of the litigation. However, it was subsequently discovered that Frontier had provided certain guarantees and indemnities that might compromise such a defence.

Following a series of communications between the parties, Frontier evidently concluded that Holly was not prepared to close, and so brought an action claiming that Holly had repudiated the contract. One day after that action was filed, Holly delivered notice to Frontier indicating that the lawsuit involving its subsidiary gave rise to a material adverse effect. On this MAE issue, the court emphasized that the MAE

---

43   *Ibid.* at 68.
44   2005 Del. Ch. Lexis 57.
45   *Ibid.* at *16.

concept is "imprecise" and "varies both with the context of the transaction and its parties and with the words chosen by the parties."[46]

The court concluded, based on expert evidence, that likely defence
costs for Frontier (even ignoring ultimate liability) would fall in the
range of $15 million to $20 million.[47] Would such an amount be "material"? Interestingly, the court held that "the question of whether a
particular 'problem' would have an MAE has both quantitative and
qualitative aspects."[48] Because the parties had chosen a "forward-look-
ing basis" for determining whether or not an event was an MAE, the
court reasoned that it was obliged to assess the effect of an obligation
over the long term. And over the long term, in the court's view, "it is
reasonable to conclude that Frontier could absorb the projected defense
costs without experiencing an MAE."[49] As for the potentially disastrous
effect of an ultimate finding against Frontier in the litigation itself, the
court found that Holly had not demonstrated in any way the *likelihood*
of such an outcome. Accordingly, the possibility of a massive (even perhaps firm-ending) verdict was a matter of mere speculation and could
not justify invoking the MAE clause at this point.

Again, as in *Tyson*, the precise wording of the MAE and the context
in which it was drafted became crucial to the court's decision, and, accordingly, an important reminder to merger parties and their solicitors.

The third key Delaware case was *Hexion Speciality Chemicals, Inc.
v. Huntsman Corp.*[50] The *Hexion* case involved a merger that had been
negotiated in July 2007—unbeknownst to the parties, on the very eve
of the "credit crunch" that would eventually herald an international financial crisis. The price to be paid by the buyer, Hexion, was generous,
and the deal contained very few "outs" other than a material adverse effect clause. The transaction required a number of regulatory approvals
which delayed closing. During this period of delay, the target reported
lackluster quarterly results. Hexion was no longer enthusiastic about
completing the deal.

Under the terms of the contract, Hexion had agreed to pay a significant "reverse break fee"[51] (of $325 million in the context of a deal

---

46 *Ibid.* at *127.
47 *Ibid.* at *141.
48 *Ibid.* at *142.
49 *Ibid.*
50 Above note 39.
51 This payment—due from the purchaser to the seller in the event that the trans-
    action does not close—is referred to as a *reverse* break fee because a conven-
    tional break fee is paid by the seller to the buyer in the event that the deal is not
    completed. Break fees are discussed further in Chapter 7.

with a total transaction value of $10.6 billion) if the deal failed to close. However, if failure to close was due to "knowing and intentional breach" of its covenants, Hexion's liability would not be limited to payment of this $325 million. Conversely, if the business of the target had suffered a "material adverse effect" within the meaning of the agreement, Hexion could terminate the agreement with impunity and would not be obliged even to pay the $325 million termination fee.

The court found that there had been no MAE. Determining whether or not an MAE had occurred called for a consideration of the context of the transaction, the court reasoned, noting that,

> In the absence of evidence to the contrary, a corporate acquirer may be assumed to be purchasing the target as part of a long-term strategy. The important consideration therefore is whether there has been an adverse change in the target's business that is consequential to the company's long-term earnings power over a commercially reasonable period, which one would expect to be measured in years rather than months. A buyer faces a heavy burden when it attempts to invoke a material adverse effect clause in order to avoid its obligation to close. *Many commentators have noted that Delaware courts have never found a material adverse effect to have occurred in the context of a merger agreement. This is not a coincidence.*[52]

The court found that the burden of proof for establishing that a material adverse effect has occurred, in the absence of clear language in the contract to the contrary, rests on the party seeking to invoke the clause to relieve it from its contractual obligations—in this case, the buyer, Hexion. To discharge that burden in this case, the court held, among other things, that the purchaser would be required to show a material deterioration in the target's operating performance. In evaluating the operational performance of an acquisition target, the court stated it was more appropriate to consider the firm's EBITDA (earnings before interest taxes depreciation and amortization) rather than (accounting) earnings per share, since earnings per share may be distorted by a firm's financing decisions.[53]

The target company's performance had, indisputably, fallen well short of its own projections. However, the buyer had not bargained for a provision that would have allowed it to terminate the contract

---

52   *Ibid.* [emphasis added].
53   For a more detailed discussion of how a firm's earnings per share may be changed by a firms' capital structure, see Stephen A. Ross, Randloph W. Westerfield, & Jeffrey Jaffe, *Corporate Finance*, 7th ed. (Boston: McGraw-Hill/Irwin, 2005) at 450*ff*.

on the basis of the target's failure to meet its projections. Thus, the court concluded, the reference in the MAE clause to the firm's "financial condition, business, or results of operations" should be given the same meaning as the phrase bears for purposes of certain U.S. federal securities regulatory filings, including Reg S-X and Item 7 of the M D & A accompanying a reporting company's financial statements. In that context, the key issue is how a company's quarterly performance compares to its performance in the same quarter of the previous year. On that basis, the court concluded, it could not be said that an MAE had occurred.

The court did acknowledge that it was relevant to consider expected future performance as well. On that issue, however, the court was persuaded that the target's expected future earnings were not likely to be as weak as the purchaser contended, a conclusion that seemed to reflect a recognition of a series of unusually unfavourable macroeconomic conditions that had recently been adversely affecting the target's operations. To end, the court concluded that there had been no MAE and that Hexion had knowingly and intentionally committed numerous contractual breaches. The court ordered specific performance of Hexion's contractual obligations, other than the obligation to close the merger itself—a remedy that seemed to be precluded by an express (albeit somewhat unclear) clause in the contract.

c.   Representations and Warranties Insurance

One relatively recent innovation that deserves brief mention here is the advent and proliferation of representations and warranties (R & W) insurance. Although, evidently, such insurance has existed for over a decade, it has recently gained greater profile in private M & A transactions and has been advocated as an important technique to consider in transactions involving public companies as well.[54]

As the website of one R & W insurance underwriter explains,[55] "coverage is optimally suited to transactions involving companies valued between $25 million to $1 billion." The premium for such insur-

---

54   See, for example, Abbe Dinkstag, Howard Spilko, & Stephanie Dinkes, "Escrows and Insurance Protections in Public Deals" *N.Y.L.J.* (8 November 2004); and Howard T. Spilko, "United States: Bridging the Gap: Representations and Warranties Insurance" 2005 Int'l Fin. L. Rev., online: www.iflr.com/Article/2027913/Channel/193438/United-States-Bridging-the-gap-representations-and-warranties-insurance.html; *IFLR Guide to Mergers and Acquisitions 2005*, online: www.iflr.com.

55   See Chartis, Mergers & Acquisitions Insurance Group, *Representations & Warranties Insurance*, online: www.chartisinsurance.com/ncglobalweb/internet/US/en/files/Representations_and_Warranties_HS_4_2010_tcm295-202212.pdf.

ance is said to be between 2 and 5 percent of the amount purchased, with a deductible ranging from 1 to 3 percent of the transaction value.[56] Such insurance is available for both buyers and sellers, and, in addition to the expected insurance benefits of certainty, and risk reduction, it has even been suggested that the use of such insurance may give buyers an edge when participating in an auction because it allows a bidder to accept "a lower than customary indemnification"[57] in the acquisition agreement, without reducing its bid price, since any shortfall may be covered by the insurance. It is not clear to what extent R & W insurance is used in Canadian M & A transactions, although to be sure the product is available and has been used in Canadian deals.

d.   Other M & A Insurance Products

There are a host of other insurance products that are relevant to M & A transactions (although not always in the context of friendly deals). For example, some insurance underwriters offer "aborted bid cost" insurance, providing coverage to a party for costs incurred in connection with a terminated merger transaction.[58] Insurance against tax, litigation and other risks may also be available.

e.   Privacy Concerns

Privacy laws have become of increasing importance in Canada in many contexts, and M & A deals are no exception. Prospective purchasers need to make sure any business they seek to acquire is truly an asset and not a liability. And they need to ensure that the price to be paid for that asset is not excessive. Assessments like these require information, and acquiring that information requires a detailed investigation or, in the parlance of M & A lawyers and bankers, "due diligence." In the course of conducting one's due diligence investigations, one is bound to require access to employee information. But access to such information may raise privacy concerns. In some provinces, provincial privacy legislation provides express exemptions for the use of personal information in connection with business acquisitions. Consider, for example, the following section of Alberta's *Personal Information Protection Act:*

> 22(1) In this section,
>
> (a) "business transaction" means a transaction consisting of the purchase, sale, lease, merger or amalgamation or any other type of acquisition or disposal of, or the taking of a security interest

---

56   *Ibid.*
57   *Ibid.*
58   See, for example, online: www.hkmb.com/risk/mergers.asp.

in respect of, an organization or a portion of an organization or any business or activity or business asset of an organization and includes a prospective transaction of such a nature;

(b) "party" includes a prospective party.

(2) Notwithstanding anything in this Act other than this section, an organization may, for the purposes of a business transaction between itself and one or more other organizations, collect, use and disclose personal information in accordance with this section.

(3) Organizations that are parties to a business transaction may,

(a) during the period leading up to and including the completion, if any, of the business transaction, collect, use and disclose personal information about individuals without the consent of the individuals if

  (i) the parties have entered into an agreement under which the collection, use and disclosure of the information is restricted to those purposes that relate to the business transaction, and

  (ii) the information is necessary

   (A) for the parties to determine whether to proceed with the business transaction, and

   (B) if the determination is to proceed with the business transaction, for the parties to carry out and complete the business transaction, and

(b) where the business transaction is completed, collect, use and disclose personal information about individuals without the consent of the individuals if

  (i) the parties have entered into an agreement under which the parties undertake to use and disclose the information only for those purposes for which the information was initially collected from or in respect of the individuals, and

  (ii) the information relates solely to the carrying on of the business or activity or the carrying out of the objects for which the business transaction took place.

(4) If a business transaction does not proceed or is not completed, the party to whom the personal information was disclosed must, if the information is still in the custody of or under the control

of that party, either destroy the information or turn it over to the party that disclosed the information.

(5) Nothing in this section is to be construed so as to restrict a party to a business transaction from obtaining consent of an individual to the collection, use or disclosure of personal information about the individual for purposes that are beyond the purposes for which the party obtained the information under this section.

(6) This section does not apply to a business transaction where the primary purpose, objective or result of the transaction is the purchase, sale, lease, transfer, disposal or disclosure of personal information.[59]

Even where the protective provisions of the Alberta statute are available, privacy breaches can still occur. The Alberta Information and Privacy Commissioner recently investigated an alleged breach of the Alberta *Personal Information Protection Act* that arose in the context of a business acquisition.[60] In 2004, an Alberta company, "Builders," entered into agreements to purchase nine other companies. The purchase agreements drafted for these transactions included representations and warranties relating to the employees of the purchased businesses. Builders requested the sellers to provide certain basic information about the employees of the purchased firms pursuant to these representations and warranties. One of the purchased companies ("Remote") provided employee information to its solicitors which included the home addresses and social insurance numbers of those employees. This information was, in turn, provided to Builders' solicitors and the information subsequently was appended to the purchase agreement. Builders was a public corporation and the purchase agreement was considered a material contract. Accordingly, the purchase agreement was posted on the SEDAR website—a publicly available website on which the public documents of reporting issuers in Canada are filed. The document—including the home address and social insurance number of the employees—remained on the website from 25 January 2005 until, after being spotted by a Remote employee, it was removed on 11 February 2005.

Although it is clear under the Alberta Act that certain information about employees can be disclosed where the information is "necessary"

---

59 *Personal Information Protection Act* (Alberta), S.A. 2003, c. P-6.5.
60 *Report of an Investigation into the Disclosure of Personal Information During the Course of a Business Transaction* (12 July 2005), Investigation Report P2005-IR-005, online: www.oipc.ab.ca/ims/client/upload/P2005_IR_005.pdf.

for a business transaction, the commissioner found that disclosure of the employees' home addresses and social insurance numbers was not necessary. The commissioner concluded that disclosure of this information was not in compliance with the *Personal Information Protection Act*. The commissioner was especially concerned with the role of the lawyers in this matter, noting, "We suggest generally that [the solicitors involved] and other law firms have shown a lack of attention to the impact of privacy laws on the myriad legal processes involving the collection, use and disclosure of personal information, including client information and third party information that are common in the type of work they perform on behalf of their clients . . . We believe that lawyers and law firms require heightened awareness and knowledge of privacy laws in order to properly recognize these implications."[61] The commissioner's recommendations included specific recommendations relating to enhanced privacy training for the law firms involved and the development of awareness and knowledge of privacy laws.

It should also be noted that not all Canadian privacy legislation includes business transaction exceptions such as those found in the Alberta statute. In particular, the federal *Personal Information Protection and Electronic Documents Act*[62] ("PIPEDA") currently includes no such provisions. The Office of the Privacy Commissioner of Canada, in its 18 July 2006 *PIPEDA Review Discussion Document*,[63] noted that PIPEDA "contains no provision to allow an organization to disclose personal information to prospective purchasers or business partners without the consent of the individual involved."[64] The document raised the question of whether such provisions ought to be added to the Act and, if so, what conditions or restrictions ought to apply in connection with such disclosures. On May 25, 2010, the federal government introduced a bill proposing amendments to PIPEDA, including a proposed "business transactions" exception.[65] The bill passed second reading in October of that year, but was not ultimately enacted. The bill was reintroduced as Bill C-12 in September 2011.[66]

---

61   *Ibid.* at paras. 47 and 57.

62   S.C. 2000, c. 5.

63   Office of the Privacy Commissioner of Canada, "Protecting Privacy in an Intrusive World" (18 July 2006), online: www.privcom.gc.ca/information/pub/pipeda_review_060718_e.asp.

64   *Ibid.* at s. 3.

65   Bill C-29, *An Act to Amend the Personal Information Protection and Electronic Documents Act*, 3d Sess., 40th Parl., 2010.

66   Bill C-12, *An Act to Amend the Personal Information Protection and Electronic Documents Act*, 1st Sess., 41st Parl., 2011.

In sum, then, privacy concerns can raise important practical issues for both buyers and sellers of firms and those concerns are especially acute in the absence of express legislative provisions allowing for disclosure in connection with business transactions.

ii) Hostile Bids

For reasons that will be explored in Chapter 7, the legal environment in Canada has been considered by many practitioners to make hostile bids easier to undertake than in some other jurisdictions, particularly the United States. This fact, among others, was thought to account for the proliferation of hostile deals in Canada prior to the recent financial crisis. From January 2002 until mid-September 2005, there were a total of ten hostile bids in Canada. Then, in the last three and one half months of 2005 there were an additional ten bids, and there were nine more such bids in the first three quarters of 2006.[67] Deal volume generally fell during the "credit crunch" and the ensuing financial crisis, and hostile bids in particular were thought to be unattractive, with a considerably higher rate of non-completion than friendly transactions. However, unsolicited bids have by no means disappeared. The Canadian law firm Blake, Cassels & Graydon LLP, in its recent review of unsolicited bids launched in the period between 1 January 2006 and 30 June 2010, reported 52 such transactions with a transaction value of at least $50 million each.[68]

The legal and public policy issues raised by hostile takeover bids are especially intriguing. When a bidder offers to purchase a corporation's shares, that offer is not made to the corporation's directors or managers; it is made to the corporation's shareholders. Why, then, should it matter so very much whether or not the directors or officers of a "target" corporation support or oppose a bid that is made for the outstanding shares of that corporation? This question is explored in some detail in Chapter 7.

---

67 Presentation by Peter Buzzi, Managing Director and Co-Head, Mergers and Acquisitions, RBC Capital Markets, "Latest Developments in Mergers and Acquisitions" *Dialogue with the OSC 2006* (10 November 2006). See online: www. osc.gov.on.ca/Media/Dialogue/2006/dwo_20061110_mergers-acquisitions.pdf.

68 See *Blakes Canadian Hostile Bids Study*, First Edition (Winter 2010/11), online: www.blakes.com/english/legal_updates/reference_guides/Hostile_take_over_bid_study_2011.pdf.

3) Corporate and Securities Law

The three principal sources in Canada of the corporate and securities law applicable to corporate mergers, acquisitions, and takeover bids are:

- *Canadian corporate statutes (both provincial and federal)*: Canada is a federal state and, for reasons that need not concern us here,[69] corporate law in Canada is a matter over which Canada's provinces and Canada's federal government have virtually concurrent jurisdiction. As a result, each of Canada's ten provinces and three territories has promulgated its own business corporation statute, and the federal government has also enacted a business corporation statute, the *Canada Business Corporations Act* ("CBCA").[70] Federal corporate legislation had existed long before the enactment of the CBCA in 1975. However, the introduction of the CBCA is considered a landmark event in Canadian corporate law history because of its modernizing, and ultimately harmonizing, influence. The CBCA was enacted following the detailed recommendations of a special committee under the chairmanship of Robert Dickerson (the "Dickerson Committee").[71] The Dickerson Committee's report is a rich source of insight into the development of Canadian corporate law, and is referred to from time to time throughout this book. With some exceptions (notably, including much of the corporate legislation in place in the provinces of Nova Scotia, Prince Edward Island, and B.C.), the development of corporate law throughout Canada has been significantly influenced by the federal CBCA, and significant portions of many provincial corporate statutes are largely modelled on the CBCA's provisions. The CBCA is also the statute under which a majority of Canada's largest publicly traded corporations have been incorporated.[72]

- *Provincial securities regulation*: In Canada, unlike the United States, there is, at the date of writing, no federal securities legislation and no federal securities regulator comparable to the U.S. Securities and Exchange Commission. Instead, securities law has, to date, been regu-

---

69 For a discussion of the topic of federal and provincial legislative authority with respect to corporate law in Canada, see Christopher C. Nicholls, *Corporate Law* (Toronto: Emond Montgomery, 2005) at 15–16 and 39–43.

70 R.S.C. 1985, c. C-44.

71 Robert W.V. Dickerson, John L. Howard, & Leon Getz, *Proposals for a New Business Corporations Law for Canada*, vol. 1, *Commentary* (Ottawa: Information Canada, 1971).

72 Based on data compiled as of August 2005, there were 250 Canadian reporting issuers (i.e., public corporations) in Canada recorded in the SEDAR system with more than $1 billion in assets. Of those 250 reporting issuers, 128 (just over 50 percent) were incorporated under the CBCA.

lated at the provincial level.[73] Each of Canada's ten provinces and three territories has its own securities legislation and its own securities administrator. For practical purposes, however, the securities legislation and regulators in four of Canada's largest provinces—Ontario, Quebec, British Columbia, and Alberta—are especially influential. As well, all of Canada's provincial and territorial securities regulators are members of the Canadian Securities Administrators (CSA), an umbrella organization that works to attempt to harmonize and co-ordinate Canadian securities regulation where possible.[74] As a result, considerable uniformity has been achieved among the provinces in many aspects of securities regulation, including takeover bid regulation. In June 2009, the federal government announced an initiative to create a new national securities regulator. A proposed federal Canadian *Securities Act* was released in May 2010.[75] To determine the constitutionality of the proposed legislation, the Act was referred by the federal government to the Supreme Court of Canada.[76] Oral argument on the reference took place in April 2011, and the Supreme Court reserved judgment. In the meantime, separate references had been launched by the governments of Alberta and Quebec to their respective courts of appeal. On 8 March 2011, the Alberta Court of Appeal released its decision, holding that the federal

---

73   There has long been debate in Canada over whether the fragmented provincial securities regulatory scheme ought to be replaced, either with federal legislation administered by a federal regulator or by co-ordinated federal/provincial legislation administered by a "national" securities commission exercising powers delegated to it by the provincial and federal governments. Among recent contributions to this debate were the 2009 report of the Expert Panel on Securities Regulation (*Creating an Advantage in Global Capital Markets: Final Report and Recommendations*, online: www.expertpanel.ca); the 2006 Crawford Panel on a Single Canadian Securities Regulator, *Blueprint for a Canadian Securities Commission* (7 June 2006), online: at www.crawfordpanel.ca, and the December 2003 report of the "Wise Persons' Committee to Review the Structure of Securities Regulation in Canada," established by the federal Minister of Finance Wise Persons' Committee, *It's Time* (Ottawa: Finance Canada, 2003).

74   In 2003, the CSA, which had long operated on a somewhat informal basis, took steps to formalize its operational structure. In 2004, a permanent CSA Secretariat was established in Montreal. See the CSA website, www.csa-acvm.ca/html_CSA/about.html. See also the January 2006 publication of the CSA, *Introduction to the CSA*.

75   See *House of Commons Debates*, 40th Parliament, 3d Session, No. 049 (26 May 2010).

76   *In the Matter of a Reference by Governor in Council concerning the proposed Canadian Securities Act, as set out in Order of Council P.C. 2010-667, dated 26 May 2010*, Supreme Court of Canada Docket No. 33718.

government did not have legislative authority to enact the proposed Canadian *Securities Act*.[77] On 31 March 2011, the Quebec Court of Appeal released its decision, also holding that the federal government did not have legislative authority to enact the statute.[78] The Supreme Court of Canada released its long-awaited decision in the proposed Canadian *Securities Act* reference on 22 December 2011. In a unanimous decision, the Court held that the federal *Securities Act*, as drafted, was not constitutionally valid under the so-called "general brand" of the federal trade and commerce power set out in section 91(2) of the *Constitution Act, 1867*.[79]

• *Caselaw (including not only court decisions, but also decisions of Canada's provincial securities commissions)*: Canadian courts are frequently called upon to adjudicate disputes that arise in the context of takeover bids and other major corporate acquisitions and business combinations. Provincial securities commissions also have a statutorily recognized role in the administration of provincial securities laws, and often sit as tribunals resolving issues emerging in the case of disputed transactions, especially contested takeover bids. As a result, a significant securities commission "jurisprudence" has developed in a number of key areas, notably with respect to defensive measures such as shareholder rights plans (or "poison pills") put in place by directors of corporations that are the targets of hostile takeover bids.

H. CONCLUSION

The Canadian law of mergers and acquisitions comprises a complex pastiche of legislation, regulation, administrative and judicial decision-making and standard practices developed over time from domestic and international precedents. This short book will not presume to deal with the topic exhaustively, but will offer an introduction to the subject and signposts for further investigation and study.

---

77   *Reference Re Securities Act (Canada)*, 2011 ABCA 77.
78   *Québec (Procureure générale) c. Canada (Procureure générale)*, 2011 QCCA 591.
79   2011 SCC 66.

CHAPTER 2

COMPETITION ACT AND INVESTMENT CANADA ACT CONSIDERATIONS

A. INTRODUCTION

There are two federal statutes of which Canadian lawyers must be especially wary when advising on a large business acquisition: the *Competition Act*[1] and the *Investment Canada Act*.[2]

B. *COMPETITION ACT*

1) Anti-Trust

The federal *Competition Act* (once called the *Combines Investigation Act*) is the primary source in Canada today for what is often called "anti-trust" law. The purpose of anti-trust law is to regulate mergers to prevent the formation of monopolies or oligopolies in which a small number of companies come to dominate an industry. Firms with market dominance, it is feared, may be in a position to abuse their market power, chiefly by charging higher prices for their goods and services than would be possible if they were subject to effective competition.[3]

---

1 R.S.C. 1985, c. C-34.
2 R.S.C. 1985 (1st supp.), c. 28.
3 Of course, there are other potential detrimental effects of decreasing competition, beyond simple increases in nominal prices. Thus, for example, the

It may seem peculiar that legislation aimed mainly at preventing anti-competitive actions of *corporations* should be known as anti-*trust* law. The origin of the term anti-*trust* is American. In the late nineteenth and early twentieth centuries, firms in a number of American industries consolidated their operations using structures that included trust agreements. Melvin Urofsky has explained these early industry-consolidating structures in this way: "A *trust* is an organizational device through which a number of firms combine. In practice, shareholders in the individual firms turn in their stock and receive trust certificates. The affairs of all the companies are then run by trustees."[4]

The facts in the key 1911 U.S. Supreme Court anti-trust decision, *Standard Oil Co. v. U.S.* provide an illustration of this technique.[5] There, it was alleged that the defendants had "entered into a contract and trust agreement, by which various independent firms engaged in . . . [aspects of the oil business] turned over the management of their business to nine trustees . . . which said trust agreement was in restraint of trade and commerce, and in violation of law."[6] Becht, Bolton, and Röell note that, in response to early American anti-trust legislation (the *Sherman Anti-Trust Act of 1890*[7]), many voting trusts "converted themselves into New Jersey registered holding companies . . . that were identical in function but escaped the initial round of antitrust legislation."[8]

Today, the sort of business combination that may threaten to lessen competition almost invariably involves corporations and rarely, if ever, involves a trust structure.

Competition Bureau, in its *Merger Enforcement Guidelines*, uses references to an increase in price to include "an increase in the nominal price, but may also refer to a reduction in quality, product choice, service, innovation or other dimensions of competition that buyers value." See Competition Bureau, *Merger Enforcement Guidelines* at para. 2.2, online: www.competitionbureau.gc.ca/eic/site/cb-bc.nsf/vwapj/cb-meg-2011-e.pdf/$FILE/cb-meg-2011-e.pdf. The *Merger Enforcement Guidelines* were issued by the Competition Bureau "to provide general direction on its analytical approach to merger review." See *Merger Enforcement Guidelines*, Foreword, at 1. The most recent version of the *Merger Enforcement Guidelines* was published in October 2011.

4   Melvin I. Urofsky, "Louis D. Brandeis, Progressivism, and the Money Trust" in Louis D. Brandeis, *Other People's Money and How the Bankers Use It*, ed. by Melvin I. Urofsky (New York: Bedford Books, 1995) at 5n [emphasis in original].

5   31 S. Ct. 502 (1910).

6   *Ibid.* at 505.

7   15 U.S.C. §§ 1–7.

8   Marco Brecht, Patrick Bolton, & Ailsa Röell, "Corporate Governance and Control" in George M. Constantinides, Milton Harris, & René M Stulz, *Handbook of the Economics of Finance*, vol. 1A (North Holland: Elsevier, 2003) 1 at 6n.

Canada's foray into anti-competition law came early. In 1889, Parliament enacted *An Act for the Prevention and Suppression of Combinations Formed in Restraint of Trade*,[9] a statute that was, evidently, "the first of its kind anywhere in the world."[10]

2) The Problem of Monopoly Power

The concerns raised by monopoly power and agreements made in restraint of trade have been recognized for centuries. Adam Smith famously observed that "People of the same trade seldom meet together, even for merriment and diversion, but the conversation ends in a conspiracy against the public, or in some contrivance to raise prices."[11] The problem raised by monopolies is an intuitive one. Economists often try to illustrate the problem that monopolies pose for consumers with a little more precision, enlisting the aid of graphs depicting "marginal cost" curves, "marginal revenue" curves, demand curves, and so on. Arguments that can be reduced to graphs rarely persuade lawyers. But these particular graphs are well worth a look.[12] They help to show, pictorially, why monopolists (who have the luxury of being "price setters" rather than "price takers") will have an incentive to restrict output to the point where the cost of producing one additional item for sale (the marginal cost) is just equal to the additional amount to be earned if the monopolist sells that one additional item (marginal revenue). But there is an important assumption built into this calculation, namely, that the monopolist must sell *every unit for the same price*.

In other words, it is assumed that the monopolist cannot discriminate between buyers—charging a higher price to those buyers who would be willing to pay more for an item, and a lower price to those buyers who do not value the item so highly. Once it is assumed that the monopolist must charge a single price for every item sold, one can begin to see why a monopolist might have an incentive to limit the number of items he or she supplies to the market. Simply put, producing fewer items and selling them to those buyers willing to pay a

---

9   1889 (U.K.), 52 Vic., c. 41.

10   "Introduction," *Interim Report on the* Competition Act, *Seventh Report of the Standing Committee on Industry* (Susan Whelan, Chair), June 2000, online: www. parl.gc.ca.

11   Adam Smith, *Wealth of Nations* (Amherst: Prometheus Books, 1991) Book I, c. 10 at 137.

12   Examples may be found in any introductory microeconomics text. See, for example, Robert H. Frank *et al.*, *Principles of Microeconomics*, 2d Canadian ed. (Toronto: McGraw-Hill Ryerson, 2005) at 235, 237, & 238.

high price for them will be more profitable than producing a larger number of items and charging a lower price for each and every one of them. More formally, the monopolist's marginal revenue—that is, the amount earned by selling an additional item—will *not* simply be the price which that additional item would fetch in the marketplace. It is on this point that a market dominated by a monopolist differs critically from a competitive market: in a competitive market, of course, the market price of each additional item sold *would* indeed be equal to the supplier's marginal revenue. But, because we assume that the monopolist must sell each and every item he or she produces at the same price, the more items the monopolist sells, the *lower the price the monopolist must charge on every item sold.*

This idea is easy to understand although a little difficult to explain. To illustrate how a hypothetical monopolist might have to determine how many units to produce, consider this (wildly exaggerated) example. Suppose a producer ("Widgetmaker") has a monopoly in the market for widgets. There simply are no other widget suppliers to be found. Equally important, for some reason assume that it is very difficult for any new widget suppliers to emerge. (There are, in the economists' vernacular, high "barriers to entry" in the widget-making market.)

Let us suppose that Widgetmaker's marginal cost for producing each widget is exactly $10.[13] Buyer A would happily pay a full $1000 for a widget. Buyers B and C, however, would each only be willing to pay $500 for a widget. There are twenty-three other prospective widget buyers in the world: Buyers D through Z. Each of these buyers would be willing to pay only $10.01 per widget. (There may well be additional prospective widget buyers who would only be interested in purchasing widgets at some price below $10 each, but since the cost of producing each widget is $10, Widgetmaker can hardly sell for less than $10.)

Now, in a competitive market, where Widgetmaker was subject to competitive pressures,[14] Widgetmaker would have no choice but to accept the price set by the market. If that market price was, say, $10.01 per widget, we would expect widgetmakers, collectively, to produce and sell twenty-six widgets. We know this because for each one of those twenty-six widgets sold, Widgetmaker would earn $10.01 in revenue, and yet the cost of producing each widget would only be $10. (Put another way, Widgetmaker's marginal revenue from producing each one

---

13   Marginal cost is not simply assumed by economists to be constant; but we will make such an assumption here to simplify the explanation.

14   Those pressures could take the form of actual competitors or, at the very least, low barriers to entry that would make it easy for prospective competitors to enter the market easily if Widgetmaker appeared to be extracting monopoly rents.

of those widgets would be $10.01, and Widgetmaker's marginal cost would be $10.)

But the situation is very different if Widgetmaker has a monopoly. As Widgetmaker ponders how many widgets to supply to the market, he realizes that if he were to produce three (and only three) widgets— to be sold to Buyers A, B, and C—each of these three widgets would be sold at a price of $500. (That is the highest price that can be charged in order for B and C to be prepared to buy widgets. Remember, we are assuming that Widgetmaker must sell at the same price to all buyers. So, if Widgetmaker wishes to make sales to B and C, B and C cannot be charged more than $500. Therefore, the price of the widget sold to A will also have to be set at $500, regardless of the fact that A would have been *willing* to pay a higher price.)

Yet, look what happens as Widgetmaker calculates whether or not to produce more than just these three widgets. If Widgetmaker produces, say, four widgets, instead of just three, that fourth widget can only be sold for $10.01. Any higher price and it will go unsold and there will have been no point in producing it in the first place. But, again, remember that we have said that Widgetmaker must charge the *same price* to each and every buyer. So if Widgetmaker intends to produce and sell four widgets instead of three, the price to be charged *for all four widgets* will have to be just $10.01—the highest price at which a buyer (namely, D), is prepared to buy that fourth widget. (A, B, and C will, of course, be delighted if Widgetmaker decides to produce and sell four widgets rather than just three. They would all have been *willing* to pay much more than $10.01; but now they will not need to. If Widgetmaker chooses to sell four widgets, he will not be able to charge A, B, or C any higher price than the price charged to D.)

So, what would Widgetmaker's marginal revenue from the sale of this fourth widget to D be? Here is the crucial insight: marginal revenue would *not* be $10.01 (even though that will be the *price* Widgetmaker will receive from D when he sells this fourth widget). The reason marginal revenue will not be $10.01, is that in calculating *marginal* revenue (that is, the additional revenue derived from selling one more unit), Widgetmaker must perform a calculation that is slightly more complicated than simply determining how much revenue will be earned from the sale of the fourth unit. Instead, he must compare (a) the total amount of revenue he will earn from selling four units, to (b) the total amount of revenue he would have earned had he decided to sell only three units instead. And that calculation results in a number very different from $10.01.

If Widgetmaker had produced and sold just three units, his total revenue would have been:

$$3 \times \$500 = \$1,500$$

If, instead, he chose to produce and sell four units, his total revenue would be:

$$4 \times \$10.01 = \$40.04$$

Therefore, the marginal revenue derived from producing that fourth unit is far less than Widgetmaker's marginal cost of $10. In fact, it is a large *negative* number (–$1,439.96). In other words, the decision to sell a fourth widget means Widgetmaker will have $1,439.96 *less* money in his pocket than if he had decided to produce and sell just three (higher-priced) widgets.

Obviously, it would make no sense for Widgetmaker to spend another $10 to produce that fourth widget. Taking into account how much the price would have to be lowered *on the other three widgets to be sold*, Widgetmaker would be made worse off. (Keep in mind that we are assuming that Widgetmaker is determining how many widgets to supply *before he has produced even a single widget*. In other words, when we calculate how much Widgetmaker would make by selling four widgets instead of three, we are certainly *not* assuming that he has already sold those first three widgets for the high prices A, B, and C would have been willing to pay. Obviously, once products have been sold it is not necessary for the seller to refund part of the purchase price when additional units are sold to other buyers at a lower cost. But we are assuming here that Widgetmaker is performing these calculations before launching his products for sale at all, and so before he has yet produced or sold any widgets. He is therefore performing these calculations explicitly for the purpose of determining how many widgets to produce and sell in the first place.)

So if Widgetmaker is a monopolist in a market with high barriers to entry, he has an incentive to restrict output: to produce and sell only three widgets in total rather than twenty-six. To reiterate, the reason there is no similar incentive for suppliers to restrict their output in a competitive market is that suppliers in a competitive market must simply accept the market price for the goods they sell; whether they choose to sell one widget or 1,000, they will receive the same sale price per unit. That price will be determined by market forces over which no individual supplier has control. That is the reason that, in a competitive market, a supplier's marginal revenue is simply equal to the market price for the goods sold. But when output is restricted (as it will be when a supplier enjoys a monopoly and wants to maximize its profit), there will be losses in total social welfare (or deadweight losses). What happens, basically, is that the monopoly seller—by charging a price that is higher than the price that would have been set in a competitive market—scoops up a significant portion of what would otherwise have been consumer surplus;[15] and some surplus simply disappears altogether. The monopoly supplier, of course, is better off. But consumers, in total, will lose *more* than the monopoly supplier gains. So society, as a whole, will be poorer.

Economists assure us that all sellers—whether in competitive markets or otherwise—will continue producing until marginal cost equals marginal revenue;[16] but the unique feature of markets where there is a monopoly seller is that a monopoly seller's marginal revenue is not equivalent to the price of each additional unit sold, for the reason explained earlier. As a result, monopoly sellers can earn *economic profits*; sellers in a competitive market cannot.

The notion that sellers in a competitive market earn zero economic profits is well-understood by students of economics, but often seems puzzling to those who have carefully avoided any course of study where graphs and equations might threaten to spoil otherwise perfectly tidy pages of printed text. The key to unravelling this (apparent) puzzle is to realize that economic profits are *not* what businesspeople (and financial newspapers, and most of the rest of us) usually refer to as profits. When businesspeople refer to "profits," they usually mean simply accounting profits. Accounting profits (or earnings) refer to the amount by which the revenue a business has earned exceeds the business's expenses, as recorded on the firm's income statement. Economic profit means something quite different. Economic profit refers to the amount by which a supplier's revenues exceed *all* costs—including an important cost that is *not* found on any income statement, "opportunity cost." Opportunity cost, as the name suggests, refers to the value of the opportunity that one sacrifices whenever one chooses to use productive capacity in one way rather than another. For example, suppose a certain machine could be used to produce either ten widgets per day or ten gidgets per day. If the owner of the machine chooses to produce ten widgets, the opportunity cost would be the amount that owner *could* have earned had she, instead, used the same machine at the same time to produce gidgets. When we say that, in a competitive market, firms

---

15   *Consumer surplus* essentially means the benefit that consumers enjoy when the market price for a good is lower than the price they would otherwise have been prepared to pay.

16   See Frank *et al.*, above note 12 at 230.

earn no "economic profits," we do not mean, of course, that they have no accounting earnings. Any business firm that does not generate any accounting earnings will—sooner or later—collapse. Instead, when we say a firm in a perfectly competitive market will not earn economic profits we essentially mean that the revenues produced less the costs incurred to produce them will not be higher than the amounts that would be generated if the firm's assets were deployed in the next most profitable alternative venture.

3) Reviewable and Notifiable Transactions

Although the *Competition Act* is based on economic principles, ultimately its rules must be interpreted and applied by lawyers. Today, under the federal *Competition Act,* a proposed business acquisition may be subject to scrutiny whether it is structured as a share sale, an asset sale, an amalgamation, an arrangement, or otherwise. For purposes of the *Competition Act,* there are two concepts that are of particular significance for M & A lawyers:

* reviewable transactions; and
* notifiable transactions.

a) Reviewable Transactions and the Efficiency Defence

Most *every* "merger" in Canada (subject to a few exceptions) is, technically, reviewable under section 92 of the *Competition Act*, regardless of the size of the businesses involved. As a practical matter, however, federal competition authorities do not enjoy the luxury of unlimited resources; so it is large mergers that are typically of most interest to the regulators. (The term *merger,* as it is used in the *Competition Act,* is explained later in this section.)

The "review" of a transaction referred to in section 92 is carried out by the Competition Tribunal, an administrative tribunal established by section 3 of the *Competition Tribunal Act.*[17] The purpose of such a review would be to determine whether or not the business combination was "likely to prevent or lessen, competition substantially"; and, where necessary, to make an appropriate order to prevent any such anti-competitive effects. Such a review is triggered by an application made to the tribunal by the commissioner of competition (the "Commissioner"), an official appointed by the governor in council pursuant to section 7 of the *Competition Act.*

---

17   R.S.C. 1985 (2d Supp.), c. 19, ss. 1–17.

The *Competition Act* also provides for the appointment of deputy commissioners. Further, to provide the necessary infrastructure and support for the Commissioner to carry out her functions, Industry Canada has established the Competition Bureau. The Competition Bureau, which is headed by the Commissioner, is described on its website as "an independent law enforcement agency responsible for the administration and enforcement" (among other things) "of the *Competition Act*."[18]

The term *merger* is defined in section 91 of the *Competition Act*. The definition is cast in wide terms. It means "the acquisition or establishment, direct or indirect, by one or more persons, whether by purchase or lease of shares or assets, by amalgamation or by combination or otherwise, of control over or significant interest in the whole or a part of a business of a competitor, supplier, customer or other person."

One unique, and sometimes controversial, feature of the Canadian *Competition Act* is the availability of an "efficiency defence." Attempting to operationalize the efficiency defence is an intriguing exercise in the integration of economic principles and traditional legal techniques of statutory interpretation. It may be tempting to assume that, because the *Competition Act* is economic legislation which frequently requires regulators to apply the sophisticated analysis of economic experts, that the interpretation of its provisions ought to be animated by economic analysis. But what must not be forgotten is that the *Competition Act*, like all legislation, is the product of a complex set of competing political forces. It is by no means certain that Parliament intended to fully endorse any particular economist's view of "efficiency," and so the words of the statute must be carefully analyzed to ensure that it is Parliament's will—whether economically optimal or not—that is given effect.

The efficiency defence is found in section 96 of the *Competition Act*. Although, the consideration of merger efficiencies is undertaken by competition regulators in other jurisdictions, including the United States and the European Union,[19] the Canadian approach is unusual, although not, perhaps, unique.[20] In U.S. and European merger review,

---

18   See Competition Bureau website, online: www.competitionbureau.gc.ca/eic/site/cb-bc.nsf/eng/01241.html.

19   See, for example, U.S. Department of Justice and Federal Trade Commission, *Horizontal Merger Guidelines* (19 August 2010) at 29ff., online: www.justice.gov/atr/public/guidelines/hmg-2010.pdf; European Commission, *Guidelines on the assessment of horizontal mergers under the Council Regulation on the control of concentrations between undertakings* (2004/C 31/03), Part VII, online: http://eur-lex.europa.eu/LexUriServ/LexUriServ.do?uri=OJ:C:2004:031:0005:0018:EN:PDF.

20   In 2005, the Competition Bureau released a report, "Report of the International Roundtable on Efficiencies" which included, among other things, a summary

consideration of the promised efficiencies of a merger transaction is integrated within an overall assessment of the anti-competitive effects of the transaction. Under the Canadian *Competition Act*, the regulatory assessment of efficiency gains is a separate exercise, distinct from the determination of the effect of a transaction on preventing or lessening of competition.

The words of the statute's efficiency defence are cumbersome but are the essential starting point for this discussion:

> 96(1) The Tribunal shall not make an order under section 92 if it finds that the merger or proposed merger in respect of which the application is made has brought about or is likely to bring about gains in efficiency that will be greater than, and will offset, the effects of any prevention or lessening of competition that will result or is likely to result from the merger or proposed merger and that the gains in efficiency would not likely be attained if the order were made.
>
> (2) In considering whether a merger or proposed merger is likely to bring about gains in efficiency described in subsection (1), the Tribunal shall consider whether such gains will result in
>
> (a)   a significant increase in the real value of exports; or
>
> (b)   a significant substitution of domestic products for imported products.
>
> (3) For the purposes of this section, the Tribunal shall not find that a merger or proposed merger has brought about or is likely to bring about gains in efficiency by reason only of a redistribution of income between two or more persons.

These words seem to tell us that there is to be no order made to prevent a merger in any case where the "gains in efficiency" promised by the merger or proposed merger outweigh (and, specifically "offset") the "effects of any prevention or lessening of competition." One might draw the simple conclusion that section 96 has been included so that mergers will be allowed to proceed where they are shown to do more

---

of the role of efficiencies in the competition policies of Australia, the European Union, Mexico, and the United Kingdom, as well as a summary note on practices in Germany, Japan, Norway, Sweden, and South Africa. Based on this review, the bureau concluded that, "With Canada, South Africa is the only other country with an explicit legislative efficiency defence." Online: www.competitionbureau.gc.ca/eic/site/cb-bc.nsf/eng/03212.html.

economic good than harm. Even pursuing that apparently simple principle, however, calls for some complicated mathematics.

There are some definitional questions, too. Precisely what sort of "efficiency" did the drafters have in mind? Allocative efficiency? Productive efficiency? Dynamic efficiency?[21] Does (or should) the concept of efficiency be measured only in terms of total welfare gains—that is, the expansion of the total economic "pie"? Or should due account also be taken of distribution effects—that is, the extent to which consumers' and producers' individual pieces of that pie grow or shrink? A standard of efficiency could well be economically sensible, yet politically controversial to the extent that it appeared to ignore (or downplay) distribution effects. In other words, some critics fear that a robust efficiency defence might be used to allow producers (invariably large corporations) to make gains at the expense of consumers (typically, human beings, or perhaps smaller business corporations) provided the producers' gains were greater than the consumers' total losses. Could an exclusive focus on total wealth (no matter how unevenly distributed) have been the intention of the *Competition Act*? Or should some consideration be given, as well, to *who* must shoulder the burdens, and *who* will enjoy the benefits of an efficiency-enhancing but competition-lessening merger?[22]

The scope of the efficiency defence, which was first introduced into Canada's federal competition legislation in 1985, has been discussed by the Competition Bureau in its *Merger Enforcement Guidelines*, but has been subject to very little scrutiny by the Competition Tribunal or the courts. In fact, the efficiency defence has been the subject of only one Canadian judicial decision to date. It was also discussed in an earlier

---

21 For a recent article discussing these differing concepts of efficiency in the antitrust context, see, for example, Barak Y. Orbach, "The Antitrust Consumer Welfare Paradox" (2011) 7 Journal of Competition Law and Economics 133 at 141.

22 One of the early discussions of a proposed efficiency defence under U.S. antitrust law appeared in a 1968 paper by economist Oliver Williamson (who would later win the Nobel Prize for Economics in 2009). In that paper, Williamson identified the possibility that "we might not always wish to regard consumer and producer interests symmetrically," noting that, if they were not regarded symmetrically, "while economies would remain a defense, any undesirable income distribution effects associated with market power would be counted against the merger rather than enter neutrally . . . ." Williamson did note, however, that "since, arguably, antitrust is an activity better suited to promote allocative efficiency than income distribution objectives (the latter falling more clearly within the province of taxation, expenditure, and transfer payment activities), such income distribution adjustments might routinely be suppressed." See Oliver E. Williamson, "Economies as an Antitrust Defense: The Welfare Tradeoffs" (1968) 58 American Economic Review 18 at 28.

Competition Tribunal decision, though the tribunal's comments on the defence were not, strictly speaking, relevant to the tribunal's decision.

The key tribunal decision was *Canada (Director of Investigation and Research, Competition Act) v. Hillsdown Holdings Canada Ltd.*[23] Because the tribunal in that case was not satisfied, on a balance of probabilities, that the proposed merger would result in a substantial lessening of competition in any event, there was, technically, no need to go on to consider the availability of the efficiencies defence. Despite this, the tribunal's discussion of the efficiency defence, as Renckens notes, was "useful as it initiated a debate with respect to the meaning of Section 96 . . . ."[24]

The *Hillsdown* tribunal reviewed the *Merger Enforcement Guidelines* in effect at that time, noting that those guidelines stated that section 96 called for a measurement of efficiency gains only against deadweight losses—that is, losses arising from the reduction of the total sum of consumer surplus and producer surplus, without regard to redistribution effects. The tribunal indicated its "difficulty"[25] with this interpretation noting, among other things, that versions of the efficiency defence language that had been proposed in earlier bills (but not enacted) explicitly provided that mergers were not to be prohibited where they would result in efficiency gains. In other words, these earlier draft versions did seem to envision the approach advocated by the *Merger Enforcement Guidelines*—an approach that did not call for any weighing of prospective gains against the effects of a substantial lessening of competition. Thus, the tribunal argued, if Parliament had intended this efficiency-trumps-all approach to be the appropriate test, the language used in these earlier bills would have been preserved in the final version of the defence as actually enacted by Parliament. Further, the tribunal looked to the "purpose clause" of the *Competition Act* (section 1.1) as an aid to interpretation of section 96. The purpose clause recites four goals of Canadian competition laws, one of which is indeed "to promote the efficiency . . . of the Canadian economy." However, other stated goals include "to provide consumers with competitive prices and product choices" and "to ensure that small and medium-sized enterprises have an equitable opportunity to participate in the Canadian economy." The tribunal reasoned that it would be wrong to privilege one of these goals—the promotion of efficiency—over the others in

---

23   (1992), 41 C.P.R. (3d) 289.

24   An Renckens, "Welfare Standards, Substantive Tests and Efficiency Considerations in Merger Policy: Defining the Efficiency Defense" (2007) 3 Journal of Competition Law and Economics 149 at 156n.

25   Above note 23.

interpreting the efficiency defence. Briefly reviewing the legislative history of the efficiency defence provision, the tribunal also adverted to the ambiguity of the efficiency defence, since it called for a balancing of non-comparable factors: efficiency, on the one hand (which could be measured in terms of actual economic gains), and income redistribution (which could not be assessed in the absence of some normative qualitative criteria). The tribunal also took issue with the assumption that wealth transfers (for example, from consumers to producers) should be regarded as neutral.

Several months after the tribunal's *Hillsdown* decision, Howard Wetston, then the Bureau of Competition Policy's Director of Investigation and Research (the office was later renamed Commissioner of Competition) spoke at the Fordham Corporate Law Institute in New York City about recent developments in Canadian competition law.[26] In his speech, Mr. Wetston noted that the *Hillsdown* treatment of the efficiency defence had "generated considerable attention." Despite the tribunal's clear reservations about the treatment of efficiencies in the then current version of the *Merger Enforcement Guidelines*, Mr Wetston stated that "from the enforcement perspective it is preferable not to depart at this time from the approach adopted in the Merger Enforcement guidelines."

Though the *Hillsdown* tribunal's discussion of the efficiency defence was extensive, it was essentially *obiter dicta*. Consequently, the most significant judicial analysis of the efficiency defence is that of the Federal Court of Appeal in *Canada (Commissioner of Competition)* v. *Superior Propane Inc.*,[27] a case that arose out of the 1998 acquisition by Superior Propane Inc. of ICG Propane Inc. The procedural history of the *Superior Propane* case was somewhat complicated. Initially, the Competition Tribunal determined that the merger between Superior Propane and ICG would lessen competition but found that the efficiency gains of the merger would offset those negative effects, and so denied the application of the Commissioner for an order to dissolve the merger. The Competition Tribunal, in coming to its conclusion, had applied the so-called total surplus standard—an economic test that measures the total potential economic

---

26   Howard Wetston, "Developments and Emerging Challenges in Canadian Competition Law" (22 October 1992), online: www.competitionbureau.gc.ca/eic/site/cb-bc.nsf/eng/01070.html. It might be noted that Howard Wetston is currently Chair of the Ontario Securities Commission.

27   2003 FCA 53, aff'g (2002), 18 C.P.R. (4th) 417 (Comp. Tribunal) [*Superior Propane*]. The Competition Tribunal decision followed redetermination proceedings, and the issue before the Federal Court of Appeal in the 2003 case was whether or not the Court of Appeal's earlier directions, [2001] 3 F.C. 185, had been adhered to.

gains from the transaction against the estimated losses—without regard to distribution effects. Put simply, if the producer would gain $2, and consumers would lose (in total) less than $2, the merger should be allowed. As the Federal Court of Appeal explained the approach in its 2003 decision: "Under the total surplus standard, there is no economic reason for favouring a dollar in the hands of consumers over a dollar in the hands of the shareholders of the merged entity who are also consumers."[28]

The Federal Court of Appeal initially determined that the tribunal had erred in law by, in effect, codifying the total surplus standard as the basis for the efficiency defence. In the court's view, the tribunal ought to have considered "a wider range of effects" and "have regard for the purposes set out in section 1.1."[29] However, in the tribunal's re-determination decision, the Federal Court of Appeal was satisfied that the tribunal had considered other factors and the purposes of section 1.1 in accordance with the Federal Court of Appeal's earlier directions. Consequently, the court dismissed an appeal from this redetermination decision, notwithstanding that—as in the original tribunal decision—the tribunal determined that the merger should be allowed, based upon the efficiency defence.

In a comment on the *Superior Propane* decision, Roman, Piaskoski and Wong note that by including the efficiency defence in the *Competition Act,* the drafters have indicated "that the preservation of competition is not the only objective to be achieved by the Act . . . Efficiency is the goal, while competition is, in most cases, the best means for achieving that goal."[30] But, as they note, competition need not always be the best means of enhancing efficiency. Moreover, the authors warn against falling into the trap of assuming that "all consumers are 'good' or more

---

28   *Ibid.* at para. 14 (FCA).
29   *Ibid.* at para. 16.
30   Andrew J. Roman, Michael E. Piaskoski, & Michelle Wong, "Legal Principles Versus Economic Principles: The Battle Over Efficiencies in Canadian Merger Review" (2006) 44 Can. Bus. L.J. 173 at 175. In August 2005, the Advisory Panel on Efficiencies submitted its final report to the Commissioner of Competition. The Advisory Panel concluded, among other things, that Canada continues to face "a major productivity problem" which calls for efforts to promote economic efficiency. In some cases, they concluded, mergers may lead to gains in both "productive and dynamic efficiency" that could offset anti-competitive effects. Accordingly, the Panel recommended that the efficiency defence be retained in the statute. However, the Panel found that the "current standard for weighing efficiency gains against competition effects is not satisfactory" and so recommended that Parliament define the appropriate standard for evaluating any such trade-off. See online: www.competitionbureau.gc.ca/PDFs/FinalPanelReportEfficiencies_e.pdf.

'worthy' . . . and that all producers are 'bad' or less worthy,"[31] a trap
that could lead to economic inefficiency and unintended and adverse
distributional consequences as well. In short, the *Competition Act* was
intended to promote efficiency through effective competition. However,
it was not intended to preserve competition at all costs. Courts and
the Competition Tribunal should be mindful of this sound economic
objective and not attempt to rewrite the *Competition Act* in an attempt
to cater to distributional goals that may be intuitively or politically
appealing, but could prove economically harmful. Yet, it is equally important to recall the important distinction between what legislation
ought to say, and what legislation actually says. The fact that Parliament
may have given the tribunal an onerous task couched in ambiguous language cannot justify ignoring the complexities of the statute in favour
of a presumed economically superior and easier to apply standard that,
nonetheless, is not fully reflective of the legislators' intent—however
messy and frustrating sincerely attempting to give effect to that intent
might prove to be. The shortcomings of the language in the Act should
be identified and rectified through the legislative amendment process,
not ignored in favour of eminently sensible approaches that require *ad
hoc* judicial or administrative rewriting of the troublesome statute.

Following the *Superior Propane* decision,[32] a private member's bill,
supported by the Commissioner, was introduced into Parliament proposing to amend the *Competition Act*'s efficiency defence.[33] If enacted,
this legislation would have amended section 96 in two key ways. First,
it would have eliminated efficiency as a free-standing "defence" in favour of an integrated approach that would make a consideration of efficiency a factor to be taken into account when making a determination
as to the anti-competitive effects of a proposed merger under section
93.[34] Second, it purported to introduce what the Competition Bureau
described as a "consumer benefit" requirement.[35] That is, the Competition Tribunal would be permitted to consider the possible efficiency
gains of a proposed merger where those gains would "provide benefits
to consumers, including competitive prices or product choices, and that
would not likely be attained in the absence of the merger or proposed

---

31   *Ibid*. at 197.

32   Above note 27.

33   Bill C-249, *An Act to amend the Competition Act*, 2nd Sess., 37th Parl., 2002.

34   This mirrors the approach taken in most other major jurisdictions. See above
      note 20.

35   See Competition Bureau, "Treatment of Efficiencies under the *Competition Act*—
      Consultation Paper," Introduction, online: www.competitionbureau.gc.ca/eic/
      site/cb-bc.nsf/eng/01602.html.

merger." This legislation died on the order paper in May 2004, and no further amendment to section 96 has been proposed since. Instead, following a process of policy consultation,[36] the Competition Bureau refined its approach to section 96, as first indicated in its March 2009 bulletin, "Efficiencies in Merger Review,"[37] a document which offers to "provide, as a supplement to the [bureau's 2004 *Merger Enforcement Guidelines*[38]], practical guidance to assist parties in understanding the Bureau's enforcement approach in this area."[39] That bulletin was subsequently superseded when a new version of the *Merger Enforcement Guidelines* was issued in October 2011.[40]

b) Notifiable Transactions

Although in theory any merger in Canada is subject to review by the Competition Bureau, in practice it is the largest transactions that are of most interest to Canadian competition regulators. Accordingly, the *Competition Act* requires parties planning to undertake large transactions to notify the Commissioner in advance, and provide the Commissioner with information about the proposed transaction.[41] The purpose of this pre-merger notification is to alert the Commissioner to major transactions so that the Commissioner can decide whether or not to make an application to the Competition Tribunal under section 92 of the Act for review of the transaction.

The requirement for parties to large mergers to notify competition regulators in advance was added to Canada's competition legislation following the adoption of a similar initiative in the United States. In 1976, the U.S. Congress enacted the *Hart-Scott-Rodino Antitrust Improvements Act of 1976*.[42] The *Hart-Scott-Rodino Act* added a new section, section 7A, to the principal federal U.S. anti-trust statute, the *Clayton Act*. This new section required that, where acquisitions above a certain size involved parties above a certain size, advance notification of such acquisitions must be filed with the Federal Trade Commission (FTC) (specifically,

---

36   The consultation process was launched with the publication of "Treatment of Efficiencies under the *Competition Act*," *ibid*.

37   Online: www.competitionbureau.gc.ca/eic/site/cb-bc.nsf/eng/02982.html.

38   The 2004 *Merger Enforcement Guidelines* superseded an earlier set of guidelines released by the bureau in 1991, online: www.competitionbureau.gc.ca/eic/site/cb-bc.nsf/vwapj/meg_part5.pdf/$FILE/meg_part5.pdf.

39   Above note 2.

40   See online: www.competitionbureau.gc.ca/eic/site/cb-bc.nsf/vwapj/cb-meg-2011-e.pdf/$FILE/cb-meg-2011-e.pdf. The treatment of the efficiency defence is dealt with in Part 12 of the new guidelines.

41   *Competition Act*, s. 114(1).

42   15 U.S.C. §18a.

the Premerger Notification Office of the FTC's Bureau of Competition) and the Department of Justice (specifically, the director of operations and merger enforcement, antitrust division). The pre-merger notification rules were introduced in response to concerns raised by studies indicating that anti-trust enforcement actions taken *after* mergers had been completed did not result in restoring competition in the relevant markets to the levels that had existed prior to the mergers.[43] Accordingly, if competition regulators were to operate effectively to preserve competition, they would need to be able to restrain non-competitive mergers before they had been completed. And to do that, they would need to be alerted in advance about such proposed mergers. However, requiring parties to every transaction, no matter how small, to make government filings would not only be unnecessary, but would actually clog the administrative processing pipeline. Large transactions by major players were the primary focus of the regulators' attention.

How "large" must a transaction be before it triggers the notification obligation? There are two sorts of prescribed-size thresholds. They are found in the *Competition Act*, as read in conjunction with the *Notifiable Transactions Regulations*:[44] one is based upon the *total size of the parties* to the transaction, and one is based upon the *total size of the transaction* itself. Parties are only required to provide advance notice of a merger if the proposed transaction falls within the parameters of *both* these thresholds.

i)   *Mergers Are Notifiable Only If Parties Involved Have Significant Assets or Significant Revenues ("Party-size" or "Size-of-Person Test")*[45]
A transaction is only notifiable if the parties to the transaction, together with their affiliates:

---

43   Ronald J. Gilson & Bernard S. Black, *The Law and Finance of Corporate Acquisitions*, 2d ed. (Westbury, NY: Foundation Press, 1995) at 1473.
44   S.O.R./87-348.
45   The term *size of person* test is used by the U.S. Federal Trade Commission to describe certain requirements in s. 7A(a)2 of the *Clayton Act*, 15 U.S.C. §12. See, for example, Federal Trade Commission, *Introductory Guide II—To File or Not to File—When You Must File a Premerger Notification Report* (Revised September 2008) at 2, online: www.ftc.gov. The equivalent term "party-size" is used in the Canadian Competition Bureau's 2012 *Merger Review Process Guidelines* at 2, online: www.competitionbureau.gc.ca/eic/site/cb-bc.nsf/vwapj/merger-review-process-2012-e.pdf/$FILE/merger-review-process-2012-e.pdf.

- have assets in Canada of more than $400 million;[46] or
- had gross annual revenues from sales "in, from, or into Canada" of more than $400 million.[47]

The determination of the assets of the parties and their affiliates is normally made as of the last day of the accounting period covered by the party's most recent audited financial statements, provided that the most recent audited financial statements are not "stale"—specifically, as long as they do not relate to an accounting period that ended more than fifteen months before the date of the determination.[48] The value of assets for this purpose is normally to be based upon values as they appear on each party's audited balance sheet,[49] even though it is well-understood that asset values recorded on a firm's balance sheet need not reflect the market value of these assets.[50] Finally, it is the value of the assets themselves that matters, rather than the unencumbered value (or the owner's "equity" in the assets). In other words, if the parties have assets with a total value of more than $400 million, the transaction will be notifiable, regardless of the amount of any corresponding liabilities.[51]

The determination of the parties' gross annual revenues from sales is also based on the parties' audited financial statements.[52] Specifically, annual gross sales revenues would be the amounts so recorded on each party's income statement for that year. Just as the assets test is to be determined without taking into account corresponding liabilities, similarly the regulations provide that the gross sales calculation is to be made "without deducting any expenses or other amounts incurred or provided for in relation to the sale or lease of goods or the rendering of services."[53]

Of course, even if the parties to a proposed merger are large enough to trigger one of these "party-size" tests, that is not the end of the matter. The transaction will only be notifiable if, *in addition to this*

---

46 *Competition Act*, s. 109(1)(a).
47 *Ibid.*, s. 109(1)(b).
48 *Notifiable Transactions Regulations*, s. 6.
49 *Ibid.*, s. 8.
50 For a discussion of the divergence of balance sheet values and market values, see Christopher C. Nicholls, *Corporate Finance and Canadian Law* (Toronto: Carswell, 2001) at 125.
51 *Notifiable Transactions Regulations*, s. 4(2). An amount may be deducted, however, for depreciation or diminution in value. See *ibid.*, s. 4(1)(c).
52 *Ibid.*, s. 9(2).
53 *Ibid.*, s. 5(1).

"party-size" threshold, *the transaction itself* exceeds certain dollar value thresholds. It is to these transaction-based tests that we now turn.

ii) *Mergers Are Notifiable Only If the Transaction Itself Is of a Certain Minimum Size ("Transaction Size" or "Size-of-Transaction Test")*[54]

Even where very large parties are involved in a merger, they will not need to notify the Competition Bureau in advance of their proposed transaction unless the transaction itself is of significant size. The *Competition Act* distinguishes between five different types of transactions, and prescribes the dollar threshold that will determine if transactions of each type will be notifiable. The five transaction types and the corresponding dollar thresholds as of 2011 are set out in Table 1.

Table 1   Transactions Determining Notifiable Mergers

Type of Transaction	Dollar Value Threshold for Determining if Transaction is Notifiable
Acquisition of assets of operating business	Total value of assets or gross annual revenues from sales in or from Canada generated from those assets exceeds $73 million,[1] subject to annual adjustment by the Minister of Industry in accordance with a formula prescribed in the statute and linked to changes in Gross Domestic Product[2]

---

54   The term "size of transaction test" is used by the U.S. Federal Trade Commission to describe certain requirements in s. 7A(a)2 of the *Clayton Act*. See *Introductory Guide II*, above note 45 at 2. The equivalent term "transaction size" used in the Canadian Competition Bureau's 2012 *Merger Review Process Guidelines* at 2. See above note 45.

Type of Transaction	Dollar Value Threshold for Determining if Transaction is Notifiable
Acquisition of voting shares of a corporation that carries on operating business, or owns another corporation that carries on operating business [Share acquisitions are only included if the purchaser will own a large block of shares in the acquired company: 20% of the voting shares in the case of a public corporation; 35% of the voting shares in the case of a private corporation. If the proposed purchaser already owns a block of shares this large before the proposed merger, then the transaction will only be included if the transaction will result in the purchaser (together with its affiliates) owning more than 50% of the shares.][3]	Total value of assets owned by corporation being acquired or corporations it controls or gross annual revenues from sales in or from Canada generated from those assets exceeds $73 million,[4] subject to annual adjustment by the Minister of Industry in accordance with a formula prescribed in the statute and linked to changes in Gross Domestic Product
Amalgamation	Total value of assets of corporation continuing after the amalgamation or corporations it controls or gross annual revenues from sales in or from Canada generated from those assets exceeds $73 million,[5] subject to annual adjustment by the Minister of Industry in accordance with a formula prescribed in the statute and linked to changes in Gross Domestic Product
Combination to carry on business other than through a corporation	Total value of the assets that are the subject of the transaction or gross annual revenues from sales in or from Canada generated from those assets exceeds $73 million,[6] subject to annual adjustment by the Minister of Industry in accordance with a formula prescribed in the statute and linked to changes in Gross Domestic Product

Type of Transaction	Dollar Value Threshold for Determining if Transaction is Notifiable
Acquisition of an interest in a combination that carries on business other than through a corporation [*An acquisition of this sort of interest is only included "where, as a result of the proposed acquisition of the interest, the person or persons acquiring the interest, together with their affiliates, would hold an aggregate interest in the combination that entitles the person or persons to receive more than 35% of the profits of the combination, or more than 35% of its assets on dissolution or, if the person or persons acquiring the interest are already so entitled, to receive more than 50% of such profits or assets."]*[7]	Total value of the assets that are the subject of the transaction or gross annual revenues from sales in or from Canada generated from those assets exceeds $73 million,[8] subject to annual adjustment by the Minister of Industry in accordance with a formula prescribed in the statute and linked to changes in Gross Domestic Product

[1]   *Competition Act*, s. 110(2); *Notifiable Transactions Regulations*, s. 14.1.
[2]   *Competition Act*, s. 110(8).
[3]   *Ibid.*, s.110(3)(b). In its October 2011 *Merger Enforcement Guidelines*, the Competition Bureau has explained the rationale for setting a higher ownership threshold in the case of private companies than in the case of public companies. Simply put, the bureau recognizes the practical need to hold a higher percentage of a private company's voting securities in order to materially influence that company. See *Merger Enforcement Guidelines*, above note 3 at para. 1.10.
[4]   *Competition Act*, *ibid.*, s. 110(3)(a); *Notifiable Transactions Regulations*, s. 14.1.
[5]   *Competition Act*, *ibid.*, s. 110(7), which came into effect in March 2009, specified that the relevant amount for the year in which the section came into force was $70 million. Thereafter, the Minister of Industry could amend the amount based on a formula tied to Gross Domestic Product (s. 110(8)). The current amount of $73 million (for 2011) was published in the Canada Gazette Part I, Vol. 145, No. 7 (12 February 2011) at 237. This threshold was to be reviewed at the end of 2011, to determine the amount for 2012. At the date of writing, no revised amount for 2012 has been announced.
[6]   *Ibid.*, s. 110(5); *Notifiable Transactions Regulations*, s. 14.1.
[7]   *Competition Act*, *ibid.*, s. 110(6)(b).
[8]   *Ibid.*, s. 110(6)(a); *Notifiable Transactions Regulations*, s. 14.1

iii) *Procedure for Notifying Commissioner*

When a proposed merger is a notifiable transaction, the parties must notify the Commissioner before the transaction is completed, and provide information about the transaction to the Commissioner. Once the notification has been filed, a "waiting period" begins. The parties are not permitted to complete their proposed transaction until the waiting period has elapsed or has been waived. Prior to significant amendments to the *Competition Act* enacted in 2009, the length of the waiting period depended on whether the parties to a proposed merger made a "short form" filing or a "long form" filing.[55] The notification procedure has now been changed, however. "Short form" and "long form" filings are gone. Now all notifiable transactions are subject to a two-stage merger review process which involves a minimum 30-day waiting period for all notifiable transactions (subject to prior waiver by the Commissioner.)

The first stage of the process begins with the filing of notice of a proposed merger.[56] This notice begins the initial 30-day waiting period within which the bureau will review the transaction. If the bureau takes no further steps within that 30-day period, the transaction may be closed at the end of the 30-day period,[57] or earlier, if the Commissioner waives the waiting period by indicating before the 30 days has elapsed that she does not intend to challenge the transaction under section 92.[58]

However, the Commissioner may choose to request additional information about the transaction during the initial 30-day period.[59] If the Commissioner makes such a request (dubbed a "supplementary information request" or "SIR" in the bureau's 2012 *Merger Review Process Guidelines*[60]) then the transaction becomes subject to a second 30-day waiting period that begins to run *after* the Commissioner has received all the information requested.[61] The Competition Bureau has indicated that "the majority of mergers do not raise competition concerns,"[62] suggesting that the use of SIRs should be relatively infrequent. However, the two-stage review process nevertheless introduces the potential for delay and uncertainty into the Canadian M & A market.

---

55 The waiting period in the case of a short form filing was fourteen days, and in the case of a long form filing was forty-two days.
56 *Competition Act*, s. 114(1).
57 *Ibid.*, s. 123(1).
58 *Ibid.*, s.123(2).
59 *Ibid*, s. 114(2).
60 Above note 45 at 1.
61 *Competition Act*, s. 123(1)(b).
62 *Merger Review Process Guidelines*, above note 45 at 1.

iv) *Advance Ruling Certificates and No Action Letters*

Noah sheltered within an ark during a famous forty-day waiting period.[63] Canadian competition lawyers, by contrast, seek the shelter of advance ruling certificates ("ARCs") to avoid waiting periods altogether. ARCs are specifically provided for under section 102 of the *Competition Act*. The idea behind seeking (and granting) such certificates is simple. To quote the words of section 102: "Where the Commissioner is satisfied by a party or parties to a proposed transaction that he would not have sufficient grounds on which to apply to the Tribunal under section 92, the Commissioner may issue a certificate to the effect that he is so satisfied."

Applying for an ARC is a good way to ensure that the parties to a proposed merger need not worry about clearing *Competition Act* hurdles. Where an ARC has been obtained, the transaction is exempt from the "notifiable transaction" provisions of the Act,[64] and, provided the transaction is completed within one year, the Commissioner may not apply to the Competition Tribunal for an order under section 92, except on the basis of information that was not provided when seeking the ARC.[65]

Occasionally, when an application for an ARC is made, the Commissioner will not be prepared to grant an ARC even though the Commissioner has no current intention to seek to block the proposed merger. In such cases, the Commissioner may issue a "no action letter"[66]—a document that, as the name suggests, indicates that the Commissioner does not intend to take any action that would impede the merger although, unlike the ARC, does not actually preclude the Commissioner from having a later change of heart.

---

63 According to the Biblical book of Genesis, Noah was, of course, aboard the ark much longer than forty days, waiting for the floodwater to subside after the initial forty days and nights of rain. His "waiting period," in fact, was apparently just over a year—a delay, it might be noted, that was not occasioned, as delays are often thought to be today, by the involvement of lawyers (Genesis 7:11, 14–16).

64 *Competition Act*, s. 113(b).

65 *Ibid.*, s. 103.

66 See Competition Bureau, "Procedures Guide for Notifiable Transactions and Avoidance Ruling Certificates under the *Competition Act*," online: www.competitionbureau.gc.ca/eic/site/cb-bc.nsf/vwapj/Final-Procedures-guideline-Oct-2010-e.pdf/$fILE/Final-Procedures-guideline-Oct-2010-e.pdf.

4) *Merger Enforcement Guidelines*

In 1991, the Competition Bureau published a set of guidelines, the *Merger Enforcement Guidelines*, providing guidance on the bureau's "analytical approach to merger review."[67] These guidelines were updated in September 2004 and, more recently, in October 2011.[68]

5) Other Issues

Competition, or "anti-trust," concerns are raised when firms in the same industry consolidate. But several years ago, in the halcyon days of private equity investment, many potential purchasers were financial buyers rather than strategic buyers operating in the same industry as the target company. There will generally be a greater risk that a strategic buyer, as opposed to a financial buyer, may not be able to close a proposed acquisition owing to anti-competition concerns. Accordingly, even if the strategic buyer's offered price is higher than a competing financial buyer's bid, the directors of the target company may still be perfectly justified in rejecting the strategic buyer's offer. The directors may justify their decision by pointing to "closing risk," that is, the risk that the proposed purchaser will not actually be able to complete or close the deal.

Two responses emerged to deal with this closing risk problem. The first was the offer by purchasers of what might be termed "reverse break-up fees." They are considered "reverse" fees because traditionally, break-up fees, as discussed in Chapter 7, were paid *to* unsuccessful prospective buyers by selling firms, rather than *by* buying firms. (As explained in Chapter 7, a traditional break-up fee is a deal protection device that serves both to entice a buyer to make a purchase offer, and to provide the buyer with assurances that its deal will either be completed, or that it will receive compensation.) A high-profile example of a reverse break-up fee occurred when Whirlpool Corporation offered to purchase Maytag Corporation in 2005. Whirlpool agreed to pay $120 million if its proposed offer for Maytag Corporation failed to close owing to a failure to obtain a regulatory approval.[69] The Delaware Court of Chancery had the opportunity to consider the implications of a reverse break-up fee

---

67   See *Merger Enforcement Guidelines*, above note 3 at 1.

68   Above note 3.

69   See Whirlpool Corporation, Press Release, "Whirlpool Corporation Submits Formal Proposal to Acquire Maytag Corporation for $20 Per Share" (8 August 2005), online: www.whirlpoolcorp.com.

in *United Rentals Inc. v. RAM Holdings Inc.*[70] (The *United Rentals* case is discussed in Chapter 7.)

A second response to closing risk is what is sometimes called a "hell or high water" clause—a provision that would obligate a purchaser to close a transaction, regardless of the conditions that might be imposed by anti-trust authorities.[71]

The delays and closing uncertainties caused by pre-merger competition reviews can become especially significant in the context of hostile acquisitions, where a purchaser is seeking to acquire the shares of a target corporation against the wishes of the target corporation's directors. Hostile acquisitions are dealt with in detail in Chapter 7. Target corporation directors could, among other things, attempt to use the merger review process as a convenient, government-funded defensive tactic. The Competition Bureau, needless to say, has no interest in having its review process used in this way to tip the balance in a contested acquisition. Accordingly, in 2011, the Commissioner of Competition released two interpretation guidelines dealing specifically with issues arising in the context of hostile acquisitions.[72] The first of the guidelines deals with disclosure of update information by the bureau on the status of its pre-merger review. The second glosses the provisions in sections 114 and 123 of the *Competition Act* that vary the normal rules for the running of waiting periods in the case of hostile takeovers in order to ensure, as the guideline explains, that "the target is not able to affect the commencement of the relevant waiting period under subsection 123(1)."[73]

---

70   937 A.2d 810 (Del. Ch. 2007).

71   According to press reports, such a clause was to have been included in the purchase agreement pursuant to which Vivendi was to acquire BMG, but it did not find favour with European competition authorities. See Siobhan Kennedy & Jeffrey Goldfarb, "BMG Music Sale Reworked after EU Balks at Structure" (5 October 2006), online: www.msnbc.msn.com/id/15143888.

72   Competition Bureau, *Hostile Transactions Interpretation Guideline Number 1: Bureau Policy on Disclosure of Information*, online: www.competitionbureau.gc.ca/eic/site/cb-bc.nsf/vwapj/Merger-Hostile-Transactions-01-e.pdf/$FILE/Merger-Hostile-Transactions-01-e.pdf; Competition Bureau, *Hostile Transactions Interpretation Guideline Number 2: Bureau Policy on Running of Subsection 123(1) Waiting Periods*, online: www.competitionbureau.gc.ca/eic/site/cb-bc.nsf/vwapj/Merger-Hostile-Transactions-02-e.pdf/$FILE/Merger-Hostile-Transactions-02-e.pdf.

73   *Hostile Transactions Interpretation Guideline Number 2, ibid.* at 2.

C. *INVESTMENT CANADA ACT*

1) Overview

When a foreign purchaser seeks to acquire control of a Canadian busi-
ness, the provisions of the *Investment Canada Act*[74] are engaged. The
Investment Canada Act is a rather less protectionist successor to the
Foreign Investment Review Act ("FIRA").

The stated purpose of the *Investment Canada Act* is expressed not in
a recital, but in section 2 of the statute itself as follows:

> Recognizing that increased capital and technology benefits Canada,
> and recognizing the importance of protecting national security, the
> purposes of this Act are to provide for the review of significant in-
> vestments in Canada by non-Canadians in a manner that encour-
> ages investment, economic growth and employment opportunities
> in Canada and to provide for the review of investments in Canada by
> non-Canadians that could be injurious to national security.[75]

The references in section 2 to national security were added in 2009
as part of a series of amendments to the Act. In announcing these
amendments, Industry Canada stated that the changes were intended
to "respond to the core recommendations of the Competition Policy
Review Panel."[76] That panel, under the chairmanship of L.R. Wilson,
had been established by the federal Ministers of Industry and Finance
in 2007, and released its final report, *Compete to Win*,[77] in June 2008.

Where there are no issues of national security, the acquisition of
significant Canadian business assets by non-Canadians is to be permitted—even encouraged—so long as those investments provide net
benefits to Canada. Under the *Investment Canada Act* investments by
"non-Canadians" (as defined in section 3), are subject either to *notification* or to *review*.

---

74   Above note 2.
75   *Ibid.*, s. 2.
76   See Industry Canada, "Regulations Amending the Investment Canada Regula-
      tions and National Security Review of Investments Regulations," online: www.
      ic.gc.ca/eic/site/ica-lic.nsf/eng/lk50926.html.
77   Online: www.ic.gc.ca/eic/site/cprp-gepmc.nsf/vwapj/Compete_to_Win.
      pdf/$FILE/Compete_to_Win.pdf.

2) Investments Subject to Notification

Two types of investments by non-Canadians are subject to notification under the *Investment Canada Act:*

- an investment to establish a new Canadian business;[78] and
- an investment to acquire control of an existing Canadian business, whether directly or indirectly (as described more specifically in section 28 of the Act), unless the transaction is reviewable, as discussed further below[79]

When an investment is subject to notification, the person making the investment is required to provide information about the investment to the Director of Investments, appointed under section 6 of the Act, either before making the investment, or within thirty days afterwards.[80] The notification requirement is not onerous. The information required is prescribed in Schedule I to the *Investment Canada Regulations*,[81] and, as a practical matter, may be provided on relatively short forms available at the Industry Canada website.[82]

Once the Director has received notice of the transaction (and assuming that the notice contained all of the required information), the Director sends a *receipt*[83] to the non-Canadian that filed the notice. The principal purpose of the receipt is to tell the person who has filed the notice whether or not the investment is subject to the Act's "review" process. The receipt may simply say that the investment is *not* reviewable.[84] Alternatively, the receipt may say that the Director has an additional twenty-one days to send to the filer a notice of review.[85] Of course, if no notice of review is sent within that twenty-one-day period, the transaction is not reviewable. In that case (again, assuming the notification contained accurate and complete information) then the transaction is not reviewable,[86] and the parties to the transaction need no longer be concerned about the *Investment Canada Act*. However, if the Director does send a notice of review within the twenty-one-day period, the investment will be subject to the Act's review process. That process is discussed in the next section.

---

78   Above note 2, s. 11(a).
79   *Ibid.*, s. 11(b).
80   *Ibid.*, s. 12.
81   s. 5 and Schedule I.
82   Online: www.ic.gc.ca/eic/site/ica-lic.nsf/eng/h_lk00010.html.
83   *Investment Canada Act*, s. 13.
84   *Ibid.*, s. 13(1)(b)(i).
85   *Ibid.*, s. 13(1)(b)(ii).
86   *Ibid.*, s. 13(3).

3) Investments Subject to Review

a) Introduction

Some investments by non-Canadians are subject not simply to noti-fication, but to substantive "review." The purpose of such a review is to determine whether the investment is "likely to be of net benefit to Canada";[87] the consequence of a finding that the investment is *not* likely to be of net benefit to Canada is that the investment may be disallowed (and if the investment has already been implemented, may have to be unwound).[88]

There are two basic factors that determine whether or not an invest-ment by a non-Canadian will be subject to review under the *Investment Canada Act:*

- the investment is to acquire control of a business in one of four speci-fied culturally sensitive industries ("business activity . . . related to Canada's cultural heritage or national identity");[89] or
- the investment exceeds certain specified dollar thresholds.

b) Culturally Sensitive Industries

Generally, investments by non-Canadians must be a specified min-imum size before they may be subject to *Investment Canada Act* review. But there has long been especial concern in Canada about the level of foreign control over "cultural industries," that is, the businesses that produce the books, magazines, and newspapers Canadians read, the music Canadians play or to which they listen, and the films or videos Canadians watch.

The *Investment Canada Act* provides two layers of special safeguards for these sorts of businesses. First, five specific activities are defined as *cultural businesses* for the purpose of section 14.1 of the Act. This is important, because section 14.1 raises the bar on what would other-wise be the dollar level of reviewable investments by non-Canadian investors in Canadian businesses where those investors are from coun-tries that are, like Canada, members of the World Trade Organization ("WTO"). In other words, investors from WTO countries may normally make larger investments in Canadian businesses than investors from non-WTO countries before those investments are subject to *Investment Canada Act* review.

The five "cultural businesses" specified for this purpose are, predictably:

---

87   *Ibid.*, ss. 16 and 21(1).
88   *Ibid.*, s. 24(1).
89   *Ibid.*, s. 15(a).

- book, magazine, periodical or newspaper publication, distribution or sale;
- film or video recording production, distribution, sale, or exhibition;
- audio or video music recording production, distribution, sale, or exhibition;
- "sheet" music (in print or machine readable form) publication, distribution, or sale; and
- radio and television (including cable television broadcasting and satellite programming and broadcast network services).[90]

For businesses in these industries, investments by non-Canadians above a certain specified dollar threshold (discussed below, under the heading "Specified Dollar Thresholds for Review") are reviewable regardless of whether the investor is a WTO investor. The more relaxed thresholds that apply to investments by WTO investors in other Canadian businesses, in other words, do not apply in the case of cultural businesses.

There are additional protections for culturally sensitive businesses too. Certain business activities are prescribed by the *Investment Canada Regulations* as business activities that are "related to Canada's cultural heritage or national identity."[91] When a non-Canadian seeks to make an investment either to establish or to acquire control of an existing Canadian business in one of these industries, the investment is potentially subject to review under the Act, even though—had an investment of the same type and magnitude been made in another industry—the transaction would only have been subject to the statute's notification requirement. To be sure, such an investment is not automatically subject to review. However, the investment *may* be subject to review if the governor in council (that is, the federal cabinet) "considers it in the public interest on the recommendation of the Minister" to issue an order for review of the investment.[92]

The four prescribed business activities subject to this additional level of scrutiny are very similar to four of the five activities defined as cultural businesses as discussed above. Specifically, the four businesses that are listed in Schedule IV of the *Investment Canada Regulations* are:

- book, magazine, periodical, or newspaper publication, distribution or sale;
- film or video product production, distribution, sale, or exhibition;
- audio or video music recording production, distribution, sale, or exhibition; and

---

90   *Ibid.*, s. 14.1(6).
91   *Ibid.*, s. 15(a); *Investment Canada Regulations*, s. 8; Schedule IV.
92   *Investment Canada Act, ibid.*, s. 15 (b).

- "sheet" music (in print or machine readable form) publication, distribution, or sale.

Review of proposed investments in these culturally sensitive industries is undertaken by the Minister of Canadian Heritage rather than the Minister of Industry.

c) Other Politically Sensitive Industries

Prior to the 2009 amendments to the *Investment Canada Act,* businesses in three other sectors that were considered politically sensitive had also been subject to lower review thresholds: uranium, financial services, and transportation services. The Competition Policy Review Panel recommended in its 2008 report that the low review threshold for businesses in these sectors be raised to the level applicable to other businesses.[93]

d) Specified Dollar Thresholds for Review

Not all investments in Canadian businesses by non-Canadians are subject to substantive regulatory review. It would hardly make sense if they were. Instead, only larger transactions are normally subject to review (except, potentially, in the case of businesses related to "Canada's cultural heritage or national identity"). The dollar thresholds that determine whether an acquisition by a non-Canadian will or will not be reviewable vary depending on these (somewhat simplified) three factors:

- *Whether the acquisition is direct or indirect:* The Act does not use this simple classification. Instead, section 28(1) describes four methods by which a non-Canadian may acquire control of a Canadian business. The wording of parts of section 28(1) is somewhat technical. However, in simplest terms, a direct acquisition refers to the acquisition of the shares or assets of a Canadian business, and an indirect acquisition essentially refers to the acquisition of a non-Canadian entity that directly or indirectly controls an entity carrying on a Canadian business.
- *Whether the investor is a "WTO Investor":* The phrase "WTO Investor" is defined in section 14.1 of the Act. It is a term of surprising complexity but, at its simplest, it refers, among other things, to a national or permanent resident of one of the 153 countries that are members of the World Trade Organization.[94] If the investor is a corporation, the term applies if the corporation is either controlled by WTO In-

---

93   Above note 77 at 36.
94   As of 23 July 2008, with the accession of Cape Verde to the WTO, the total number of WTO members is 153. See online: www.wto.org.

vestors or has a board of directors of which at least two-thirds of the members are any combination of Canadians and WTO Investors.[95]

- *Whether the subject business is a "cultural business":* These are the five Canadian "cultural businesses" specified in section 14.1(6) and referred to above.

Table 2 provides an overview of the *Investment Canada Act* review thresholds:

Table 2 Thresholds for Review under the *Investment Canada Act*

	Cultural Businesses[9]		All other Businesses	
	Direct (Value of assets)	Indirect (Value of assets)	Direct (Value of assets)	Indirect (Value of assets)
WTO Investor	$ 5 million	$50 million	$330 million[10]	Not reviewable[11]
Non-WTO Investor	$5 million	$50 million	$5 million	$50 million

[9]   These are the four industries referred to in s. 14.1(5) of the *Investment Canada Act*, ibid.

[10]   This is the amount Industry Canada has indicated is expected to be the threshold amount for 2012, although at the date of writing, this amount has not yet been officially published in the Canada Gazette. See online: www.ic.gc.ca/eic/site/ica-lic.nsf/eng/h_lk00050.html. The published threshold for 2011 was $312 million. This amount is subject to adjustment each year, in accordance with a formula set out in s. 14.1(2) of the *Investment Canada Act*. The revised amount is published in the Canada Gazette, and is also posted on Industry Canada's website. It should be noted that these monetary thresholds will be significantly increased when s. 448 of the *Budget Implementation Act, 2009*, S.C. 2009, c. 2 is eventually proclaimed into force. In addition, the higher monetary thresholds will be based not on the value of the assets being acquired but on enterprise value, as determined in accordance with yet-to-be promulgated regulations. The concept of enterprise value is well known to investment bankers and private equity funds and, essentially, refers to the total value of a firm's equity and debt—a measure of value that, in the simplest sense, indicates the total value of the claims to a firm's cash flows, without any distortions that could arise from a firm's particular financing choices. The decision to base the monetary thresholds on enterprise value was based on a recommendation of the Competition Policy Review Panel (above note 77 at 31). The panel defined enterprise value as "the sum of the price to be paid for the equity of an acquired business and the assumption of liabilities on its balance sheet minus its current cash assets." (*Ibid.* at 111.) The panel considered this to be a better measure than the "out of date" gross assets measure because it "better reflects the increasing importance to our modern economy of service and knowledge-based industries in which much of the value of an enterprise is not recorded on its balance sheet because it resides in people, know-how, intellectual property and other intangible assets not recognized in a balance sheet by current accounting methods."(*Ibid.* at 31.)

[11]   *Investment Canada Act*, s. 14.1(4).

---

95   *Investment Canada Act*, s. 14.1, definition of "WTO Investor."

e) Undertakings

The *Investment Canada Act* provides that, where the minister is not satisfied that a proposed investment is of net benefit to Canada, the minister may, among other things, give the applicant an opportunity to make "undertakings" (that is, promises) to address such concerns.[96] Typical undertakings might relate, for example, to commitments regarding employment or the conduct of certain activities in Canada in the future. If the undertakings are not fulfilled, the Act authorizes the minister to take steps to seek a court order for enforcement.[97] The Federal Court of Appeal recently considered the legal nature of the legislative provisions for enforcement of *Investment Canada Act* undertakings. In *Canada (Attorney General) v. United States Steel Corp.*[98] United States Steel Corporation and U.S. Steel Canada Inc. (collectively "U.S. Steel") argued that sections 39 and 40 of the *Investment Canada Act* were, among other things, contrary to the presumption of innocence and the right to a fair hearing prescribed by subsection 11(d) of the *Canadian Charter of Rights and Freedoms*,[99] and were thus invalid. The case arose from the Minister of Industry's decision to seek enforcement of certain undertakings provided by U.S. Steel in connection with its acquisition of Stelco Inc. in 2007. The undertakings related to the maintenance of levels of production and employment in Canada. U.S. Steel did not dispute that it had not complied with these undertakings, but had advised the Minister by letter that it had been facing "difficulties . . . due to the unexpected economic downturn."[100] The Minister sought an order compelling U.S. Steel to comply, imposing a penalty of $10,000 per day per breach until it had complied.

The Federal Court of Appeal rejected U.S. Steel's arguments, holding, among other things, that sections 39 and 40 did not violate section 11(d) of the *Charter* because the protections of section 11 were only engaged when a person had been "charged with an offence." In the court's view, a person subject to proceedings contemplated by sections 39 and 40 could not be said to have been "charged with an offence" as that concept had been interpreted for the purposes of section 11 of the *Charter*. The court also rejected U.S. Steel's argument that sections 39 and 40 violated section 2(e) of the *Bill of Rights*.[101] In December 2011,

---

96   *Ibid.*, s. 23.

97   *Ibid.*, ss. 39(1), 39(3), and 40(2)(c).

98   2011 FCA 176.

99   Part I of the *Constitution Act, 1982*, being Schedule B to the *Canada Act 1982* (U.K.), 1982, c. 11.

100   Above note 98 at para 7.

101   S.C. 1960, c. 44, Pt. I, reprinted R.S.C. 1970, App. III.

the minister of industry announced that agreement had been reached with United States Steel Corp. to provide "new and enhanced undertakings under the *Investment Canada Act*" and that the court action against the company was, accordingly, to be discontinued.[102]

4) Exemptions

There are eleven specified transactions that are exempt from the provisions of the *Investment Canada Act*.[103] These exemptions cover transactions where the sovereignty concerns underlying the statute generally appear to be less acute, or are outweighed by other commercial or financial considerations. So, for example, the provisions of the Act will not be engaged when a venture capitalist acquires a voting interest "not inconsistent with such terms and conditions as may be fixed by the Minister";[104] certain acquisitions related to financing or realization on security interests"; involuntary acquisitions" as, for example, in estate transfers; and in eight other situations.

5) Foreign Direct Investment and National Security

One of the most significant recent changes to the *Investment Canada Act* was the introduction of references to "national security" in 2009 amendments to the statute, and the introduction of a new national security review. These new provisions represent the culmination of a process of reflection and review of Canada's foreign investment review policy, a process reflecting an ongoing debate in which policymakers seek to balance the benefits of attracting foreign capital against concerns of maintaining economic sovereignty, and informed by international developments that have highlighted the need to guard against perceived threats to national security.

The federal Minister of Finance, in his November 2006 economic plan entitled *Advantage Canada*,[105] noted that "Canada's share of total inward foreign investment directed to the G7 and OECD countries has been falling. No other country in the G7 comes close to matching Canada's

102 Industry Canada, News Release, "Industry Minister Paradis Reaches an Out-of-Court Settlement in the U.S. Steel Litigation" (12 December 2011), online: www.ic.gc.ca/eic/site/ic1.nsf/eng/07011.html.

103 Above note 2, s. 10(1).

104 *Ibid.*, s. 10(1)(b).

105 Department of Finance, *Advantage Canada: Building a Strong Economy for Canadians* (2006), online: www.fin.gc.ca/ec2006/plan/pltoc-eng.asp [*Advantage Canada*].

decline . . . "[106] The document argues that Canada's restrictive foreign investment policies have contributed to this decline, citing an OECD study indicating that "Canada has the highest level of explicit restrictions on foreign-equity ownership in the G7—primarily in the transportation and telecommunications sectors."[107] The Competition Policy Review Panel took issue with the OECD's assessment.

Accordingly, the government indicated its intention to review the *Investment Canada Act* with the goal of increasing foreign investment. However, the desire to increase foreign investment is tempered by (real or imagined) concerns of national security. The link between foreign investment and issues of national security is not new. In the United States, for example, legislation already exists (the so-called *Exon-Florio Amendment*[108]) permitting the President to take steps to prevent acquisitions by foreign persons or companies that threaten U.S. national security. In Canada, a widely-publicized proposed acquisition in late 2004 of all the shares of Noranda Inc. by China Minmetals Corp., a firm owned by the Chinese state, prompted the then Liberal government to introduce Bill C-59. This bill proposed an amendment to the *Investment Canada Act* that would have permitted the review of foreign investments in Canadian firms on national security grounds, regardless of the size of such proposed investments. That bill was never passed. However, the concerns raised by proposed acquisitions of this kind persist. The current Minister of Finance has indicated that "foreign investments by large state-owned enterprises with non-commercial objectives and unclear corporate governance and reporting may not be beneficial to Canadians."[109] Accordingly, it has been suggested that "while such cases are very much the exception rather than the rule, the Government needs a principles-based approach to address these situations."[110] To be sure, however, as the minister's statement makes clear, when foreign state enterprises (or sovereign wealth funds) acquire controlling interests in Canadian businesses, economic concerns weigh at least as heavily as national security issues.

---

106 *Ibid.* at 87.
107 *Ibid.* The most recent version of that OECD study reiterates the concern that, in Canada, "[r]estrictions on foreign direct investment . . . remain higher than in the majority of OECD countries, discouraging productivity-enhancing capital deepening." OECD, *Economic Policy Reforms 2011: Going for Growth*, Part I (Paris: OECD, 2011) c. 2 at 78.
108 Section 721 of the *Defense Production Act of 1950*, 50 U.S.C. § 2061*ff*, as added by *The Omnibus Trade and Competitiveness Act of 1988*.
109 *Advantage Canada*, above note 105 at 87.
110 *Ibid.*

Amendments to the *Investment Canada Act* enacted in 2009 added Part IV.1 to the statute. Part IV.1 provides for the review of investments by non-Canadians under circumstances where the Minister, after consultation with the Minister of Public Safety and Emergency Preparedness, "considers that the investment could be injurious to national security and the Governor in Council, on the recommendation of the Minister, makes an order within the prescribed period for the review of the investment."[111]

6) Canada: Open for Business?

Many Canadian business leaders have also voiced their desire for a more protective approach to foreign investment.[112] No doubt these arguments are sincere, although one is mindful of the possibility at least that some senior Canadian executives may find it convenient to use the Canadian flag as a form of camouflage for arguments favouring their own economic self-interest. Recent research has suggested that increased foreign investment has not led to the much-feared "hollowing out" of corporate Canada. To the contrary, a 2007 Conference Board of Canada paper concluded that there has been an increase in the number of head offices in Canada between 1999 and 2005.[113]

Nevertheless, concerns about the effects of foreign control of Canadian resources persist. In 2010, for example, BHP Billiton PLc, a British company that was part of the Australian-headquartered BHP Billiton Group, launched a hostile takeover bid for the shares of Potash Corporation of Saskatchewan Inc.[114] ("PotashCorp"), the world's largest producer of potash. The bid, opposed by the directors of PotashCorp, triggered vigorous national debate over foreign investment in major Canadian industries. On 3 November 2010, Industry Canada Minister Tony Clement announced that he had delivered a notice to BHP Billiton indicating that he was "not satisfied that the proposed transaction is likely to be of net benefit to Canada."[115] Although BHP Billiton was per-

---

111 *Investment Canada Act,* s. 25.3. See also the *National Security Review of Investments Regulations,* S.O.R. 2009/271.

112 See, for example, Gordon Pitts, "Manulife CEO Issues a Call to Arms" *Globe and Mail* (19 January 2007) B1.

113 Glen Hodgson, "Is Corporate Canada Being Hollowed Out? It Depends Where You Look" (Ottawa: Conference Board of Canada, 2007) Publication no. 149-07.

114 See BHP Billiton Takeover Bid Circular (20 August 2010), online: www.sedar.com.

115 See News Release, "Minister of Industry Confirms Notice Sent to BHP Billiton Regarding Proposed Acquisition of Potash Corporation," online: www.ic.gc.ca/eic/site/ic1.nsf/eng/06031.html.

mitted within a 30-day period to make additional representations or undertakings, shortly after the Minister's announcement, BHP Billiton announced that it was withdrawing its bid.[116]

116 See BHP Billiton, News Release, "BHP Billiton Withdraws its Offer to Acquire PotashCorp And Reactivates its Buyback Program" (15 November 2010), online: www.bhpbilliton.com/home/investors/news/Pages/Articles/BHP%20Billiton%20 Withdraws%20Its%20Offer%20To%20Acquire%20PotashCorp%20And%20Re- activates%20Its%20Buy-back%20Program.aspx

CHAPTER 3

ASSET PURCHASES

A. INTRODUCTION

Most of this book deals with major share transactions. However, a business acquisition can also be structured as a purchase of the assets used in a business. A number of the key legal considerations triggered by asset purchases will be canvassed briefly in this chapter.

B. PURCHASING ASSETS VS. PURCHASING HIDDEN OR CONTINGENT LIABILITIES

Why are some business acquisitions structured as share transactions, and others as asset purchases? It has become a matter of received wisdom: all else equal, purchasers of a business prefer to buy assets. But, again, all else equal, sellers prefer to sell shares. This general "rule" must allow for so many real-world exceptions that it hardly qualifies as a rule at all. The kernel of truth embedded in this otherwise potentially misleading generalization is that an asset sale enables the purchaser to identify specifically the business assets he or she wishes to purchase, and to exclude the assets which he or she does not need (and, importantly, does not wish to pay for). Perhaps most important of all, when assets are being acquired, rather than shares in the corporate entity that owns those assets, the purchaser does not unknowingly inherit liabilities of the vendor corporation.

A particularly dramatic—though hardly commonplace—illustration of the potential risk of inheriting unwanted corporate liabilities in a share purchase transaction may be found in the peculiar case of *Sherwood Design Services Ltd. v. 872935 Ontario Ltd.*[1] The *Sherwood Design* case, to be sure, did not involve a conventional sale of a business. Rather, the "Purchasers" of the shares very likely supposed that a freshly minted (numbered) corporation was being formed by their lawyers expressly for them to be used in a new business venture. However, unbeknownst to the Purchasers, that apparently pristine numbered corporation actually had an unfortunate past.

Sometime earlier, in connection with a different transaction about which the Purchasers knew nothing, the corporation had been identified by the law firm that had created it as the entity that was to adopt a pre-incorporation contract entered into between a client of the law firm and another party. A letter to that effect, identifying the corporation by its (number)name, had been sent by a lawyer at the firm to a lawyer acting for the other party to the deal. It was only when the transaction to which this earlier pre-incorporation contract related cratered, that the corporation was returned to the law firm's inventory of such shelf corporations. And there it sat—its articles and organizational documents, no doubt, neatly encased in a black or maroon-coloured minute book with the corporate name brightly embossed in gold on the spine. It would have been indistinguishable from dozens of other similarly embossed minute books organized for dozens of other numbered shelf companies, all ready to be assigned to the next client of the firm who might be able to put them to use.

And so it was that this particular numbered company (872935 Ontario Limited) was, in fact, assigned to other clients—the Purchasers. They used the corporation for a wholly unrelated commercial real estate acquisition. As a result of that acquisition, the numbered company became the owner of a valuable piece of real property.

In the meantime, the disgruntled counterparty to the earlier pre-incorporation contract had decided to sue the numbered company for breach of that earlier contract. The lawsuit engaged the problematic pre-incorporation contract provisions of Ontario's *Business Corporations Act.*[2] In the end, the majority in the Ontario Court of Appeal held

---

1   (1998), 39 O.R. (3d) 576 (C.A.), application for leave to appeal to S.C.C. discontinued, [1998] S.C.C.A. No. 318.

2   *Business Corporations Act*, s. 21 [OBCA]. For a detailed discussion of this case, and of the problematic law of pre-incorporation contracts generally, see

that the corporation was, indeed, liable. In other words, although the Purchasers of the corporation's shares were quite innocent (and indeed quite unaware) of any contractual breach by the corporation (pre-incorporation or otherwise), the corporate entity itself was not blameless.

Sherwood Design is an unusual case. But it does help to illustrate, in the starkest way, that when one buys the shares of a corporation, that corporation remains subject to liability for all acts or omissions of the corporation that occurred before the sale.

C. ADDITIONAL OBLIGATIONS IN AN ASSET SALE

An asset sale may trigger a host of filing and other obligations. If the sale involves real property, for example, the transfer of ownership will need to be registered with the appropriate government land registration office. Such a transfer may, in turn, trigger an obligation to pay land transfer taxes and so on. Where the assets being sold include automobiles, ownership records will need to be changed in accordance with applicable provincial legislation.[3] Also, where the business being acquired involves material contracts, those contracts will need to be assigned to the purchaser, a step that is not required when shares of the business are acquired (although even a share sale may, in some cases, trigger "change of control" provisions in material contracts).

D. *BULK SALES ACT*

In Ontario, an asset sale engages the provisions of the archaic and troublesome *Bulk Sales Act*.[4] At one time, other Canadian jurisdictions had similar legislation in place, but they have since found these laws unnecessary and have wisely chosen to repeal them.[5] The purpose of bulk sales legislation is to protect the creditors of a business by preventing the owner of that business from selling his or her assets out

---

Christopher C. Nicholls, *Corporate Law* (Toronto: Emond Montgomery, 2005) at 130–60.

3   See, for example, *Highway Traffic Act* (Ontario), s. 11(2).

4   *Bulk Sales Act* (Ontario).

5   The provinces that most recently repealed their bulk sales legislation are New Brunswick, where the statute was repealed as of 1 August 2004, and Newfoundland and Labrador, where the statute was repealed as of 4 June 2008.

of the ordinary course of business without regard to the creditors' interests. Essentially, the *Bulk Sales Act* applies whenever there is a sale of assets "in bulk." This obviously does not include sales made from inventory in the ordinary course of the seller's business. Rather, as the legislation states, the Act applies only to sales of goods "in bulk out of the usual course of business or trade of the seller."[6] How large a sale must be to constitute a sale "in bulk" is not entirely clear, but certainly the courts have held that a sale by no means must involve all or even substantially all of the assets of the seller to engage the provisions of the *Bulk Sales Act*.

When the Act does apply, the interests of the sellers' creditors must be protected in one of three ways:

1. The buyer, before making payment, must require the seller to produce a statement listing all of the seller's creditors, and certain details about the debts owed to them.[7] After receiving this statement, the buyer is permitted to complete the purchase, provided the seller's statement disclosed (a) that the total debts owing to unsecured trade creditors did not exceed $2,500 and the total debts owing to secured creditors did not exceed $2,500 (and the buyer has no notice of claims above these amounts); or (b) all claims of trade creditors have been paid in full; or (c) adequate provision has been made for payment in full of all creditors (other than creditors who have delivered a waiver in prescribed form);[8] *or*
2. The buyer, after receiving from the seller the statement of creditors referred to above, may pay the proceeds of the sale to a trustee appointed either by the seller, with the consent of at least 60 percent (both in number and in dollar value) of the seller's creditors, or by the court;[9] *or*
3. The seller has applied to the court for an exemption order from *Bulk Sales Act* compliance, an order that may be granted where the court is satisfied, "that the sale is advantageous to the seller and will not impair the seller's ability to pay creditors in full."[10]

Each of these methods is cumbersome, potentially expensive, and likely to delay or impede commercial transactions. Yet, if none of these steps has been taken to comply with, or obtain an exemption from, the *Bulk Sales Act*, then the purchaser is at risk of having the sale declared

6   *Bulk Sales Act* (Ontario), s. 1, definition of "sale in bulk."
7   See, for example, *ibid.*, s. 4.
8   *Ibid.*, s. 8(1).
9   *Ibid.*, s. 8(2). Appointment of the trustee is dealt with in s. 9.
10   *Ibid.*, s. 3.

void and may be held personally liable to account to the creditors of the seller.[11]

Compliance with the *Bulk Sales Act* is so cumbersome that frequently parties to an asset sale agree to "waive" compliance with the statute; then, to protect the buyer, the seller provides the buyer with an indemnity for any losses arising from failure to comply. Such an indemnity may well have value in protecting the purchaser from becoming entangled in disagreements between the seller and its creditors over disputed debts. However, there is an obvious problem with such indemnities in other contexts. Purchasers will most frequently seek to rely on them in cases where the seller is not simply disputing a debt, but is actually unable to satisfy the claims of his or her creditors. And if the seller does not have the resources to satisfy his or her creditors, it is probable that he or she will also lack the resources to honour an indemnity in favour of the buyer. One way for purchasers to increase the value of such an indemnity is to require it to be given not only by the seller itself, but also by one or more principals of the seller, such as a major shareholder of a seller that is a corporation.

Relying on such waivers, however, though not uncommon can involve some risk for asset purchasers. Moreover, the arcane drafting of the *Bulk Sales Act* has perplexed some courts and led to judicial decisions that should make purchasers somewhat wary about closing asset sale transactions without complying with the terms of the *Bulk Sales Act*.

In *Sidaplex-Plastic Suppliers Inc. v. Elta Group Inc.*,[12] for instance, the Ontario Court of Appeal noted a peculiar feature of the Ontario *Bulk Sales Act*. Under section 4 of the Act, the buyer is required to demand that the seller produce a statement with the names of the seller's "unsecured trade creditors" and "secured trade creditors," together with details about the debts owing to them. However, the Act does not require that provision be made with respect to *all* secured trade creditors, but only with respect to the claims of those secured trade creditors "that are or become due and payable upon completion of the sale of which the buyer has notice."[13] Because of a series of complex arrangements, the complaining creditor in *Sidaplex* did not have a claim that was or would "become due and payable upon completion of the sale." Accordingly, the complaining creditor was *not* a secured trade creditor for whom provision had to be made under section 4. In other words, even if the parties had complied with the *Bulk Sales Act*, the creditor

---

11   See *ibid.*, s. 16.
12   (1998), 40 O.R. (3d) 563 (C.A.) [*Sidaplex*].
13   *Bulk Sales Act* (Ontario), s. 8(1)(c).

in question would not have been entitled to the legislation's protective provisions.

The parties to the impugned sale had not in fact complied with the Act. And section 17 of the Act provided that an action to have a sale in bulk declared void for failure to comply with the statute could be commenced "by a creditor of the seller"[14]—even a creditor, as in this case, *for whom no provision under the Act needed to be made*. Nor was this right of mere academic interest, because the Court of Appeal went on to give a narrow interpretation to section 16(1) of the Act, which provides that "A sale in bulk is voidable unless the buyer has complied with this Act." In the view of the court, these words meant just what they said: the sale was voidable where there was non-compliance with the Act, and except in limited cases where the non-compliance was "technical," "the court does not have a discretion to refuse to declare a sale void."[15]

The suggestion that the court has no discretion on the matter was subsequently rejected by the Supreme Court of Canada in the most significant *Bulk Sales Act* case to date, *National Trust Co. v. H & R Block Canada Inc.*[16]

The *National Trust* case, once again, concerned a business transaction where the parties—undoubtedly for reasons of commercial expediency—chose not to comply with the onerous provisions of the Ontario *Bulk Sales Act*. It was clear that the sale transaction was in no way intended to hinder or defeat the creditors of the seller. The seller, Tax Time, had a number of secured and unsecured creditors at the time of the sale. The entire amount of the proceeds of the bulk sale transaction, $800,000 in total, was applied by the seller against the debts it owed to its two most senior secured creditors. However, one of the seller's unpaid *unsecured* creditors launched a proceeding under section 17(1) of the Ontario *Bulk Sales Act* seeking to have the purchaser account as a result of failure to comply with the provisions of the Act.

At first glance, the complaining creditor's claim seems somewhat improbable: if provision had been made for payment of the seller's debts, as required by the *Bulk Sales Act*, senior ranking creditors would have been paid before junior ranking creditors such as the complaining shareholder. Accordingly, if the purchaser were to be held personally liable for amounts that the junior ranking creditors would not have received *even if the Act had been complied with*, then those junior ranking creditors might appear to be reaping something of a windfall. Indeed, if it were possible for junior ranking creditors to recover in such cases,

---

14   *Ibid.*, s. 17(1).
15   *Sidaplex*, above note 12 at 573.
16   [2003] 3 S.C.R. 160 [*National Trust*].

then one might assume that such creditors should be delighted to see the *Bulk Sales Act* regularly ignored by debtors.

In fact, the majority in the Supreme Court of Canada recognized this anomaly. To require a purchaser to account to a junior ranking creditor when the sale proceeds had not been spirited away but had, in fact, been applied to pay down the debts owing by the seller to its senior creditors would improperly place the junior creditor "in a better position than it would have been in had the buyer complied with the Act."[17] Moreover, the majority expressly rejected the proposition advanced by the Ontario Court of Appeal in *Sidaplex*, that the court had no discretion to refuse to compel the purchaser to pay whenever there is non-compliance with the Act (other than technical non-compliance).[18] Nevertheless, the trial judge in the *National Trust* case, as well as the majority in the Court of Appeal, and two dissenting judges in the Supreme Court of Canada would all have imposed personal liability on the purchaser. This, despite the fact that there seemed to be no doubt as to the *bona fides* of the transaction under consideration, or as to the good faith shown by the seller in applying all of the proceeds of the sale to the repayment of its debts. Accordingly, despite the comforting assurances by the majority in the Supreme Court of Canada that the *Bulk Sales Act* ought to be interpreted in light of "the true purpose of the Act and of commercial realities,"[19] asset purchasers must still continue to be mindful of bulk sales legislation in Ontario and be fully aware of the risks that may be involved in closing an asset purchase transaction without complying with the *Bulk Sales Act* rules.

As the Alberta Law Reform Institute put it in 1990, "The [*Bulk Sales*] Act does more harm than good."[20] It is a vestige of a bygone era where unscrupulous debtors could sell their assets in bulk to unsuspecting buyers, steal away, and leave their creditors unpaid, with no recourse against the non-collusive buyer. With today's panoply of creditor protections, these concerns of yesteryear may be compared to pedestrian fears of being run over by a horse and carriage. In the United States, the National Conference of Commissioners on Uniform State Laws and the American Law Institute recommended repeal of the U.S. equivalent of the Ontario *Bulk Sales Act*, Article 6 of the Uniform Commercial Code, in 1988 (although, it must be acknowledged, a few states have clung

---

17   *Ibid.* at para. 47.
18   *Ibid.* at para. 37.
19   *Ibid.* at para. 47.
20   Alberta Law Reform Institute, *The Bulk Sales Act*, Report No. 56 (January 1990) at 2, online: www.law.ualberta.ca/alri/docs/fr056.pdf.

to the relic.)[21] One can only hope that by the time the next edition of this book is released, the government of Ontario will have joined the other provinces and abolished the antiquated and irksome *Bulk Sales Act* altogether.

E. EMPLOYEES OF THE BUSINESS

As a technical matter, when the business assets of one corporation are acquired by a second (different) corporation, the employment of all of the employees of the first corporation is terminated, even if those employees continue to work for the new business under its new owner. However, this technical employment termination is typically overridden by provincial legislation. So, for example, section 9 of the Ontario *Employment Standards Act, 2000*[22] states:

> If an employer sells a business or a part of a business and the purchaser employs an employee of the seller, the employment of the employee shall be deemed not to have been terminated or severed for the purposes of this Act and his or her employment with the seller shall be deemed to have been employment with the purchaser for the purpose of any subsequent calculation of the employee's length or period of employment.[23]

When employees are unionized, the "successor employer" provisions of applicable labour relations legislation come into play. So, for example, section 69 of Ontario's *Labour Relations Act, 1995*[24] provides that where an employer that is party to a collective agreement with a union sells his, her, or its business, the purchaser becomes bound by the collective agreement until the Ontario Labour Relations Board (OLRB) declares otherwise. Subsection 69(5) permits the OLRB, on application of any "person, trade union or council of trade unions concerned" to terminate a collective agreement if "in the opinion of the Board, the person to whom the business was sold has changed its character so that it is substantially different from the business of the pre-

---

21   See Fred H. Miller & William B. Davenport, "Introduction to the Special Issue on the Uniform Commercial Code" (1990) 45 Business Lawyer 1389 at 1391.
22   S.O. 2000, c. 41.
23   *Ibid.*, s. 9(1).
24   S.O. 1995, c. 1, Sch. A.

decessor employer." There are similar successor employer provisions in other provincial labour statutes[25] and the federal *Canada Labour Code*.[26]

There may, nevertheless, be various administrative consequences arising from this change of employer that provincial employment standards legislation do not address. For example, employers are required to withhold and remit amounts from their employees' income in respect of unemployment insurance, under the federal *Employment Insurance Act* as well as under the federal *Canada Pension Plan*. Employers are required to deduct specific amounts from their employees' paycheques each pay period, subject to a maximum annual amount. Once the maximum annual amount has been reached, no further deductions in respect of unemployment insurance or the *Canada Pension Plan* (or *Quebec Pension Plan* in Quebec) are necessary; so, from that date forward (as most Canadian employees are well aware) the employees' take-home pay is higher. However, if an employee then changes employment partway through the year, the new employer must normally begin withholding amounts in respect of Canada Pension Plan and unemployment insurance premiums, without regard to the amounts already withheld by the previous employer. To be sure, these double payments are not lost forever to the employee; they will be refunded the following spring when he or she calculates his or her personal income tax for the year. But in the meantime, the employee will experience the disappointment of an apparently shrinking paycheque.

Prior to 2004, employees of businesses that were sold by way of asset sales often suffered this sort of double deduction. However, as of 1 January 2004, the *Employment Insurance Act*[27] and the *Canada Pension Plan*[28] have been amended to try to alleviate this problem.[29]

F. TAX

The income tax implications of an asset sale are very different from those of a share sale. For example, in an asset sale, it is possible for the buyer and the seller to agree to a reasonable allocation of the purchase

---

25   See *Labour Relations Code* (B.C.), s. 35; *Labour Relations Code* (Alta.), s. 46; *Trade Union Act* (Sask.), s. 37; *Labour Relations Act* (Man.), s. 56; *Labour Code* (Que.), s. 45; *Industrial Relations Act* (N.B.), s. 60; *Labour Act* (P.E.I.), s. 39; *Trade Union Act* (N.S.), s. 31; *Labour Relations Act* (N.L.), s. 93.

26   Section 44*ff.*

27   S.C. 1996, c. 23.

28   R.S.C. 1985, c. C-8.

29   See *Canada Pension Plan*, s. 9(2), and *Employment Insurance Act*, s. 82.1.

price among the assets being acquired. This allocation of the purchase price is significant since it can affect the tax liabilities of both the buyer and the seller. The buyer may, for example, be able to step up the tax basis of depreciable assets purchased from the seller and maximize the availability of depreciation deductions in taxation years following the sale. On the other hand, where the selling company has accumulated non-capital losses, a purchasing company may be able to use those losses to reduce tax by first purchasing the shares of that company, and then amalgamating with it. The legal effect of amalgamation, as discussed in Chapter 4, is that the two amalgamating corporations become one. Thus, the accumulated non-capital losses of one of the amalgamating corporations (subject to certain limitations in the *Income Tax Act* aimed at preventing unrestricted trafficking in such losses)[30] may be used to reduce the taxable income of the amalgamated corporation.[31]

Structuring an acquisition as an asset sale can have sales tax consequences, too, both under provincial retail sales tax legislation and the federal goods and services tax.

Needless to say, the tax consequences—both as a matter of law and administrative practice—of any major transaction can be inordinately complex and are best left to be dealt with in more specialized tax sources.

G. SALE OF "ALL OR SUBSTANTIALLY ALL" OF A CORPORATION'S PROPERTY

Under most Canadian corporate law statutes, when a corporation proposes to sell, lease, or exchange all or substantially all of its property, other than in the ordinary course of business, the sale must be approved by the corporation's shareholders.[32]

---

30 See *Income Tax Act*, s. 111(5).

31 For an illustration of a transaction structured to take advantage of the ability to use accumulated tax losses of one company to reduce future taxable income of an amalgamated corporation, see *Duha Printers (Western) Ltd. v. Canada*, [1998] 1 S.C.R. 795.

32 See, for example, *Canada Business Corporations Act*, s. 189(3) [CBCA]; Alberta *Business Corporations Act*, s. 190 [ABCA]; British Columbia *Business Corporations Act*, s. 301(1) [BCBCA]; *The Corporations Act* (Manitoba), s. 183 [MCA]; New Brunswick *Business Corporations Act*, s. 130(1) [NBBCA]; Newfoundland and Labrador *Corporations Act*, s. 303 [NLCA]; Nova Scotia *Companies Act*, s. 135A, Third Sch., s. 12(1) [NSCA] [The NSCA also includes a provision (s. 26(9)) stating that a company may not "sell or dispose of its undertaking, or a substantial part thereof" without shareholder approval by way of "special

That approval must typically be by way of special resolution (that is, by two-thirds majority vote).[33] Moreover, many Canadian corporate statutes decree that every share of the corporation is entitled to vote on a resolution to approve such a sale, even if such shares do not otherwise carry the right to vote.[34] Further, if any class or series of share is affected differently by the proposed transaction, holders of that class or series may be entitled to a separate class vote, with approval of the

resolution"—a term defined differently in the NSCA than in most other Canadian statutes. See below note 33 as that term is defined in the NSCA. However, this provision is less significant than s. 12(1) of the Third Schedule of the NSCA because, unlike the Third Schedule protections, s. 26(9) does not apply if the corporation's memorandum says otherwise. (Ibid., s. 26(11)]; OBCA, s. 184(3); Prince Edward Island *Companies Act*, s. 15(1)(m) [PEICA]; Saskatchewan *Business Corporations Act*, s. 183(2) [SBCA]; Northwest Territories *Business Corporations Act*, s. 192 [NWBCA]; Nunavut *Business Corporations Act*, s. 192 [NuBCA]; Yukon *Business Corporations Act*, s. 192 [YBCA]. There is a comparable provision in the Quebec *Business Corporations Act*, R.S.Q. c. S-31.1, although the approach of the Quebec statute is somewhat different. First, the Quebec rules are triggered where a sale would result in a corporation being "unable to retain a significant part of its business activity" (s. 271). Then, unlike the regime in other Canadian provinces, the question of what constitutes a "significant part of its business activity" is not left to the courts. Rather, s. 274 deems that a corporation has retained a significant part of its business activity if, after the relevant alienation, the business activity retained: "(1) required the use of at least 25% of the value of the corporation's assets as at the date of the end of the most recently completed fiscal year; and (2) generated at least 25% of either the corporation's revenues or its income before taxes during the most recently completed fiscal year."

33   See, for example, CBCA, s. 189(8); ABCA, s. 190(4); MCA, s. 183(6); NBBCA, s. 130(4); NLCA, s. 303(5); NSCA, s. 135A, Third Sch., s. 12(1) (As a technical matter, the approval requirement under this provision in the mandatory Third Schedule of the NSCA is a two-thirds shareholder vote rather than a "special resolution" because the term "special resolution" under the NSCA has a different definition from most other Canadian corporate statutes, and the shareholder protections provided in the Third Schedule are intended to mirror the protections found in the CBCA.); SBCA, s. 183(5); NWBCA, s. 192(4); NuBCA, s. 192(4); YBCA, s. 192(4). (Note that not every provincial statute provides to holders of shares that are normally non-voting the same rights as the CBCA in the context of a "sale of all or substantially all" of a corporation's assets.)

34   See, for example, CBCA, s. 189(6); ABCA, s. 190(4); MCA, s. 183.6; NBBCA, s. 130(4); NSCA, s. 135A, Third Sch., ss. 2(1)(e) and 12(1); SBCA, s. 183(5); NWBCA, s. 192(4); NuBCA, s. 192(4); YBCA, s. 192(4). While the OBCA does not require the holders of non-voting shares to approve every sale of all or substantially all of a corporation's property, it does provide that if such a sale would affect a particular class or series of shares differently from the shares of another class or series entitled to vote, then holders of those shares will be entitled to a class vote, even where their shares are not otherwise entitled to vote (OBCA, s. 184(6)).

transaction depending upon the passing of a special resolution by each such separate class. Finally, even if the sale, lease, or exchange is approved, dissenting shareholders are entitled to be paid the fair value of their shares by the corporation.[35]

In the case of corporations with publicly traded shares, the corporation must comply with the normal public shareholder meeting requirements, including the requirement to solicit proxies and to prepare and deliver a detailed information circular to the shareholders to enable them to cast informed votes.

There have been a number of cases in which the meaning of the phrase *all or substantially all* has been considered. These cases typically arise in situations where a corporation is selling not all but only some major portion of its business. Canadian courts have held that, in determining whether or not a sale of assets by a corporation constitutes "all or substantially all" of its property, one must apply not only a quantitative, but also a qualitative test.[36] Indeed, at least one Canadian court has opined that the qualitative is to be "preferred as the acid test."[37]

In a recent decision of the Ontario Court of Appeal, Cronk J.A. explained the rationale underlying the qualitative test in this way:

> [Q]ualitative analysis seeks to determine the nature of the transferor's core business activities, and the property involved in carrying out such activities. The purpose of the inquiry is to assess whether the transferred property is integral to the transferor's traditional business, such that its disposition or transfer strikes at the heart of the transferor's existence and primary corporate purpose.[38]

---

35   See, for example, CBCA, s. 190(1)(e) and (3); ABCA, s. 191(e); BCBCA, s. 301(5); MCA, s. 184(1)(e); NBBCA, s. 131(1)(f); NLCA, s. 304(1)(e); NSCA, s. 135A, Third Sch., s. 2(1)(e); OBCA, s. 185(1)(e); SBCA, s. 184(1)(e); NWBCA, s. 193(1)(e); NuBCA, s. 193(1)(e); YBCA, s. 193(1)(e).

36   See, for example, *85956 Holdings Ltd. v. Fayerman Brothers Ltd.* (1986), 46 Sask. R. 75 (C.A.); *Martin v. F.P. Bourgault Industries Air Seeder Division Ltd.* (1987), 45 D.L.R. (4th) 296 (Sask. C.A.); *Lindzon v. International Sterling Holdings Inc.* (1989), 45 B.L.R. 57 (B.C.S.C.); *GATX v. Hawker Siddely Canada Inc.* (1996), 27 B.L.R. (2d) 251 (Ont. Ct. Gen. Div.); *Benson v. Third Canadian General Investments Trust Ltd.* (1993), 14 O.R. (3d) 493 (Gen. Div.) [*Benson*]; *Cogeco Cable Inc. v. CFCF Inc.* (1998), 136 D.L.R. (4th) 243 (Que. C.A.); *Hovsepian v. Westfair Foods Inc.* (2003), 37 B.L.R. (3d) 178 (Alta. Q.B.); *Amaranth LLC v. Counsel Corp.* (2007), 84 O.R.(3d) 361 (S.C.J.).

37   *Benson, ibid.* at 506.

38   *Canadian Broadcasting Corporation Pension Plan (Trustee of) v. BF Realty Holdings Ltd.* (2002), 214 D.L.R. (4th) 121 at para. 45 (Ont. C.A.).

In some respects, a qualitative test tied to the transferor's "primary corporate purpose" is peculiar given that modern Canadian corporate statutes typically do not require a corporation's constating documents to state business objects or purposes of any kind. In any event, as important as the qualitative test appears to be, it must be considered carefully within the context of each individual transaction, and in the light of developing jurisprudence not only in Canada but elsewhere. For example, a 2004 decision of the Delaware Court of Chancery suggests that, in applying the qualitative test, the courts should focus not on amorphous concepts of fundamental nature but rather upon "economic quality."[39]

One additional interesting issue that may arise in the "all or substantially all" context is the question of whether a series of sales, in the aggregate, may be found to constitute a sale of "all or substantially all" of a corporation's assets. This issue was considered by the Delaware Supreme Court in a recent case, *Bank of New York Mellon Trust Co. v. Liberty Media Corporation.*[40] This case involved the interpretation of the phrase "all or substantially all" in the context of a bond indenture rather than a corporate statute, but in the Court of Chancery decision, which the Supreme Court affirmed, Laster V-C expressly found that the phrase would have the same meaning in both contexts. Liberty had engaged in a series of "spinoff transactions" which involved rolling out certain assets to its shareholders. Although no single transaction could be said to constitute a sale of "all or substantially all" of Liberty's assets, bondholders argued that, when aggregated, these transactions amounted to such a sale. The court disagreed with the bondholders, holding that the sales in question should not be aggregated. Citing with approval a decision of the United States Court of Appeals for the Second Circuit, *Sharon Steel Corp. v. Chase Manhattan Bank, N.A.,*[41] determining "that aggregation is appropriate only when a series of transactions are part of a 'plan of piecemeal liquidation' and an 'overall scheme to liquidate' and not where each transaction stands on its own merits without reference to the others."[42]

---

39   *Hollinger Inc. v. Hollinger International Inc.*, 858 A.2d 342 (Del. Ch. 2004). For further discussion of the holding in this case, and the topic of "sale of all or substantially all" more generally, see Nicholls, *Corporate Law*, above note 2 at 449–53.

40   29 A.3d 225 (Del S.C.), aff'g CA 5702-VCL (Del. Ch. Ct. 29 April 2011).

41   691 F.2d 1039 at 1050 (2d Cir. 1982).

42   Above note 40 at 243 (Del. S.C.).

H. CONCLUSION

Most major business acquisitions in Canada are, in fact, accomplished by way of share-based rather than asset-based transaction structures. Accordingly, most of the remainder of this book will focus on share deals. One only notes in conclusion, here, that despite the conventional wisdom that purchasers prefer asset sales and vendors prefer share sales, the complex effect of income tax and other considerations demand a very careful analysis of every proposed business acquisition to determine the optimal method, on balance, of structuring the transaction.

CHAPTER 4

"MERGERS"/ AMALGAMATIONS AND STATUTORY PLANS OF ARRANGEMENT

A. INTRODUCTION

As discussed in Chapter 1, when parties enter into a "friendly" or negotiated transaction, they may choose a deal structure that best accommodates their respective interests. Two forms of share transaction that
may be chosen by friendly "merger" parties in Canada (in addition
to structuring the deal as a takeover bid, as discussed in Chapters 5
through 7) are amalgamations and plans of arrangement.[1]

B. AMALGAMATION

1) Legal Effect of Amalgamation

The legal concept of "amalgamation" in Canada involves the fusion of
two or more amalgamating corporations to become a single entity—the

---

1   The word *merger*, although regularly used by lawyers and investment bankers in
    Canada, is not a term of art either in Canadian corporate or Canadian secur-
    ities law. The word is used in the Canadian *Competition Act* but in a very broad
    sense that is not intended to connote any legally unique form of transaction
    for corporate law purposes. See Christopher C. Nicholls, *Corporate Finance and
    Canadian Law* (Toronto: Carswell, 2000) at 297.

"amalgamated corporation."[2] The Supreme Court of Canada has famously described the theory underlying the Canadian concept of corporate amalgamation by drawing the analogy of "a river formed by the confluence of two streams, or the creation of a single rope through the intertwining of strands."[3]

This legal effect differs from the Delaware corporate law concept of a "merger." In Delaware, the merger of two or more corporations essentially results in the continuation of one of the constituent corporations, into which the other constituent corporations are merged.[4] (The Delaware corporate law transaction that appears to be closer conceptually to the Canadian concept of amalgamation is "consolidation.")[5] Canadian amalgamation does not simply involve the continuation of one of the amalgamating corporations, even though the newly formed amalgamated corporation is permitted to adopt the name of any of the amalgamating corporations.[6]

The legal effect of a corporate amalgamation is notionally to continue the existence of each of the predecessor (amalgamating) corporations through the new (amalgamated) corporation. Thus, all of the property of the amalgamating corporations becomes the property of the amalgamated corporation.[7] Equally important, all liabilities—including any existing causes of action—are unaffected by the amalgamation.[8]

---

2   See, for example, *Canada Business Corporations Act*, s. 181 [CBCA]; Alberta *Business Corporations Act*, s. 181 [ABCA]; British Columbia *Business Corporations Act*, s. 269 [BCBCA]; *The Corporations Act* (Manitoba), s. 175(1)[MCA]; New Brunswick *Business Corporations Act*, c. B-9.1, s. 120 [NBBCA]; Newfoundland and Labrador *Corporations Act*, s. 288 [NLCA]; Nova Scotia *Companies Act*, s. 134 [NSCA]; Ontario *Business Corporations Act*, s. 174 [OBCA]; Prince Edward Island *Companies Act*, s. 77(1) [PEICA]; Saskatchewan *Business Corporations Act*, s. 175 [SBCA]; Northwest Territories *Business Corporations Act*, s. 183 [NWBCA]; Nunavut *Business Corporations Act*, s. 183 [NuBCA]; Yukon *Business Corporations Act*, s. 183 [YBCA].
3   *R. v. Black & Decker Manufacturing Corp.*, [1975] 1 S.C.R. 411 at 421.
4   *Delaware General Corporation Law*, Delaware Code, Title 8, Chapter 1, s. 251(a).
5   *Ibid.*
6   See, for example, *Canada Business Corporations Regulations, 2001*, s. 31(2).
7   CBCA, s. 186(b); ABCA, s. 186(b); BCBCA, s. 282(1)(g); MCA, s. 180(b); NBBCA, s. 125(b); NLCA, s. 294(1)(b); NSCA, s. 134(12); OBCA, s. 179(b); PEICA, s. 77(4); SBCA, s. 180(b); NWBCA, s. 188(b); NuBCA, s. 188(b); YBCA, s. 188(b).
8   CBCA, ss. 186(c) & (d); ABCA, ss. 186(c) & (d); BCBCA, ss. 282(1)(h)–(j); MCA, ss. 180(c) & (d); NBBCA, s. 125(b); NLCA, ss. 294(1)(c) & (d); NSCA, s. 134(12); OBCA, s. 179(b); PEICA, s. 77(4); SBCA, ss. 180(c) & (d); NWBCA, ss. 188(c) & (d); NuBCA, ss. 188(c) & (d); YBCA, ss. 188(c) & (d).

Accordingly, convictions or judgments against any of the amalgamating corporations may be enforced against the amalgamated corporation.[9]

The existence of predecessor (or amalgamating) corporations theoretically continues after amalgamation, but only through the new amalgamated corporation. In other words, the predecessor corporations should not be thought to maintain some independent existence following the amalgamation. It might seem that this point is rather abstract and theoretical, but the issue has practical implications as well, as the Ontario Court of Appeal's judgment in the 2002 case, *Charter Financial Company v. Royal Bank of Canada*[10] illustrated.

In *Charter Financial* the Court of Appeal held that an amalgamating corporation "continued after the amalgamation to have sufficient existence to enter into valid and binding agreements . . . ."[11] Thus, the Court held that a financing statement registered under the *Personal Property Security Act*[12](PPSA) under the name of an amalgamating corporation was valid, despite the fact that the registration did not occur until after the debtor corporation had amalgamated with a second corporation, to form a new corporation with a different corporate name. With the greatest respect to the Ontario Court of Appeal, this decision appears to be in error both as a matter of law and in terms of the policy underlying the *PPSA*.[13]

Following the *Charter Financial* decision, the Ontario legislature amended the Ontario *Business Corporations Act* ("OBCA") to clarify that following amalgamation, "the amalgamating corporations cease to exist as entities separate from the amalgamated corporation."[14] This statutory amendment—which Gray *et al.* note appears merely to "[codify] existing law on the legal effect of an amalgamation"[15]—should nevertheless serve to overrule *Charter Financial* in the case of corporations incorporated under the OBCA. There remains a risk that in the case of amalgamations involving corporations incorporated under other Canadian

---

9   CBCA, ss. 186(e) & (f); ABCA, ss. 186(e) & (f); BCBCA, s. 282(1)(k); MCA, s. 180(f); NBBCA, s. 125(c); NLCA, ss. 294(1)(e) & (f); OBCA, s. 179(c); SBCA, ss. 180(e) & (f); NWBCA, ss. 188(e) & (f); NuBCA, ss. 188(e) & (f); YBCA, ss. 188(e) & (f).

10   2002 CanLII 41852 (Ont. C.A.).

11   *Ibid.* at para. 6.

12   R.S.O. 1990, c. P.10.

13   For a detailed critique of the decision, see Wayne D. Gray, David L. Denomme, & Jacob S. Ziegel, "Perfection Under a Predecessor Debtor Name—Comment on *Charter Financial Company v. Royal Bank of Canada*" (2005) 41 Can. Bus. L.J. 431.

14   OBCA, s. 179(a.1), as am. by S.O. 2004, c.19, s. 3.

15   Above note 13 at 448.

corporate statutes without this language, courts might apply *Charter Financial*'s problematic reasoning.

2) Structuring a Transaction as an Amalgamation

Various factors might lead merger parties to choose to amalgamate, although it has been said that the use of direct amalgamation as a one-step merger structure "is extremely unusual."[16] For example, at one time a corporation with substantial operating earnings could amalgamate with another corporation that had accumulated significant unused tax losses and apply those losses to reduce income tax. Although the Canada Revenue Agency has subsequently taken steps to curtail unrestrained trafficking in tax losses, amalgamation may still offer key tax advantages. In addition, amalgamation is the method frequently used to implement the second stage of a two-step takeover bid/going-private transaction as discussed further in Chapter 8.

3) Two Basic Methods (or Forms) of Amalgamation

The amalgamation provisions in most Canadian corporate statutes are similar. They typically provide for two types of amalgamations:

- short form amalgamations; and
- long form amalgamations.

a) Short Form Amalgamations

Short form amalgamations, as the name suggests, involve an expedited procedure, with fewer required formalities and documentation. However, corporations are only permitted to amalgamate using the simpler short form procedures in two cases:

- *Vertical short form amalgamations:* A corporation is permitted to use the short form amalgamation rules to amalgamate with one or more of its subsidiary corporations, provided that all the shares of any amalgamating corporation are held by one or more of the amalgamating corporations.[17]

---

16   See *McEwen v. Goldcorp Inc.*, 2006 CanLII 35985 at para. 45 (Ont. S.C.J.), aff'd 2006 CanLII 37415 (Ont. Div. Ct.), summarizing the evidence of a leading Canadian mergers and acquisitions lawyer.

17   See, for example, CBCA, s. 184(1); ABCA, s. 184(1); BCBCA, s. 273; MCA, s. 178 (1); NBBCA, s. 123(1); NLCA, s. 291; NSCA, s. 134(23); OBCA, s. 177(1); SBCA, s. 178(1); NWBCA, s. 186(1); NuBCA, s. 186(1); YBCA, s. 186(1).

- *Horizontal short form amalgamations:* Two or more wholly owned subsidiaries of the same corporation may use the short form amalgamation rules to amalgamate with one another.[18]

The short form amalgamation procedures permit eligible corporations to authorize amalgamation by simple directors' resolution. No shareholder vote is required. Nor is it usually necessary for the two amalgamating corporations to enter into an amalgamation agreement.[19] Corporate statutes do typically mandate some formal requirements concerning cancellation of the shares of all but one of the amalgamating corporations[20] and the calculation of the stated capital account of the amalgamated corporation.[21]

b) Long Form Amalgamations

Where corporations are not eligible to use the short form amalgamation procedures, the amalgamation process is somewhat more cumbersome. The amalgamating corporations must enter into an amalgamation agreement, dealing with a number of specified matters detailed in the corporate legislation.[22] The directors of each amalgamating corporation must then submit the amalgamation agreement to the corporation's shareholders for approval.[23]

---

18 See, for example, CBCA, s. 184(2); ABCA, s. 184(2); BCBCA, s. 274; MCA, s. 178(2); NBBCA, s. 123(2); NLCA, s. 292; NSCA, s. 134(24); OBCA, s. 177(2); SBCA, s. 178(2); NWBCA, s. 186(2); NuBCA, s. 186(2); YBCA, s. 186(2).

19 See, however, NSCA, ss. 134(23) & (24) which provide for an amalgamation agreement; however, that agreement may be approved by the directors rather than the shareholders.

20 See, for example, CBCA, ss. 184(1)(b)(i) and (2)(b)(i); ABCA, ss. 184(1)(b)(i) and (2)(b)(i); BCBCA, ss. 273(1)(d)(i) and 274(1)(c)(i); MCA, ss. 178(1)(b)(i) and (2)(b)(i); NBBCA, s. 123(1)(b)(i) and (2)(b)(i); NLCA, ss. 291(b)(i) and 292(b)(i); NSCA, ss.134(23)(c)(i) and 134(24)(b)(i); OBCA, ss. 177(1)(b)(i) and (2)(b)(i); SBCA, ss. 178(1)(b)(i) and (2)(b)(i); NWBCA, ss. 186(1)(c)(i) and (2)(b)(i); NuBCA, ss. 186(1)(c)(i) and (2)(b)(i); YBCA, ss. 186(1)(b)(i) and (2)(b)(i).

21 See, for example, CBCA, ss. 184(1)(b)(iii) and (2)(b)(iii); ABCA, ss. 184(1)(b)(iv) and (2)(b)(iii); BCBCA, s. 273(2) and 274(3); MCA, s. 178(2)(b)(iii); NBBCA, s. 123(2)(b)(iii); NLCA, s. 292(b)(iii); NSCA, ss. 134(23)(c)(iii) and (24)(b)(iii); OBCA, s. 177(2)(b)(iii); SBCA, s. 178(1)(b)(iii) and (2)(b)(iii); NWBCA, ss. 186(1)(c)(iv) and (2)(b)(iii); NuBCA, ss. 186(1)(c)(iv) and (2)(b)(iii); YBCA, s. 186(2)(b)(iii).

22 See CBCA, s. 182(1); ABCA, s. 182(1); BCBCA, s. 270(2); MCA, s. 176(1); NBBCA, s. 121(1); NLCA, s. 289(1); NSCA, ss. 134(2) & (3); OBCA, s. 175(1); PEICA, s. 77(2); SBCA, s.176(1); NWBCA, s. 184(1); NuBCA, s. 184(1); YBCA, s. 184(1).

23 See CBCA, s. 183(1); ABCA, s. 183(1); BCBCA, s. 271; MCA, s. 177(1); NBBCA, s. 122(1); NLCA, s. 290(1); NSCA, s. 134(4); OBCA, s. 176(1); PEICA, s. 77(3);

The statutory requirements for approval of the amalgamation agreement are somewhat onerous. The shareholders of each amalgamating corporation must typically approve the agreement by super majority vote, usually by special resolution[24] (that is, by a two-thirds vote). Further, under certain Canadian corporate statutes, including the CBCA, every shareholder of each amalgamating corporation is entitled to vote, even if the class of share he or she holds does not normally carry voting rights.[25] Finally, if the amalgamation agreement includes a provision that would entitle holders of a class or series of shares to a separate class or series vote if that provision had been included in a proposed amendment to the corporation's articles, then the holders of such class or series of shares will also be entitled to a separate vote with respect to the amalgamation agreement.[26] Not every Canadian corporate statute includes such broad protection for the holders of non-voting shares.[27]

In addition, any shareholder of any amalgamating corporation that opposes the amalgamation is entitled to exercise dissent rights.[28] If

---

SBCA, s. 177(1); NWBCA, s. 185(1); NuBCA, s. 185(1); YBCA, s. 185(1).

24 See CBCA, s. 183(5); ABCA, s. 183(5); compare BCBCA, s. 271(6) (vote must be by "special majority" where shareholders not otherwise entitled to vote are permitted, by s. 271(7), to vote on the amalgamation); MCA, s. 177(5); NBBCA, s. 122(5); NLCA, s. 290(4); NSCA, s. 134(4) (Until recently the definition of "special resolution" under the NSCA differed from the definition under the CBCA and most other Canadian corporate statutes. The older definition still applies to corporations incorporated before recent amendments to s. 87 of the NSCA, which now defines "special resolution" as a two-thirds vote of the shareholders, unless those older corporations have chosen to adopt the newer definition.); OBCA, s. 176(4); PEICA, s. 77(3) (requiring approval of three-quarters of votes cast); SBCA, s. 177(5); NWBCA, s. 185(5); NuBCA, s. 185(5); YBCA, s. 185(5).

25 See CBCA, s. 183(3); ABCA, s. 183(3); BCBCA, s.271(7); MCA, s. 177(3); NBBCA, s. 122(3); SBCA, s. 177(3); NWBCA, s. 185(3); NuBCA, s. 185(3); YBCA, s. 185(3).

26 See CBCA, s. 183(4); ABCA, s. 183(4); BCBCA, s. 271(6)(b); MCA, s. 177(4); NBBCA, s. 122(4); NLCA, s. 290(3); OBCA, s. 176(3) (see description below in note 27); SBCA, s. 177(4); NWBCA, s. 185(4); NuBCA, s. 185(4); YBCA, s. 185(4).

27 For example, s. 176(3) of the OBCA provides for a separate class vote for holders of shares, including non-voting shares, only if the amalgamation agreement includes an amendment to the corporation's articles that would trigger a class vote under the amendment provisions of s. 170. However, the OBCA, unlike the CBCA, does not otherwise require non-voting shareholders to approve an amalgamation.

28 See CBCA, s. 190(1)(c); ABCA, s. 191(1)(c); BCBCA, ss. 272 and 238(1)(b); MCA, s. 184(1)(c); NBBCA, s. 131(1)(d); NLCA, ss. 290(2)(b) and 304(1)(c); NSCA, s. 135A, Third Sch., s. 2(1)(c); OBCA, s. 185(1)(c); SBCA, s. 184(1)(c); NWBCA, s. 193(1)(c); NuBCA, s. 193(1)(c); YBCA, s. 193(1)(c). Note that shareholders are *not* entitled to exercise dissent rights when the amalgamation is completed using the short form procedures.

the amalgamation is subsequently approved by the other shareholders, such dissenting shareholders are entitled to be paid the fair value of their shares by the corporation.[29] The risk of triggering these dissent and appraisal rights is thought to impose some constraint on corporate managers contemplating an amalgamation. The possibility that a significant number (potentially up to one-third) of a corporation's shareholders might object to an amalgamation approved by the remaining two-thirds means that the managers must carefully consider the potential impact of making a cash distribution to all these shareholders of an amount representing the "fair value" of their shares.

The Dickerson Committee expressly acknowledged the potentially constraining effect of the existence of dissent rights (not only in the amalgamation context, but more generally in the context of proposed fundamental corporate changes).[30] The extent to which the spectre of large payments that may have to be made to dissenting shareholders does or does not pose an impediment to efficient managerial decision-making is a matter of some debate.[31] In any event, most Canadian corporate statutes specifically allow an amalgamation agreement to include a provision permitting the directors of the amalgamating corporations to terminate the agreement, regardless of whether the shareholders of any or all of the amalgamating corporations have voted to approve the transaction.[32]

Where one or more of the amalgamating corporations has publicly traded shares, approval of the amalgamation agreement will need to take place at a special meeting of shareholders. The process of convening the necessary shareholders' meeting involves complying with additional notice and information requirements. Notice of the meeting must be accompanied by a form of proxy[33] and an information circular (management proxy circular) in the form prescribed by legislation,[34] providing

---

29   See CBCA, s. 190(3); ABCA, s. 191(3); BCBCA, s. 245; MCA, s. 184(3); NBBCA, s. 131(3); NLCA, s. 304(4); NSCA, Third Sch., s. 2(4); OBCA, s. 185(4); SBCA, s. 184(3); NWBCA, s. 193(3); NuBCA, s. 193(3); YBCA, s. 193(3).

30   Robert W.V. Dickerson et al., *Proposals for a New Business Corporations Law for Canada*, vol. 1, *Commentary* (Ottawa: Information Canada, 1971) at para. 347.

31   See, for example, Christopher C. Nicholls, *Corporate Law* (Toronto: Emond Montgomery, 2005) at 441.

32   See CBCA, s. 183(6); ABCA, s. 183(6); MCA, s. 177(6); NBBCA, s. 122(6); NLCA, s. 290(5); OBCA, s. 176(5); SBCA, s. 177(6); NWBCA, s. 185(6); NuBCA, s. 185(6); YBCA, s. 185(6).

33   See, for example, CBCA, s. 149(1).

34   *Ibid.*, s. 150(1)(a). There are parallel proxy/information circular requirements in provincial securities legislation. See, for example, *Securities Act* (Ontario), Part XIX; National Instrument 51-102, Part 9. (The proxy and information circular requirements of Part XIX do not apply where a reporting issuer complies with

shareholders with sufficient information about the proposed amalgamation to enable them to cast their vote in an informed manner. Where the amalgamation involves a change, exchange, issuance or distribution of securities, the information circular must include prospectus-level disclosure.[35]

Where an amalgamation involving a publicly traded company is initiated following a successful takeover bid in an effort to eliminate the interests of any remaining shareholders who did not tender their shares to the bid, specific provincial securities rules also apply.[36] Use of an amalgamation to effect such a second-step going-private transaction is often referred to as an "amalgamation squeeze," and is discussed in greater detail in Chapter 8.

The final point to be observed about amalgamation is that it provides considerable flexibility. For example, the articles of amalgamation, which function as the articles of the new amalgamated corporation, need not simply mirror the articles of one of the amalgamating corporations[37] so that, upon amalgamation, the corporation can, as it were, reinvent itself. The same flexibility exists with respect to the amalgamated corporation's by-laws.[38] Finally, an amalgamation agreement may include terms pursuant to which shares of an amalgamating corporation are *not* converted into shares of the new amalgamated corporation but, instead, entitle the holders to receive cash or securities in some other entity.[39] It is this feature of the corporate law amalgamation provisions that facilitates, among other things, the elimination of minor-

---

the comparable provisions in NI 51-102. See OSC Rule 51-801. ss. 3.11–3.13.) To avoid duplication or overlap with corporate law requirements, the *Securities Act* and NI 51-102 provide that where a corporation complies with the proxy solicitation laws of its incorporating jurisdiction, and those laws are similar to the requirements of the *Securities Act* or NI 51-102, as the case may be, the requirements of the Act or of the National Instrument do not apply (*Securities Act* (Ontario), s. 88(1); NI 51-102, s. 9.5).

35   Form 51-102F5, Item 14.2.

36   See Multilateral Instrument 61-101.

37   See CBCA, s. 182(1)(a), specifying that the articles of amalgamation are to include the provisions required by s. 6 of the Act to be included in articles of incorporation. See also ABCA, s. 182(1)(a); BCBCA, s. 270(2)(d); MCA, s. 176(1)(a); NBBCA, s. 121(1)(a); NLCA, s. 289(1)(a); NSCA, ss.134(14) & (15); OBCA, s. 175(1)(a); SBCA, s. 176(1)(a); NWBCA, s. 184(1)(a); NuBCA, s. 184(1)(a); YBCA, s. 184(1)(a).

38   See CBCA, s. 182(1)(f); ABCA, s. 182(1)(f); MCA, s. 176(1)(f); NBBCA, s. 121(1)(d); NLCA, s. 289(1)(f); OBCA, s,175(1)(d); SBCA , s.176(1)(f); NWBCA, s. 184(1)(f); NuBCA, s. 184(1)(f); YBCA, s. 184(1)(f).

39   See CBCA, s. 182(1)(d); ABCA, s. 182(1)(d); BCBCA, ss. 270(2)(b)(ii) & (iii); MCA, s. 176(1)(d); NBBCA, ss. 121(1)(b)(ii) & (iii); NLCA, s. 289(1)(d); NSCA, s.

ity shareholder interests in a post takeover bid amalgamation squeeze transaction as discussed in Chapter 8.

C. STATUTORY PLAN OF ARRANGEMENT

1) Introduction

One important method of effecting a major corporate share acquisition in Canada is by way of a statutory plan of arrangement. An arrangement is a court-approved transaction provided for under many Canadian corporate statutes.[40] Such an arrangement may include, among other things, an amalgamation, a transfer of all or substantially all the property of a corporation, or a going-private or squeeze-out transaction. The arrangement provision first entered Canadian corporate law in 1923, derived from a similar provision in the English corporate statute. Wegenast noted that such a provision was "anomalous"[41] in the Canadian Act, because changes to corporate constitutional documents were generally determined by the relevant government department, not the courts.[42] The provision was not included in the CBCA when it was first enacted in 1975, evidently because of concerns that it was "superfluous and that it could be invoked to squeeze out minority shareholders unfairly."[43] However, the federal government subsequently recognized that "complicated situations do arise where no one and no combination of the fundamental change institutions . . . set out in the [CBCA] can be invoked to resolve all the problems in a practical matter."[44] Accordingly, in 1978 the CBCA was amended to include the arrangement provision.

134(2)(h); OBCA, ss. 175(1)(b)(ii) & (iii); SBCA, s. 176(1)(d); NWBCA, s. 184(1)(d); NuBCA, s. 184(1)(d); YBCA, s. 184(1)(d).

40   See, for example, CBCA, s. 192; ABCA, s. 193; BCBCA, ss. 288–99; MCA, s. 185; NBBCA, ss. 128 & 129; NLCA, s. 315; NSCA, ss. 130 & 131; OBCA, ss. 182 & 183; SBCA , s. 186.1; NWBCA, s. 195; NuBCA, s. 195; YBCA; s. 195.

41   F.W. Wegenast, *The Law of Canadian Companies* (Toronto: Carswell, 1979, reprinted from original 1931 publication) at 476.

42   *Ibid.*

43   Canada, Department of Consumer and Corporate Affairs, *Detailed Background Paper for an Act to Amend the Canada Business Corporations Act* (Ottawa: Consumer and Corporate Affairs Canada, 1977) at 5. See also Simon Scott, Timothy O. Buckley, & Andrew Harrison, "The Arrangement Procedure under Section 192 of the *Canada Business Corporations Act* and the Reorganization of Dome Petroleum Limited" (1990) 16 Can. Bus. L.J. 296 at 299.

44   See *Detailed Background Paper, ibid.* at 5.

The term "arrangement" is often associated with workout or re-organizations of companies that are insolvent or in financial distress. The CBCA's arrangement provision, however, is not such an insolvency measure. In fact, it may only be used by corporations that are *not* insolvent (although, as explained below, this restriction has been broadly interpreted). Many parties to complex corporate change of control transactions have found the plan of arrangement provisions useful because among other things they offer, generally speaking:

- *Flexibility:* Complex transactions may consist of many different steps that must be undertaken simultaneously, and may affect the holders of diverse financial interests in one or more affected corporations. In the acquisition context specifically, arrangements can make it possible for an acquisition to be completed in a single-step transaction rather than, for example, a two-step (takeover bid followed by a going-private transaction) process.
- *Comprehensiveness:* A transaction completed by way of arrangement can deal, simultaneously and comprehensively, with both debt and equity of a target corporation. Other methods of completing an acquisition, such as amalgamations or takeover bids, involve only the equity securities of the target corporation.
- *Certainty:* The arrangement procedure involves a court process and, ultimately, court approval. Thus, once an arrangement is complete, the parties have great comfort that their transaction cannot subsequently be impugned.
- *Tax and Securities Law Advantages:* The arrangement procedure allows a corporate transaction to be completed in a way that solves timing and other contingencies that could lead, among other things, to adverse tax implications. In addition, where a corporation has U.S. securityholders who are to receive securities as part of the change of control transaction, use of the arrangement procedure permits those securities to be issued without the costly and time-consuming requirement to file a registration statement under U.S. federal securities laws, thanks to the registration exemption available under section 3(a)(10) of the U.S. *Securities Act of 1933.*[45]
- *Other Advantages in Cross-Border Deals:* In addition to the benefit of exemption from U.S. securities law registration requirements, for

---

45   15 USC § 77*aff*. Staff of the U.S. Securities and Exchange Commission's Division of Corporate Finance have provided their views on the use of the s. 3(a)(10) exemption, as well as the resale status of securities issued pursuant to that exemption, in "Staff Legal Bulletin No. 3A" (18 June 2008), online: www.sec.gov/interps/legal/cfslb3a.htm.

certain specific types of transactions, including transactions involving Canadian corporations with U.S. shareholders, or acquisitions of Canadian corporations by U.S. corporations, the arrangement offers other advantages as well. In cross-border deals, for example, involving an acquisition of a Canadian corporation by a U.S. corporation, the plan of arrangement technique facilitates a seamless one-step transaction in which the Canadian shareholders may receive exchangeable shares. The purpose of an exchangeable share structure is to avoid triggering the capital gains tax that Canadian shareholders would be required to pay (assuming the proceeds of disposition they realized exceeded the adjusted cost base of their shares) if they were to receive shares of the American acquiror outright in exchange for their shares in the Canadian company being acquired. Under an exchangeable share structure, the Canadian shareholders receive, instead, shares of a Canadian corporation that essentially mirror the rights and attributes of shares in the American parent, but, because they are issued by a Canadian corporation, permit a tax "rollover," that is, a deferral of the capital gains tax that would otherwise be payable.

Such shares are also, typically, exchangeable, at the option of the holder, for actual shares of the American parent. At the point of such exchange, the issue of shares to the Canadian shareholders would constitute a "distribution"; and, under Canadian securities laws, when there is a distribution of securities, normally the seller must prepare and file a prospectus, unless there is an available prospectus exemption.[46] Canadian securities laws do provide a prospectus exemption in the case of a "distribution of a security in connection with . . . an . . . arrangement that is under a statutory procedure."[47] Clearly, this exemption would apply to exempt the original issue of the exchangeable shares in the Canadian corporation. However, there had been, apparently, some concerns raised that the exemption (and its predecessors) might not be broad enough to extend to the subsequent issue to Canadian shareholders of the shares of the American parent upon exercise of the previously granted exchange right since that issuance could occur many months after the original transaction. To try to put to rest any such concerns, Companion Policy 45-106 CP specifically provides that:

> The securities regulatory authorities or regulators take the position that the statutory procedure exemptions contained in section 2.11

---

46   See, for example, *Securities Act* (Ontario), s. 53.
47   National Instrument 45-106, s. 2.11(1)(a).

and 3.11 of NI 45-106 refer to all distributions or trades of securities that are necessary to complete an exchangeable share transaction involving a procedure described in section 2.11 or section 3.11, *even where such distributions or trades occur several months or years after the transaction.*[48]

The opportunities for creative and effective transaction design made available by the plan of arrangement provisions in the CBCA and other Canadian corporate statutes have been long recognized by Canadian legal practitioners, and acknowledged by regulators. For example, in a policy statement issued by the Director under the CBCA (the current version of which is dated 4 January 2010), the Director endorsed

> the view that the arrangement provisions of the Act are intended to be facilitative and [noted] that the arrangement provisions of the Act have been utilized by corporations to effect a wide range of different types of transactions, such as "spin offs" of business enterprises, combinations of business enterprises, continuances of corporations to or from other jurisdictions and so-called "going-private" transactions.[49]

2) Basic Steps Involved in an Arrangement

A fairly well-defined process has developed for completing arrangements under section 192 of the CBCA (and similar provisions in other Canadian corporation statutes). First, the party seeking approval of the arrangement applies to the court for an interim order. The interim order deals principally with the procedure the applicant intends to follow in order to seek approval of the proposed arrangement from shareholders and other interested stakeholders. The court would thus be asked to approve the applicant's proposal to hold various meetings of affected stakeholders, and to seek various specified voting approval thresholds, class voting rights (where appropriate), quorum thresholds, any dissent and appraisal rights, and notice and disclosure requirements. The Director has indicated that, despite the fact that section 192 does not mandate the granting of dissent and appraisal rights to dissenting shareholders, such rights should normally be granted,[50] and the Supreme Court of Canada has also alluded to the fact that courts,

---

48   Companion Policy, 45-106 CP, s. 4.2(3) [emphasis added].

49   "Policy 15.1—Policy of the Director Concerning Arrangements under Section 192 of the CBCA," s. 2.01, online: http://strategis.ic.gc.ca/eic/site/cd-dgc.nsf/vwapj/15-1_04-01-10-eng.pdf/$FILE/15-1_04-01-10-eng.pdf [Policy 15.1].

50   Policy 15.1, *ibid.*, s. 4.06.

in reviewing the indicia of fairness of proposed arrangements, have considered, among other things, whether affected shareholders have recourse to dissent and appraisal rights.[51] However, it is clear that the court does have the discretion not to grant such rights in appropriate cases, as the 1998 decision of Spence J. of the Ontario Court General Division (as it was then called) illustrates.[52]

Section 192 of the CBCA does not, in fact, mandate a particular (or any) level of securityholder approval for a plan of arrangement. In this respect, the CBCA differs from some of its counterparts in provincial corporate law statutes.[53] However, the CBCA Director has indicated that "as a minimum, all security holders whose legal rights are affected by a proposed arrangement are entitled to vote on the arrangement."[54]

The question of whether voting rights should also be granted to securityholders whose *legal* rights are not being affected (or arranged) but whose economic interests may be impacted by the arrangement has been the subject of comment not only by the CBCA Director, but also by the Supreme Court of Canada. The Director has suggested that there may be cases where securityholders whose legal rights are unchanged but whose economic or other rights have been affected ought to be permitted to vote.[55] However, the Director is mindful of the fact that in the case of debt securities, governed by contractual terms in which the parties themselves have negotiated their own pattern of debt holder protections, those contractual terms should govern, "absent extraordinary circumstances."[56] This view echoes the judgment of the Supreme Court

---

51   *BCE Inc. v. 1976 Debentureholders*, 2008 SCC 69 at para. 152 [*BCE*].
52   *Re Electrohome Ltd.* (1998), 40 B.L.R. (2d) 210 (Gen. Div.).
53   See, for example, ABCA, ss. 193(4)(a) & (b); BCBCA, ss. 289(1)(a) & (2); NSCA, s. 130(2); OBCA, ss.182(3) &(4); NWBCA, ss. 195(4) and (6); NuBCA, ss. 195(4) and (6); YBCA, ss. 195(4) and (6). Commenting on this difference between the OBCA and the CBCA, Farley J., in *Re Stelco Inc.*, 2006 CanLII 4500 (Ont. S.C.J.), suggested at para. 11 "That may well be a distinction without a difference if one analyzes the situation in light of *Re Loewen Group Inc.*, 2001 CarswellOnt. 4910 (SCJ [Commercial List]) at paras. 2 and 14. It is also clear that it is the court process which is important to ensuring that the issue of fairness and reasonableness is met: See *Olympia & York Developments Ltd. v. Royal Trust Co.* (1993), 18 C.B.R. (3d) 176 (Ont. Gen. Div.) pp. at 191–2. See also *Re Teddy Bear Valley Mines Ltd.* (1993), 1 C.C.L.S. 97 (Ont. Gen. Div.) which indicates, albeit in a quite different fact situation, that shareholder approval of an arrangement is not a *sine qua non* prerequisite to court approval of an arrangement under the OBCA but rather the mechanism by which an arrangement is achieved is [sic] the court process rather than approval by security holders."
54   Policy 15.1, above note 49, s. 3.09.
55   *Ibid.*, s. 3.09.
56   *Ibid.*

of Canada in *BCE Inc. v. 1976 Debentureholders*, where the court held that "The purpose of s. 192, discussed above, suggests that only security holders whose legal rights stand to be affected by the proposal are envisioned".[57] The Court acknowledged that "This general rule, however, does not preclude the possibility that in some circumstances, for example threat of insolvency or claims by certain minority shareholders, interests that are not strictly legal should be considered."[58] The *BCE* case involved an action brought by debentureholders protesting a proposed arrangement that would result in a material fall in the market value of their debentures, but involved no change whatsoever in their legal rights. These facts, the court determined, did not constitute the sort of "extraordinary circumstances" that would be necessary to consider the non-legal interests of the debentureholders for purposes of a CBCA section 192 application.[59]

Again, although the CBCA itself specifies no particular voting thresholds, the CBCA Director has expressed the opinion that, where debtholders rights are affected, "the appropriate voting level for debtholders is two thirds in value of the total debt held by all the debtholders of each class present, personally or by proxy."[60] The Director has also indicated that in certain instances it will be necessary to obtain approval of disinterested securityholders and, to that end, adherence to the same "majority of minority" voting rules that would apply under provincial securities laws (specifically Multilateral Instrument 61-101) will suffice.[61]

Once the interim order has been granted by the court, the applicant must then proceed to hold the meetings and seek the approvals in accordance with the procedure approved at the interim order stage. The applicant then returns to court to seek a final order approving the arrangement.

3) Tests to Be Satisfied

In considering whether or not to approve a plan of arrangement, Canadian courts generally adopt a three-part test to answer the following questions:[62]

---

57   Above note 51 at para. 133.
58   *Ibid.* at para. 134.
59   *Ibid.* at para. 135.
60   Policy 15.1, above note 49, s. 3.10.
61   *Ibid.*, s. 3.11.
62   See, for example, *BCE*, above note 51 at para. 137. This three-pronged test has a venerable history. Wegenast refers to the 1891 judgment of Lindley L.J. in *In re Alabama, New Orleans, Texas and Pacific Junction Ry Co.*, [1891] 1 Ch. 213 at 238,

- Have the statutory procedures been complied with?
- Has the application been put forward in good faith?
- Is the arrangement fair and reasonable? (Prior to the Supreme Court of Canada's decision in *BCE Inc. v. 1976 Debentureholders*, courts often referred to this third criteria as the "business judgment test"[63] because it was often held that, in this context, the question of whether the arrangement was fair and reasonable was to be to determined by asking whether "an intelligent and honest business person, as a member of the class concerned and acting in his or her own interest, might reasonably approve of the plan?"[64] The Supreme Court of Canada concluded that the so-called "business judgment test" was "not useful"[65] and, indeed, in part because it sounds confusingly similar to the very different concept of the "business judgment rule," it could lead to confusion.[66]) In *BCE*, the Court indicated that to determine whether an arrangement was fair and reasonable "involves two inquiries: first, whether the arrangement has a valid business purpose; and second, whether it resolves the objections of those whose rights are being arranged in a fair and balanced way."[67]

Technically, a corporation may only apply to the court for an order approving an arrangement under the CBCA "where it is not practicable for a corporation that is not insolvent to effect a fundamental change in the nature of an arrangement under any other provision" of the corporate statute.[68] But Canadian courts have interpreted both the "not insolvent" and the "impracticability" requirement broadly. The CBCA Director, in Policy 15.1, has expressly endorsed the view that "the impractic-

---

in which the court interpreted the arrangement section in the English corporate statute upon which the Canadian arrangement provisions were originally based: "What the Court has to do is to see, first of all, that the provisions of that statute have been complied with; and, secondly, that the majority has been acting *bona fide*. The Court also has to see that the minority is not being overridden by a majority having interests of its own clashing with those of the minority whom they seek to coerce. Further than that, the Court has to look at the scheme and see whether it is one as to which persons acting honestly, and viewing the scheme laid before them in the interests of those whom they represent, take a view which can be reasonably taken by business men." Cited in Wegenast, above note 41 at 477.

63   See, for example, *Pacifica Papers Inc. (Re)*, 2001 BCSC 1069 at para. 23.
64   *PetroKazakhstan Inc. v. Lukoil Overseas Kumkol B.V.*, 2005 ABQB 789; see also *Re Trizec Corp.* (1994), 21 Alta. L.R. (3d) 435 (Q.B.); *Pacifica Papers Inc. (Re)*, ibid.
65   Above note 51 at para. 142.
66   *Ibid.*
67   *Ibid.* at para. 143.
68   CBCA, s. 192(3).

ability requirement means something less than 'impossible' and, generally, that the test would be satisfied by demonstrating that it would be inconvenient or less advantageous to the corporation to proceed under other provisions of the Act."[69]

This broad interpretation of the term *impracticability* accords with the CBCA Director's more general view "that the arrangement provisions of the Act . . . should not be construed narrowly."[70] As discussed earlier in this chapter, corporations have found that arrangements can be a very useful means of completing complex corporate mergers for a variety of reasons including, among others, flexibility, avoidance of provincial takeover bid rules, and the certainty afforded the transaction by the court approval process. Likewise, the solvency requirement has been interpreted so as to allow use of the provision where the applicant is solvent, even if another major party to the transaction is not.[71]

As the CBCA Director's Policy Statement indicates, it has become customary for applicants to obtain a "fairness opinion" from a financial firm, in which the firm opines that the transaction or, perhaps more specifically, the consideration to be received by securityholders, "is fair from a financial point of view" to those affected.[72] Although there is no legal requirement to provide such an opinion, and indeed the Director acknowledges that there might well be circumstances where no such opinion is needed, nevertheless the Director has recognized the value of fairness opinions, and has indicated that when an arrangement applicant has chosen not to obtain such an opinion, the applicant "should be prepared to justify its position to the Director."[73] Obtaining such an opinion also provides considerable comfort to those putting forward the proposal and, for that matter, the court that the arrangement is fair and reasonable.

4) Articles of Arrangement

Once the court has given its final approval to the arrangement, the applicant will file its articles of arrangement. The form of articles of arrangement currently fixed by the CBCA is Form 14.1. The plan of

---

69   Policy 15.1, above note 49 s. 2.06.
70   *Ibid.*, s. 1.02.
71   The groundbreaking case on this issue was *Savage v. Amoco Acquisition Co.* (1988), 87 A.R. 321 (C.A.). See also *Re St Lawrence & Hudson Railway Co.*, [1998] O.J. No. 3934 (Gen. Div.). Both of these cases are referred to in the discussion of the solvency limitation in the CBCA Director's Policy 15.1, *ibid*, s. 2.03.
72   *Ibid.*, s. 4.03.
73   *Ibid.*

arrangement, which may include amendments to the applicant corporation's articles of incorporation, is attached to the articles of arrangement filed with the CBCA Director. The Director then issues a certificate of arrangement to the applicant,[74] making the arrangement effective,[75] and the articles of arrangement become the corporation's "articles" for purposes of the CBCA.

5) Arrangement vs. Takeover Bid

The increasing use of arrangements as a device for structuring a corporate change of control transaction without the requirement to comply with formal takeover bid rules has attracted some attention from Canadian securities regulators.

From time to time it has been suggested that certain arrangements ought to be regulated in the same way as takeover bids, since some arrangements are functionally similar to takeover bids. The Quebec Securities Commission (as it then was)[76] issued a notice for comment in 2001 on the issue of whether or not transactions such as arrangements that resulted in the change of control of public corporations ought to be regulated in the same way as takeover bids. This issue was considered by Ontario's Five Year Review Committee, a panel struck by the Ontario government to conduct a review of Ontario's securities laws which was completed in 2003. The Five Year Review Committee concluded, in its final report, that "the two types of transactions need not be regulated in an identical manner."[77] In their view, "as a matter of public policy, parties to commercial transactions should have the freedom to structure transactions to achieve their business purposes as long as these transactions, and the legislation that governs these transactions, are fair to all interested parties."[78] As the committee pointed out, arrangements are subject to court approval and provide dissent rights to minority shareholders who regard the offered price as inadequate. Moreover, they noted, the Securities Commission retained the power to curb abusive transactions by invoking its public interest jurisdiction under section 127 of the *Securities Act*.

---

74   See, for example, CBCA, ss. 192(7) and 262.

75   *Ibid.*, s. 192(8).

76   As of 1 February 2004, the Commission des valeurs mobilières du Québec has been merged with four other Quebec financial regulators to form the Autorité des marchés financiers.

77   *Five Year Review Committee Final Report-Reviewing the* Securities Act *(Ontario)* (Toronto: Queen's Printer for Ontario, 2003) at 182.

78   *Ibid.* at 183.

It is interesting to observe that this issue is not unique to Canada. Concerns that corporate law arrangement provisions could be used inappropriately to avoid the protective rules and procedures of the formal takeover bid regime have also been raised in other jurisdictions with comparable statutory provisions.[79]

6) No Deemed Arrangements

A business transaction that is not explicitly undertaken as an arrangement cannot be deemed to be an arrangement, and thereby made subject to all of the legislative procedures applicable to arrangements. This conclusion was confirmed by the Ontario Divisional Court in *McEwen v. Goldcorp Inc.*[80] In 2006, Goldcorp Inc. and Glamis Gold Ltd. entered into a transaction pursuant to which Goldcorp agreed to acquire the shares of Glamis in exchange for shares of Goldcorp. Although this transaction involved a plan of arrangement *from the perspective of Glamis*, Goldcorp's role in the transaction did not involve an arrangement. Indeed because of the way in which the transaction was structured, no approval of Goldcorp's shareholders was needed. One of Goldcorp's shareholders was opposed to the deal, and applied to the court seeking relief under sections 253, 106, and 248 of the OBCA. Among other things, the shareholder argued that the proposed transaction constituted an "arrangement" with respect to *Goldcorp* within the meaning of section 182 of the OBCA, and therefore required the approval of Goldcorp's shareholders. The court disagreed. Pepall J., at first instance, held that

> an arrangement must be proposed . . . a corporation should not find itself within the ambit of these provisions by inadvertence. To suggest otherwise would result in considerable uncertainty. Any disenchanted investor would feel free to parse language regardless of context or business purposes in an attempt to try and squeeze a transaction into the purview of section 182.[81]

Such an outcome, in the court's view, was contrary to the intent of the legislation and would undermine the directors' mandate to manage the business and affairs of the corporation. The Divisional Court concurred with the application judge that "a corporation must propose a

---

79   See, for example, Scott Clune, "Amalgamations, Schemes of Arrangement and Takeovers Regulation: Concerns of the Takeover Panel and the Need for Reform" (2007) 13 Canterbury L. Rev. 91.

80   Above note 16.

81   *Ibid.* at para. 32 (S.C.J.).

plan of arrangement to attract s. 182—that is, the section is facilitative and not mandatory."[82]

Accordingly, it is clear that parties must explicitly propose a plan of arrangement under the relevant statutory provisions; they cannot stumble into the arrangement procedure through inadvertence.

D. CONCLUSION

The one-step amalgamation technique (as opposed to amalgamations completed in the context of post-takeover bid squeeze transactions as discussed in Chapter 8) are a relatively rare method of undertaking a major share transaction between two or more public corporations. The arrangement, however, is widely-used, and has become an integral part of Canadian M & A practice. Although practitioners occasionally moot the possibility of undertaking an arrangement on a hostile basis, to date no such use of the arrangement provision has, to the knowledge of the author, ever been attempted. Accordingly, based on well established practice, it may be said that both amalgamations and arrangements are only available in the case of friendly transactions; that is transactions in which the directors of both the purchasing and the selling corporations support the deal and are working together to bring it to fruition. As long as the corporation sought to be acquired is actively resisting the overtures of a would-be purchaser, it is not feasible to structure a transaction as an amalgamation or a plan of arrangement. In such cases, the purchaser must resort to launching a takeover bid or, if control of the board of directors is the principal objective, perhaps a proxy contest. The remainder of the book considers these complex and important methods of seeking corporate control.

---

82   *Ibid.* at para. 11 (Div. Ct.).

CHAPTER 5

TAKEOVER BIDS (PART 1): FORMAL BID RULES

A. INTRODUCTION

The phrase *takeover bid* is sometimes used by American lawyers as an imprecise synonym for "corporate acquisition," and sometimes as a synonym for the particular acquisition technique known in the United States as a "tender offer." In Canada the term *tender offer* is not used or defined in securities or corporate law statutes, but the phrase *take-over bid* has a very specific meaning under provincial securities legislation. That technical statutory definition will be considered at length later in this chapter. For the moment, it will be sufficient to say that "take-over bids," in Canada, refer to purchases of shares (or offers to purchase) under certain statutorily defined circumstances that the legislators have decided could likely result in the purchaser attaining *practical* or effective control over a corporation.[1]

Make no mistake: the general description in the preceding paragraph is only intended to suggest to the reader an intuitive explanation of *why* we regulate "takeover bids." The actual definition of takeover bid found in the statute books does not rely on any vague, subjective concepts. It uses a clear "bright-line" test, namely, a purchase (or offer to purchase) shares that will constitute at least 20 percent of a class of a corporation's outstanding voting or equity shares, when combined

---

[1]   For a more detailed review of Canadian takeover bid rules, see Jeffrey G. MacIntosh & Christopher C. Nicholls, *Securities Law* (Toronto: Irwin Law, 2002) c. 10.

with any shares of that class that the purchaser or offeror already owns. Such a bright-line test markedly distinguishes Canadian takeover law from otherwise comparable U.S. federal "tender offer" legislation.

In the United States, the Williams Act[2] (which refers to sections 13(d)–(e) and 14(d)–(e) of the *Securities Exchange Act of 1934*) contains many provisions and protections that are similar to those found in Canadian takeover bid legislation. In the case of the U.S. rules, these provisions are triggered when a share acquisition is made by way of a "tender offer." Yet, the U.S. legislation does not actually define the term *tender offer*. To leave undefined what is arguably the most pivotal concept in the legislation may well strike a Canadian reader as peculiar. Many leading American commentators have also puzzled over this deliberate legislative omission.[3] In 1979, the U.S. Securities and Exchange Commission did propose a rule that would have defined the term *tender offer*,[4] but this attempt was ultimately abandoned. Why did Congress choose not to define a phrase upon which so much of the Williams Act depended? It may well have been thought that a bright-line test might have pulled more transactions into the Williams Act orbit than either Congress desired or the business community could tolerate.

There is an additional wrinkle in the fabric of U.S. takeover bid regulation. The principal source of securities regulation for publicly traded corporations in the United States is federal,[5] whereas corporate law is exclusively a state matter. Thus, there have been many important U.S. state corporate law developments relating to business combinations and control share acquisitions that significantly affect the way in which the control of corporations changes hands. No more will be said of the U.S. regime here, although in the material that follows it will be useful from time to time to draw insights and comparisons from the rich American experience.

---

2   These provisions are referred to collectively as the "Williams Act" after the original sponsor of the legislation, Senator Harrison Williams.

3   See, for example, Louis Loss & Joel Seligman, *Securities Regulation*, 3d ed., vol. 5 (New York: Aspen Law & Business, 1989) c. 6 at 2198: "[I]t is odd that, with everything in 14(d)–(f) turning on the existence of a 'tender offer,' that term is defined by neither statute nor rule."

4   See Ronald J. Gilson & Bernard S. Black, *The Law and Finance of Corporate Acquisitions*, 2d ed. (Westbury, NY: Foundation Press, 1995) at 981.

5   As Roberta Romano of the Yale Law School has noted, although there certainly is state-level securities legislation in the United States, "as a generalization, it would be most descriptively accurate to say that federal securities law has occupied the securities field and that state law development has been marginal." Roberta Romano, *The Advantage of Competitive Federalism for Securities Regulation* (Washington: The AEI Press, 2002) at 2.

The regulation of takeover bids in Canada has a lengthy history. Philip Anisman has chronicled this history in some depth.[6] Only a few of the more recent highlights will be touched on here. At one time, many decades ago, Canada had a *Code of Procedure on "Takeover Bids"* developed by self-regulatory organizations.[7] Since 1966, however, securities legislation in Ontario, Canada's largest province, has included detailed takeover bid rules, and other Canadian provinces have followed suit.

Prior to 2001, the federal business corporation statute, the *Canada Business Corporations Act* ("CBCA"), also contained its own takeover bid provisions. These rules applied, of course, only to takeovers of corporations incorporated under the CBCA. With the repeal of those provisions, however, provincial securities regulation is now the sole source of Canadian formal takeover bid legislation. A perceived need for greater consistency and harmonization of takeover bid regulation across Canada has prompted significant co-operative efforts amongst Canada's securities regulators. In April 2006 the Canadian Securities Administrators, the umbrella organization to which all of Canada's provincial and territorial securities regulators belong, released for comment proposed National Instrument 62-104.[8] In 2008, a successor to this instrument, Multilateral Instrument 62-104, was adopted in every province and territory in Canada except Ontario. Although Ontario chose not to adopt Multilateral Instrument 62-104, concurrent amendments to the takeover bid provisions in Ontario's *Securities Act* and related OSC Rule have led to essential national uniformity in takeover regulation.

As the Dickerson Committee noted in 1971, most of the provisions on takeover bids originally set out in Ontario's *Securities Act* were "derived from the United Kingdom 'City Code on Takeovers and Mergers' of March 27, 1968 and its predecessors."[9] The common ancestry of Canada's current takeover rules and the most recent version of the City

---

6   Philip Anisman, *Takeover Bid Legislation in Canada: A Comparative Analysis* (Toronto: CCH Canadian Limited, 1974).

7   *Ibid.* at 4. This code of procedure, "A Recommended Code of Procedure to be applied in connection with Takeover Bids" was produced in 1963 with input from various industry groups, including the Investment Dealers Association of Canada and Canadian stock exchanges. However, the Kimber Committee, writing in 1965, indicated that this voluntary code "appears not to have been followed in many cases." See *Report of the Attorney General's Committee on Securities Legislation in Ontario* (J.R. Kimber, Chair) (Toronto: Ministry of the Attorney General, March 1965) at 3.06 [Kimber Report].

8   (2006), 29 OSCB 3533 [Proposed NI 62-104].

9   Robert W.V. Dickerson, John L. Howard, & Leon Getz, *Proposals for a New Business Corporations Law for Canada*, vol. 1, *Commentary* (Ottawa: Information Canada, 1971) at para. 427.

Code (now called the Takeover Code) is still discernible; but there have been significant developments on both sides of the Atlantic that have resulted in a number of critical differences between Canadian and U.K. takeover rules today.

With the promulgation of Multilateral Instrument 62-104 and concurrent amendments to Ontario legislation and regulation, all provinces and territories are now subject to a harmonized takeover bid regime. (The core of Ontario's takeover bid rules is found in Part XX of the Ontario *Securities Act*[10] and in OSC Rule 62-504.)

The primary (though not sole) objective of Canadian takeover bid rules has traditionally been expressed as the protection of the shareholders of corporations that are the target of takeover bids.[11] To achieve this general objective, the takeover bid rules seek, more specifically, to ensure that all shareholders of the target corporation are treated .equally, that they receive adequate time to assess a bid so that they are not unfairly pressured into accepting an offer, and that they are given adequate information to make an informed decision about whether to accept the bid. These three specific goals were expressly stated in the proposed companion policy (Companion Policy 62-104 CP) that was issued with proposed National Instrument 62-104.[12]

National Policy 62-203 includes a statement of the "primary objectives" of the Canadian takeover bid regime which reflects two of these goals (equal treatment and adequate information) as well as a third: "an

---

10   R.S.O. 1990, c. S.5, as amended [*Securities Act* (Ontario)].

11   In National Policy 62-202 (1997), 20 OSCB 3525 [NP 62-202], a policy statement adopted by the Canadian securities regulators, the following statement appears:

> The primary objective of the take-over bid provisions of Canadian securities legislation is the protection of the bona fide interests of the shareholders of the target company. A secondary objective is to provide a regulatory framework within which take-over bids may proceed in an open and even-handed environment. The take-over bid provisions should favour neither the offeror nor the management of the target company, and should leave the shareholders of the target company free to make a fully informed decision.

> The Kimber Committee, in 1965, had concluded that "the primary objective of any recommendations for legislation with respect to the takeover bid transaction should be the protection of the bona fide interests of the shareholders of the offeree company." However, the Committee was also concerned to ensure that its recommendations "would not unduly impede potential bidders or put them in a commercially disadvantageous position vis-à-vis an entrenched and possibly hostile board of directors of an offeree company." Kimber Report, above note 7 at 3.10.

12   See Proposed Companion Policy 62-104CP, s. 2.1 [Proposed 62-104CP].

open and even-handed bid process."[13] Accordingly, takeover regulation today is aimed at ensuring a fair environment. But it is clear that the impetus for detailed takeover regulation was a perceived proliferation of high-handed tactics by aggressive bidders, and target company shareholders are, under NP 62-202, at the very least first among equals from a takeover regulation perspective. It is therefore worth saying something about the target shareholder protection rationale, for although the explanation is regularly repeated, the underlying logic is neither intuitive nor unassailable.

First, one notes that many profoundly important corporate decisions are—indeed must necessarily be—taken by corporate managers, without the benefit of shareholder input, or the inconvenience of shareholder approval. Further, the sale by a minority shareholder of his or her shares in a public corporation is typically undertaken as a routine matter, concluded on the basis of a call to one's broker or the tap of a few keys on a computer. No elaborate statutory protective mechanism is engaged by such trades. Is it necessarily clear that the regulatory scheme ought to be so dramatically different when *all* the shareholders simultaneously receive offers to purchase their shares—offers, it should be remembered, that are typically made at a significant premium to the current trading price? Put another way, should the opportunity to sell at a significant (and probably unexpected) profit trigger *greater* protective regulatory machinery than independent decisions taken to sell at (lower) prevailing market prices? At what special mischief is such protective legislation directed?

Although protection of the shareholders of target companies may be the *primary* objective of takeover bid rules, it is not the only objective. Securities regulators are well aware that most companies that launch takeover bids have public shareholders of their own. It would certainly be strange if Canada's securities commissions saw it as their exclusive duty to ensure that bidding companies (and therefore, indirectly, the public shareholders of bidding companies) paid the highest price possible to shareholders of target companies. In fact, some commentators have even audaciously suggested that, if anything, regulators ought to be *more* mindful of the concerns of shareholders of bidding companies than of target companies.[14]

Securities regulators are also acutely aware that hostile takeover bids—that is, bids that are opposed by the managers of the target com-

---

13   National Policy 62-203 (2008), 31 OSCB 1319 [NP 62-203].
14   For a glimpse of the reasoning underlying this provocative position see Christopher C. Nicholls, *Corporate Finance and Canadian Law* (Toronto: Carswell, 2000) at 360.

pany—are often economically beneficial, as inefficient managers of a target company may be replaced by the company's new owners. The buying and selling of enough shares of a corporation to give the buyer sufficient voting power to replace all of the corporation's directors (and therefore its chief executive officer and other senior managers who are hired and may be fired by those directors) lies at the heart of what has come to be called the "market for corporate control" by financial economists and legal scholars. This market for corporate control in the minds of many, beginning with legal scholar Henry Manne, represents one of the most important ways in which managers of publicly traded corporations who might otherwise be tempted to lounge or to loot (or, to use more common terminology, "to shirk or to shark") may be kept on their toes.[15]

Canadian takeover regulation reflects a balance of these competing interests. Though originally prompted by concerns that shareholders of target companies might sometimes be bamboozled or unfairly pressured[16] by aggressive, better-informed bidders, the takeover rules as applied by Canadian securities regulators today aim at creating a fair environment, rather than one in which the interests of any one group of shareholders are overly favoured over those of others.

Further, even the "target-shareholder protection" rationale for takeover bid regulation has been challenged. The terms of the debate are complex. But at its core, the matter comes down to these three essential propositions: First, do shareholders of target companies need to be protected from opportunistic bidders? Second, if they do need such protection, can directors and managers of target companies be relied upon to provide that protection? Or will their desire to entrench themselves overwhelm the sense of loyalty and responsibility that, one assumes, has otherwise tempered their self-interest in the conduct of the corporation's affairs? Finally, are takeover bids in general, and hostile bids in particular, to be regarded as healthy and positive signs of a dynamic and efficient economy where assets flow to their most highly valued and efficient use? Or are they, rather, acts of corporate pillage

---

15   Henry G. Manne, "Mergers and the Market for Corporate Control" (1965) 73 J. Pol. Econ. 110. Manne's idea has been enthusiastically embraced and subjected to various empirical tests by a number of financial economists. See, for example, Michael C. Jensen & Richard S. Ruback, "The Market for Corporate Control: The Scientific Evidence" (1983) 11 J. Fin. Econ. 5.

16   It is interesting to note that the phrase "or exert pressure on" which originally appeared in the language outlining the objectives of Canadian takeover bid regulation in section 2.1 of the predecessor of NP 62-203 was deleted from the final version of the policy. See CSA Notice, NP 62-203, Take-over Bids and Issuer Bids (2007), 30 OSCB Supp-6 at 41.

and displacement serving the narrow interests of a few "raiders" while bringing ruin to employees, shareholders, communities, and the public interest generally? Of this debate, and its implications for the legal treatment of takeover bids in general and hostile bids in particular, more will be said in Chapter 7.

For the remainder of this chapter, the emphasis will be upon explicating the Canadian securities law rules surrounding takeover bids, rules that apply whether such bids are undertaken with or without the support of the target company's directors and officers.

B. FUNDAMENTAL FEATURES OF THE CANADIAN TAKEOVER BID REGIME

The takeover bid requirements found in Multilateral Instrument 62-104, Ontario legislation and rules, and related regulatory instruments are detailed and complex. However, the most fundamental features of the rules may be summarized as follows.

1) Broad Definition of Takeover Bid

a) Twenty Percent Threshold

The term *take-over bid* is defined in Multilateral Instrument 62-104 and the Ontario *Securities Act* in specific terms. The definition has a very broad reach.[17] It captures almost every attempted purchase of outstanding equity or voting securities where the purchaser is expected to own at least 20 percent of the outstanding securities of the class after the proposed purchase is completed. The rules cannot be easily skirted. One cannot, for example, "game" the rules by structuring a proposed deal as an offer made by securityholders to *sell* rather than as an offer by the bidder to *purchase* because the definition of takeover bid applies to any "offer to acquire." The latter term expressly includes offers to purchase, solicitations, or acceptances, of offers to sell, "or any combination thereof."[18] Multilateral Instrument 62-104 and the Ontario *Securities Act* also include rules that require parties who are acting "jointly

---

17   See Multilateral Instrument 62-104 [MI 62-104], s. 1.1, definition of "take-over bid," online: www.albertasecurities.com/securitiesLaw/Regulatory%20Instruments/6/13983/2698059%20v1%20-%20MI%2062-104%20Pub%20Nov%2016,%202007.pdf [MI 62-104] and *Securities Act* (Ontario), s. 89(1), definition of "take-over bid."

18   *Ibid.*, definition of "offer to acquire."

or in concert" to lump all of their security holdings together when calculating whether the crucial 20 percent line has been crossed so as to prevent bidders from using clever "club" strategies in an effort to evade the takeover bid requirements.

Any prospective purchase that meets this 20 percent bright-line quantitative test will trigger the formal takeover bid rules, unless a specific statutory exemption is available. (Those exemptions will be discussed in Chapter 6.) Such an objective test avoids squabbles over the issue of whether a particular transaction is or is not subject to the formal takeover bid rules.

Notice that the definition of takeover bid turns on how many shares (or other voting or equity securities) a bidder would ultimately *own* if a proposed purchase were completed; it does not depend at all on how many securities a bidder actually proposes to buy. What this means, among other things, is that if a bidder already owns 20 percent of the outstanding voting or equity shares of a company, every additional purchase of shares of that class by that bidder—whether of one single share or of one million shares—would constitute a takeover bid.

Of course, it would be wasteful and absurd to require a controlling shareholder to prepare a formal takeover bid circular every time he or she wanted to purchase a single additional share. The takeover bid rules therefore, sensibly, include special exemptions to prevent such undesirable results. But the point to be remembered is that such a purchase would, in the first instance, constitute a takeover bid (as defined by the statute), even though the bidder might well be able to take advantage of an *exemption* relieving him or her from the otherwise onerous consequences that usually apply when one launches a formal takeover bid.

Why did Canadian legislators (and regulators) choose 20 percent as the level at which the formal takeover bid requirements would be triggered? Why not, for example, 50 percent, the point beyond which legal control of a corporation is acquired? The answer lies in the recognition of a practical reality. Corporations can be effectively controlled by holders of far less than 50 percent of the outstanding shares. Many Canadian corporations are, in fact, effectively controlled by holders of large blocks of shares that constitute less than 50 percent of the total. Indeed, securities laws consider a holder of more than a 20 percent block of outstanding voting securities to be a control person for several purposes.[19] The goal was, therefore, to ensure that transactions that were apt to result in a change of *effective* control of a public corporation would

---

19   See, for example, *Securities Act* (Ontario), s. 1(1), definition of "control person."

be subject to the formal bid requirements, even if such transactions did not necessarily involve a sufficient interest to constitute a change of *legal* control.[20] Whether 20 percent is too high a threshold or too low to achieve this goal cannot be determined with certainty. Undoubtedly, in some firms—particularly if there is another holder with an equal or even larger block of shares—it is too low. Yet in other firms, if shareholdings are especially widely dispersed, it may well be too high.

Prior to 2001, the CBCA contained its own takeover bid rules that were triggered by any offer to purchase shares of a CBCA corporation which, when combined with the offeror's shares, would exceed just 10 percent of the class. A proposal was made in 1982 to lower the takeover bid threshold in the Ontario *Securities Act* to 10 percent as well,[21] a threshold that was endorsed in 1983 in a report to the Ontario Securities Commission completed by three leading Ontario securities law practitioners ("Practitioners Report").[22] However, the relevant threshold in every Canadian jurisdiction continues to be 20 percent of the voting or equity securities. The 20 percent threshold is, of course, similar (though not identical) to the test used elsewhere in the Act and the rules to deem a shareholder of a corporation to be a control person.[23]

b)   Acting "Jointly or in Concert"

One of the most important concepts in takeover bid regulation is that of "acting jointly or in concert." The concept is significant in at least two contexts. First, it is used in determining whether or not a takeover bid has been made in the first place. Second, it becomes relevant when determining voting thresholds to approve going-private transactions undertaken after a takeover bid has been completed.

The 20 percent threshold is crossed if the number of shares under offer, when added to the "offeror's securities," constitute 20 percent or more of the outstanding securities of the class. The phrase *offeror's securities*, in turn, is defined to include not only securities owned by the offeror itself, but also any securities of the class owned by "any person

---

20   See Kimber Report, above note 7 at 3.11.

21   Ontario, Bill 176, *An Act to Amend the Securities Act*, 2d Sess., 32d Parliament, 1982.

22   Gordon Coleman, Garfield Emerson, & David Jackson, *Report of the Committee to Review the Provisions of the* Securities Act *(Ontario) Relating to Takeover Bids and Issuer Bids* (Toronto: Ontario Securities Commission, 1983) [Practitioner's Report]. (While this report is often referred to as the Practitioner's Report, it is also referred to in some sources as the "report of the 'Three Wise Men.'") See, for example, *Five Year Review Committee Final Report: Reviewing the* Securities Act *(Ontario)* (Toronto: Queen's Printer, 2003) at 22 [Crawford Report].

23   See above note 19.

or company acting jointly or in concert with the offeror." The term *jointly or in concert* is then glossed in section 1.9 of Multilateral Instrument 62-104 and section 91(1) of the Ontario *Securities Act.*

Under these provisions, whether a person or company is or is not a person who is acting jointly or in concert with the offeror (a "joint actor") is said to be a question of fact. Two specific instances are then set out in which it will be "deemed" that persons or companies are acting jointly or in concert with the offeror:

- persons or companies who agree with the offeror or with any other joint actor with the offeror to acquire or offer to acquire the target company's securities,[24] and
- affiliates of the offeror.[25]

In addition to these two "deeming" provisions, the rules provide that the following persons or companies will be "presumed" to be acting jointly or in concert with the offeror:

- persons or companies who agree with the offeror or with any other joint actor with the offeror to exercise jointly or in concert voting rights of the target company's securities,[26] and
- associates of the offeror.[27]

The distinction between the terms *presumed* and *deemed* is significant. If parties were merely "presumed" to be acting jointly or in concert, it remains possible to rebut this presumption in appropriate cases. If, however, parties were "deemed" to be acting "jointly or in concert," offerors wishing to avoid the implications of acting "jointly or in concert" would be obliged to apply to the securities regulatory authorities for an exemption from the deeming provision. Prior to the promulgation of the nationally harmonized takeover bid rules, not all Canadian provincial Securities Acts dealt with the "jointly or in concert" issue in exactly the same way, and this fact was adverted to in the Canadian Securities Administrators (CSA) notice and request for comments that accompanied the release of the draft of proposed National Instrument 62-104.[28]

---

24 *Securities Act* (Ontario), s. 91(1)(a)(i); MI 62-104, s. 1.9(1)(a)(i).
25 *Securities Act* (Ontario), s. 91(1)(a)(ii); MI 62-104, s. 1.9(1)(a)(ii). The term "affiliate" is defined, for purposes of Ontario's takeover bid rules, in ss. 89(2) & (3) of the *Securities Act* (Ontario), and for purposes of the takeover bid rules in other Canadian jurisdictions in ss. 1.3 & 1.4 of MI 62-104.
26 *Securities Act* (Ontario), s. 91(1)(b)(i); MI 62-104, s. 1.9(1)(b)(i).
27 *Securities Act* (Ontario), s. 91(1)(b)(ii); MI 62-104, s. 1.9(1)(b)(ii).
28 Under an early draft of proposed NI 62-104, persons or companies referred to in the bulletted items above were *deemed* (not merely presumed) to be acting

c) Outstanding Securities

The formal takeover bid rules apply only in the cases of offers to acquire *outstanding* securities—that is, previously issued securities already in the hands of other securityholders, rather than new securities issued from treasury. In other words, an offer to subscribe for shares of a corporation—no matter how great a percentage of the corporation's shares the subscriber expects to hold when those shares are issued—does not constitute a takeover bid. (The Ontario Securities Commission ("OSC") confirmed that the takeover bid rules apply only to the purchase of outstanding securities in *Re Trizec Equities Limited and Bramalea Limited*.)[29]

The purchase of shares directly from the issuing corporation does not engage the formal takeover bid rules because such purchases do not raise the same kinds of concerns that prompted legislators to regulate takeover bids in the first place. It is unlikely that a subscriber, for example, has better information about the issuer than the issuer itself; it is unlikely that the issuer can be pressured into accepting a share subscription without adequate time to consider the matter (indeed, it is more likely that the *purchaser* of treasury shares is at risk of being pressured and uninformed, as the need for prospectus rules governing securities issues indicates); and the price paid for newly issued shares cannot (by definition) unfairly favour one selling securityholder over another. That is not to say that the issuance of large blocks of shares by the issuer does not raise important legal and policy issues; clearly it does, as cases such as *Teck Corporation Ltd. v. Millar*[30] and, more recently, *Icahn Partners LP v. Lions Gate Entertainment*,[31] discussed in Chapter 7, indicate. However, the concerns raised by such share issuances differ from the concerns to which the formal takeover bid rules in the Ontario *Securities Act* and Multilateral Instrument 62-104 were intended to respond.

However, if an offeror has acquired the right to obtain newly issued shares of a corporation and, at the same time, makes an offer to acquire outstanding securities of the same class, then the number of newly

---

jointly or in concert with the offeror, with the exception of associates of the offeror, who were only *presumed* to be joint actors. (proposed NI 62-104, s. 1.7.) In the notice accompanying the release of the draft of NI 62-104, the CSA explained that associates of the offeror were treated differently "due to the range of entities that might be caught by a deeming provision including persons who have no relevant connection to the acquisition activities of the offeror." See above note 8 at 3535.

29 (1984), 7 OSCB 2033.
30 [1973] 2 W.W.R. 385 (B.C.S.C.).
31 2011 BCCA 228.

issued shares to be acquired may be included in calculating whether or not the offer to acquire the outstanding shares constitutes a takeover bid. This is so because section 90(1) of the Ontario *Securities Act* and section 1.8 of Multilateral Instrument 62-104 deem an offeror to have beneficial ownership of any securities that the offeror has the right or obligation to acquire within sixty days of the calculation date, including unissued securities. Simultaneous subscriptions and offers to purchase outstanding securities could also engage the formal bid rules. Moreover, such issuances are certainly relevant for purposes of the "early warning rules," discussed later in this chapter.

d) "Voting or Equity Securities"

Although the Canadian definition of takeover bid is broad in many ways, it does not catch every major purchase of securities. It applies only to a purchase of outstanding *voting* or *equity* securities. Those terms are defined in the Ontario *Securities Act*. Multilateral Instrument 62-104 includes a definition of *equity security* that is identical to that found in the current Ontario statute.[32] The multilateral instrument does not define the term *voting security*, a phrase typically defined in provincial securities statutes not only for purposes of the takeover bid rules but also in other contexts.[33] Thus, for example, the term *voting security* in the Ontario Act is found not in Part XX but rather in the general definition section of the Act, section 1(1). Nevertheless, it might have been preferable, in Multilateral Instrument 62-104, to add *voting security* as an expressly defined term.

An *equity security* is a security[34] "that carries a residual right to participate in the earnings of the [target] *and*, upon the liquidation

---

32 MI 62-104, s. 1.1.

33 See, for example, *Securities Act* (Alberta), s. 1(lll); *Securities Act* (British Columbia), s. 1(1); *Securities Act* (New Brunswick), s. 1(1); *Securities Act* (Newfoundland and Labrador), s. 2(1)(uu); *Securities Act* (Nova Scotia), s. 2(1)(au); *Securities Act* (Ontario), s. 1(1); *Securities Act* (Prince Edward Island), s. 1(jjj); *Securities Act* (Quebec), s. 5; *Securities Act, 1988* (Saskatchewan), s. 2(1)(xx); *Securities Act* (Northwest Territories), s. 1(1); *Securities Act* (Nunavut), s. 1(1); *Securities Act* (Yukon), s. 1(1).

34 The meaning of the word *security* is not discussed here. The word is defined expansively, and yet not exhaustively, in provincial securities legislation. See, for example, s. 1(1) of the *Securities Act* (Ontario). For a discussion of that definition and some of the leading cases in which it has been considered, see MacIntosh & Nicholls, *Securities Law*, above note 1 at 23–55. For the purposes of this chapter, it is sufficient to note that the definition of security includes shares of a corporation.

or winding up of the [target], in its assets."[35] The word *and* has been italicized to emphasize that a share must carry a residual participation right with respect to both dividends and distributions of the corporation's assets upon liquidation (after outstanding debts have been satisfied). One commenter on the original proposed draft of National Instrument 62-104, the predecessor of Multilateral Instrument 62-104, rightly noted a technical ambiguity that has always plagued this definition of equity security.[36] Because Canadian corporate law has always treated the declaration and payment of dividends on shares as a matter within the discretion of a corporation's board of directors, it is not entirely clear what it means to say that a share must carry a "right" with respect to dividends. Nonetheless, a reasonable interpretation of the language is that it refers to a right to dividends when and if declared by the corporation, a reading that would accord, for example, with one of the fundamental rights attached to shares of a CBCA corporation with only one class of shares.[37] A traditional "common" or "ordinary" share would, therefore, be an equity security. But so, too, would a non-voting share that entitled the holder to such residual participation rights.

The definition of voting security in the Ontario statute (and the other provincial statutes noted) has two critical components.[38] First, a debt security (such as a bond, a debenture, or a note) can never be a voting security, as defined, even if it does, in fact, confer upon the holder the right to vote. Corporate debt instruments, such as debentures, typically do confer upon their holders voting rights of a sort. Such rights are typically found in the trust indenture under which corporate debt instruments are usually issued. A trust indenture is an agreement between two parties: the corporation issuing debt instruments and an indenture trustee (a trust company that has been retained by the corporation to serve as the indenture trustee). The trust indenture contains all of the terms and conditions of the debt instrument—the interest rate, when and how interest is payable, the maturity date of the debt, the details of any collateral security given by the issuer to secure payment of the debentures, covenants on the part of the issuer in favour of the debentureholders, and so on. The purpose of the trust indenture is to provide a method by which the corporation issuing debt securities can

---

35   MI 62-104, s. 1.1; *Securities Act* (Ontario), s. 89(1) [emphasis added].

36   See NI 62-104, "Comment Letter to Alberta Securities Commission *et al.*, from Simon Romano" (20 October 2006), online: www.albertasecurities.com/securitiesLaw/Regulatory%20Instruments/6/13983/All%20Final%20Comment%20Letters.pdf.

37   *Canada Business Corporations Act*, s. 24(3)(b) [CBCA].

38   *Securities Act* (Ontario), s. 1(1).

effectively enter into binding contractual commitments with all of the holders of those debt securities, even if the instruments are sold publicly to hundreds or even thousands of investors all over the country.

Trust indentures typically include voting provisions. Debenture-holders are given the right to vote, for example, on proposals to amend the provisions of the trust indenture itself. But this conventional voting right is not the sort of voting right with which takeover law is usually concerned. Rather, it is the right to vote to elect members to the corporation's board of directors that matters for takeover law purposes, since the right to replace directors links voting to the power to effect changes in corporate control. And the right to elect directors, in Canada, is a right enjoyed by shareholders.[39]

The second critical component of the voting security definition is this. If a non-debt security only confers upon the holder the right to vote *in certain circumstances*, it will nevertheless be considered a voting security *while those certain circumstances prevail*. Perhaps the most common example of such a security would be a non-voting preferred share with a stated dividend rate. Such shares frequently include a share condition that entitles holders to vote if, but only if, the issuing company had failed to pay the stated dividend for a particular period of time (perhaps eight consecutive quarters, or two years). If an issuer of such preference shares had defaulted on its dividend payment obligations, and the shares, accordingly, entitled their holders to vote, such shares would become "voting securities." Any offer to purchase these shares, while they continued to enjoy such a voting right, would constitute a "take-over bid" if the 20 percent threshold test were met.

Why does the legislation attach so much significance to voting and equity securities? Why are there no similar protections for the holders of non-voting shares or debt instruments? The answer must relate to the mischief to which the takeover bid rules are directed. The purchase of fixed-income securities such as debentures does not raise the same concerns that the purchase of voting or equity securities raises. To understand why, it is helpful to remember how the value (and therefore the market price) of securities is determined.

The value of a fixed-income security such as a debt instrument is a function of the coupon (that is, the interest) rate, considered in the context of (a) market interest rates generally; and (b) the particular issuer's creditworthiness. Specifically, to determine the value of a debt instrument, one must calculate the present value of that instrument's expected future cash flows, using a discount rate that reflects the issu-

---

39   See, for example, CBCA, ss. 106(3) and 109(1).

ing corporation's creditworthiness. Future cash flows would certainly include all expected interest payments, but would also include the expected repayment of the principal amount of the debt when the debt instrument matures.

Now, reasonable people could well differ as to what discount rate ought to be used in calculating the present value of such future cash flows. But such differences of opinion are not likely to result in the same kind of large disparities as are often found between competing valuations of equity securities. And of course, there is an absolute ceiling on the value to be ascribed to any debt instrument, namely, the present value of that instrument discounted at the appropriate risk-free interest rate. A holder of debt securities, in other words, can fairly readily assess whether an offer to purchase those securities is or is not an attractive one.

Moreover, there is considerably less scope for a purchaser of debt securities to gain a meaningful informational advantage over a seller of those securities. At most, a prospective purchaser might have better information than the seller as to the probability that the issuing company will or will not default on its future payment obligations. (The purchaser might, of course, have more sophisticated ways to estimate the future direction of market interest rates, but outguessing the market in forecasting the future direction of interest rates is an elusive [some would say self-delusive] talent. In any event, it is not the sort of inside informational "advantage" that is thought to merit regulatory protection in a market economy.)

The "knowledge" (or perhaps merely the "belief") that a particular company is actually more creditworthy than it might appear to less-informed outsiders is a far cry from the expectations of increased equity values motivating purchasers of equity securities. In the case of equity purchases, the most probable source of anticipated future increases in value is the prospective change of control itself. Much of takeover law is directed toward assisting shareholders of target companies to extract a greater share of those anticipated gains.

One also suspects that the drafters of Canadian takeover bid law did not envision that anyone would seek to gain influence over the operation of a corporation by accumulating large blocks of its outstanding debt securities participating in restructuring negotiations or perhaps "agitating for change," although this is a strategy that has, in fact, from time to time proven profitable for those organizations known to their detractors as "vulture funds" or, as they sometimes more generously describe themselves, "catalysts for value." (Indeed, it is often remarked that modern hedge funds frequently "loan to own"—that is, lend money to corporations in anticipation of being able to acquire equity of the company when the borrower defaults.[40])

In short, the purchase of debt securities has not historically been thought to engage the same policy considerations as the purchase of voting or equity securities, and therefore is not subject to takeover bid regulation.

A more interesting question is raised, however, with respect to convertible securities—that is, securities that are neither voting nor equity securities but that may be converted by the holder, at some future date, into voting or equity securities of the issuer. A very formalistic, literal reading of securities legislation would appear to suggest that an offer to acquire non-voting, non-equity securities is *not* a takeover bid, even where such securities may later be converted into voting or equity securities.[41] This is a reading, however, that does not sit well with many regulators and troubles many shareholders as well.

Consider a hypothetical public company with 10 million issued and outstanding common shares. Assume that this company has also issued, at some point in the past, $100 million in aggregate principal amount of convertible debentures. These debentures may be converted into shares of the issuing company at any time, at a conversion price of $10 per share. Thus, if the holders of these debentures were to choose to exercise their conversion rights, they would hold 10 million shares of the corporation. If all debentures were converted, there would be 20 million shares in total outstanding, such that the 10 million shares into which the debentures had been converted would represent 50 percent of the equity of the company. Now suppose that, before a single debenture has yet been converted, a purchaser wishes to acquire effective control of this issuer. This purchaser, wishing to avoid the formal takeover bid rules, agrees to purchase all of the outstanding convertible debentures for $120 million. (We will assume that the purchaser is prepared to pay a premium over the face value of the debentures either because market interest rates have fallen since the debentures were originally issued, or because the value of the embedded option represented by the conversion privilege justifies the payment of such a premium or both.)

If the purchaser's offer to purchase these debentures is accepted, the purchaser can promptly convert them into common shares. After that conversion, the purchaser will hold 50 percent of the corporation's voting shares—well in excess of the 20 percent takeover bid threshold. It

---

40   See, for example, Jonathan M. Landers, "Reflections on Loan-to-Own Trends" (2007) 26 American Bankruptcy Institute Journal 1.

41   The *Securities Act* (Ontario) requires the bid to be delivered to holders of convertible securities (s. 94). MI 62-104 has the same requirement (s. 2.8), but this requirement has no impact on the definition of takeover bid itself.

seems clear, as a matter of policy, that such a purchase ought to be subject to the same mandatory formal bid requirements that would apply if
the purchaser had simply made an offer to acquire 10 million outstanding shares of a corporation with a total of 20 million shares outstanding. Yet, a narrow technical reading of the *Securities Act* or Multilateral
Instrument 62-104 might suggest otherwise. The debentures would be
neither "voting" nor "equity" securities as those terms are defined in
the legislation. There are special deeming rules that apply to convertible securities,[42] but they would not appear to apply in any way that
would affect this analysis. Nor, in this example, would a takeover bid be
deemed to occur at the moment the new owner of the debentures exercised his or her conversion privilege, since the common shares acquired
pursuant to the exercise of that conversion right would be acquired directly from the issuer. In other words, these common shares would be
"previously unissued" securities rather than "outstanding securities";
and, as discussed above, it is clear from the definition of takeover bid
in section 89(1) of the Ontario *Securities Act* and in Multilateral Instrument 62-104 that the formal takeover bid rules are triggered only when
there is an offer to acquire *outstanding* securities.

This apparent gap in the drafting of the takeover bid rules was identified some time ago. Securities regulators have argued that, although
there may be no specific provision to catch the purchase of convertible
securities, the broad language in section 92[43] of the *Securities Act*—ex-
tending the reach of the takeover bid rules to "direct *or indirect*" offers
to acquire securities—is sufficient, in light of the underlying policy
considerations, to cover such purchases if the intention of such a purchase is primarily to acquire the underlying shares.[44]

---

42   Subsection 90(1) of the *Securities Act* (Ontario) provides that, "in determining
     the beneficial ownership of securities of an offeror . . . the offeror . . . shall be
     deemed to have acquired and to be the beneficial owner of a security, includ-
     ing an unissued security, if the offeror . . . is the beneficial owner of a security
     convertible into the security within 60 days following that date . . ." (MI 62-104,
     s. 1.8(1) contains similar language.) However, note that this deeming provision
     would *not* apply on the date on which the offeror made an offer for the convert-
     ible debentures, since the offeror would not, on that date, be the beneficial
     owner of the debentures. After acquiring the debentures the purchaser would
     be deemed to own the underlying shares for purposes of Part XX, but that
     deemed ownership would occur as a result of the operation of the statute, not
     as a result of any offer to acquire on the part of the purchaser. Accordingly, the
     mere fact that the statute deemed the purchaser to own the underlying secur-
     ities would not constitute a takeover bid in respect of those securities.
43   MI 62-104 has comparable language in s. 1.10.
44   See, for example, *Submission of the Take-Over Bid Team at the Ontario Securities Com-
     mission in Connection with the Five-Year Review of Securities Legislation in Ontario* (11

Former OSC Chair Stanley Beck reportedly commented once that if the purchase of convertibles were excluded from the operation of the takeover bid rules, then one could "drive a coach and four" through the provisions of Part XX of the *Securities Act*.[45] Other commentators have expressed differing views. Some years before his appointment as Vice Chair of the Ontario Securities Commission, James Turner argued that section 92 should not be interpreted to apply to the purchase of convertible securities.[46] He noted that earlier proposals to amend the *Securities Act* so that the takeover bid rules would explicitly apply to convertible securities were never enacted, that purchases of securities from treasury are not, in any event, subject to the takeover bid rules, and that determining the premium paid for the underlying securities in the case of a purchase of convertible securities would be problematic. Moreover, he noted that if the takeover provisions were intended to apply to the purchase of convertible securities, the Act would surely need to include provisions that would make the calculation of the 20 percent takeover bid threshold intelligible in the case of an offer to purchase convertible securities. In other words, one would expect to see a provision deeming to be outstanding any unissued voting or equity securities into which convertible securities subject to an offer to acquire for purposes of determining whether or not the offer constituted a takeover bid. Currently the Act (section 90(2)) and Multilateral Instrument 62-104 (section 1.8(2)) do include provisions deeming such unissued securities to be outstanding in a different context, namely *for purposes of calculating the number of securities held by an offeror at the time of making an offer*, but there is no similar provision that applies when convertible securities are actually the subject of the offer. That legislative omission, he argued, is both deliberate and sensible.

The issue of the application of the *Securities Act* takeover bid rules to convertible securities was discussed in 2000 in the *Five Year Review Committee Final Report* (the "Crawford Report"). The Crawford Report noted that there were competing views among securities practitioners as to whether the takeover bid rules extended to a purchase of convertible securities. Some practitioners argued that section 92 operates to subject a purchase of convertible securities to the statute's formal

---

August 2000), online: www.osc.gov.on.ca/documents/en/Securities/fyr_20000811_list_com_take-over-bid.pdf at 8 [*OSC Take-Over Bid Team Submission*].

45   *Ibid.* at 8, n 15.

46   James E.A. Turner, "Purchasing Convertible Securities: Getting More Than You Bargained For," Submission to Five Year Review Committee (October 2000), online: www.osc.gov.on.ca/documents/en/Securities/fyr_20001000_list_com_turner.pdf.

takeover bid rules only where the purchaser has a subjective intention to acquire the underlying securities. Others were less certain of the application of the legislation, and would favour greater clarity.

The Five Year Review Committee concluded that "providing absolute certainty in this area would not be constructive,"[47] noting that the "purpose for acquiring convertible securities will vary from transaction to transaction"[48] and therefore, in their view, only those transactions in which the acquiror's true intent was to acquire the underlying securities ought to be subject to the formal takeover bid rules. Accordingly, they recommended no change to the wording of the statute itself, implying that, as currently drafted, the formal bid rules would apply to a purchase of convertible securities if the purchaser had the requisite intention at the time to ultimately acquire an interest in the underlying voting or equity securities. Of course, in cases where the animating spirit or policy of the Act is being violated, even in the absence of specific provisions, it is clear that the securities commission may take appropriate action within its broad public interest jurisdiction.[49]

Closely related to the question of how takeover bid rules ought to apply to a purchase of convertible securities, is the question of how these same rules ought to operate in the context of the grant of share purchase options. In 1984, the Ontario Securities Commission ruled, in *Re Trizec Equities Limited*,[50] that a takeover bid did *not* occur at the time that a purchaser acquired call options (that is, options to purchase shares) in a target corporation. Instead, the rules would be triggered only later when the purchaser actually exercised the call options. (Note that when call options are exercised, it is the writer [or seller] of the call option, *not the target company itself*, that must deliver target company shares to the buyer. It is for this reason that the purchase of options does not lead to the same legislative gap that may occur in the case of convertible securities where it is the target company itself that issues new securities from treasury, rather than outstanding securities, upon exercise of the conversion privilege.)

The issue in the *Trizec* case was whether the private agreement exemption from the formal takeover bid rules (the current version of which is now found in section 100.1 of the Ontario *Securities Act* and section 4.2 of Multilateral Instrument 62-104) was available in connection with the purchase and subsequent exercise of call options. As discussed in Chapter 6, the private agreement exemption may be

---

47   Crawford Report, above note 22 at 188.
48   *Ibid.*
49   See, for example, *Securities Act* (Ontario), s. 127.
50   Above note 29.

relied upon only if the price paid for the securities is not more than 15 percent above the market price. Of course, the market price of shares might well change from the date on which the call option is purchased and the date on which it is exercised. Thus, the exercise price (that is, the price at which the holder of the option has the right, but not the obligation, to purchase shares) might be set at an amount that is more than 15 percent above the market price of the shares when the call option itself was first purchased, yet might prove to be less than 15 percent above market price by the time the holder of the call chooses to exercise the option. The commission ruled that the private agreement exemption would be available in connection with the exercise of a call option provided that the exercise price did not exceed 115 percent of the market price *calculated at the time of exercise*. It did not matter that the exercise price might have significantly exceeded the market price of the target company shares at the time the call option was first written (that is, sold).

In 1990, in *In the Matter of the Enfield Corporation Limited, Schneider Canada Inc. and Federal Pioneer Limited*,[51] the commission was invited to consider whether this same reasoning applied in the case of a put option (that is, an option that entitles, but does not require, the holder to *sell* securities of the target company to the option writer, at a specified price, on or before a date specified in the option contract). *Federal Pioneer* involved a takeover bid by Schneider of Federal Pioneer Limited. Enfield had held 53 percent of Federal Pioneer's shares. Federal Pioneer, in turn, held a large block of shares in Consumers Packaging Inc. equal to about 5 percent of all of Consumers Packaging's outstanding shares. Schneider wished to buy all of the shares of Federal Pioneer (including the 53 percent interest held by Enfield) but did *not* want exposure to some of Federal Pioneer's investments, including its significant holding of Consumers Packaging shares. To entice Schneider to purchase the outstanding shares of Federal Pioneer, Enfield offered Schneider a way to protect itself from these unwanted investments. Enfield agreed to grant to Schneider a put option on those shares. The put option would permit Schneider, if it chose to do so, to sell to Enfield (and would obligate Enfield in such a case to purchase) all of the shares in Consumers Packaging held by Federal Pioneer at any time during a ninety-day period commencing on the date on which Schneider's bid for Federal Pioneer was completed. But there was a problem with this plan. Enfield already owned about 45 percent of Consumers Packaging shares. Ac-

---

51   (1990), 13 OSCB 3364.

cordingly, any agreement by Enfield to purchase an additional 5 percent of those shares would constitute a "take-over bid."

As in *Trizec*, the question was whether the private agreement takeover bid exemption would be available to exempt this takeover bid from the formal takeover bid rules. The answer to that question turned on whether the price paid by Enfield for the Consumers Packaging shares was or was not more than 15 percent above the market price. The exercise price under the put (that is, the price that Enfield would have to pay for each share if Schneider were to exercise the option) was $14.25. The market price of the Consumers Packaging shares on the day the put was granted was actually higher than this price; so if the date of acquiring the option was regarded as the date of the takeover bid, the private agreement exemption would certainly have been available. However, by the time Schneider actually decided to exercise the put option, the market price of Consumers Packaging shares had fallen to just $9.15. Accordingly, the exercise price—the price that Enfield had agreed to pay for each Consumers Packaging share—was now considerably more than 115 percent of the market price.

If the reasoning in *Trizec* applied to put options as well as call options, then the purchase of shares by Enfield upon the exercise by Schneider of the put would constitute a takeover bid for Consumers Packaging by Enfield, for which the private agreement exemption would not be available. The Securities Commission determined, however, that in the case of a put option the "offer to purchase" (for purposes of the takeover bid definition) occurs at the date on which the put is granted, rather than at the date of exercise of the put. The rationale is clear. When a put option is granted, the seller of the put (who, if the put is eventually exercised, will become the buyer of the underlying shares, or, in takeover bid terms, the "offeror") no longer has any choice about buying the shares of the target company. That choice, from the instant the put is granted, rests entirely in the hands of the holder of the put (in this case, Schneider). Thus, as the commission explained, "It is on the date of its grant of the put that the offeror's [that is, Enfield's] investment decision has been made."[52]

Of course, the matter is very different when the offeror acquires shares pursuant to a previously granted *call* option—that is, an option to *buy* shares on or before some future date, as in *Trizec*. The holder of the call option may acquire the target company shares at a time of his or her choosing. Thus her or his investment decision is made *not* on the date on which the option contract itself is entered into, but only later (indeed, if at all) at the date on which the call option is exercised, and the shares are

---

52   *Ibid*. at 3369.

then purchased. Although it would seem that this important distinction between put and call options should almost always guide the interpretation of the bid-timing issue, the commission in its *Federal Pioneer* decision very clearly resisted laying down a bright-line test, cautioning that it would "continue to look at both put and call options . . . in the full context of the whole transaction and, in particular, the business purposes which are claimed for them."[53]

Another conceptual method of analyzing the option cases might have been to consider not simply whether the price paid for the shares was significantly above market value, but rather whether the price paid for the option itself was significantly above market value. If, for example, the price paid for a call option was well in excess of the expected price for such an option (based, for example, on the Black-Scholes formula[54] or some other option pricing model) then one might regard the excess as a takeover premium, regardless of the market price of the underlying shares at the time of exercise. Needless to say, such an alternative approach is not possible under current securities laws which provide only for the calculation of the market price of shares, not options, and link the control premium question expressly to the purchase of shares.

2) All Non-exempt Takeover Bids Subject to a Series of Formal Takeover Bid Rules

a) "Follow-up Offers" No Longer Used
Canadian securities legislation today requires that any offer that is a "take-over bid" must be made strictly in accordance with the formal takeover bid rules, unless an exemption from those rules is provided for in the legislation or rules (or is granted by the securities regulators, upon application for such an exemption order by an interested party). Prior to 1987, Ontario's takeover rules worked a little differently, at least in the case of private purchases of securities where the buyer paid a premium over the market price. These above-market private purchases were not expressly prohibited by the old Act (as they now are, except in specified circumstances).[55] Instead, the old Act relied on the

---

53   *Ibid.* at 3374–75.
54   The Black-Scholes (or Black-Scholes-Merton) option pricing model refers to the groundbreaking method for pricing options developed by Fischer Black, Myron Scholes, and Robert Merton in the 1970s. See Fischer Black & Myron S. Scholes, "The Pricing of Options and Corporate Liabilities" (1973) 81 Journal of Political Economy 637; Robert C. Merton, "Theory of Rational Optional Pricing" (1973) 4 Bell Journal of Economics and Management Science 141.
55   *Securities Act* (Ontario), s. 100.1.

concept of a mandatory follow-up offer. When a bidder made an offer to certain securityholders such that the statute's takeover bid rules were triggered, the bidder was required *subsequently* to make a follow-up offer to all other securityholders on the same terms and conditions.

A requirement for mandatory follow-up offers is still found in the U.K. Takeover Panel's Takeover Code.[56] However, the mandatory follow-up offer structure was abandoned in Ontario, following the 1983 recommendations of a special committee of three securities practitioners appointed by the chairman of the Ontario Securities Commission, Henry Knowles.[57] That committee argued that the follow-up offer mechanism was "inappropriate and impracticable" for at least three reasons.[58] First, the gap in time between the private exempt purchase and the subsequent takeover bid meant that market conditions could change, making it practically difficult to launch a bid of equal value.[59] Second, the obligation had led to costly litigation both in the courts and before the securities commission.[60] Finally, they argued that the existence of the follow-up offer probably reduced the number of Canadian public companies and therefore the number of potential equity investments for Canadian investors, since the requirement made it very difficult for purchasers simply to purchase a controlling interest (rather than a 100 percent interest) in public companies.[61] In place of the follow-up offer, the legislators introduced the current express requirement that every non-exempt takeover bid be made in compliance with the formal bid rules discussed further below.

---

56   *The Takeover Code*, Section F, Rule 9.1, online: www.thetakeoverpanel.org.uk/wp-content/uploads/2008/11/code.pdf.

57   Practitioner's Report, above note 22. By the time the committee issued its report in 1983, Henry Knowles had been succeeded as chair of the commission by Peter Dey.

58   *Ibid.* at para. 5.05.

59   *Ibid.*

60   *Ibid.* at para. 5.06.

61   *Ibid.* at para. 5.07. This last point is intriguing because it suggests that partial bids (that is, bids for anything less than all of the target company's outstanding shares) ought to be encouraged. Such a suggestion runs counter to the views of many commentators who have suggested that partial bids should, in fact, be regarded with great wariness because they can be structured in coercive ways. Occasionally, it has even been suggested that partial bids are inherently coercive since target shareholders may feel compelled to tender their shares to a partial bid rather than risk being left owning a small, illiquid (and so, essentially, unmarketable) number of shares. To be sure, the notion that partial bids are inherently, rather than merely potentially, coercive is by no means the predominant view.

b) A Formal Bid Must Be Made to All Securityholders of the Class Subject to the Bid

If a purchase (or a proposed purchase) of securities meets the definition of *take-over bid* as set out in the Ontario *Securities Act* and Multilateral Instrument 62-104, and if no statutory exemption from the formal take-over bid rules is available, then the bidder must make the takeover bid to all holders of the class of securities subject to the bid. To be clear, it is *not* sufficient for the bidder to make a subsequent follow-up offer to all of the shareholders. The point of the current legislation is that if the bidder has planned to make a purchase that would constitute a non-exempt takeover bid, then the bidder must make that bid from the outset to *all* holders of shares of the class. If the bidder is not prepared to give every shareholder the opportunity to participate, then plans for the bid must be abandoned. As the following section explains, the obligation to make the *offer* to all shareholders does not mean that the bidder must offer to buy every outstanding share. It only means that each shareholder of the target company must be given the opportunity to sell the same *proportion* of his or her shares as every other shareholder.

In fact, the bid must be delivered not only to each shareholder of the class subject to the bid, but also to anyone in the (local) jurisdiction[62] that holds securities that are convertible into the class of securities that are the subject of the offeror's bid.[63] The distinction between (i) *making* the bid to all subject securityholders and (ii) simply *delivering* the bid to holders of convertible securities is that if holders of convertible securities wish to tender to the bid, they will first have to exercise their conversion rights so that they become holders of the type of securities that the offeror has offered to buy. As discussed earlier, the takeover bid rules do not expressly sweep convertible securities into the definition of "voting or equity securities" although it has been argued that in certain circumstances, it may be that the indirect offer rules in the Ontario *Securities Act* and Multilateral Instrument 62-104 would be found to apply to purchasers of convertible securities.

c) Proportionate Take-up of Securities by the Offeror (When the Bid Is For Less Than 100 Percent of a Class of Shares)

The bidder's offer to purchase shares must be made to every shareholder, but the offer does *not* have to extend to *all* of the shares held by every shareholder. If the offeror decides to make a bid for less than all of the

---

62   That is, Ontario, in the case of the *Securities Act* (Ontario), and the relevant province or territory in the case of MI 62-104.

63   *Securities Act* (Ontario), s. 94; MI 62-104, s. 2.8.

outstanding securities of a class, the offeror must give every holder the chance to sell the same proportion of his or her shares; and if there are more shares "tendered" to the bid than the offeror is prepared to buy, the offeror must purchase shares on a pro rata basis from all security-holders who tender to the bid.[64]

Consider this simple example. Offerco wishes to purchase 67 percent of Target Ltd.'s shares. With 67 percent of the voting shares, Offerco will be able to pass special resolutions[65] and so effectively control the corporation. Offerco does not have the financial means to acquire 100 percent of Target's shares. Offerco's offer to purchase must be made to each and every one of Target Ltd.'s shareholders. Suppose there are 1,000 Target Ltd. shareholders in all, and each shareholder holds exactly 100 shares. There are, therefore, 100,000 outstanding shares of Target in total. Offerco, we are assuming, wishes to buy (and is only willing to buy) 67,000 of those shares. If the price that Offerco is willing to pay for each share is much higher than the current market price, it may happen that every Target Ltd. shareholder will decide that he or she would very much like to sell all of his or her shares to Offerco.

When a selling shareholder agrees to sell his or shares in response to a formal takeover bid, the shareholder is said to "tender" his or her shares to the bid.[66] If all the Target Ltd. shareholders tendered, then 100,000 shares would be tendered to Offerco's bid. But Offerco is only prepared to buy 67,000 shares. The Ontario *Securities Act* and Multilateral Instrument 62-104 would therefore require Offerco in this hypothetical case to purchase 670 shares from each of the 1,000 tendering shareholders. Offerco would be forbidden from choosing to purchase a larger number of shares (or, for that matter, a smaller number) from any holder. Thus, for example, Offerco could not favour one holder (Holder A) by purchasing all 1,000 of Holder A's tendered shares at the attractively high bid price, while choosing to discriminate against another holder (Holder B)

---

64 *Securities Act* (Ontario), s. 97.2; MI 62-104, s. 2.26.

65 A "special resolution" under most Canadian corporate statutes means a resolution passed by at least two-thirds of the shareholders who vote in respect of the matter at a shareholders' meeting. (See, for example, CBCA, s. 2, definition of special resolution.) Approval by special resolution is generally required for most amendments to the corporation's articles and certain other fundamental changes.

66 This terminology may seem a trifle confusing. After all, since the word *tender* essentially means offer, it appears that the shareholders are "offering" their shares in response to an "offer." Basic contract law suggests that we ought to see an "acceptance" from someone rather than yet another offer. The complexities of the regulated tender offer process, however, complicate the simple "offer/acceptance" paradigm.

by purchasing no shares at all from him, even though Holder B had also tendered all 1,000 of his shares to Offerco's bid.

d) Identical Consideration

The offeror must pay each securityholder who tenders to the bid the same price for each purchased security.[67] The Act also contains three special rules that are intended to prevent avoidance of this equal price requirement:

- the pre-bid integration rule;
- the post-bid purchase restriction; and
- the no "collateral benefit" provision.

i)   Pre-Bid Integration

The first of these restrictions is the pre-bid integration rule.[68] If an offeror makes a formal takeover bid, and has purchased securities of the same class within ninety days before making that bid, then the takeover bid will have to satisfy two special requirements. First, the price offered in the takeover bid must be at least as high (and in the same form) as the highest per security price paid in any of those pre-bid transactions, or the cash equivalent of that consideration. Second, the percentage of shares that the offeror offers to acquire in the takeover bid must be at least as high as the highest percentage of shares purchased from a seller in any of those pre-bid transactions. In other words, if the offeror had purchased 100 percent of the shares owned by a shareholder within the ninety-day period preceding the launch of a formal takeover bid, the offeror will be required to offer to purchase 100 percent of all the remaining shares of the class in the subsequent takeover bid. If, instead, the offeror purchased no more than, say, 80 percent of the shares held by any one shareholder in that ninety-day period, the offeror will only be required to offer to purchase at least 80 percent of the remaining outstanding shares.

The pre-bid integration rules had their genesis in an Ontario Securities Commission practice that predated the current legislative regime. Under (old) OSC Policy 9.3, the OSC presumed that a purchaser who acquired shares by way of private agreement had done so with the intention of making a subsequent takeover bid if a takeover bid was launched within 180 days of the private purchase. The Practitioner's Report expressly endorsed the OSC's approach,[69] and so recommended

---

67   *Securities Act* (Ontario), s. 97(1); MI 62-104, s. 2.23.
68   *Securities Act* (Ontario), s. 93.2; MI 62-104, s. 2.4.
69   Practitioner's Report, above note 22 at para. 6.03.

that the *Securities Act* include a provision comparable to what is now found in section 93.2, but applicable in the case of private agreements made in the 180-day (rather than the ninety-day) period preceding a takeover bid. The Practitioner's Report also recommended that the pre-bid integration rules ought not to apply when the bidder already owned at least 50 percent of the outstanding shares. The rationale was simple: if a purchaser already controlled the corporation, any premium paid to the seller in the pre-bid transaction could not reasonably be considered a premium for control, and so did not call for legislative protections to ensure that premium was made available to shareholders generally.

These pre-bid integration rules are simple to apply when all the share purchases—both in the pre-bid transaction and the bid itself—are settled in cash. They become more complicated when some or all of the purchases include non-cash consideration, such as shares of the purchasing company issued to shareholders of the target corporation in exchange for target corporation shares. In those cases, the pre-bid integration rules require that the offeror offer, in exchange for securities deposited under the subsequent bid, either consideration "at least equal to the highest consideration that was paid" in a pre-bid transaction *and in the same form*, or "at least the cash equivalent of that consideration."

The phrase 'and in the same form' was added to the *Securities Act* in 2007 to address the situation where a pre-bid acquisition was a cash deal and to clarify that the bidder in such a case must subsequently make a cash takeover bid. It is not sufficient in such a case for the bidder to make a securities exchange takeover bid, even if the market value of the securities offered to target shareholders is at least equal to the cash paid in the pre-bid transaction. In its 2000 submission to the Five Year Review Committee in 2000, the OSC Take-Over Bid Team noted a possible ambiguity in the pre-bid integration language in the *Securities Act* as it then was, and recommended that the Act be clarified to ensure that a takeover bid offer shareholders consideration not only of equal value, but in the same form, as the consideration paid in pre-bid acquisitions.[70]

There are two exceptions to the pre-bid integration rules. They will not apply when:

---

70   OSC Take-Over Bid Team Submission, above note 44 at 24–25. The submission noted that s. 103(1) of the British Columbia *Securities Act* includes more specific language on this point.

- the pre-bid purchase is a normal course purchase under certain prescribed conditions made on a published market[71] such as the Toronto Stock Exchange, or
- the securities purchased in the pre-bid transaction were previously unissued securities (that is, securities issued from treasury by the target issuer, rather than outstanding shares) or securities that had been previously issued but had then been redeemed, purchased by, or donated to the issuer.

Neither normal course market purchases nor purchases from the issuer itself raise the concern of possible unequal treatment of holders of outstanding securities that the pre-bid integration rules were designed to prevent. In 1988, an issue arose as to whether a block purchase of shares made through the facilities of the Toronto Stock Exchange but in the "upstairs market"[72] was subject to the pre-bid integration rules. In an OSC staff notice,[73] staff expressed its view that "customary 'upstairs market' activities by brokers on behalf of clients may fall within the pre-bid integration rules in the event that such a client were to make a formal takeover bid within 90 days of such a transaction."[74]

ii)   Post-Bid Purchase Restriction

The second "anti-avoidance" rule is the post-bid purchase restriction found in section 93.3 of the Ontario *Securities Act* and section 2.5 of Multilateral Instrument 62-104. An offeror that has made a formal takeover bid is prohibited from acquiring additional securities of the same class as those that were subject to the bid for a twenty-business-day period after the expiry of the bid in a transaction not generally available on identical terms to target shareholders. The 1983 Practitioners Report had recommended a much longer post-bid restricted period of 180 days.[75] However, that recommendation was made in the context of

---

71   *Securities Act* (Ontario), s. 93.2(2); OSC Rule 62-504, s. 2.3; MI 62-104, s. 2.6.4(7). A published market is defined in s. 89(1) to mean "any market on which such securities are traded if the prices at which they have been traded on that market are regularly published in a newspaper or business or financial publication of general and regular paid circulation."

72   The "upstairs market" refers to transactions involving the shares of exchange-listed companies that brokers undertake by matching buy and sell orders on their books, without running the orders through the exchange's order books.

73   "OSC Staff Concludes Pre-Bid Integration Rules Applicable to Proposed Stock Exchange Bid by Noranda, Inc." (1988), 11 OSCB 4367, later amended and numbered OSC Staff Notice 62-702 (2001), 24 OSCB 2405.

74   *Ibid.*

75   Practitioner's Report, above note 22 at para. 6.08.

the same report's recommendation that the pre-bid integration period should also apply to purchases made during a 180 day period prior to the commencement of a takeover bid.[76] The post-bid restrictions do not apply to normal course purchases on a public market.[77] Market purchases do not raise concern about unequal treatment or the favouring of specific target company shareholders; an offer to purchase made in an anonymous market is, indeed, akin to an offer made on identical terms to all shareholders.

iii) "No Collateral Benefit" Provision

The third statutory provision intended to preserve the integrity of the identical consideration rule is the "no collateral benefit" restriction.[78] There is a risk that the offeror might try to induce a target company shareholder to sell his or her shares by offering him or her some other contractual benefit on the side. Although supposedly unrelated to the purchase of the target company shares, such benefits, as a practical matter, may well be aimed at (or have the effect of) encouraging the shareholder to sell to the bidder. Any such benefits that are not available to all target shareholders would clearly undermine the principle that all target company shareholders are to be treated alike. Moreover, arrangements of this sort could also make it possible for one favoured shareholder to receive part of a "control premium," which other shareholders would not enjoy. Accordingly, section 97.1 of the Ontario *Securities Act* and section 2.24 of Multilateral Instrument 62-104 prohibit the offeror from entering into any collateral agreement with any target company shareholder "that has the effect, directly or indirectly, of providing a security holder . . . with consideration of greater value than that offered to the other security holders of the same class of securities." National Policy 62-203 indicates that this restriction "includes participation by the holder in another transaction with the offeror that has the effect of providing consideration of greater value to the holder than that offered to other security holders of the same class."[79] Not surprisingly, it is not always a straightforward task to distinguish an acceptable transaction from the sort of collateral agreement this rule is intended to prohibit.

In *Re Genstar Corp.*,[80] the Ontario Securities Commission offered its definition of the term *collateral agreement* as an agreement that is

---

76   *Ibid.* at 6.03.
77   *Securities Act* (Ontario), s. 93.3(2); OSC Rule 62-504, s. 2.4; MI 62-104, s. 2.6.
78   *Securities Act* (Ontario), s. 97.1; MI 62-104, s. 2.24.
79   NP 62-203, s. 2.5.
80   (1982), 4 OSCB 326C.

"separate and apart from any agreement resulting from acceptance of the offeree's take-over bid itself."[81]

One intriguing issue that has come before securities regulators on several occasions is whether or not the prohibition against providing additional consideration to one or more shareholders by way of a collateral agreement is limited to consideration that will be received only if the "favoured" shareholders tender their shares to the bid. In other words, is the "no collateral agreement" provision limited to situations where the effect of such an agreement is to entice a shareholder to tender to the bid (and so receive additional value that other tendering shareholders will receive), or does it extend more broadly to prevent an offeror from offering *any* special benefits to specific shareholders, even if those extra benefits will only be realized if the shareholder chooses *not* to tender his, her, or its shares to the bid? If the purpose of the "no collateral agreement" provision is only to ensure that the offeror does not "buy off" some shareholders to entice them to tender when they would otherwise have rejected the price to be received by all other shareholders, then the only "benefits" that should be prohibited are those that the shareholder will receive if he, she, or it chooses to tender to the bid. If, on the other hand, the purpose of the "no collateral agreement" provision is to ensure that all shareholders of the same class are treated equally—not just in the sense that they will receive the same price if they choose to tender their shares, but also in the sense that they will receive the same deal if they choose *not* to tender their shares—then the "no collateral agreement" provision should also prohibit special deals even where they do not take effect unless a shareholder chooses not to tender.

To appreciate this distinction, it is helpful to consider some examples. In *Re CDC Life Sciences Inc.*[82] a takeover bidder, Institut Merieux S.A., entered into an agreement with the largest shareholder of the target company. Under that agreement, the shareholder, La Caisse de depot et placement du Québec (the "Caisse") was granted a put option in respect of its shares in the target that would become effective more than a year after the date of the takeover bid. In addition, the agreement included a "covenant for co-operation" between the Caisse and Institut Merieux with respect to material decisions regarding the target, and also provided for mutual rights of first refusal with respect to the target shares held by the Caisse and Institut Merieux. Clearly, none of these three terms would be of any effect if the Caisse were to tender its shares

---

81   *Ibid.* at 338C.
82   (1988), 11 OSCB 2541 [*CDC Life Sciences*].

in the target to Institut Merieux. Accordingly, in order for the securities commission to find that the agreement violated the "no collateral
agreement" provision, it would need to conclude that the prohibition
against providing consideration of greater value than that offered to
other holders of shares of the target company meant something more
than consideration to be received upon selling shares.

The Ontario Securities Commission determined that "through the
agreement, the Caisse received a consideration different from that offered generally by Merieux to the holders of CDC common shares and
that consideration had value."[83] Accordingly, in the Commission's view,
the agreement was in breach of the "no collateral agreement" prohibition. The fact that the Caisse "had more choices available to it than did
the other CDC shareholders" offended the "principle requiring identical
treatment of holders of the same class of securities in a take-over bid."[84]

The facts in *CDC Life Sciences* were unusual in at least two respects.
First, the bidder in that case was not attempting through its takeover
bid to acquire legal control of the target. The bidder held about 12.6
percent of the shares of the target before commencing the bid, and the
bid itself was for a maximum of 20 percent of the outstanding shares.
Accordingly, at most the bidder could expect to hold no more than 32.6
percent of the shares at the conclusion of its bid. The Caisse, in the
meantime, held 19.5 percent of the target's shares. Thus, if the bidder's bid was successful, the bidder and the Caisse—in the aggregate—
would hold just over 50 percent of the shares of the bidder. To the extent
that they agreed to co-operate with respect to their holdings thereafter,
they would have "jointly" acquired a controlling interest, potentially
without the need to pay a control premium. By including mutual rights
of first refusal in their agreement, the parties may have been able to
preserve the possibility of realizing a control premium in a future sale
to which the other shareholders would not have been entitled. Thus,
the *CDC Life Sciences* case need not necessarily be understood as a
case which stands for the broad proposition that all shareholders of
a corporation that is subject to a takeover bid must always be treated
"identically"—not only with respect to the amount they will receive for
tendered shares (which must be the law) but also with respect to value
they will receive if they do *not* tender their shares (a more controversial
proposition.) Rather, the case might better be interpreted as an appropriate restriction on the use of a collateral agreement where the effect of
such an agreement could be to deny shareholders a chance to share in

83   *Ibid.*
84   *Ibid.*

an additional premium in the future, where the opportunity to realize such a premium was created by a transaction that effectively consolidated control in two co-operating parties.

In 2006, the British Columbia Securities Commission[85] considered the application of the "no collateral agreement" provision as it then appeared in the B.C. *Securities Act*[86] to certain terms included in a lock-up agreement, an agreement frequently negotiated between bidders and major shareholders of target corporations in advance of a takeover bid to increase the likelihood that the bid will succeed. In that case, the takeover bidder had entered into a so-called "hard" lock-up agreement[87] with the majority shareholder of the target company; that is, the majority shareholder was committed to tendering its shares to the bidder, even if a higher, competing bid were to emerge. The lock-up agreement also provided that if the bidder abandoned its bid, it would be required to pay the majority shareholder $2 million. (The agreement was subsequently amended to provide that the fee, if paid, would be shared by all shareholders of the target company.)

This fee, which the B.C. Securities Commission referred to as a "penalty provision," was similar in *intent* to a break-up fee (discussed further in Chapter 7), but fundamentally differed from a break-up fee in at least three respects: first, the $2 million fee was to be paid to a *shareholder* rather than (as in the case of a typical break-up fee) to the bidding corporation itself; second, the party that would be liable to pay this fee was to be the bidder, not (as in the case of a break-up fee) the target or (in the case of mergers of equals) whichever of the two merging parties did not proceed with the deal;[88] third, break-up fees are a deal protection measure included in merger agreements in the case of *friendly* takeover bids. Although in this case, of course, the majority shareholder had agreed to sell its shares to the bidder, the bid itself was a hostile bid—that is, a bid that was opposed by the management of the target company.

---

85   *Stornoway Diamond Corporation et al. (Re)*, 2006 BCSECCOM 533, application for leave to appeal dismissed, (*sub nom. Ashton Mining of Canada Inc. v. Stornoway Diamond Corp.*) 2006 BCCA 406.

86   Section 107(2).

87   For a more detailed discussion of lock-up agreements, including the distinction between "hard" lock-ups and "soft" lock-ups, see Christopher C. Nicholls, "Lock-Ups, Squeeze-Outs and Canadian Takeover Bid Law: A Curious Interplay of Public and Private Interests" (2006) 51 McGill L.J. 407.

88   There have been examples, however, of "reverse break-up fees," where it is the bidder, not the target, that must pay a fee if the takeover is not consummated. See Chapter 2, text accompanying note 69.

The B.C. Securities Commission found that the lock-up agreement did not offend the "no collateral agreement" rules, either before or after its terms had been amended to provide for the "penalty" payment to be made to all shareholders of the target company. Even before the lock-up agreement was amended, the penalty amount would only be paid if the bid did *not* proceed (and therefore no shares in the target were ever acquired). Accordingly, it could not be said that the penalty payment was consideration "connected to the ultimate acquisition of the shares by the offeror."[89] In any event, the commission noted, after the lock-up agreement was amended to provide that all target company shareholders would share equally if any penalty were paid, there could certainly be no violation of the collateral contract rule since all shareholders would be treated alike in any event. Nor was the commission persuaded that this conclusion was in any way changed by the fact that only the major shareholder who was a party to the lock-up agreement would be able to trigger payment of the penalty. In other words, what mattered was that that all shareholders would be treated identically whether the provision was triggered or not. The ability to trigger payment was not, in the Panel's view, a benefit in and of itself. This conclusion was reached in the context of considering whether all shareholders had received "identical consideration." However, although the right to trigger the payment was not explicitly considered by the Panel in their discussion of the prohibition on collateral benefits, it seems probable that a similar analysis would have applied in that context as well.

The B.C. Securities Commission, thus, expressly rejected the notion that benefits to be received only if a shareholder does *not* tender its shares can be included in determining whether that shareholder has received impermissible collateral benefits within the meaning of the "no collateral agreement" restriction. The B.C. Securities Commission did refer to the *CDC Life Sciences* case in its decision, but made no attempt to reconcile its holding with the Ontario Securities Commission's earlier finding on this point.

The Ontario Securities Commission addressed the "identical treatment" vs. "identical price for tendered shares" issue squarely in 2009 in *Re Patheon Inc.*[90] There, a bidder ("JLL") had launched an "any and all"[91] takeover bid for the restricted voting shares of the target, Patheon.

---

89 Above note 85 at para. 45.

90 (2009), 32 OSCB 6445.

91 The significance of an "any and all" bid is that the bidder does not include in its offer any minimum tender condition. In other words, it does not make its obligation to complete its acquisition of shares conditional upon a specified minimum of shares being tendered (such as, for example, sufficient shares to ensure

A small group of insiders of Patheon (the "MOVA Group") held, in the aggregate, about 13.7 percent of the outstanding shares. The bidder entered into an agreement with the MOVA Group just before formally launching the bid. This agreement did not provide for any additional consideration to be paid to the MOVA Group if it tendered its shares to the bid. However, it did provide certain protections to the MOVA Group, as minority shareholders of Patheon, that would arise if, but only if, the MOVA Group remained minority shareholders of Patheon and did *not* tender their shares to the bid.

Although the bidder had, in fact, proposed to terminate the impugned agreement in any event, the Panel was still called upon to discuss the propriety of such an agreement because, among other things, an issue had arisen as to whether or not a similar agreement might be entered into within the 120 day period following expiry of the bid.

The Panel noted that the MOVA Group would receive through the agreement "an opportunity and benefits not available to other shareholders of Patheon."[92] Emphasizing that the term "consideration" in subsections 97(1) and 97(1.1) of the Act "should be interpreted broadly,"[93] the Panel went on to assert "it is not an answer to say that, if the MOVA Group accepts the Offer, they will receive the identical cash consideration as the public shareholders. That response ignores the legal and economic reality of the circumstances and what we consider to be the proper interpretation of the term 'consideration' used in subsections 97(1) and 97.1(1) of the Act. It also ignores the opportunity and benefits the MOVA Group is receiving through the Voting Agreement."[94]

A decision that all shareholders should be treated identically has intuitive appeal. What could seem more fair, after all, than identical treatment? Yet, it should not be forgotten that such ensurance of identical outcomes can, paradoxically, undermine arguably more essential principles of identical treatment of citizens' property rights and freedom of contract. Identical treatment of shareholders of a company that is the target of a bid is not an end in itself. The bidder is typically a shareholder, too, as are others acting jointly or in concert with the bidder.

---

that the bidder will own at least two-thirds of all outstanding shares, or more than 50 percent of all outstanding shares). A bidder's decision not to include a minimum bid condition is often regarded with some suspicion although, as a practical matter, minimum tender conditions are typically conditions included for the "sole benefit" of the bidder and thus could, in any event, be waived by a bidder.

92 *Ibid.* at para. 97.
93 *Ibid.* at para. 105.
94 *Ibid.* at para. 106.

Statutory interference with the rights of bidders and shareholders to contract freely can only be justified to the extent that such interference is necessary for the protection of investors and the proper functioning of our capital markets (including, of course, the fairness of those markets and confidence in those markets.) One might argue that investors will perceive that markets are more "fair" if all shareholders are treated identically—not only with respect to the price they receive for their shares (which is, of course, justifiable), but also with respect to their "options" where they choose not to tender their shares. But this argument, with respect, is facile. Employees might well regard the labour markets as more fair if all employees—from the CEO to the junior sales associate—received the same income. But a law ensuring such "fairness" would undermine our economic system. It must be remembered that the identical consideration requirement in the *Securities Act* does represent an interference with the normal rule that parties are entitled to contract freely and so ought to be interpreted narrowly, not broadly. Where a collateral agreement has the effect either of enticing favoured shareholders to tender their shares where they would not otherwise do so, such an agreement is rightly prohibited. Where a collateral agreement may reasonably be seen as a device to enable favoured shareholders to preserve for themselves a premium on the eventual sale of their shares, that too is rightly prohibited. But a private agreement between a bidder and shareholder that provides no additional benefit—present or future—for the sale of their shares would not appear to offend the underlying purpose of the takeover provisions of our securities laws and so the right of private parties to freely contract with respect to their own property should be respected in such cases.

Thus, the somewhat sweeping language of the OSC in *Re Patheon* may perhaps go further than is desirable, although on the facts of *Re Patheon* itself the holding of the Panel is entirely defensible since the agreement in question included "tag along/drag along" rights that could be triggered on a later future sale of the securities that were subject to the bid. In other words, the agreement provided for just the possibility of the realization of a premium on the eventual sale of the shares that would not be available to tendering shareholders, precisely the sort of advantage that the takeover rules were intended to prevent.[95]

---

95   There have been at least two other cases—both referred to in the *Re Patheon* decision, above note 90—in which the Ontario Securities Commission considered the application of the "identical consideration" requirement to benefits other than specific consideration payable for target securities. See *Re Noverco Inc.* (1990), 13 OSCB 3243 and *Re NCG Acquisition Corp. et al.* (1992), 15 OSCB 5355.

It is apparent that an agreement between a bidder and a target company shareholder can be found to violate the no collateral benefit rules in cases where that agreement provides only that the shareholder in question is entitled to receive consideration in a different *form* from that available to other shareholders, even if the *value* of the consideration is no greater.[96] In the Ontario Securities Commission's decision in *Sears Canada Inc. (Re)*[97] the Panel considered this intriguing issue in the context of the no collateral benefit rule then found in section 97(2) of the Ontario *Securities Act*.

The issue in the *Sears Canada* case arose in this way. Sears Holdings Corporation, the majority shareholder of Sears Canada, held about 53.8 percent of Sears Canada's outstanding shares, and wished to launch a takeover bid to acquire the remaining shares of Sears Canada. Sears Holdings intended, following its takeover bid, to undertake a second-stage going-private transaction (as discussed in greater detail in Chapter 8) to eliminate the share interests of any shareholders who had not tendered to the bid. Certain significant shareholders of Sears Canada were financial institutions that had acquired their shares less than one year earlier. These institutions faced significant adverse tax consequences if they were to dispose of their shares before they had held them for a full year.[98]

Accordingly, to induce those shareholders to support its bid to gain control of Sears Canada, Sears Holdings Corporation negotiated support agreements with these shareholders. The support agreements provided that the shareholders would not tender their shares to the bid itself, but would agree, on certain conditions, to vote their shares at a subsequent shareholders' meeting in favour of a going-private transaction to be undertaken after the takeover bid had expired. That vote would be held at a date late enough to ensure that the shareholders would be able to retain their shares for a full year, and so avoid the adverse consequences of the *Income Tax Act*'s stop loss rule.

Sears Holdings also agreed to structure the post-bid going-private transaction so as to accommodate these shareholders. Specifically, the transaction would be completed either by way of a statutory plan of arrangement or a share consolidation. Two additional forms of transaction—amalgamation and capital reorganization—had also been dis-

---

96   See, for example, *Re Royal Trustco Limited and Campeau Corporation (No. 2)* (1980), 11 B.L.R. 298 (O.S.C.).

97   *Sears Canada Inc. (Re)* (2006), 22 B.L.R. (4th) 267, aff'd (*sub nom. Sears Holdings Corporation v. Ontario Securities Commission*), 2006 CanLII 34453 (Ont. Div. Ct.), leave to appeal to Ont. C.A. refused 15 November 2006 [*Sears Canada*].

98   The adverse tax consequences arose as a result of the so-called stop loss rules in the *Income Tax Act*.

closed as possibilities in the takeover bid circular. The significance of committing to one of these first two forms of transaction was, evidently, that a transaction in such form would be treated as a redemption of the shares for tax purposes. Again, this would result in desirable tax treatment for the shareholders. Put more simply, then, although these shareholders would receive exactly the same consideration for their shares as every other shareholder—both in amount, and in form—the timing and, to some extent, the structure of the transaction had been carefully tailored to accommodate the shareholders who were parties to these support agreements.

Finally, Sears Holdings entered into a deposit agreement with a Sears Canada shareholder pursuant to which that shareholder agreed to tender its shares to the Sears Canada bid. Sears Holdings, in turn, provided this shareholder with "price protection" and also agreed to provide a release from all claims that might arise from the shareholder's actions in connection with the transaction. (Sears Holdings evidently believed that it had no cause of action against this shareholder in any event and, accordingly, that this release was of no real value.)[99]

The OSC panel hearing the case found that providing a release to one shareholder, in exchange for that shareholder's agreement to tender to the bid, did, indeed, constitute an impermissible collateral agreement contrary to section 97(2). Although the bidder may not have regarded the release as having value, the tendering shareholder evidently did regard it as valuable, even, perhaps, "of critical importance."[100] And, regardless of Sears Holdings' subjective assessment of the value of the release, "even where the validity of a claim is in doubt, the courts have held that forbearance to enforce it can be good consideration."[101] In any event, the panel held, "for purposes of subsection 97(2) it is not necessary to determine whether the quantum of the consideration is large or small."[102] Accordingly, the panel determined that granting the release was, indeed, a violation of section 97(2).

With respect to the support agreements that had been entered into between the bidder and certain financial institutions, the panel made a number of important findings. Among other things, the panel stated its view that section 97(2) "does not expressly require that the consideration of greater value, if it is found to exist, must emanate from the offeror or the person acting jointly or in concert with the offeror. Rather [it] requires a determination of whether a collateral agreement . . . has

---

99   *Sears Canada* (OSC), above note 97 at para. 209.

100   *Ibid.* at para. 193.

101   *Ibid.* at para. 219, citing *D.C.B. v. Arkin* (1996), 138 D.L.R. (4th) 309 (Man. Q.B.).

102   *Sears Canada, ibid.* at para. 213.

the 'effect' of providing to a shareholder consideration of greater value than that offered to other shareholders."[103]

The panel also observed that the section 97(2) prohibition would apply even to agreements to acquire securities outside of the takeover bid itself. That determination was relevant in the case of the support agreements. Unlike typical support or lock-up agreements that bind shareholders to tender their shares to a bid, the support agreements in the *Sears Holdings* case anticipated that the shareholders would *not* tender their shares to the bid, but would subsequently vote their shares in favour of a post-bid going-private transaction. The panel ultimately considered that the bidder's agreement to structure and time the transaction in a way that had favourable tax consequences for the shareholders who had entered into the support agreements also constituted impermissible collateral agreements with those shareholders. Indeed, the Panel was dogmatic on the point, stating that "no other conclusion, in the unique circumstances of this case, would be consistent with the wording, spirit and intent underlying the Collateral Benefits Prohibition which is a fundamental element of the protections afforded under Part XX of the Act."[104]

One wonders, however, if the matter was really so entirely free from doubt. It is interesting to note that, although the Divisional Court dismissed an appeal from the commission's decision, finding that the decision as a whole satisfied the "reasonableness" standard of review, the court's comments on this particular aspect of the panel's findings fell well short of a ringing endorsement. Indeed, when discussing these matters, the Divisional Court noted "that does not mean that the determinations of the OSC on these questions were unreasonable *even if members of this court might have come to a different conclusion. The standard of review of reasonableness encompasses the 'right to be wrong'.*"[105] This language contrasts sharply with the court's later statement on a different aspect of the OSC decision. Referring to the OSC's finding of abuse, the court stated, "In our view, it was eminently reasonable, and in fact almost inevitable, for the OSC to conclude that such heavy-handed tactics were abusive of the minority shareholders of Sears Canada and of the capital markets and should not be condoned . . . ."[106]

The OSC's decision on the collateral benefit issue raises several questions. One notes, for example, that the panel's decision is based upon an assessment of after-tax rather than pre-tax consideration. Of

---

103   *Ibid.* at para. 240.
104   *Ibid.* at para. 70.
105   *Sears Canada* (Div. Ct.), above note 97 at para. 13 [emphasis added].
106   *Ibid.* at para. 17.

course, as a matter of business economics this is eminently sensible—it is after-tax dollars that count, and for a buyer to structure a deal so as to provide more after-tax dollars to a seller unequivocally confers a benefit upon the seller. But as a matter of securities regulatory policy, to consider the after-tax effect of a transaction structure for particular shareholders (in situations where, as in *Sears*, the pre-tax price paid to all shareholders would be identical) introduces uncertainties that may be unnecessary and even undesirable. Assume, for example, a takeover bidder—who, by educated guess or diligent investigation—determined that a significant number of shareholders would gain a particular tax or other benefit if a transaction were structured in one way rather than another. The bidder would be perfectly free to structure the transaction in just that advantageous way. His or her decision to do so would be unassailable, despite the fact that the effect of that decision would be that some shareholders would receive a higher (after-tax) price than they might have otherwise. And note, too, that such an effect could not be dismissed as either unintended or serendipitous: the bidder would have fully intended to confer such (unbargained for) benefits on favoured shareholders. Equality of treatment, in other words, has never been understood to mean equality of *after-tax* treatment (a fact acknowledged by the OSC in the *Sears Canada* decision).[107] Should the outcome be so dramatically different simply because the bidder has formally agreed rather than unilaterally acted to structure a transaction in a way that—although providing identical pre-tax consideration to all—happens to prove favourable to certain shareholders after taxes?

Indeed, in the *Sears Canada* case itself, Sears Holdings could presumably have unilaterally announced—even publicly committed to—a deal structure and a timetable that would, in fact, have proved attractive to the selling shareholders.[108] Should the fact that the structure and timing were settled by negotiations between shareholders and the bidder rather than determined by artful guesswork on the bidder's part really have such starkly different legal consequences? Subsection 97(2) is surely intended to prevent bidders from succeeding with a bid launched at an inferior price by unfairly inducing some shareholders to sell: "unfairly" in the sense that they are not happy with the share price itself, but agree to sell nonetheless because they hope to gain the benefits of an additional side agreement that has not been made available to the other shareholders. Structuring a transaction so that certain

---

107 *Sears Canada* (OSC), above note 97 at para. 234.

108 The OSC Panel conceded that, "[a]s a general proposition, there is nothing wrong with bidders taking into account the tax planning objectives of shareholders generally in the course of structuring their bids." *Ibid.* at para. 235.

shareholders—receiving the same price, at the same time, on the same terms and subject to the same conditions as every other shareholder—nevertheless happen to avoid adverse tax consequences does not seem to involve the sort of problems at which section 97(2) was aimed.

In fact, one of the arguments advanced by commission staff in support of its view that the support agreements violated section 97(2) actually seems to suggest that the policy concern underlying section 97(2) was *not* engaged. Commission staff had argued:

> It is clear from the evidence that the Banks would have suffered severe tax losses if the Offer and the SAT had been completed within the timeframe and in the form originally contemplated by Sears Holdings *and if Sears Holdings had chosen not to enter into the Support Agreements and had simply raised the bid price under the Offer.*[109]

The point of the argument appears to be that, but for the support agreement, Sears Holdings might have raised the offer price, to the general benefit of the shareholders. But surely there is another more probable conclusion: that is, that *even by* raising the bid price somewhat Sears Holdings could not have persuaded the banks to sell (or to support a second-step going-private transaction) because, on an after-tax basis, the price would have continued to be unattractive. In such a case, *there would have been no point in raising the price* or perhaps in offering the shareholders any deal at all. In other words, the entering into of the support agreements was *not* an action taken that enabled the bidder to achieve success without offering a higher price to all shareholders. On the contrary, entering into the support agreements made it possible for Sears Holdings to undertake the bid in the first place, at a price that many shareholders—not simply the "favoured" shareholders—evidently regarded as advantageous.

It is true, as the panel stated, that the effect of the support agreements was that "the Banks agreed to support the SAT in circumstances where they would not, in fact, have tendered to the bid because they received consideration of greater value in exchange for entering into the Support Agreements."[110] However, it is surely not the case that section 97(2) is only aimed at prohibiting agreements that entice shareholders to tender their shares (provided, it must again be emphasized, that all shareholders receive equal consideration). Rather, it is aimed at prohibiting such agreements *only if the effect of such agreements is that the*

---

109 *Ibid.* at para. 243 [emphasis added].
110 *Ibid.* at para. 244.

bidder chooses to enter into such agreements instead of offering a higher bid price to the shareholders generally.[111]

Even before the *Sears Canada* decision, the broad wording of section 97(2) had led many cautious offerors (or, to be more precise, their legal counsel) to seek exemption orders from the securities commission in connection with innocuous agreements that might, nevertheless, possibly appear to run afoul of the provision. The Ontario *Securities Act* provides specific authority to the commission to decide that a particular instrument does not violate the restriction on collateral agreements,[112] and the OSC set out an approach for dealing with such exemption applications in a number of cases in the 1980s.[113]

When the Canadian Securities Administrators issued proposed National Instrument 62-104, they noted that it is frequently the case that offerors do wish to enter into employment contracts with employees of a target corporation who are also shareholders under circumstances where there is no reason to believe that the contractual arrangements have been made in an attempt to avoid the identical consideration rule. The discretionary exemptive relief sought from securities regulators for such arrangements was routinely granted.[114] Accordingly, to obviate the need for offerors to seek such routine exemptions, Multilateral Instrument 62-104 and OSC Rule 62-504 now make clear that the "no collateral benefit" rule does not prevent employees of the target corporation (who are also shareholders) from receiving an enhancement in employee benefits as a result of participating in a group plan made available to a successor employer of the target corporation.[115] Nor does it prevent an employee, director, or consultant of the target (who is also a shareholder) from receiving a benefit solely in connection with their services to the target corporation provided certain conditions are satisfied.[116] Those conditions include a requirement that the benefit is not made conditional upon an agreement of the shareholder to support the bid and a further requirement that either (a) the shareholder's interest represents less than 1 percent of the outstanding securities of the

---

111 One notes that, in dismissing an appeal from the OSC decision, the Divisional Court deferred to the OSC, applying the administrative law "reasonableness" standard of review. On certain aspects of the decision, however, the court did not suggest that the court itself would necessarily have come to the same conclusion. Above note 97 at para. 13 (Div. Ct.).

112 *Securities Act* (Ontario), s. 104(2)(a).

113 See, especially, *CDC Life Sciences Inc.*, above note 82; *Re Bank of Montreal Securities Canada Limited and Nesbitt, Thomson Inc.* (1987), 10 OSCB 5173.

114 Above note 8 at 3536.

115 MI 62-104, s. 2.25(1)(a); OSC Rule 62-504, s. 4.1(a).

116 MI 62-104, s. 2.25(1)(b); OSC Rule 62-504, s. 4.1(b).

class subject to the bid; or (b) an independent committee[117] of the target company's board of directors, to whom disclosure of the benefit has been made, has determined that the net value of the consideration to be received by the shareholder is less than 5 percent of the total value to be received by the securityholder for his or her shares under the bid, or that the securityholder is providing equivalent value[118] for the benefit. That determination, and full particulars of the benefit, must also be disclosed in the takeover bid circular or the director's circular delivered in connection with the formal bid.[119]

e) Bidder Purchasing Shares during the Bid

As a general rule, once a bidder has announced its intention to make a formal takeover bid, it is not permitted until the bid expires to acquire securities of the same class as those subject to the bid except pursuant to the formal bid itself.[120] The Practitioner's Report, which recommended this provision, acknowledged that it could place one bidder at a disadvantage relative to a rival who had not yet commenced a bid (or announced its intention to do so). Nevertheless, in the view of the authors of that report, the restriction was "a necessary ingredient to ensure that all holders of voting securities of the offeree issuer are treated equally."[121] This purchase restriction also extends to securities that are convertible into securities of the class subject to the bid.

---

117 NP 62-203 indicates that an independent director, for these purposes, should be "disinterested in the bid or any related transactions," and that the definitions of independent director and independent committee set out in Multilateral Instrument 61-101 provide "relevant guidance on determining director independence." See NP 62-203, s. 2.6.

118 NP 62-203, s. 2.7 states that in making the "equivalent value" determination, the independent committee should consider whether the arrangements are consistent with "arrangements made with individuals holding comparable positions (i) with the offeror and (ii) in the industry generally."

119 MI 62-104, ss. 2.25(1)(b), (2), & (3); OSC Rule 62-504, ss. 4.1(1)(b), (2), & (3). It should be noted that the U.S. Securities and Exchange Commission also recently dealt with the issue of employment arrangements in the context of tender offers. As of December 2006, the so-called "third-party and issuer tender offer best price rules" in Rules 133-4 and 14d-10 under the *Securities Exchange Act of 1934* were amended to provide a safe harbour provision to enable employment and other compensation arrangements approved by independent directors to be entered into without violating the best-price rule. See SEC Release No. 34-54684, online: www.sec.gov/rules/final/2006/34-54684.pdf.

120 MI 62-104, s. 2.2(1); *Securities Act* (Ontario), s. 93.1(1).

121 Practitioner's Report, above note 22 at para. 6.06.

i)   Application to Lock-up or Support Agreements

It is common practice for bidders to enter into agreements ("lock-up agreements") with one or more large shareholders of a target company prior to launching a formal takeover bid. Such lock-up agreements typically provide that the shareholders will agree to tender their shares to the proposed bid provided the bid price is not less than some stated minimum amount. The agreement may or may not allow the shareholders to tender their shares to another rival bid, if such a bid should later emerge offering a higher price. Some of the legal and regulatory implications of lock-up agreements are discussed later in this chapter. At this point, it is only noted that entering into such lock-up agreements is a well-established, practical, business-like method of reducing the bidder's risk and does not violate the general prohibition against purchasing securities other than pursuant to the bid itself. (The 1983 Practitioners Report clearly envisioned that lock-up agreements entered into prior to launching a bid ought not to be restricted, although they raised this issue in the context of the private agreement exemption.)[122] Multilateral Instrument 62-104 and OSC Rule 62-504 both state that the prohibition against a bidder acquiring securities of the same class as those subject to the bid, other than under the bid itself, does not apply to "an agreement between a security holder and the offeror to the effect that the security holder will, in accordance with the terms and conditions of a [take-over bid], deposit the security holder's securities under the bid."[123]

In *Sears Canada*, the OSC was asked to consider whether section 94(2) of the *Securities Act* (the predecessor to section 93.1) applied to support agreements signed by major shareholders of the target company in favour of the takeover bidder. These support agreements differed from conventional lock-up agreements because they did not commit the shareholders to tender their shares to the bid. Instead, they provided that the shareholders—who, in fact, were *not* going to tender their shares to the bid—would vote their shares in favour of a planned going-private transaction[124] to be undertaken by the bidder after the bid itself had been completed. The panel conceded that support agreements of this sort "do not 'technically' appear to offend subsection 94(2),"[125] though they went on to suggest that the "true substance and intended

---

122 *Ibid.* at para. 5.13: "The private agreement restriction should not preclude an agreement with a significant holder with respect to the deposit of his securities under a bid made to security holders generally in compliance with Part XIX."

123 MI 62-104, s. 2.2(2); OSC Rule 62-504, s. 2.1(2).

124 Going-private transactions are discussed further in Chapter 8.

125 *Sears Canada*, above note 97 at para. 174 (O.S.C.).

effect" of these agreements might well be seen as a violation of section 94(2). Ultimately, however, they did not need to rule on the point.

The critical question, surely, is whether or not such an agreement constitutes an attempt by the bidder to enter into a purchase agreement with one shareholder on terms more favourable than those available to the other shareholders under the bid, undermining the critical objective of equal treatment for target company shareholders. It might be argued that such an interpretation of section 93.1 would make the section redundant, since section 97(1) already includes an express requirement that all holders of target securities receive identical consideration. However, the section 97(1) provision appears to govern the terms of the formal bid itself, an interpretation that seems consistent with the statutory inclusion of a prohibition against collateral agreements. In the *Sears Canada* case, the agreement in question did not appear to offer the securityholders terms superior to those offered to the other shareholders (except, arguably, by virtue of the tax advantage to the securityholders discussed earlier—an advantage which is best analyzed as a putative "collateral benefit"—if, indeed, an inappropriate benefit at all.

ii) Exemption for 5 Percent Market Purchases

The Ontario *Securities Act* and Multilateral Instrument 62-104 provide an exception from the rule prohibiting share purchases by a bidder other than by way of the bid itself in the case of normal course purchases on a published market that do not exceed 5 percent of the outstanding securities of the class subject to the bid.[126] In order to take advantage of this exception, the bidder must specifically disclose its intention to make such purchases in the takeover bid circular, must issue and file a news release after the close of business of the relevant exchange on each day on which securities have been purchased in reliance upon this exception, and must pay no unusual brokerage fees or commissions or make any arrangements to solicit offers to sell.[127] This "5 percent permitted purchase" provision raises a number of interesting legal and strategic issues.

First, bidders must consider carefully whether or not they wish to take advantage of the permitted purchase provision. Takeover bidders often plan to carry out "clean-up" going-private transactions after their takeover bid has been completed to eliminate the interests of any minority shareholders who chose not to tender their shares. As discussed in

---

126 MI 62-104, s. 2.2(3); *Securities Act* (Ontario), s. 93.1(2), OSC Rule 62-504, s.
      2.1(1).
127 *Ibid.*

more detail in Chapter 8, such going-private transactions (or "business combinations") are permitted in Canada provided the bidder follows certain procedures, prescribed by securities law. One of the requirements in connection with certain post-bid going-private transactions is that the transaction must be approved by a majority of the minority shareholders—in other words, by a majority of those shareholders *other than* the takeover bidder itself.

For reasons explained in Chapter 8, Ontario law permits a successful takeover bidder to include any shares that were tendered to the bid to be included in this post-bid majority of the minority vote, even though such shares are, of course, held by the bidder itself by the time the vote is held. What this means, however, is that a bidder must be sensitive to the number of shares it acquires in a target company *before* commencing its takeover bid as well as the number of shares it chooses to acquire through permitted market purchases during the takeover bid. Obtaining a significant block of shares before launching the bid (sometimes called a "toehold position") or by way of permitted purchases during the bid may well increase the likelihood that the bidder will end up with a controlling interest in the target company. But this strategic advantage comes at a price: the bidder will not be able to count any of the shares it has acquired in this way in any subsequent going-private minority approval vote.

The requirement that permitted market purchases must be made "in the normal course," and without unusual brokerage fees or solicitations of offers to sell was found in an earlier OSC rule, Rule 62-501. The requirement was first proposed in 1995,[128] though it was not enacted until 2002, following the decision of the OSC in *In the Matter of Chapters Inc. and Trilogy Retail Enterprises L.P.*[129] The panel in *Chapters/Trilogy* determined that section 94(3) of the *Securities Act* (the forerunner of section 93.1) permitted the bidder in that case to acquire shares of the target corporation while its formal bid was ongoing in three "block purchases" initiated in the so-called upstairs market.[130]

The *Chapters/Trilogy* decision was controversial because permitting such block purchases would appear to make it possible to evade the requirement in section 97(1) of the *Securities Act* (and section 2.23(1) of Multilateral Instrument 62-104) that all holders of the class of securities subject to a takeover bid are to be offered identical consideration. The OSC noted that, in fact, the trades in question were all carried out

---

128 (1995), 18 OSCB 4915.
129 (2001), 24 OSCB 1663.
130 For a brief explanation of the upstairs market, see above note 72.

at prices equal to or lower than the bid price.[131] That fact obviates the concern that the bidder had completed these trades at a higher price than would generally have been available to shareholders tendering to the bid.

However, while this fact may have provided comfort to the panel that these specific trades did not violate the spirit of the Act, it was ultimately irrelevant to the Panel's interpretation of the language of section 94(3). As they noted, the section 94(3) exception simply does not require that the permitted purchases be completed at a price identical to the bid price. Put another way, the panel determined that the requirement in section 97(1) that "all holders of the same class of securities shall be offered identical consideration" does *not* apply to purchases made, during the course of the bid, in full compliance with section 94(3). Accordingly, the crucial issue was whether the block purchases in this case met the requirements of section 94(3) or whether, instead, 94(3) was only intended to permit "normal course" purchases through the facilities of the exchange. The panel held that section 94(3), by its terms, permitted purchases made "through the facilities of a stock exchange" regardless of whether or not those purchases were normal course purchases. The panel noted that section 94(3) simply did not include language limiting its availability to normal course purchases unlike, for example, section 94(7) (now sections 93.2 and 93.3), which makes clear that market trades are exempt from the pre-bid integration and post-bid restriction rules only if they are trades in the normal course.

Fittingly, perhaps, for a case involving book retailers, the *Chapters/Trilogy* case was not the final chapter in this story. Shortly after the decision was released (and indeed at the urging of the panel itself) the OSC adopted OSC Rule 62-501[132] (a rule that had been proposed more than five years before the *Chapters/Trilogy* case, but had languished since). Rule 62-501 dealt expressly with the matter and effectively overruled the *Chapters/Trilogy* decision, stating, among other things, that the exemption in section 94(3) was only available if "the purchases are made in the normal course on a stock exchange."[133] Finally, when the current takeover rules took effect, the 5 percent market purchase exemption was expressly limited to normal course market purchases.[134]

The Ontario Securities Commission also had occasion to consider the possibility that the 5% market purchase exemption might be used to undertake a "creeping takeover." The term creeping takeover usually

131 Above note 129 at 1665.
132 OSC Rule 62-501 (2002), 25 OSCB 5356.
133 *Ibid.*, s. 2.2 a.
134 See above note 126.

refers to the gradual acquisition, through market purchases, of enough shares of a target corporation to gain control. It was a technique that sometimes proved troublesome in the United States because American federal takeover rules do not use the kind of bright-line "take-over bid" test that characterizes Canadian takeover law.

American style creeping takeovers are not generally thought to pose a threat in Canada because the formal bid rules are normally triggered when an acquiror reaches the 20 percent ownership threshold, whether gradually or in one fell swoop. However, in *In the Matter of Falconbridge Limited*[135] a concern was raised that a hostile takeover bidder that held 19.8 percent of the target company's shares before launching its bid, might be able to use the normal course purchase exemption to acquire just enough shares in the market to effectively block a competing friendly bid, ending the takeover auction, and leaving the target company shareholders with no opportunity to tender their shares at a premium. The Ontario Securities Commission concluded that the hostile bidder should not be permitted to acquire shares pursuant to the 5 percent market purchases exemption, reasoning that such market purchases "in combination with [the hostile bidder's] ability to waive its minimum tender condition, would have had the potential to end the take-over bid auction early."[136]

A second issue was raised in the *Falconbridge* case relating to the requirement that an offeror seeking to rely on the 5 percent market purchase exemption must specify in its takeover bid circular its intent to make such purchases. In the circular in question, the offeror had stated that it had no present intention to make such market purchases, but retained the right to do so in future. Although such language was conventional, and indeed commission staff took no exception to it, it was suggested that on the unique facts of this case such disclosure might be considered inadequate to the extent that it suggested an ambiguity of intention that may not have been wholly accurate. In the end, the commission did not need to resolve this issue, since it was prepared to deny use of the exemption to the hostile bidder under its general section 127 public interest power. However, the panel did suggest that the commission should consider the issue of what would constitute sufficient wording of intent in a takeover bid circular for purposes of the market purchases exemption.

---

135 (2006), 29 OSCB 6784.
136 *Ibid.* at para. 79.

f) Restrictions on Sales by Offeror during Bid

Once a takeover bid is launched, the bidder is normally prohibited from making any sales of securities of the class subject to the bid until the bid has expired.[137] This restriction on sales by the offeror appears to be aimed at preventing share price manipulation (or at least potential distortion) from the launching of a takeover bid. In the absence of this rule, if the launch of a takeover bid caused the target company's share price to rise, a bidder could take advantage of that rise by opportunistically selling its own shares into the market while the bid was outstanding then ultimately withdrawing its bid, perhaps citing the failure of some condition to be satisfied.[138] It is worth noting that in the case of an issuer bid—that is, a bid made by a corporation to buy back its own outstanding shares—this prohibition would not prevent the issuer from issuing new securities of the same class pursuant to dividend plans, dividend reinvestment plans, employee stock purchase plans, or similar plans.[139]

g) Financing the Bid

When shareholders of a target corporation are trying to decide whether or not to tender their shares to a takeover bid, they will generally be most interested in the price that the bidder has offered. Needless to say, in assessing the attractiveness of that price the shareholder assumes that the bidder will, indeed, be able to pay all amounts due to shareholders who tender their shares. Bidders, in turn, will often need to obtain financing for their bids.

The issue of financing is important because it affects the issue of "deal certainty"—the likelihood that a prospective acquisition will actually be completed. Multilateral Instrument 62-104 and the Ontario *Securities Act* state that when a bid provides that the bid price is to be paid in whole or in part in cash, the offeror must "make adequate arrangements before the bid to ensure that the required funds are available"[140] to make the necessary payments. (No such financing re-

---

137 MI 62-104, s. 2.7; *Securities Act* (Ontario), s. 93.4. If disclosed in the takeover bid circular, the offeror may enter into agreements, before the bid expires, to sell securities taken up under the bid after the bid expires. MI 62-104, s. 2.7 (2); *Securities Act* (Ontario), s. 93.4(2).

138 The Canadian Securities Administrators have recognized the problems that may arise from the price impact of a takeover bid that is subsequently withdrawn in another context—the variance of bid terms. See CSA Staff Notice 62-305 (2009), 32 OSCB 10449.

139 MI 62-104, s. 2.7(3); OSC Rule 62-504, s. 2.5.

140 MI 62-104, s. 2.27(1); *Securities Act* (Ontario), s. 97.3(1).

quirement is necessary, of course, when the bidder makes a "paper" or securities exchange takeover bid—that is, when the bid price is to be satisfied by newly issued shares of the bidder rather than by the payment of cash.) A takeover bid, in other words, may not be made conditional on obtaining financing.

A bidder's financing arrangements themselves may be subject to conditions so long as the bidder believes the possibility that it will be unable to complete the bid as a result of failure to satisfy such conditions to be "remote."[141] This express reference to financing conditions was introduced at the time the Canadian takeover bid regime rules were harmonized. The provision has an interesting history. Even before the express permissibility of such financing conditions, the broad adequate financing requirement was not generally regarded as imposing an onerous burden on bidders. In particular, it had been widely assumed by practitioners that customary conditions imposed by a bidder's lenders would not mean that financing arrangements would fail to satisfy the bid financing requirements. This assumption was challenged, however, in a 2005 decision of the Ontario Superior Court of Justice in *BNY Capital Corp. v. Katotakis*.[142] An appeal of this decision to the Court of Appeal was dismissed, but the Court of Appeal expressly declined to comment on the financing issue.

The *Katotakis* decision prompted the Canadian Securities Administrators to issue a staff notice indicating the view of CSA staff that the financing requirement would be satisfied, "if the offeror reasonably believes the possibility is remote that it will not be able to pay for tendered securities because of a financing condition not being satisfied."[143] The Ontario Securities Commission also made a new rule, Rule 62-503,[144] dealing with the financing requirement. Rule 62-503 consists of a single section stating:

> [F]or the purposes of section 96 [the forerunner to s. 97.3(1)] . . . the financing arrangements required to be made by the offeror prior to a bid may be subject to conditions if, at the time the bid is commenced, the offeror reasonably believes the possibility to be remote that, if the conditions of the bid are satisfied or waived, the offeror will be unable to pay for securities deposited under the bid due to a financing condition not being satisfied.

---

141 MI 62-104, s. 2.27(2); *Securities Act* (Ontario), s. 97.3(2).
142 (2005), 2 B.L.R. (4th) 71 (Ont. S.C.J.), aff'd (2005) 1 B.L.R. (4th) 168 (Ont. C.A.).
143 CSA Staff Notice 62-304 (2005), 28 OSCB 7305.
144 (2005), 28 OSCB 8677.

It is that language that later became the basis for section 97.3(2) of the Ontario *Securities Act* and section 2.27(2) of Multilateral Instrument 62-104.

h) Takeover Bid Circular

i) *Form of Circular*

When an offeror makes a formal takeover bid, it is required to produce a takeover bid circular. The circular is a detailed disclosure document that must be delivered to every holder of the securities of the class subject to the bid and filed with securities regulators.[145] The circular is required to contain certain information specified by the *Securities Act*, Multilateral Instrument 62-104, and OSC Rule 62-504. Multilateral Instrument 62-104 and OSC Rule 62-504 prescribe the form for the circular—Form 62-104F1/62-504F1.[146]

The takeover bid circular must include a certificate signed (where the bidder is a corporation) by the chief executive officer, the chief financial officer, and on behalf of the board of directors of the offeror, by two members of the board,[147] attesting to the accuracy and completeness of the circular.[148] This certification requirement is very similar to the prospectus certificate required in the case of a public offering of securities.[149] If the takeover bid circular contains a misrepresentation, provincial securities laws provide for statutory civil liability similar to the regime that applies in the case of misrepresentations in a prospectus,[150] and the circular must contain a statement of these statutory civil liability rights.[151] (These statutory rights are in addition to any common law remedies that may be available to aggrieved security holders.)

---

145 MI 62-104, s. 2.10; *Securities Act* (Ontario), s. 94.2.
146 MI 62-104, s. 2.10(1)(a); OSC Rule 62-504, s. 3.1(a).
147 Where the corporation has fewer than four directors and officers, all directors and officers must sign: MI 62-104, s. 3.3(2); *Securities Act* (Ontario), s. 99(2).
148 MI 62-104, s. 3.3; *Securities Act* (Ontario), s. 99; Form 62-104F1/62-504F1, Item 26.
149 See, for example, *Securities Act* (Ontario), s. 58(1).
150 See, for example, *Securities Act* (Alberta), s. 205; *Securities Act* (British Columbia), s. 132; *Securities Act* (New Brunswick), s. 153; *Securities Act* (Newfoundland and Labrador), s. 131; *Securities Act* (Nova Scotia), s. 139; *Securities Act* (Ontario), s. 131; *Securities Act* (Prince Edward Island), s. 114; *Securities Act* (Québec), ss. 222, 223, and 225; *Securities Act, 1988* (Saskatchewan), s. 139; *Securities Act* (Northwest Territories), s. 114; *Securities Act* (Nunavut), s. 114; *Securities Act* (Yukon), s. 114.
151 Form 62-104F1/Form 62-504F1, Item 25.

ii) Evolving Purpose of Circular

The nature and purpose of the takeover bid circular has evolved considerably since the Kimber Report's original proposals for mandatory takeover bid legislation. Today, the emphasis is on full disclosure. The Kimber Committee, by contrast, had proposed that, in the case of cash bids, bidders should be permitted to keep their identity a secret from target shareholders because, in their view, a rule that required all bidders to disclose their identities might deter the launching of many bids that would be of benefit to public company shareholders![152]

iii) Incorporation of Acquisition Entity

Frequently, an entity launching a takeover bid prefers to launch its bid through a single-purpose subsidiary that the bidder has incorporated expressly for the purpose of completing the transaction. There are many reasons for adopting this approach. For example, if the "true" bidder is a U.S. corporation, it may be useful to incorporate an acquisition entity under Canadian law so that the bid may be structured in a tax-efficient way. Further, using a single-purpose entity to purchase the target's shares may facilitate a subsequent going-private transaction, as discussed in Chapter 8.

Regulators have been concerned, however, that in some takeover bids in which an acquisition entity like this has been used, the takeover bid circular has been signed only on behalf of that single-purpose entity and not on behalf of the parent company. Accordingly, in 2003 the Canadian Securities Administrators issued Staff Notice 62-303,[153] in which they stated the view of staff:

> Where a take-over bid is made by a wholly-owned entity, CSA staff regard the entity's parent to be a joint offeror. In that case, both parties must sign the circular as offerors. If the named offeror is not a wholly-owned entity, CSA staff will consider whether the primary party is a joint offeror under the bid by examining its role in that bid.[154]

In 2008, these views were reiterated in National Policy 62-203.[155]

iv) Regulatory Review of Circulars

One issue of recurring interest in Canadian takeover bid regulation is the question of whether or not takeover bid circulars ought to be sub-

---

152 Kimber Report, above note 7 at 3.18.
153 (2003), 26 OSCB 5972.
154 *Ibid.*
155 NP 62-203, s. 2.1.

ject to prior regulatory review (similar to prospectus review) at least in cases of a securities exchange bid (that is, a bid in which the offeror offers to pay for the target company's shares not with cash, but by issuing securities in itself). After all, the issuance of new shares by the bidder in such a case is a "distribution"[156] within the meaning of securities laws and issuers are normally obliged to issue and file a prospectus, which is subject to prior regulatory review, when a distribution is made.

Securities rules do provide exemptions from the prospectus requirement in certain cases, and such an exemption is available when a bidder issues its securities in connection with a securities exchange takeover bid.[157] The rationale for this prospectus exemption is presumably that shareholders of the target company to whom the bidder's securities are being offered will have access to prospectus-level disclosure in any event because a takeover bid circular, in the case of a securities exchange bid, is required to provide prospectus-type disclosure.[158] Moreover, as noted above, the takeover bid circular must include a certificate of the directors and officers similar to the certificate that accompanies a prospectus, and the *Securities Act* provides for liability in the case of a misrepresentation in a circular.[159]

The existence of these various safeguards, however, does not completely explain why there is no prior review of securities exchange takeover bid circulars. Certificate and liability provisions apply to prospectus offerings too, and yet prospectuses are subject to prior regulatory review. If a prescribed form of disclosure buttressed by certificate and liability provisions render prior regulatory review superfluous in the case of securities offered by a takeover bidder, why is such review not equally superfluous in the case of *all* prospectus offerings? Conversely, if certificate and liability provisions are not thought to offer investors adequate protection, in the absence of prior regulatory review of the offering document, why are takeover bid circulars that are used in securities exchange takeover bids exempt from such review in Canada?[160]

---

156 For a discussion of the general obligation to prepare and file a prospectus when securities are distributed, see Jeffrey G. MacIntosh & Christopher C. Nicholls, *Securities Law* (Toronto: Irwin, 2002) c. 6.

157 See National Instrument 45-106, s. 2.16.

158 See, in particular, Form 62-104F1/Form 62-504F1, Item 19.

159 See above note 150.

160 In the United States, prior to 2000, a bidder making a share exchange "tender offer" (the functional U.S. equivalent to a Canadian formal takeover bid) was required to register the securities to be offered to target shareholders and the tender offer could not be launched until the Securities and Exchange Commission declared the registration statement effective (a process that is function-

The Kimber Committee, in 1965, specifically considered whether or not takeover bid circulars ought to be subject to prior review, ultimately recommending against such a requirement, in part owing to a concern that cash and securities exchange bids ought to be treated alike and in part "because of the importance of speed and secrecy to the success of a takeover bid."[161] It seems fair to say that securities regulators today are less concerned with facilitating the "speed" of bids, and are not at all interested in fostering their secrecy.

Certainly, if securities exchange takeover bids were subject to prior regulatory review, while cash bids were not, cash bids could enjoy a considerable tactical advantage, an advantage that such bids were said to have enjoyed in the United States especially prior to the changes in the registration requirement for exchange offers made in 2000.[162] Placing securities exchange bids at such a disadvantage could deter potential bidders from launching such bids in the first place, to the general disadvantage of minority shareholders of public companies. Alternatively, regulators could decide to subject all takeover bid circulars to prior regulatory review. However, it is not entirely clear how such a review process would operate. Would bidders be permitted to deliver to target shareholders a "preliminary" offeror's circular, similar to a "preliminary prospectus," pending obtaining a receipt for a final circular? What information, if any, could be excluded from such a preliminary document? How would the minimum bid periods relate to the time required by regulators to complete their review? During periods of increased takeover bid activity, regulatory resources might be strained, leading not only to delays for all filers but, potentially, longer delays for some bidders than for others—jeopardizing the conduct of M & A deals. Accordingly, although there might well be some advantages to subjecting offerors' circulars to prior regulatory review, on balance those advantages are outweighed by the potential problems posed by such review.

---

ally equivalent to obtaining a receipt for a final prospectus in Canada). This is no longer the case in the United States. Under Rule 162, "offerors may solicit tenders of securities in an exchange offer . . . before a registration statement is effective as to the security offered, so long as no securities are purchased until the registration statement is effective and the tender offer has expired in accordance with the tender offer rules." 64 FR 61408, 61450, 10 November 1999.

161 Kimber Report, above note 7 at 3.24. Of course the "secrecy" of takeover bids is not protected under current law in the way that the Kimber Committee had envisioned.

162 See, for example, Meredith M. Brown, Paul S. Bird, & William D. Regner, "Introduction to Hostile Takeovers" in *Contests for Corporate Control 2005* (New York: Practising Law Institute, 2005) 345 at 368.

In any event, where a takeover bidder (or its parent) is a seasoned public issuer, suggestions that circulars be subject to prior regulatory review may be regarded as outmoded. Increasingly, securities regulation is moving away from its traditional transaction-based focus to become more issuer-based. Increasing emphasis is being placed upon an issuer's periodic and continuous disclosure record rather than exclusively, or even primarily, upon prospectus disclosure. The advent of the various alternative forms of prospectus in Canada—the short form,[163] the shelf,[164] and the post-receipt pricing (PREP)[165] systems—the adoption by regulators of selective prospectus review and, most recently, in the United States, the introduction of the Well-Known Seasoned Issuer ("WKSI")[166] streamlined rules all demonstrate the increasing importance of such issuer-based regulation. In that context, a move to prior regulatory review of takeover bid circulars for seasoned issuers seems to represent a step backward.

i)   Commencing the Bid

There are two ways for an offeror to commence a takeover bid: by delivery of the takeover bid circular to the target company's securityholders (including holders of securities convertible into the target securities) or by publishing an advertisement in a major daily newspaper.[167]

At one time, it was only possible to commence a takeover bid by sending the circular to the target shareholders. This requirement, however, posed a particular logistical challenge for hostile bidders. In order to send the circular to shareholders, bidders first needed access to the target corporation's shareholder list. The shareholder list is not a public document, although most corporate statutes provide that a corporation must make the list available upon request in certain circumstances, including in cases where the list is requested by a party for the purpose of launching a takeover bid. Those same corporate statutes, though, allow the target corporation a certain minimum number of days to produce the list. For example, for publicly traded (or "distributing") corporations incorporated under the CBCA, section 21(3) of the CBCA states that a corporation must provide a shareholder list to any person who has paid a reasonable fee and delivered an affidavit stating, among other things, that the shareholder list will only be used for a purpose

---

163   See National Instrument 44-101.
164   See National Instrument 44-102.
165   See National Instrument 44-103.
166   See "Securities Offering Reform" SEC Release No. 33-8591, 34-52056, 70 Fed. Reg. 44,722 (3 August 2005).
167   MI 62-104, s. 2.9; *Securities Act* (Ontario), s. 94.1.

permitted by the statute.[168] However, the corporation has until up to ten days following receipt of the affidavit to supply this list.[169]

It would be unusual today for a publicly traded corporation to maintain its own shareholders' list. Typically, the list would be maintained by the corporation's registrar and transfer agent—a specialized company that would perform similar services for many other publicly traded corporations. The shareholders' list would be in computerized form and, subject to any other demands to which the transfer agent might be subject from time to time, could be generated promptly—almost literally at the push of a button. However, in the case of a hostile takeover bid, the directors of the target corporation will have an incentive to try to hinder the bidder by delaying delivery of the list until the last possible minute.

This potential for delay was recognized by the Zimmerman Committee, a committee established by the Investment Dealers Association in 1996 to review takeover bid time limits.[170] The committee concluded that it was "inappropriate to allow this tactical delay in the process to acquire companies" and suggested that it would be "far better for shareholders if this period of non-public activity were converted into more time for the bid to be exposed to the market."[171] The committee, accordingly, considered the possibility of reducing the period within which corporations were required to deliver shareholder lists from ten to three days, but ultimately concluded, instead, to propose that bids could be launched immediately by publication,[172] as the Canadian takeover bid regime now provides.

The takeover rules also attempt to provide some uniformity in the provision of securityholders' lists. Section 3.4 of Multilateral Instrument 62-104 and section 99.1 of the Ontario *Securities Act* provide that a target issuer must provide its list of securityholders to a prospective bidder to enable the bid to be made (where it would not otherwise be required by law to do so), and to that end incorporates by reference the

---

168   The purposes for which a shareholder list may be used are: (a) in connection with an effort to influence shareholder voting; (b) in connection with an offer to acquire securities of the corporation; and (c) in connection with "any other matter relating to the affairs of the corporation." CBCA, s. 21(9).

169   *Ibid.*, s. 21(3).

170   Investment Dealers Association of Canada, Committee to Review Takeover Bid Time Limits (Adam Zimmerman, Chair), *Report of the Committee to Review Takeover Bid Time Limits* (May 1996) at 2, reproduced at (1996), 19 OSCB 4469.

171   *Ibid.*

172   *Ibid.*

securityholder list request procedures of section 21 of the CBCA ("with necessary modifications").[173]

j) Minimum Bid Period/Withdrawal Rights

A takeover bid must remain open for at least thirty-five calendar days.[174] Securities tendered to the bid within that thirty-five-day period may not be taken up by the offeror until the expiry of that thirty-five-day period,[175] and securityholders who have tendered their shares within that period are permitted to withdraw them during this period if they wish.[176] These withdrawal rights not only ensure that shareholders have a significant amount of time to consider the terms of the bid and to seek legal and financial advice about it if they wish, but they also permit a securityholder to tender to a higher competing bid if one emerges before the expiry of the first bid's minimum-bid period.

For many years in Ontario (and other Canadian jurisdictions) the mandatory minimum-bid period imposed by statute was just twenty-one days. Then, in 1996, the Zimmerman Committee[177] recommended that the minimum-bid period be increased from twenty-one to thirty-five days, an increase—as was well understood by the Zimmerman Committee, by experienced practitioners and by regulators—that, as a practical matter, would really involve an extension of only about four days, rather than fourteen.[178]

A legal requirement that takeover bids remain open for a minimum number of days not only provides target shareholders more time to consider the adequacy of a bid, but also gives the directors and officers of the target corporation sufficient time, in the case of an unsolicited or hostile bid, to try to craft an alternative strategy. That strategy might involve identifying an alternative bidder who can be induced to make an even more attractive bid and so, perhaps, trigger an auction for the target corporation's shares, or could consist of developing some other method of maximizing shareholder value, subject to the considerations raised by the Supreme Court of Canada in *BCE v. 1976 Debentureholders*[179] discussed in Chapter 7.

---

173 MI 62-104, s. 3.4; *Securities Act* (Ontario), s. 99. 1..
174 MI 62-104, s. 2.28; *Securities Act* (Ontario), s. 98(1).
175 MI 62-104, s. 2.29; *Securities Act* (Ontario), s. 98(2).
176 MI 62-104, s. 2.30; *Securities Act* (Ontario), s. 98.1.
177 Above note 170.
178 The explanation for this relates to the ten-day delay that managers of a target corporation could effectively impose upon hostile bidders in responding to the bidders' request for a shareholders list, as explained above.
179 2008 SCC 69.

In fact, it is likely that allowing directors of a target corporation sufficient time to generate alternatives to an unsolicited bid is today considered the most important rationale for mandatory bid periods, although it seems equally clear that the Kimber Committee, which first proposed mandatory bid periods, did not consider the generation of competing bids to be a necessary or even desirable outcome of such requirements.[180]

No more will be said here about the duty of the directors of a corporation that is subject to a hostile takeover bid. This is a complex topic that is discussed in somewhat greater detail later in Chapter 7.

k) Directors' Circular

To help securityholders of the target company make an informed decision about whether or not to tender their securities, the directors of the target company must prepare and send to their securityholders a circular of their own within fifteen days after the takeover bid is commenced.[181] In that circular, the directors must normally make a recommendation to their securityholders either to accept or to reject the bid (with supporting reasons), or, if unable to make such a recommendation, they must provide reasons for this.[182] In some cases, directors may require more time to determine whether or not to recommend acceptance or rejection of a bid. The legislation allows them to take that extra time by indicating in the directors' circular that they are considering their recommendation, stating their reasons for not making a recommendation, and advising holders to await further communication before tendering their securities.[183] If they do choose to include such a provision in the directors' circular, the directors must subsequently deliver a recommendation (or a statement that they are unable to make a recommendation) to the securityholders, with supporting reasons, at least seven days before the outstanding bid expires.[184] Where the views of an individual director or officer differ from those of the majority of

---

180   The Kimber Report states, for example, that the mandatory bid and withdrawal periods "will ensure that the shareholders of the offeree company are afforded an adequate opportunity to form a reasoned judgment as to whether or not they should sell their shares, *without working a hardship on bidders by unreasonably exposing them to counter bids whether from management or others.*" Kimber Report, above note 7 at 3.16 [emphasis added].

181   MI 62-104, s. 2.17(1); *Securities Act* (Ontario), s. 95(1).

182   MI 62-104, s. 2.17(2); *Securities Act* (Ontario), s. 95(2).

183   MI 62-104, s. 2.17(2)(c); *Securities Act* (Ontario), s. 95(2)(c).

184   MI 62-104, s. 2.17(3); *Securities Act* (Ontario), s. 95(3). The director's circular must contain the information prescribed in Form 62-104F3/Form 62-504F3. See MI 62-104, s. 2.17(4); OSC Rule 62-504, s. 3.2.

the board, that individual may issue his or her own recommendation accompanied by an individual director's or officer's circular.[185] A statutory civil liability remedy is available in the event of misrepresentations in a directors' circular.[186]

The preparation of this directors' circular represents essentially the only express *securities law* obligation to which directors of a target corporation are subject. They are, however, always obliged, under corporate law, to act honestly, in good faith and with a view to the best interests of the corporation,[187] duties that can be especially challenging to interpret in the heat of a contested control transaction. Shareholders of large, publicly traded corporations depend upon the knowledge and expertise of the directors when attempting to evaluate the adequacy of a proposed takeover bid. Ultimately, however, the bid is made to the shareholders, not to the directors. Further, commentators and regulators have long worried that managers of a corporation that is the subject of a hostile takeover bid might well be influenced by considerations other than the desire to achieve the best possible deal for their shareholders, as discussed later in Chapter 7.

C. EARLY WARNING DISCLOSURE SYSTEM

In addition to the formal takeover bid requirements, Canadian securities statutes also provide for an "early warning" disclosure system modelled on similar U.S. federal securities law requirements.[188] It is thought that by compelling public disclosure of major share acquisitions (even where such acquisitions fall short of the 20 percent threshold that would trigger the takeover bid rules), the market will receive useful information and perhaps advance notice of the possibility of a bid being undertaken in the future.

---

185 MI 62-104, s. 2.20; *Securities Act* (Ontario), s. 96. The individual director's or officer's circular must be in Form 62-104F4/Form 62-504F4. See MI 62-104, s. 2.20(3); OSC Rule 62-504, s. 3.3.

186 See, for example, *Securities Act* (Alberta), s. 205(2); *Securities Act* (British Columbia), s. 132(3); *Securities Act* (New Brunswick), s. 153(2); *Securities Act* (Newfoundland and Labrador), s. 131(2); *Securities Act* (Nova Scotia), s. 139(2); *Securities Act* (Ontario), s. 131(2); *Securities Act* (Prince Edward Island), s. 114(3); *Securities Act* (Quebec), s 225; *Securities Act, 1988* (Saskatchewan), s. 139(2); *Securities Act* (Northwest Territories), s. 114(3); *Securities Act* (Nunavut), s. 114(3); *Securities Act* (Yukon), s. 114(3).

187 See, for example, CBCA, s. 122(1)(a).

188 See s. 13(d) of *Securities Exchange Act of 1934.*

Accordingly, whenever an acquiror[189] acquires securities that result in it holding 10 percent or more of a class of outstanding voting or equity securities, that acquiror must issue and file a press release and, within two business days, file a report with securities regulators.[190] An additional disclosure requirement is triggered whenever a holder of at least 10 percent of a class of a corporation's voting or equity securities purchases 2 percent or more of the securities of the same class (or securities convertible into securities of the same class).[191]

The acquiror in such cases is then prohibited from acquiring additional securities of the same class for one business day after the required disclosure is made.[192] Eligible institutional investors such as pension and mutual funds are permitted to file monthly reports as alternatives to the early warning reports required of other purchasers of securities.[193]

As noted earlier, the takeover bid rules in Multilateral Instrument 62-104 and Part XX of the Ontario *Securities Act* generally apply only where there has been an acquisition of *outstanding* securities. However, the early warning disclosure obligations in Multilateral Instrument 62-104, section 5.2 and Ontario *Securities Act*, section 102.1 are triggered by any acquisition of the relevant number of securities—whether "outstanding securities" or previously unissued securities acquired directly from the issuer, whether through subscription or through the exercise of previously acquired option or conversion rights. This conclusion is based upon the broad definition of "acquiror" in section 5.1 of Multilateral Instrument 62-104 and section 102(1) of the Ontario *Securities Act*.[194]

There is a slightly more complicated disclosure regime that comes into play when a purchaser acquires a significant block of shares of a company *after* a takeover bid has been launched by a different purchaser. In such a case, section 102.2 of the Ontario *Securities Act* states:

> If, after a formal bid has been made for voting or equity securities of a reporting issuer and before the expiry of the bid, an acquiror acquires beneficial ownership of, or the power to exercise control or direction over, securities of the class subject to the bid which, when added to the acquiror's securities of that class, constitute 5 per cent or more of

---

189 MI 62-104, s. 5.1 and *Securities Act* (Ontario), s. 102(1) define "acquiror" as someone who acquires a security other than by way of a formal takeover bid.
190 MI 62-104, s. 5.2(1); *Securities Act* (Ontario), s. 102.1; OSC Rule 62-504, s. 7.1.
191 MI 62-104, s. 5.2(2); *Securities Act* (Ontario), s. 102.1(2); OSC Rule 62-504, s. 7.1.
192 *MI* 62-104, s. 5.2(3); *Securities Act* (Ontario), s. 102.1(3).
193 See National Instrument 62-103, Part 4.
194 See above note 189.

the outstanding securities of that class, the acquiror shall disclose the acquisition in the manner and form required by regulation.[195]

OSC Rule 62-504 set out the "manner and form" of this required disclosure: the acquiror must issue and file a news release containing specific information before the opening of trading on the next business day.[196] Multilateral Instrument 62-104 includes a provision to the same effect.[197] The purpose of section 102.2, as the Ontario Securities Commission has confirmed, is "to provide a signal to the marketplace that competing bidders may be interested in making a formal bid (or blocking a formal bid) and that others are purchasing the target issuer's shares."[198]

The application of the early warning rules to joint actors and economic (but not legal) interests in shares acquired in derivatives transactions were considered by the Ontario Securities Commission in the *Sears Canada* case.[199] The facts in *Sears Canada* were outlined earlier in this chapter.[200] Briefly, Sears Holdings sought to acquire the shares of Sears Canada it did not already own, and its bid was actively opposed by a group of three hedge funds with investments in Sears Canada. Sears Holdings argued that these hedge funds had violated the early warning rules. None of the three funds *individually* held 10 percent of the outstanding shares of Sears Canada prior to the commencement of Sears Holdings' takeover bid, nor did any of the funds individually hold more than 5 percent of the shares of Sears Canada until 6 April 2006; and within one business day of the share purchase, which brought one of the fund's holdings above the 5 percent level, that fund issued a press release in accordance with section 102 (the predecessor of Ontario *Securities Act* section 102.2). Accordingly, there was clearly no violation by the funds of the early warning rules unless the funds were found to be "joint actors" with one another (and possibly with a fourth fund that subsequently entered into a Deposit Agreement with Sears Holdings) such that their holdings were required to be aggregated for purposes of determining whether they were obliged to make filings pursuant to section 101 (the predecessor of section 102.1) and 102.

The panel confirmed its agreement with the "general proposition" that a formal agreement between parties is not a prerequisite to finding

---

195 *Securities Act* (Ontario), s. 102.2(1).

196 OSC Rule 62-504, s. 7.2.

197 MI 62-104, s. 5.3.

198 *Sears Canada*, above note 97 at para. 65 (O.S.C.), citing Paul G. Findlay, ed., *Securities Law & Practice*, 3d ed., looseleaf (Toronto: Thomson Canada, 2006) vol. 2 at para. 20.15.1.

199 *Sears Canada*, ibid.

200 See text accompanying above note 97.

joint actor status.[201] However, on the particular facts of the case, the panel
was not persuaded that there was evidence to support the allegation that
the funds had been acting jointly or in concert prior to a date *following*
the filing of the April 7 press release in compliance with section 102.

A somewhat more intriguing aspect of the analysis, however, related to the interpretation of sections 101 and 102 in the context of
swap arrangements. One of the hedge funds opposed to the Sears Holdings bid had entered into a total return swap arrangement pursuant to
which it sold 5.3 million Sears Canada shares, but retained, by virtue
of the total return swap agreement with a financial institution, an economic interest in the future performance of those shares.[202] Could it be
said that the hedge fund retained a sufficient degree of direction or control over the Sears Canada shares that were the subject of these swap
arrangements that the hedge fund must be taken to be the beneficial
owner of those shares?

The panel determined that "there was no evidence . . . to support
a finding that [the hedge fund] and its Swap counterparties had an
understanding that the shares would be returned or otherwise made
available to be voted so that [the hedge fund] could be said to exercise
'control or direction' over the shares within the meaning of sections
101 and 102 of the Act."[203] Nor was the panel convinced that the use
of such swaps to allow the hedge fund to avoid the disclosure obligations of sections 101 and 102 was abusive of the capital markets, so as
to invoke the OSC's public interest jurisdiction. The OSC seemed to
look favourably on the hedge fund's argument that entering into swap
arrangements of this sort was a "common practice,"[204] and was also
satisfied with the hedge fund's explanation for initiating these swap
transactions, in particular its stated desire to maintain an economic
interest in the shares of Sears Canada, but avoid the potentially adverse tax consequences of receiving a particular dividend while owning those shares. However, the panel also issued a terse warning to

---

201 *Sears Canada*, above note 97 at para. 79 (O.S.C.).
202 A total return swap is a financial agreement between two parties pursuant to which
     one ("Party A") receives from the other ("Party B") amounts that would other-
     wise have been received by an owner of a specified reference asset (for example, a
     particular bond, share etc.), but also remains subject to the risk of loss of value of
     that asset. For example, if the reference asset were shares in ABC Corp., an amount
     equal to any dividends paid on those shares would be paid by Party B to Party A
     within a specified time period following payment of the dividends to sharehold-
     ers. In exchange, Party A pays to Party B a payment at regular intervals, typically
     calculated using a reference interest rate applied to an agreed notional value.
203 *Sears Canada*, above note 97 at para. 105 (O.S.C.).
204 *Ibid.* at para. 108.

those who might wish to undertake more aggressive derivatives-based strategies in the future:

> We wish to underscore that there might well be situations, in the context of a take-over bid, where the use of swaps to "park securities" in a deliberate effort to avoid reporting obligations under the Act and for the purpose of affecting an outstanding offer could constitute abusive conduct sufficient to engage the Commission's public interest jurisdiction.[205]

The concern alluded to by the commission relates to what Hu and Black have dubbed "hidden (morphable) ownership."[206]

D. NON-COMPLIANCE WITH THE TAKEOVER BID RULES

There are special enforcement rules that apply in cases where a person is not complying with Part XX of the *Securities Act*. Section 104 provides that an interested person may apply to the OSC for an order and such an order may be granted "if the Commission considers that a person or company has not complied with, or is not complying with, a requirement under this Part or the regulations related to this Part." Then, section 105 permits an interested person to apply to the court for an order which may be granted where a judge is "satisfied that a person or company has not complied with a requirement under this Part or the regulations related to this Part."

E. CONCLUSION

Canada's formal takeover bid rules can prove cumbersome to bidders, but also provide a significant layer of protection for shareholders of target corporations. In certain instances, however, there are sensible policy reasons for exempting bidders from the burdensome formal takeover bid rules. These exemptions are discussed in the next chapter. Takeover protections take on special significance in the case of transactions involving non-arm's length bidders and bidders who seek to acquire control of the target company over the objections of the target company's directors. Those two subjects are dealt with in Chapters 7 and 8.

---

205 *Ibid.* at para. 111.
206 See Henry T.C. Hu & Bernard S. Black, "The New Vote Buying: Empty Voting and Hidden (Morphable) Ownership" (2006) 79 S. Cal. L. Rev. 811.

CHAPTER 6

TAKEOVER BIDS (PART 2): EXEMPTIONS

A. INTRODUCTION

The definition of "take-over bid" for purposes of the Canadian take-over bid regime, as noted in Chapter 5, is extremely broad. As a result, the onerous, time-consuming, and expensive formal takeover bid rules would apply to many transactions where such requirements would be unnecessarily and inappropriately burdensome. Exemptions are therefore available in the case of share transactions where legislators and regulators have decided that, on balance, the protections of the formal takeover bid rules are not necessary. The principal takeover bid rule exemptions are these:

- normal course purchase exemption;
- private agreement exemption;
- private (target company) non-reporting issuer exemption;
- foreign bid exemption; and
- *de minimis* exemption.

Of course, securities regulators may also grant an exemption from the application of the takeover bid rules upon application by an interested party, and provided the regulators are satisfied that granting such an exemption "would not be prejudicial to the public interest."[1]

---

1   *Securities Act* (Ontario), s. 104(2).

B. NORMAL COURSE PURCHASE EXEMPTION

Once a shareholder has acquired a 20 percent voting or equity interest in a public corporation, the purchase of any additional shares—even the purchase of a single share—would constitute a "take-over bid" within the meaning of Multilateral Instrument 62-104 and the Ontario *Securities Act*. This sweeping coverage was deliberate, intended to avoid murky interpretation challenges that might weaken the protections the takeover bid rules were intended to provide.

Yet many (perhaps most) purchases of a modest number of securities do not usually raise the concerns that the statutory takeover bid rules were intended to address. The takeover bid rules therefore include an exemption from the formal bid requirements for a purchase of a modest number of securities that would otherwise constitute a takeover bid under the following conditions:[2]

1. No more than 5 percent of the outstanding securities of a class of the target may be purchased in any twelve-month period.
2. There must be a published market for the class of securities purchased.
3. The price paid for the securities acquired must not exceed the market price at the time of purchase.[3]

This exemption is referred to as the "normal course purchase exemption." Although the takeover bid rules in Multilateral Instrument 62-104 and the Ontario *Securities Act* Part XX generally apply only to the purchase of outstanding securities, rather than to purchases from the issuing company itself of newly-issued treasury securities, it has been observed that the 5 percent annual limit now found in Multilateral Instrument 62-104, section 4.1 (b) and in Ontario *Securities Act*, section 100 2 is calculated by adding the number of outstanding securities subject to the bid to the number of securities acquired in all other "acquisitions otherwise made" by the offeror and anyone acting jointly or in concert with the offeror. This broad language would appear to include not only purchases of outstanding securities, but also purchases of se-

---

2   Multilateral Instrument 62-104 [MI 62-104], s. 4.1; *Securities Act* (Ontario), s. 100.
3   "Market price" is defined for this purpose in MI 62-104, s. 1.11 and OSC Rule 62-504, s. 1.3. In the usual case, market price will mean the simple average of the closing price for the twenty business days preceding the acquisition. There are special rules in cases where this calculation cannot be applied or where the security trades on more than one published market. For further discussion of "market price" in the context of the private agreement exemption, see Section C(5), below in this chapter.

curities from treasury (that is, newly issued shares acquired directly from the target company itself) and, indeed, any other acquisition of securities of the class.[4]

C. PRIVATE AGREEMENT EXEMPTION

1) Basic Requirements

One of the most important and frequently used takeover bid exemptions is the private agreement exemption, which permits certain securities purchases (that would otherwise constitute "take-over bids") to be made from a small number of vendors without triggering the formal bid requirements, provided the premium paid for those securities does not exceed a statutorily prescribed limit. Specifically, the private agreement exemption will be available where all of the following conditions are fulfilled:[5]

- the purchase of securities is made from not more than five persons or companies;
- the bid is not made generally to all securityholders of the class; and
- the price paid does not involve a premium over the market price (where there is a published market) or the value of the securities (where there is no published market) of more than 15 percent.

2) Development and Underlying Policy of Private Agreement Exemption

The private agreement exemption in its current form represents the culmination of a long series of developments that will not be discussed in detail here. It will only be noted that, at one time, the exemption was available in the case of purchases from up to fourteen sellers, and the relevant market price against which the allowable premium was calculated was the price over the ten trading days prior to entering into the agreement.

---

4   See, for example, *Submission of the Take-Over Bid Team at the Ontario Securities Commission in Connection with the Five-Year Review of Securities Legislation in Ontario* (11 August 2000), online: www.osc.gov.on.ca/documents/en/Securities/ fyr_20000811_list_com_take-over-bid.pdf [*OSC Take-Over Bid Team Submission*].

5   MI 62-104, s, 4.2; *Securities Act* (Ontario), s. 100.1.

In a 1980 decision, the Ontario Securities Commission noted that the private agreement exemption represented a significant exception to the general rule that a takeover bid must be made on the same terms to all holders of the target securities, and so reasoned that the provision must be strictly construed.[6] It might also be noted that the treatment of privately negotiated agreements has followed a different path in the United States.[7]

The private agreement exemption gives rise to important practical, technical, theoretical, and policy considerations. As the 1983 Practitioners Report noted, the exemption "has always been controversial because of the opportunities it provides for unequal treatment of shareholders of the same class."[8] Indeed, the existence of the private agreement exemption, it is said, is often cited by corporations as a justification for adopting a shareholder rights plan (or poison pill) to ensure that all shareholders will be treated equally.[9]

The provision represents a legislative response to the question of the extent to which large shareholders of a publicly traded corporation ought to be permitted to sell their interest (including a controlling interest) and realize a premium on that sale that is not enjoyed by the other shareholders. At its simplest, the argument in favour of permitting controlling shareholders to sell their shares freely, at whatever premium they are able to negotiate, is that in an economic system that recognizes and protects private property rights, an owner of property should not be constrained from selling that property at the highest price that a willing buyer is prepared to pay. However, there is a contrary argument. To the extent that securities of the same class of a public company are intended to represent identical financial interests, the fact that holders of larger blocks of such shares are able to acquire an additional "control premium" on the sale of such blocks is regarded by some as unfair. The precise nature of this supposed unfairness has been the subject of fairly extensive commentary, and is discussed in greater detail in the following section. Finally, there is an

---

6   *Ronalds-Federated Limited (Re)*, [1980] OSCB 304.

7   See, for example, *Hanson Trust PLC v. SCM Corp.*, 774 F.2d. 47 (2d Cir. 1985) in which a purchase of 25 percent of the target company's shares from five institutional investors was held not to constitute a tender offer.

8   *Report of the Committee to Review the Provisions of the Securities Act (Ontario) Relating to Takeover Bids and Issuer Bids* (Toronto: Ontario Securities Commission, 1983) at s. 5.01 [*Practitioners Report*].

9   See, for example, *Submission of the Take-Over Bid Team at the Ontario Securities Commission in Connection with the Five-Year Review of Securities Legislation in Ontario*, above note 4.

ongoing concern about the liquidity of large control blocks of shares of public corporations—a well-recognized feature of the Canadian capital market landscape.[10]

3) Sale of Corporate Control and the Control Premium Controversy

It is often considered obvious or trite to observe that someone who purchases enough shares to obtain control of a corporation must (and will) pay a "control premium" for that interest. And it is assumed to be equally obvious that minority shareholders of a corporation with a controlling shareholder must accept a "minority discount" upon the sale of their shares. In other words, if one were able to calculate with certainty all future cash flows to be generated by a corporation's business, and were further able, with the same degree of absolute certainty, to determine the present value of those cash flows, the task of valuing each corporate share would still involve more than the simple mechanical exercise of dividing the present value of the firm by the total number of outstanding shares. Instead, each share held by a controlling shareholder would be worth something more than its strict proportionate interest (reflecting the control premium); and each share held by a minority shareholder would be worth something less (reflecting the minority discount). Not all commentators agree with this "trite" observation, but no one disputes that at least some shares of publicly traded companies trade at a minority discount.

The most benign view of the control premium is that it reflects the additional value inherent in the ability to determine a corporation's future: a superior manager is willing to pay for the privilege of being able to ensure that the corporation's assets are managed more effectively, despite the fact that the benefits of that superior management will ultimately be enjoyed equally by all shareholders. The less benign, but perhaps more realistic, view is that the control premium represents the estimated present value of the private benefits of control—that is, the value of all the benefits that a controlling shareholder can extract by diverting corporate resources to himself or herself. These benefits might, in extreme cases, take the form of egregious value diversion and may well prompt allegations that directors or officers, appointed

---

10   See, for example, Christopher C. Nicholls, "The Characteristics of Canada's Capital Markets and the Illustrative Case of Canada's Legislative and Regulatory Response to *Sarbanes-Oxley*," Research Study Commissioned by the Task Force to Modernize Securities Legislation in Canada (15 June 2006), Vol 4, 127 at 168, online: www.tfmsl.ca/docs/V4(3A)%20Nicholls.pdf.

by the controlling shareholders to do their bidding, have breached their fiduciary duties. In the most abusive instances, these practices may even lead to criminal charges. But in the real world it is (perhaps grudgingly) acknowledged that the extraction of *some* private benefits of control may very well be undertaken at a level that will fly below the fiduciary radar or, perhaps, may be tolerated by minority shareholders because they reckon that the total value contributed by the opportunistic control person actually outweighs the value of any private benefits appropriated by that control person. In this sense, private benefits of control are essentially being viewed as a form of managerial or directorial compensation.

As Gilson and Gordon have noted, it is not necessarily in the interests of minority shareholders to eliminate all opportunities for controlling shareholders to extract private benefits of control.[11] The presence of a controlling shareholder can reduce managerial agency costs. Put more simply, a controlling shareholder has the motive and the means to monitor management and ensure that managerial lounging and looting is kept to a minimum. In order to induce investors to acquire a controlling interest that will facilitate this sort of monitoring, they argue, controlling shareholders must be able to extract *some* private benefits. Thus, they argue, "[F]rom the public shareholders' point of view, the two facets of the agency problem present a tradeoff. The presence of a controlling shareholder reduces the managerial agency problem, but at the cost of the private benefits agency problem."[12] The ability, within reasonable limits, to extract private benefits of control might also serve to encourage privately held corporations to offer their securities to the public in the first place, thus providing additional investment opportunities.

If one concedes that the extraction of at least some private benefits of control is desirable, or at least tolerable, then it is not clear why capitalizing the value of such private benefits, in the form of a sale of control premium, is regarded as especially offensive. One wonders if it is all together too cynical to suggest, as I have written elsewhere, that "the 'equal treatment' supporters are like parents who say to their children, 'It's fine to *have* a treat that the other children don't have. But if you want to eat it in front of them, you will have to share.'"[13]

The "sale of control" issue arises when public corporations have a significant or controlling shareholder. Since the existence of such major

---

11   Ronald J. Gilson & Jeffrey N. Gordon, "Controlling Controlling Shareholders" (2004) 152 U. Pa. L. Rev. 785.

12   *Ibid.*

13   Christopher C. Nicholls, *Corporate Finance and Canadian Law* (Toronto: Carswell, 2000) at 331n.

or controlling shareholders is far more common in the case of Canadian public corporations than American corporations, one would expect that the control premium issue would be more salient in Canada than in the United States. Yet, although one might predict that public corporation sale of control issues would occur more frequently in Canada, one would not necessarily expect that the foundational legal principles surrounding such sales would have followed different paths in Canada and the United States. But in fact, important differences have developed. Controlling shareholders of U.S. public corporations have not been subject to any statutory limits on control premiums, unlike Canadian controlling shareholders. This is perhaps curious given that the notion that majority shareholders owe a fiduciary duty to minority shareholders is a concept that has been developed in the United States, but not in Canadian corporate law. Briefly put, then, controlling shareholders have generally been permitted in the United States to sell their shares at a premium not enjoyed by the minority shareholders, subject only to a few narrow exceptions.[14] Those exceptions are said to arise in the following cases:[15]

- sales to suspected corporate "looters" (that is, purchasers who are likely to unlawfully extract value from the corporation after the sale);

---

14   There have been a number of important and frequently cited U.S. cases dealing either explicitly or implicitly with one or more variants of this question including *Brown, Jr. et al. v. Halbert et al.* (1969), 76 Cal. Rptr. 781 (1st Cir. C.A.) (president and dominant shareholder of a savings and loan firm liable to minority shareholders for persuading a potential acquiror of the entire corporation to first buy his shares at a premium, then persuading minority shareholders to sell at a lower price by claiming new control holder would withhold dividends and pay themselves high salaries); *Perlman v. Feldmann*, 219 F.2d 173 (2d Cir. 1954) (controlling shareholder and senior officer of a steel company liable to account to minority shareholders for a premium realized on sale of his shares where that premium arose from the desire by the purchaser to obtain a secure source of supply of steel at a time of crucial steel shortages [that is, during the Korean conflict]. The fact that the company was sacrificing unusual profit was critical to the majority decision.); *Jones v. H.E. Ahmanson & Co.*, 460 P.2d 464 (Cal. 1969) (minority shareholders of a savings and loan association held to have cause of action against controlling shareholders who had transferred their control block of shares with very high market price to a holding corporation, then sold shares representing smaller interests of that holding corporation to the public at correspondingly lower market price in order to create a more liquid market for their shares, a structure that effectively eliminated any trading market for the remaining savings and loan shares held by the minority shareholders).

15   See, for example, Ronald J. Gilson & Bernard S. Black, *The Law and Finance of Corporate Acquisitions*, 2d ed. (Westbury: The Foundation Press, 1995) at 1214–18; Robert C. Clark, *Corporate Law* (New York: Aspen Law & Business, 1986) at 478–91; American Law Institute, *Principles of Corporate Governance: Analysis and Recommendations* (St. Paul, MN: American Law Institute, 1994) s. 5.16.

- sales "of office" (that is, where a seller and the seller's nominee members of the board of directors facilitate a transfer of their positions on the board of directors to the purchaser of their shares); this has been considered improper in the United States only where the sale of control involves shares that constitute less—perhaps materially less—than the number required to exert legal control—typically 50 percent plus 1 share; the reason that sale of office raises problems only in cases of sales of less than a legally controlling interest is that, with legal control, a purchaser can in any event be assured of electing anyone he or she wishes to the board of directors; and
- undisclosed sale of control transactions (that is, situations where a controlling shareholder either persuades an acquiror to buy his or her controlling interest at a premium *instead of making a general offer to all shareholders* or persuades minority shareholders to sell at a lower price, without disclosing the existence of an offer made by an acquiror to the controlling shareholder to purchase a controlling interest at a premium).[16]

The fact that controlling shareholders in the United States have generally been permitted to sell their shares at a premium not enjoyed by minority shareholders has been regarded by some commentators as troubling. It is important to consider precisely *why* selling control interests at a premium is considered by some as improper in order to avoid reducing the argument to a mere scarecrow.[17]

Those who favour allowing controlling shareholders to sell their shares at a premium typically argue that their views follow logically and inevitably from fundamental concepts of private property rights. This was essentially the view expressed by the majority of members of the Ontario 1973 Select Committee on Company Law, who stated in their final report: "Shares are a form of personal property and . . . the owner should be entitled to dispose of them by private agreement on whatever terms he may consider advisable without interference on the part of the legislature."[18]

---

16 In the Canadian (and English) tradition, this latter situation calls to mind the facts in *Percival v. Wright* (1902), 2 Ch. 421, a case in which the selling shareholders were held not to have recourse. It should be noted that more recent English and Commonwealth authorities have cast doubt if not on the correctness of *Percival v. Wright* then at least on the narrow scope of situations to which it may safely be said to apply.

17 The term *scarecrow argument* I use here as an inclusive language substitute for the older term, *strawman argument*.

18 Select Committee on Company Law, *1973 Report on Mergers, Amalgamations and Certain Related Matters* (Ontario Legislative Assembly: 3d Sess., 29th Leg.) at 30 (William Hodgson, Chair).

Owners of property are typically allowed to sell that property at whatever price they can negotiate with a willing buyer; they have no obligation to ensure that, somehow, holders of similar (even identical) property must also be given the opportunity to sell on the same terms. On the "shares as ordinary personal property" view, perhaps the law should even allow a controlling shareholder to conceal the existence of a pending offer to acquire all of the controller's shares at a price of $20 each when negotiating with minority shareholders to purchase each of their shares for just $10 each. Yes, it would be socially desirable, sporting, fair-minded, and "gentlemanly" to provide such disclosure. But why should there be any legal obligation to do so? One may, for example, generally purchase real estate from an unsuspecting owner at a low price, knowing that someone else stands ready to buy the same property from you at a higher amount. There is no legal requirement to disclose details of this lucrative pending opportunity to the current owner. Instead, we leave the matter to the private negotiations that lie at the heart of our economic system. If the current owner suspects that a buyer is going to "flip" the property at a profit, she can insist on some kind of price protection clause in the purchase agreement itself, or simply demand a higher price to begin with. That is a matter for the parties to decide as between themselves.

Are corporate shares so very different? Some argue that they are. One obvious difference is that a control premium may represent value paid to gain access to private benefits of control that represent wrongful diversions of value from the corporation to the detriment of the corporation (and therefore to the remaining minority shareholders). However, as discussed above, if the extraction of such control benefits is unlawful, surely concern should be focused on the ultimate act of seizing such benefits, not on preventing a controlling shareholder from monetizing the opportunity to seize them in future. Moreover, if the extraction of private benefits of control is possible and known to potential buyers, then one assumes that this fact is also reflected in the trading price of the minority shares. That means that the minority shareholders, presumably, acquired their shares at a discount that reflected the existence of a potentially exploitive controlling shareholder. Why, then, should these minority shareholders subsequently be entitled to share in a sale of control premium that the low price they originally paid for their shares never reflected? If fairness is the abiding principle, should the current minority shareholders who reap such a control premium windfall not be obliged, in turn, to share that windfall with the people from whom they originally purchased their shares?

Commentators have argued that there is another important difference in the case of shares. To appreciate this difference, consider the similarities between the position occupied by controlling shareholders and the position occupied by a corporation's directors. It is without doubt that a corporation's directors are neither allowed to sell their offices, nor to accept payment for voting in connection with any particular matter. Any attempt to profit from their positions would be regarded as a breach of their fiduciary duties. Yet if a controlling shareholder has, as a practical matter, effective control over the assets of the corporation, could it be said that, in exercising that power, the controlling shareholder stands in the same or at least in a similar relationship with the corporation's minority shareholders as do the corporation's directors and officers? Should that controlling shareholder not, therefore, be subject to similar duties?

Berle and Means put forward an argument along these lines in their classic 1932 work, *The Modern Corporation and Private Property*.[19] Commenting on the holding in a preliminary motion that had been brought in the case of *Stanton v. Schenk*, a case in which the final decision had not yet then been rendered, Berle and Means commented, "[I]t apparently involved too great a leap into the dark for the New York court to say that the power going with 'control' is an asset which belongs only to the corporation; and that payment for that power, if it goes anywhere, must go into the corporate treasury."[20]

This characterization of control as a "corporate asset" was taken up again by Berle.[21] The view that all shareholders ought to share in any control premium received by controlling shareholders from the sale of their shares has been echoed by other commentators as well.[22] As Robert Clark has warned, to say that control is a "corporate asset" can be somewhat misleading if interpreted literally. Rather, as Clark explains:

> [T]he phrase *corporate asset* is merely a short-hand reference to the theory's operational meaning, which is that the power to control corporate activities, even as it is represented in ownership of voting stock, should be treated for many legal purposes like the power that

---

19   Adolf A. Berle & Gardiner C. Means, *The Modern Corporation and Private Property* (originally published in 1932 by Harcourt, Brace & World) published with intr. by Murray Weidenbaum & Mark Jensen (New Brunswick, NJ: Transaction Publishers, 1968).

20   *Ibid.* at 216–17.

21   Adolf A. Berle, "The Price of Power: Sale of Corporate Control" (1965) 50 Cornell L.Q. 628.

22   See, for example, William D. Andrews, "The Stockholder's Right to Equal Opportunity in the Sale of Shares" (1965) 78 Harv. L. Rev. 505.

is given to one who occupies an official corporate position such as that of director or officer.[23]

Over time, debate over the question of whether (or to what extent) a controlling shareholder ought to be entitled to receive a premium on the sale of his or her shares that is not generally available to the corporation's minority shareholders has focused broadly upon this "control as corporate asset" theory, on the one hand, or upon a related concept often referred to as a doctrine of "equal opportunity."[24] At a broader level, those opposed to placing any restrictions on the right of controlling shareholders to sell their shares at a premium have argued that such restrictions could impede transfers of control. This would be undesirable, in their view, since sale of control transactions are economically beneficial.[25] Robert Clark has countered that legal rules that forced acquirors to treat all target shareholders alike would actually encourage the most beneficial acquisitions, and deter corporate looters.[26]

The control premium question has been the subject of considerable debate in Canada. One notes that the Kimber Committee, in its influential 1965 report, recommended that private sales of control not be the subject of securities legislation at all, despite their express recognition that such sales may result in a premium being paid for shares that is not shared by minority shareholders. For the Kimber Committee, it was better to leave to the courts "the evolution of a legal doctrine which may impose upon directors or other insiders of a company . . . a fiduciary duty toward other shareholders of such company in cases of change of control" (except in cases of insider trading).[27]

---

23   Clark, *Corporate Law*, above note 15 at 491.

24   See, for example, Bailey & Crawford, "The Takeover Bid by Private Agreement: The Follow-Up Offer Obligation" (1983) 7 Dal. L.J. 93 at 100: "Some commentators argue that corporate shares are a form of personal property which should be freely transferable at whatever price the seller can obtain, even if the consideration involves a premium paid for the sale of a controlling block of shares. On the other hand, others have argued that a premium paid for the purchase of corporate control should be shared equally amongst all shareholders of a corporation. The views of the latter group of commentators can be generally categorized under the corporate asset or the fiduciary duty theories, or the equal opportunity rule."

25   See, for example, Frank H. Easterbrook & Daniel R. Fischel, *The Economic Structure of Corporate Law* (Cambridge: Harvard University Press, 1991) at 126–34.

26   See Clark, *Corporate Law*, above note 15 at 491–98. For further discussion, see Christopher C. Nicholls, *Corporate Finance and Canadian Law*, above note 13 at 327–32.

27   *Report of the Attorney General's Committee on Securities Legislation in Ontario* (Toronto: Ministry of the Attorney General, 1965) at 3.12 (J.R. Kimber, Chair).

The fundamental policy considerations underlying sale of control premia were canvassed by the Ontario Court of Appeal in *Bell et al. v. Source Data Control Ltd. et al.*[28] *Source Data* involved a privately held corporation, rather than a public corporation. The minority shareholders of this corporation had approached a third party hoping to persuade this third party to purchase their shares. These efforts failed. The prospect of becoming a minority shareholder in a private company was, not surprisingly, of little interest to the third party.

However, the controlling shareholder of the private company later approached this same prospective purchaser, indicating that he would also be interested in selling his controlling interest. Evidently the prospect of obtaining control of the company, rather than merely a minority interest, was more appealing. The minority shareholders later agreed to sell their shares to the controlling shareholder, at the price at which they had originally offered to sell their shares to the third party. The controlling shareholder, after acquiring the minority shareholders' shares, subsequently sold them—together with his own—to the third party. The price per share received by the controlling shareholder was higher than the price per share he had previously paid to the minority shareholders. The minority shareholders had not been aware, at the time they agreed to sell their shares to the controlling shareholder, that he had already made arrangements with the third party to "flip" the shares and turn a profit in this way.

At trial, and on appeal to the Ontario Court of Appeal, the claim of the minority shareholders failed. However, in a carefully reasoned dissent in the Court of Appeal, Cory J.A. indicated that, in his view, the controlling shareholder ought to have been found to owe a fiduciary duty to the minority shareholders, a duty which, in Cory J.A.'s opinion, demanded at least that the controlling shareholder disclose to the minority the existence of the third party offer for the company's shares. In support of this view he cited, among other authorities, the British Columbia Court of Appeal's decision in *Dusik v. Newton*,[29] and the New Zealand Court of Appeal's decision in *Coleman v. Myers*,[30] a case that argued for a departure from the rigours of *Percival v. Wright*.[31]

Cory J.A.'s suggestion that controlling shareholders ought to owe a fiduciary duty to minority shareholders has not subsequently found much favour with Canadian courts. Evidently, the broad oppression remedy available under most Canadian corporate law statutes has essentially pre-

28   (1989), 40 B.L.R. 10 (Ont. C.A.) [*Source Data*].

29   (1985), 62 B.C.L.R. 1 (C.A.).

30   [1977] 2 N.Z.L.R. 225 (C.A.).

31   Above note 16.

empted any such development. As McKinlay J.A. suggested in *Brant Investments Ltd. v. Keeprite*:[32] "The enactment of [corporate law oppression remedy] provisions has rendered any argument for a broadening of the categories of fiduciary relationships in the corporate context unnecessary and, in my view, inappropriate."[33]

The current private agreement exemption in Multilateral Instrument 62-104 and the Ontario *Securities Act* may, accordingly, be understood as a workable if imperfect compromise between two competing views. Controlling shareholders of public companies will be allowed to sell their shares at a price somewhat above the prevailing market price, but the extent of that premium is subject to a cap.[34]

4) Limits on Use of the Private Agreement Exemption

Can the private agreement exemption be relied upon more than once in respect of the same target corporation? In other words, could an offeror enter into one agreement with five or fewer sellers and then, in a later, separate transaction, enter into a second agreement with five more sellers, and so on? In each case, the technical requirements of the exemption might be observed meticulously, yet the effect of such "serial" purchases would be to permit a purchaser to acquire shares from many more than five purchasers at a premium which would be denied to shareholders in general. Opinions have been divided on this issue. Although the private agreement exemption was ambiguous on this point, certain Canadian securities regulators and practitioners were long of the view that this exemption ought to be available only once in respect of any one target company. Others countered that no such express limitation appeared in the statute, and, in their view, it was unnecessary and inappropriate to read such a limitation into the legislation.

The Ontario Securities Commission considered the propriety of an aggressive use of the private agreement exemption in *In the Matter of Med-Tech Environmental Limited*.[35] There, an offeror sought to structure a takeover bid as two separate tranches in order to acquire a controlling interest in the shares of a target corporation from more than five shareholders without launching a formal takeover bid. First, the offeror acquired just under 20 percent of the target company's shares by way of

---

32   (1991), 3 O.R. (3d) 289 (C.A.).

33   *Ibid.* at 302.

34   This compromise was crafted by then OSC Chairman James C. Baillie. See D. Johnson & K.D. Rockwell, *Canadian Securities Regulation*, 2d ed. (Toronto: Butterworths, 1998) at 161, n42.

35   (1998), 21 OSCB 7607 [*Med-Tech*].

private agreements with twenty-three of the target company shareholders. Since the offeror had not previously owned any shares in the target company, this acquisition did not constitute a takeover bid, and therefore no exemption from the formal bid rules was required. Immediately after completing that purchase, the offeror purchased an additional 40 percent of the shares of the target corporation in a private agreement with five of the target company shareholders (and at a price not exceeding 115 percent of the market price). Although this second purchase clearly did constitute a takeover bid, the offeror argued that this bid was exempt from the formal takeover bid rules under the private agreement exemption, then found in section 93(1)(c) of the Ontario *Securities Act*.

The result of these two back-to-back purchases, if the offeror's reasoning were accepted, would be to permit the offeror to acquire approximately 60 percent of the target company's shares in transactions involving twenty-eight target company shareholders, without the need to comply with the formal takeover bid rules.

Following a hearing, the Ontario Securities Commission ruled that the section 93(1)(c) exemption had not "been properly relied on,"[36] finding that the offeror had actually been engaged in one continuing takeover bid, rather than separate transactions.

The commission's ruling suggested that merely complying with the technical requirements of the private agreement exemption would not always be enough. Where ostensibly separate transactions are closely linked, securities regulators may be prepared to treat them as a single or continuous transaction—aggregating the number of sellers and so potentially disallowing use of the private agreement exemption.

Applying a principles-based facts and circumstances test to the use of the private agreement exemption involves the kind of analysis with which Canadian securities law practitioners have become familiar.[37] However, regulators often prefer a more bright line rules-based regime to provide greater consistency and predictability in enforcement. Thus, in 1990, the Canadian Securities Administrators proposed imposing an

---

36   *Ibid.* at 7618.

37   The Ontario Securities Commission held as early as 1978 in *Re Cablecasting Ltd.*, [1978] OSCB 37 that it had the authority to issue a cease-trade order under its "public interest" power (s. 127 of the *Securities Act* (Ontario)) to prevent actions that contravened the intent of securities laws, even where there was no violation of the law itself. The Ontario courts have affirmed that proposition. See, for example, *Re Canadian Tire Corp.* (1987), 35 B.L.R. 56 (O.S.C.), aff'd (1987), 59 O.R. (2d) 79 (Div. Ct.). For more detailed discussion about the Commission's broad public interest jurisdiction, see Jeffrey G. MacIntosh & Christopher C. Nicholls, *Securities Law* (Toronto: Irwin Law, 2002) at 355.

express limitation on the use of the provision.[38] That proposal was not adopted. More recently, when proposed draft National Instrument 62-104 was introduced, the CSA once again attempted to explicitly limit the availability of the private agreement exemption to a single use.[39] In the notice accompanying proposed National Instrument 62-104, the CSA argued that this change was "necessary to ensure that the exemption is used for its original purpose of allowing limited transfers by groups of controlling shareholders rather than for the purpose of avoiding the formal bid requirements by characterizing the bid as a series of exempt 'private agreements.'"[40]

The changes proposed in draft National Instrument 62-104 also sought to formalize rules dealing with the timing of the negotiations of private agreements purported to be made in reliance upon the exemption. Specifically, the proposed national instrument provided that, in order for the private agreement exemption to apply, "all of the purchases . . . [must be] negotiated at approximately the same time and . . . completed within 6 months of the first purchase."[41]

These proposed changes to the private agreement were not generally well received. Although one law firm commenting on the rule supported the change, suggesting it would provide "needed clarity to the exemption and, in our view, aligns the exemption with its originally intended purpose,"[42] most other commenters were critical. One comment letter, for example, described the proposed limitations as "extreme";[43] a second argued that the changes "may not be warranted in the Canadian context";[44] a third, insisted that the changes were "not necessary";[45] a fourth contended the proposed restrictions were "not justified";[46] a fifth maintained that the proposed change would have a "negative impact without a clear positive regulatory impact"[47] and

---

38   See *OSC Take-Over Bid Team Submission*, above note 4 at 27.

39   See proposed National Instrument 62-104 [Proposed NI 62-104], s. 5.3(2).

40   (2006), 29 OSCB 3533 at 3537.

41   Proposed NI 62-104, s. 5.3(1)(b).

42   See Comments on Proposed NI 62-104, online: www.albertasecurities.com/securitiesLaw/Regulatory%20Instruments/6/13983/All%20Final%20Comment%20Letters.pdf, Comment of Fraser Milner Casgrain at 4.

43   See Comments on Proposed NI 62-104, *ibid.*, Comment of Davies Ward Phillips & Vineberg LLP at 12.

44   See Comments on Proposed NI 62-104, *ibid.*, Comment of Fasken Martineau at 3.

45   See Comments on Proposed NI 62-104, *ibid.*, Comment of Ogilvy Renault at 4.

46   See Comments on Proposed NI 62-104, *ibid.*, Comment of Ontario Bar Association at 2.

47   See Comments on Proposed NI 62-104, *ibid.*, Comment of Torys at 2.

could lead to "potentially arbitrary and unintended effects."[48] In short, as one commenter put it (after noting that "we are not aware of a compelling need to change this rule"), "if it ain't broke perhaps there is no need to fix it."[49]

When the final version of Multilateral Instrument 62-104 was released, the proposed restrictions on the use of the private agreement exemption had been removed. In the accompanying notice, the CSA said of its decision to revert to the traditional form of private agreement exemption: "Based on the comments received, we agreed that amendments to the exemption should not be made without further research and analysis."[50]

5) "Market Price" for Purposes of the Private Agreement Exemption

The private agreement exemption is available only where purchases of outstanding securities do not exceed 115 percent of the "market price." "Market price" is defined in section 1.11 of Multilateral Instrument 62-104 and section 1.3 of OSC Rule 62-504. Where there is a single published market for the securities in question, the basic rule is that market price is equal to the simple average of the closing price for the twenty business days immediately preceding the date of calculation.[51]

The authors of the Practitioners Report had argued for the use of a *weighted* average, rather than a simple average of closing prices, an eminently sensible proposal that would give greater significance to closing prices on days on which higher volumes of shares changed hands.[52] Using a weighted average lessens the risk of market manipulation for the obvious reason that it is more difficult (certainly more expensive and risky) for miscreants to attempt to create an artificial trading price for shares if the exercise requires the trading of very large numbers of shares.

The calculation of market price has led to more than a few interpretational challenges. In *In the Matter of Selkirk Communications Lim-*

---

48   *Ibid.* at 3.

49   See Comments on Proposed NI 62-104, *ibid.*, Comment of McCarthy Tétrault at 4.

50   See CSA Notice, "Multilateral Instrument 62-104 *Take-Over Bids and Issuer Bids*" (16 November 2007) at 6, online: www.albertasecurities.com/securitiesLaw/ Regulatory%20Instruments/6/13983/2698131%20v1%20-%20CSA%20NO-TICE%20Pub%20Nov%2016,%202007.pdf.

51   There are special rules in cases where this calculation cannot be applied or where the security trades on more than one published market.

52   Practitioners Report, above note 8 at para. 3.12.

ited et al.,[53] the Ontario Securities Commission was asked to consider whether a purchaser ought to be permitted to rely on the private agreement exemption under circumstances where a transaction appeared to comply with the wording of the exemption, but where special circumstances suggested that it might not be appropriate for the transaction to take place on an exempt basis. The *Selkirk* case involved a proposed purchase by Southam from five purchasers of a significant block of outstanding equity securities of Selkirk Communications Limited, a public company. Southam already held about 42 percent of the outstanding securities of the class being purchased and was—by far—the largest single shareholder of Selkirk. Although the price that had been negotiated for this purchase transaction was well within 115 percent of the market price, as defined for purposes of the private agreement exemption, there were two important complications.

First, Southam had agreed in each of the purchase agreements to provide the sellers with "upside price protection." In other words, if Southam were to resell the shares it was acquiring at a price greater than the price paid to the five sellers, Southam agreed to compensate the sellers for the excess. The effect of such a clause, of course, was that it left open the possibility that the final sale price might well exceed 115 percent of the market price of the shares. However, after the date of the original agreement, the parties agreed to "cap" the amount that could be paid as upside price protection at an amount chosen to ensure that the consideration for the shares could not exceed 115 percent of the market price.

Of greater concern was the determination of the applicable market price. On a strict reading of the statute and the accompanying regulations, market price, for the purpose of the private agreement exemption, was to be based upon the price of the shares during the twenty-business-day period ending on the date of the share purchase agreements between Southam and the five vendors. Within that twenty-business-day period, however, another firm had announced its intention to make a takeover bid for the shares of Selkirk at a price per share considerably higher than the current trading price. In response to that announcement, Selkirk's shares jumped in price, and stayed at this elevated price for several days.

Southam announced that it would not tender its block of Selkirk shares to any such bid. The party that had been proposing the bid then realized its bid was bound to fail (since Southam was by far the largest Selkirk shareholder); so it promptly abandoned its bid plans. Once the

---

53   (1988), 11 OSCB 286 [*Selkirk*].

prospect of a generous third-party bid had fallen away, Selkirk's share price, predictably, dropped. However, the effect of the short-lived spike in the price of Selkirk shares was that the average price—calculated over the twenty trading days that included the days of this unusually high price—rose. That meant that Southam, by offering to pay a 15 percent premium over this *average* market price, was actually offering substantially more to the five private vendors than a 15 percent premium over the trading price on the date of the agreements. Yet it was this lower trading price that should probably have been considered more reflective of the "true" market value of the shares at the time the agreements were signed than the "skewed" average price that included the effect of the short-term price bounce.

The *Selkirk* case was heard by a nine-member panel, and led to three separate sets of reasons. Six of the commissioners concurred that Southam should not be entitled to rely on the private agreement exemption based on this skewed market price, even though, as a technical matter, Southam's purchase agreements complied with the terms of that exemption.[54] Three of the commissioners believed:

> [T]here is prejudice to the public interest, in the sense of the public trading markets, for a dominant shareholder to take advantage of a market anomaly to enter into private agreements with a small number of relatively large shareholders that sees the premium created by that market anomaly given exclusively to those shareholders, and to the exclusion of their fellow shareholders.[55]

In separate reasons, three other commissioners harshly criticized "Southam's proposed arrogation of the premium in the market arising from the [proposed takeover bid] announcement, for the benefit of five selected sellers," and concluded that such an action was "contrary to the public interest."[56]

In a third set of reasons, three other members of the panel dissented.[57] In the view of these three commissioners, the legislation did not intend to permit the commission to, in effect, calculate its own market price for the purposes of the private agreement exemption; the relevant market price to be used was the twenty-trailing-business-day price then prescribed by the regulations. In these dissenting reasons,

---

54 Only three of these commissioners, however, were in favour of issuing a cease-trade order.

55 Above note 53, Reasons of Commissioners Beck, Holland, and Waitzer at 303.

56 *Ibid.*, Reasons of Commissioners Salter, Taschereau, and Reid at 319.

57 *Ibid.*, Reasons of Commissioners Blain, Carmichael, and Wigle at 321*ff.*

the commissioners noted that, prior to legislative amendments in 1987, the commission was expressly empowered by the statute to recalculate market price for purposes of the exemption, a power that had deliberately been removed from the Act presumably to enhance certainty.[58] Accordingly, for the dissenting commissioners, it was important that market participants be entitled to rely on the language of the exemption itself, at least in the absence of "clear abuse and perhaps manifest unfairness."[59] For them, Southam ought to have been able to rely on the calculation of market price as provided for by the regulations, with no adjustment to eliminate the effect of the supposedly anomalous prices observed while the market anticipated a rival takeover bid being launched for Selkirk's shares.

The reasons of the six concurring commissioners—that is, those who opposed Southam's use of the exemption—reflect hostility toward the payment of a premium that would not be shared by all shareholders. That hostility seems to be unjustified as a general matter, and especially unjustified on the facts of the *Selkirk* case itself. The use of a trailing average to determine market price is intended to lessen the potential impact of short-term (even one-day) pricing anomalies. Since the legislators evidently intended that market anomalies should not be allowed to distort the market price calculation, it is perhaps tempting to conclude that when a specific, known anomaly has skewed the price calculation—as in the *Selkirk* case—the regulators ought to intervene in an effort to preserve the underlying purpose of the market price test. The good intentions of the regulators, however, cannot compensate for inherent institutional limitations. Unless the party seeking to rely on the private agreement exemption has itself taken steps that have caused the anomalous spike in a target company's share price, it seems imprudent and inappropriate for securities regulators to presume to recalculate market price by choosing to exclude the effect of events to which, in its view, the market has not "validly" reacted. Indeed, the dissenting members of the panel made this very point. As it happened, the market

---

58   This legislative history was not ignored by the other members of the panel. However, among other things, it was argued that there was a distinction to be made between share price fluctuations that might arise from a "generalized expectation" of a possible takeover bid, on the one hand, and a very specific proposed bid, as in the *Selkirk* case, on the other. It was thus argued in the concurring reasons that the commission was no longer intended to recalculate "market price" where anomalies had arisen from "generalized expectations," but that it retained the power to do so where anomalies were the result of very specific proposed bids, as in *Selkirk*. See *ibid.*, Reasons of Commissioners Salter *et al.* at 315*ff.*

59   *Ibid.* at 330.

"break" of October 1987[60] had also occurred during the relevant twenty business day period in *Selkirk*. "Should some adjustment be made for this?" mused the panel.[61] "If one starts making adjustments, where does one stop?"[62]

A similar issue arose in the subsequent case, *In the Matter of H.E.R.O. Industries Ltd.*[63] In that case the panel appeared to concur with the view I have suggested above, namely, that "even if [the Commission] still [has the power to re-calculate 'market price' for purposes of the private agreement exemption], it is probably best left for the most egregious cases, such as those in which there is some evidence of collusion, or market manipulation, or some other active interference with the auction market mechanism upon which the 115 percent test is based."[64] The *H.E.R.O.* case raised an additional and more intriguing issue, however. The dispute surrounded the use of the private agreement exemption not by an offeror seeking control, but rather by a rival bidder seeking to thwart an outstanding takeover bid. H.E.R.O. was a publicly traded corporation. Gordon Capital Corporation had launched a takeover bid for the shares of H.E.R.O. at a substantial premium over the market price of H.E.R.O.'s shares. Prior to the launch of this bid, H.E.R.O. had two significant shareholders (in addition to the bidder, Gordon Capital, itself): Middlefield (which held about 29.8 percent of H.E.R.O.'s shares) and New Frontiers (which held about 18.6 percent). Following the launch of Gordon Capital's bid, the trading price of H.E.R.O.'s shares rose. Middlefield was tracking the share price rise. Each day that the price rose, of course, the market price of the shares, for purposes of the private agreement exemption, also increased. Eventually, that market price, plus the 15 percent premium permitted under the private agreement exemption, made it possible for Middlefield to offer to purchase New Frontiers' shares in H.E.R.O. at a price slightly higher than Gordon Capital's bid price, yet in a transaction that would be exempt from the formal takeover bid rules.

---

60   The market "break" or market crash of 19 October 1987 was the largest single-day stock market price fall in history—larger, even, than any single-day fall in 1929. On that day, the Dow Jones Industrial Average fell by 22.6 percent. By comparison, the largest single day fall in the Dow in 1929 (on 28 October 1929) was 12.8 percent. See *Presidential Task Force on Market Mechanisms* (the "Brady Report") (January 1988) at 1, online: http://ia700308.us.archive.org/5/items/reportofpresiden01unit/reportofpresiden01unit.pdf.

61   Above note 53, Reasons of Commissioners Blain *et al.* at 334.

62   *Ibid.*

63   (1990), 13 OSCB 3775.

64   *Ibid.* at 3785.

The issue before the commission was whether or not this proposed purchase by Middlefield (which would stymie the Gordon Capital bid) ought to be allowed to proceed. The commission actually doubted whether Middlefield's offer to purchase shares from New Frontiers was a takeover bid at all (because New Frontiers was a foreign corporation and so the offer was not made to anyone in Ontario). Moreover, even if it were a takeover bid, Middlefield's offer was, in the panel's view, at worst opportunistic, but not "collusive or manipulative."[65] Nevertheless, the commission emphasized that, regardless of the terms of the specific rules in what is now Part XX of the *Securities Act*, it was essential to take account of underlying policy considerations. In particular, they noted concern over the use of the private agreement exemption "that has the effect of defeating a rival bid made to the public at a premium price."[66] The commission regarded Middlefield's actions in this case to be "clearly prejudicial to the public interest"[67] because the minority shareholders of H.E.R.O. had been deprived of the chance to tender their shares to the Gordon Capital bid at a premium price. Accordingly, although the commission did not prevent Middlefield from acquiring the H.E.R.O. shares from New Frontiers, the panel did extend a prior temporary cease-trade order in respect of those shares, subject to certain conditions that would permit Middlefield to tender the shares to Gordon Capital's bid, or to launch a takeover bid of its own for H.E.R.O.

D. PRIVATE (TARGET) COMPANY NON-REPORTING ISSUER EXEMPTION

1) Basic Requirements

An exemption from the formal bid requirements is available where the target company is not a reporting issuer, there is no published market for its securities, and the total number of holders of the class of securities subject to the bid is not more than fifty (exclusive of employees and former employees).[68] This exemption is sometimes referred to informally as the "private company exemption" although, as a technical matter, the companies to which this exemption applies need not be "private companies" as that term is defined in section 1(1) of the *Secu-*

---

65   *Ibid.*
66   *Ibid.* at 3789.
67   *Ibid.* at 3794.
68   MI 62-104, s. 4.3; *Securities Act* (Ontario), s. 100.2; OSC Rule 62-504, s. 6.1.

rities Act, a definition, it must be said, that no longer, in fact, is of any practical use under the Ontario *Securities Act*.[69]

2) Rationale for Exemption

The purchase of the shares of companies that are not publicly traded and have a relatively limited number of shareholders would not typically involve the same risks of target shareholder exploitation that a bid for a public company might entail. Shareholders of private, closely held companies generally have access to better information about the company (and accordingly its value) than the widely dispersed shareholders of a public company. They would also typically have opportunities to meet face-to-face and discuss with other shareholders any offer that was made for their shares, making it unlikely that they could be pressured to hastily accept an inadequate, opportunistic bid. Finally, the very fact that the shares of private corporations are not traded in public markets means that there is a less compelling need for regulatory intervention aimed at protecting investors with a view to boosting confidence in the capital markets.

But not all private companies are alike. One could envision a private company with a considerable number of shareholders. If, for example, a larger private company had issued shares to a significant number of its employees, such a company could well have hundreds of shareholders—many of whom would be quite as removed from the company's decision-making process as shareholders of a public company. Yet an offer to acquire shares of such a "widely held" private company would continue to meet the exemption requirements of Multilateral Instrument 62-104, section 4.3 and Ontario *Securities Act*, section 100.2. In such a case, parties involved in an acquisition transaction might be well-advised to voluntarily adopt—with suitable modifications—some of the protective features of the Canadian takeover bid regime in order to prevent later complaints of unfairness. But it would be cumbersome and unnecessary to impose the formal takeover bid requirements in all

---

69 The phrase *private company* was originally included in the statute for purposes of a registration exemption formerly found in s. 35(2) of the *Securities Act* (Ontario), and a corresponding exemption from the prospectus requirement formerly found in s. 73(1)(a). In place of the old "private company" registration and prospectus exemptions, National Instrument 45-106 provides exemptions for certain sales of securities of a "private issuer," as defined in s. 2.4 of National Instrument 45-106. Once again, however, the sort of issuer referred to in Multilateral Instrument 62-104, s. 4.3 and *Securities Act* (Ontario), s. 100.2 need not be a "private issuer" as defined in National Instrument 45-106.

cases as a blunt weapon aimed at guarding against potential abuses in the relatively rare instances of private companies with unusually large numbers of shareholders.

3) Number of Securityholders

The availability of the private company exemption depends, among other things, on determining that the "number of holders" of the securities of the class subject to the bid "is not more than 50, exclusive of holders who are in the employment" of the target or an affiliate of the target, or were formerly in such employment (and acquired their securities while in such employment). In the case of most small issuers, there is no doubt that the number of shareholders is well within this prescribed limit. But occasionally determining the number of holders of a company's shares for purposes of the private company or non-reporting issuer exemption can be a complicated matter.

In *In the Matter of Med-Tech Environmental Limited*,[70] for example, the company in question had a total of sixty-two *registered* shareholders. It was apparent that, although only sixty-two shareholders appeared on the share register, many of those registered shareholders held shares on behalf of yet other *beneficial* owners of shares. Accordingly, in determining whether or not the private company exemption was available in the case of a purchase of more than 20 percent of the shares of this company, two critical questions needed to be answered:

- Did the reference then found in section 93(1)(d) of the Ontario *Securities Act* (the predecessor to section 100.2 and OSC Rule 62-504, section 6.1) to "holders" of securities refer to *registered* or to *beneficial* holders of securities?
- Were the shares of this corporation held by more than fifty holders *exclusive of employees and former employees*? (And, as a corollary issue, who is to be considered an "employee" for purposes of section 93(1)(d))?

On the first point, the Ontario Securities Commission expressed the view that "holders," for purposes of section 93(1)(d) means *registered* holders of securities.[71] The commission favoured this interpretation both because it was simpler and also because, in the panel's view, "absent specific language to the contrary, 'holder' normally means the person shown as the shareholder on the register of shareholders at the

---

70   *Med-Tech*, above note 35.
71   *Ibid.* at 7614.

relevant time."[72] One of the most significant effects of limiting the term *holder* in section 93(1)(d) to registered shareholders would occur in cases where the employees or former employees chose to hold their shares of a private corporation through their own holding corporations. In such cases, even if shares had originally been issued only to employees, the share register of the private corporation ("Target") might well show more than fifty shareholders, none of whom was in the employment of Target (since only the individual employees, and not their holding corporations, could be considered to be in the employment of Target). A similar outcome could occur if the registered holder were a trust or a nominee. It is possible, though uncertain, that a party seeking to rely on the section 93(1)(d) exemption might be able to persuade the commission that the exemption ought nevertheless to be available by leading specific evidence as to the identities of the beneficial owners of the shares (including the beneficial owners of the shares of incorporated registered shareholders). In the *Med-Tech* case itself, the OSC said only that "if . . . the beneficial holders test is the applicable one [a proposition that the panel appeared to reject earlier in the decision] it was incumbent on [the offeror], in claiming to have the benefit of the exemption in clause (d) available to it, to establish that there were no more than 50 beneficial holders."[73] But in fact the offeror in that case had led no evidence on this point.

On the second point, concerning the meaning of the phrase *in the employment of the offeree issuer*, the commission considered, in particular, whether officers and directors of a corporation ought to be considered employees for the purposes of section 93(1)(d). Superficially, it might at first seem obvious that corporate officers are employees of the corporation and, equally, that corporate directors—*qua* directors—are not. But the issue is not as straightforward as that. Although top officers of a corporation share many attributes with ordinary employees— they may be paid a salary, for example—it has been argued that their relationship with the corporation is materially different from the relationship between the corporation and employees. Some nominal officers, of course, may not be actively engaged in the business's operations at all. More fundamentally, as Laskin J. (as he then was) of the Supreme Court of Canada once put it, albeit in a different context: "[S]enior officers of a corporation are 'top management' and not mere employees."[74] There are technical arguments of statutory interpretation that also sup-

---

72   *Ibid.*
73   *Ibid.*
74   *Canadian Aero Service Ltd. v. O'Malley*, [1974] S.C.R. 592.

port the view that officers, for purposes of the section 93(1)(d) exemption, were not intended to be considered persons in the employment of the target corporation. As the commission panel noted in its *Med-Tech* ruling, the *Securities Act* "in various provisions, distinguishes between employees and officers and directors. See e.g., clause 76(5)(c) and subsection 118(1). The commission has treated 'mere' officers and directors as being distinct and different from employees."[75] Accordingly, the commission concluded that, for purposes of section 93(1)(d), officers and directors would *not* be considered persons "in the employment of" the target corporation. Thus, any shares held by officers and directors would count in determining whether or not the shares of the corporation were held by more than fifty holders.

What the OSC's decision did not discuss was why, as a policy matter, shares held by officers and directors ought not to be treated in the same way as shares held by rank and file employees. Presumably, the private issuer exemption exists to enable purchasers to acquire a controlling interest in a corporation in circumstances where the protections of the formal takeover bid rules are unnecessary. An unlimited number of shares may be held by employees or former employees without placing the availability of this exemption in jeopardy; surely that is because it is assumed that (a) employee shareholders have access to information about the company that makes the protections of the formal takeover bid rules unnecessary or, at least, overly burdensome relative to the benefits; and (b) legislators did not wish to discourage or inhibit the issuance of shares to corporate employees.

But if the rationale for the private company exemption derives from the notion that corporate employees—unlike outside investors—have superior information about the target company, surely the exemption ought to extend to officers and directors who would be expected to have even greater access to corporate information than other more junior employees. Nor does it seem likely that issuing shares to officers and directors is somehow less advantageous than issuing shares to junior employees. In fact, there are often compelling reasons for a corporation to seek to align the interests of its most senior officers and directors with those of the corporation itself (or its shareholders)—by issuing shares to them. The commission's technical reading of the language of section 93(1)(d) is also somewhat surprising given the frequent pronouncements in other contexts—especially the enforcement context—about the need for the underlying policy of the *Securities Act*,

---

75   *Med-Tech*, above note 35 at 7614.

rather than formal technical rules, to govern the actions of market actors and the regulatory role of the commission.

E. FOREIGN BID EXEMPTION

Canadian securities regulation could, in theory, be designed to protect Canadian securityholders in connection with any offer made to purchase their securities, even where the principal market for the issuer's securities lay elsewhere. Such broad rules, however, would very likely do more harm than good. In particular, if the number of Canadian shareholders of a company were few, and Canadian takeover rules were onerous, bidders might understandably choose not to extend offers to Canadian shareholders in the first place.

Canadian takeover rules provide an express exemption from the formal takeover bid requirements where a bid is made for securities of a company that has a relatively small number of Canadian securityholders, and for which the greatest volume of trading occurs in a published market outside of Canada. The intent of the exemption is to facilitate offers made in accordance with the laws of a foreign jurisdiction for companies that have relatively few Canadian securityholders. At one time, this exemption was limited to bids made in accordance with the laws of so-called "recognized jurisdictions,"[76] although in some cases, where there was a minimal number of securityholders in a province, and the bid was made in accordance with the laws of a foreign jurisdiction that was *not* a recognized jurisdiction, securities regulators were prepared to grant an exemption from the takeover bid rules.[77]

While it is likely that the target of most offers of this sort will be foreign companies, the exemption is not limited to offers for foreign companies, as the CSA itself pointed out in its notice accompanying the

---

76   See (former) *Securities Act* (Ontario), s. 93(1)(e). The recognized jurisdictions for this purpose included the United States and the United Kingdom, provided that the bid made in those jurisdictions was in compliance with applicable takeover laws (or, in the case of a bid in the United Kingdom, in compliance with The City Code on Takeovers and Mergers) and was not exempt from those laws or rules. Recognition Order 62-904 (1997), 20 OSCB 1035.

77   See, for example, *In the Matter of Emerson Exploration Inc. and Terra Gold Mining Inc.* (6 August 2005), OSCB, online: www.osc.gov.on.ca/en/Securities-Law_ord_20050819_2113_emersonexploration.htm. (The B.C. and Ontario Securities Commissions granted exemption in the case of a bid by an Australian company made in accordance with Australian law, where the number of shareholders in B.C. and Ontario were *de minimis*.)

release of Multilateral Instrument 62-104.[78] Specifically, such an offer will be exempt from the formal bid requirements where[79]

- less than 10 percent of the target company's registered shareholders have a Canadian address;
- the offeror reasonably believes that securityholders in Canada hold less than 10 percent of the securities subject to the bid;
- the published market on which the greatest dollar volume of trading in securities of the target class in the last twelve months is outside Canada;
- securityholders in each Canadian jurisdiction are entitled to participate in the bid on terms at least as favourable as those available to securityholders in general; and
- bid material sent to securityholders is filed with Canadian securities regulators and sent to Canadian securityholders and, where those materials are not in English, an English summary is sent to Canadian securityholders in provinces other than Quebec, and, in Quebec, a French or French and English summary is sent to Quebec securityholders, or, where a notice or advertisement of the bid has been published, an advertisement of the bid explaining how securityholders may obtain or get access to bid documents is published in the relevant Canadian jurisdictions and filed with Canadian securities regulators.

F. *DE MINIMIS* LOCAL HOLDINGS EXEMPTION

A formal bid exemption is available where there is a relatively trivial number of securityholders in any particular Canadian province or territory (that is, fewer than fifty) and where such securityholders own, in the aggregate, a *de minimis* percentage of securities of the class that is the target of the offer (that is, less than 2 percent in total).[80] To rely upon this exemption, offerors must ensure that securityholders in each jurisdiction are entitled to participate in the bid on terms at least as favourable as the terms that apply to the "general body of security hold-

---

78   Above note 50 at 6.
79   MI 62-104, s. 4.10; *Securities Act* (Ontario), s. 100.3; OSC Rule 62-504, s. 6.2.
80   MI 62-104, s. 4.5; *Securities Act* (Ontario), s. 100.4; OSC Rule 62-504, s. 6.2(2).

ers of the same class,"[81] and that material relating to the bid is sent to securityholders and filed with Canadian securities regulators.[82]

Canada's securities regulators have long been concerned about the prospect of selective bids, made to securityholders in some jurisdictions, but not in others. Such selective behaviour could have the effect of undermining one of the key goals of takeover bid regulation, ensuring that all shareholders of a target corporation are treated alike. In 1997, the CSA promulgated National Policy 62-201.[83] This National Policy indicated that if a bidder made a bid in one Canadian jurisdiction, but not in others, the securities regulator in the jurisdiction in which the bid was made may issue a cease-trade order to stop the bid from proceeding, after giving the bidder an opportunity to show, if it could, why the bid does not offend relevant public policy considerations. This view was recently reiterated in National Policy 62-203.[84]

G. HISTORICAL NOTE: THE FORMER STOCK EXCHANGE BID EXEMPTION

Until recently, Canadian provincial securities statutes provided that the formal takeover bid rules would not apply where the bid was undertaken through the facilities of a recognized stock exchange and in compliance with the exchange's own takeover bid rules.[85] At one time, the Toronto Stock Exchange had a parallel set of formal takeover bid rules that were similar, but not identical, to the formal bid rules set out in the Ontario *Securities Act*. However, little use was made of these alternative rules,[86] and the Exchange repealed them as of 1 January 2005. When the CSA adopted the final version of Multilateral Instrument 62-104, the accompanying notice explained that the stock exchange takeover bid exemption had been deleted because

---

81 MI 62-104, s. 4.5(c); *Securities Act* (Ontario), s. 100.4 (2).
82 MI 62-104, s. 4.5(d); OSC Rule 62-504, s. 6.2(2).
83 (1997), 20 OSCB 3523.
84 National Policy 62-203 (2008), 31 OSCB 1319, s. 2.3.
85 See (former) *Securities Act* (Ontario), s. 93(1)(a). An equivalent exemption was found in the original draft of proposed NI 62-104 at s. 5.10.
86 See, for example, "TSX Notice – Approval of Amendments to Parts V, VI and VII of the Toronto Stock Exchange Company Manual in respect of Non-Exempt Issuers, Changes in Structure of Issuers' Capital and Delisting Procedures" (2004), 27 OSCB 9057 at 9063: "Over the past two years, TSX has not received any applications for bids through the facilities of the exchange."

both TSX and the TSX Venture Exchange have recently repealed their rules governing take-over bids. We have decided that only normal course issuer bids will be permitted through a designated exchange but all other bids, exempt or otherwise, will have to be made in compliance with the Instrument.

H. CONCLUSION

The definition of "take-over bid" in Canadian securities legislation is deliberately cast very widely in an effort to ensure that the interests of minority shareholders of public corporations are protected when there are major share sales of public corporations. In many instances, however, it is recognized that it would be inappropriate or inefficient to require all takeover bids to comply with the complete panoply of formal takeover bid rules, and so exemptions from those rules are available. To fully appreciate the importance of these exemptions it is necessary to have a detailed understanding of the formal bid rules that apply in the case of takeover bids that are *not* exempt. Those formal takeover bid rules were discussed in Chapter 5.

Exempt takeover bids typically arise following direct negotiations between a bidder and shareholders of the target company, with directors and officers of the target company playing a minor role at most (unless, of course, they are themselves shareholders participating in the negotiations). In the next chapter, we consider those takeover bids in which the role of the target board and management team moves to centre stage: hostile bids.

CHAPTER 7

HOSTILE BIDS AND DEFENSIVE TACTICS

A. INTRODUCTION

When one corporation decides to combine with another, the transaction is usually undertaken following negotiation. Members of the management of each of the two corporate parties hammer out a deal, working with the co-operation of their respective boards of directors and anticipating both boards' enthusiastic endorsement of the final agreement. Such deals are often described as "friendly" transactions, not because the mood at the negotiating table is invariably chummy or non-confrontational, but to distinguish this sort of mutually voluntary deal from "hostile" or "unsolicited" acquisitions in which the managers of the company to be acquired are actively opposed to the transaction.

Frequently, the impetus for friendly transactions is not the acquisitive desires of the "buying" corporation, but rather a tottering "selling" corporation's struggle for self-preservation. (Schumpeter's "creative destruction"[1] has more intuitive appeal for firms offering creativity than for firms undergoing destruction.) Corporations facing competitive pressures will occasionally announce publicly that they are "pursuing financial or strategic alternatives." This genteel code phrase sometimes signals a state of increasing desperation to sell major assets to raise much-needed cash, and sometimes—more dramatically—is a

---

1   Joseph Alois Schumpeter, *Capitalism, Socialism and Democracy* (New York: Harper, 1942).

transparent appeal to prospective buyers to bid for the very company itself. Indeed, it is sometimes said that by the time a corporation publicly announces its "pursuit of alternatives," it has already exhausted efforts to find a suitable strategic partner or buyer behind the scenes. In these latter cases it is as if the company has hung a virtual "for sale" sign on its doors. It is soliciting offers. And the (hoped for) parade of potential buyers will be a welcome sight for the hapless target company's directors and officers.

There are many advantages to pursuing a deal in a "friendly" way. Not the least of these advantages is that a friendly transaction may be structured in a mutually favourable way. The players enjoy the luxury of selecting strategically from the menu of M & A structure options referred to elsewhere in this book (amalgamations, plans of arrangement, reorganizations, takeover bids) to take full and careful account of accounting, tax, securities law, and other considerations.

But not all transactions are friendly or "solicited" by the managers of target companies. Sometimes one corporation will decide it wishes to acquire control of another very much against the wishes of that target corporation's board of directors and management. Such a transaction is referred to colloquially as a "hostile" takeover (or sometimes—particularly by sanctimonious bidders themselves and their well-heeled (and well-paid) advisors—as an "unsolicited" bid). Hostile takeovers can come about in a number of ways. Often, a bidder will initially approach a prospective target hoping to pursue a friendly deal; but when these advances are rebuffed by the intended target, the bidder may switch tactics and "go hostile" instead. Or, again, a hostile takeover may be launched by a bidder immediately after the intended target has announced its own intention to complete a *friendly* deal with a different party. The fact that a company has chosen to undertake a friendly acquisition is typically understood in the business community to have placed that company on the market, or "in play."[2] Having essentially declared itself to be up for auction, a company in such a position will not be surprised to see rival bids emerge, though these interloping bids may by no means be welcome. Indeed, parties to friendly deals frequently go to some lengths to guard their transaction jealously from such outside interference. More will be said about such "deal protection measures" later in this chapter.

---

2   This is not to suggest that every proposed business combination invariably signals that either or both prospective parties to that transaction are "in play." The phrase *in play* and its ambiguous meaning in the takeover law lexicon are discussed in somewhat greater detail later in this chapter.

The remainder of this chapter will focus on hostile bids although it should be said that the distinction between hostile and friendly bids in the real world can be a little blurred. For example, many transactions that are concluded and reported in the press as friendly deals actually start as hostile transactions; only when it becomes clear to the target that no better alternative can be found do negotiations begin, leading to a transaction ultimately endorsed by the target board of directors. And some hostile bids begin as friendly transactions. Alas, negotiations that begin well may encounter some stumbling block and break down, but not before one of the parties has concluded that an acquisition would make such good business sense that the deal is worth pursuing even without the blessing or co-operation of the target board.

Empirical research on hostile bids has suggested that they have always represented a minority of takeover deals. Summarizing empirical studies on the matter, for example, Becht, Bolton, and Röell report: "Even at their pre-1990 peak hostile bids never represented more than 30% of all USA deals. . . . Between 1990 and 1998 only 4% of all USA deals were hostile at some stage and hostile bidders acquired 2.6% of the targets."[3] Weston and Weaver, studying data for the period 1985 to 2000, conclude that "the median level of hostile M & A activity to the total worldwide value of transactions is 3.3 percent."[4] Recent empirical work by Rossi and Volpin indicates that hostile bids are more frequent in countries that offer shareholders better protection. They suggest that this observation might be explained by the fact that "good protection for minority shareholders makes control more contestable by reducing the private benefits of control."[5]

In 2011, Allen & Overy reported an apparently dramatic "776% increase in value of public hostile acquisitions."[6] However, on closer scrutiny this apparently remarkable jump in hostile deal activity becomes rather less eye popping. The reported 776% increase is based on a comparison of the total value of all hostile acquisitions in the first half of 2011 with the value of hostile acquisitions for the same period in 2010. In each

---

3   Marco Becht, Patrick Bolton & Ailsa Röell, "Corporate Governance and Control" in George M. Constantinides *et al.*, eds., *Handbook of the Economics of Finance*, vol. 1A (Amsterdam: Elsevier, 2003) 1 at 51 [notes and references omitted].

4   J. Fred Weston & Samuel C. Weaver, *Mergers & Acquisitions* (New York: McGraw-Hill, 2001) at 114.

5   Stefano Rossi & Paolo Volpin, "Cross-Country Determinants of Mergers and Acquisitions," ECGI Working Paper Series in Finance, Working Paper No. 25/2003 (September 2003) at 3, online: http://ssrn.com/abstract_id=395020.

6   Allen & Overy, *The Allen & Overy M & A Index H1 2011*, online: www.allenovery.com.

case, the number of deals was modest: three for the first half of 2010, and seven for the first half of 2011.[7] To put those numbers in perspective, Allen & Overy reported a total of 1,106 transactions for the first half of 2010, and 1,206 for the first half of 2011.[8] Accordingly, hostile deals accounted for less than one-third of 1 percent of all deals in the first half of 2010, and just over one-half of 1 percent of all deals in the first half of 2011. In terms of deal values (the basis on which the 776 percent increase was calculated), the total dollar value of hostile deals in the first half of 2010 was U.S. $794 million; the total dollar value of hostile deals in the first half of 2011 was U.S. $6.953 billion.[9] But, again, as a fraction of all deals, hostile acquisitions in both periods was still quite small (less than 1 percent): about .09 percent for the first half of 2010 and about .64 percent for the first half of 2011.

Conventional wisdom once held that the Canadian takeover market, if anything, was generally characterized by fewer hostile bids than many other jurisdictions—especially the United States. But for a number of reasons the legal and regulatory environment in Canada may be more amenable to hostile takeovers than in the U.S. As indicated earlier in Chapter 1, a recent study of Canadian hostile takeover bids with a deal value in excess of U.S. $50 million indicated that there were fifty-two such transactions from 1 January 2006 to 30 June 2010.[10]

B. HOSTILE BIDS: GOOD, BAD, OR INDIFFERENT?

Hostile acquisitions were by no means an invention of the late twentieth century. Patrick Gaughan notes that one can trace the first major hostile takeover in America to the 1860s.[11] And by the 1960s, there had been enough concern in the United States over takeovers—including hostile takeovers—to prompt Senator Harrison Williams to famously proclaim the need for new federal takeover rules to stop the "white-collar pirates"

---

7   *Ibid.* at 5, "Global Deal Summary" Table.
8   *Ibid.*
9   *Ibid.*
10 See *Blakes Canadian Hostile Bids Study*, First Edition (Winter 2010/11), online: www.blakes.com/english/legal_updates/reference_guides/Hostile_take_over_bid_study_2011.pdf.
11 Patrick A. Gaughan, *Mergers, Acquisitions and Corporate Restructurings* (New York: John Wiley & Sons, 1989) at 22.

who were seizing control of "proud old companies."[12] In fact, even be-fore Senator Williams's takeover reforms were enacted in the United States, takeover bid provisions had been included in the Ontario *Securities Act*, becoming "the first of their kind adopted in North America."[13]

The concern over hostile takeover bids in the 1960s was also salient enough to lead Professor Henry Manne to write his paper "Mergers and the Market for Corporate Control."[14] (This paper, and its implications for takeover law and policy, are discussed briefly later in this chapter.) But it is generally thought that hostile takeovers were still relatively uncommon, at least among the largest industrial players, until the 1974 takeover by Inco of ESB Inc. This transaction is sometimes said to her-ald the beginning of the modern hostile tender offer phenomenon in America,[15] in large part because of the involvement of a "bulge bracket"[16] investment banker acting on behalf of the hostile bidder. That the hos-tile bidder in the case was, in fact, a Canadian (and hence, from the U.S. perspective, a foreign) company was, evidently, not lost on those who wished to garner political support in opposition to the bid.

---

12   111 Cong. Rec. 28,257 (22 October 1965). Steven Davidoff notes that concern about "abusive and coercive" tender offers in the 1960s had first been raised by the U.S. Securities and Exchange Commission, under the leadership of its then Chairman, Manuel F. Cohen. See Steven M. Davidoff, "Takeover Theory and the Law and Economics Movement,"online: http://ssrn.com/abstract=1802733.

13   Frank Iacobucci, "Planning and Implementing Defences to Takeover Bids: The Directors' Role" (1980) 5 Can. Bus. L.J. 131 at 160. At the time this article was written, Frank Iacobucci was dean of the University of Toronto's Faculty of Law. He later served as a justice of the Supreme Court of Canada.

14   Henry Manne, "Mergers and the Market for Corporate Control" (1965) 73 J. Pol. Econ. 110 [Manne, "Mergers"].

15   Bebchuk *et al.*, for example, note that prior to the Inco bid, hostile takeovers "were uncommon, particularly for large, established targets." Lucian Bebchuk, John Coates IV, & Guhan Subramanian, "The Powerful Antitakeover Force of Staggered Boards: Theory, Evidence and Policy" (2002) 54 Stan. L. Rev. 887 at 940. Lipton and Rowe have likewise described the Inco bid as a "watershed event" and "an unprecedented case of one blue-chip industrial making a hostile bid for another. The willingness of Morgan Stanley, then the pre-eminent investment banker to America's corporate establishment, to serve as adviser to the bidder was confirmation that hostile takeovers were no longer the province of the upstart or outsider." See Martin Lipton & Paul K. Rowe, "Pills, Polls and Professors: A Reply to Professor Gilson" (2002) 27 Del. J. Corp. Law 1 at 4–5.

16   The term *bulge bracket* refers to the investment banking firms that are listed at the top of the "tombstone" advertisements published after a public offering has been completed, indicating that they sold the largest part of the offering. The bulge bracket firms are the largest, most prestigious, firms at the top of the in-vestment banking hierarchy, although following the recent financial crisis there has been something of a realignment of the investment banking industry.

New financing techniques emerged to facilitate and encourage mega mergers. Accordingly, size and frequency of hostile takeover bids increased materially beginning through the late 1970s and 1980s. The directors of even the largest corporations became mindful of the possibility of becoming the target of a hostile bid. The emerging threat of management displacement became the subject of political and economic debate. Were hostile takeover bids a blessing for target company shareholders and for the economy generally? Or was there something nefarious and economically destructive about hostile takeover bids?

The terms of this debate were importantly influenced by Manne's celebrated 1965 article[17] arguing that the threat of a hostile takeover bid could act as an effective check on managerial excess, or, in economic terms, "agency costs."[18] If corporate managers performed poorly, the price of their corporation's shares would fall. If the price were to fall far enough, an astute bidder would recognize that, in the hands of better management, the value of the corporation could be greatly improved and so would be enticed to launch a takeover bid, with a view to replacing the board and senior management. There was, as Manne put it, "an active market for corporate control," and the operation of this market gave "shareholders both power and protection commensurate with their interest in corporate affairs."[19] On the "market for corporate control" view of the world, hostile takeover bids were beneficial to target company shareholders, and to the economy as a whole, as assets moved to their highest valued use. Hostile takeover bidders were not the "pirates" and "raiders" of whom Senator Williams warned. They were "catalysts for value" and heroes of the free market economy.

Many financial economists roundly endorsed the notion that hostile takeover bids were beneficial and provided an important check on man-

---

17   Manne, "Mergers," above note 14.
18   Agency problems are regarded by many contemporary scholars as the central issue in modern corporate law. Put simply, when one person (the economic principal) has the residual economic interest in business assets while a different person (the economic agent) has effective control over those assets, the interests of the agent and the principal will, predictably, diverge. Costs will therefore arise that do not exist when a single person has both ownership and control over those assets. It has become trite to observe in works aimed at a legal audience that the terms *agent* and *principal* are used in an economic sense, *not* in their legal sense. The seminal paper on the agency costs problem is Michael Jensen & William Meckling, "Theory of the Firm: Managerial Behavior, Agency Costs and Ownership Structure" (1976) 3 J.F. Econ. 305. For a discussion of agency costs theory in the Canadian corporate law context, see Christopher C. Nicholls, *Corporate Law* (Toronto: Emond Montgomery, 2005) at 27*ff.*
19   Manne, "Mergers," above note 14 at 112.

agerial lethargy and overreaching. Empirical research was undertaken demonstrating that hostile takeover bids were good news for the shareholders of target companies and the economy generally,[20] and, thus, indicting those corporate law statutes and judicial decisions that impeded takeovers as generally bad for shareholders.[21] There was significant support for the idea within the legal academy as well. As Ronald Gilson put it, "the market for corporate control is crucial to the corporate structure because neither other markets nor a fiduciary 'fairness' standard effectively constrains some forms of management self-dealing."[22] Macey and Miller have even suggested that "the market for corporate control lies at the heart of the American system of corporate governance."[23]

Even those supportive of the theory underlying the importance of the market for corporate control have acknowledged, though, that some practical limitations may constrain the effectiveness of unsolicited bids as a check on smaller-scale managerial opportunism.[24] And some scholars and legal practitioners, including, notably, Martin Lipton, the creator of the "shareholders rights plan" or "poison pill," have been critical, or even dismissive, of the claimed benefits of the "market for corporate control."[25] Critics of takeovers have alleged that the destructive effects of unconstrained corporate acquisitions could include

---

20 Michael Jensen has been an especially vigorous advocate of the benefits of hostile takeovers. See, for example, Michael Jensen, "Agency Costs of Free Cash Flow, Corporate Finance and Takeovers" (1986) 76 Am. Econ. Rev. 323; Richard Ruback & Michael Jenson, "The Market for Corporate Control: The Scientific Evidence" (1983) 11 J. Fin. Econ. 5. See also Gregor Andrade, Mark L. Mitchell, & Erik Stafford, "New Evidence and Perspectives on Mergers" (2001) Harvard Business School Working Paper No. 01-070.

21 See, for example, Robert Daines, "Does Delaware Law Improve Firm Value?" (2001) 62 J.F. Econ. 525. Roberta Romano, a strong advocate of competitive federalism in U.S. corporate law, has asserted that "because the overwhelming balance of research views takeovers favourably, the more restrictive of takeovers, the more ill-conceived the regulation." Roberta Romano, "A Guide to Takeovers: Theory, Evidence and Regulation" (1992) 9 Yale J. on Reg. 119 at 177.

22 Ronald Gilson, "A Structural Approach to Corporations: The Case against Defensive Tactics in Tender Offers" (1981) 33 Stan. L. Rev. 819 at 845.

23 Jonathan R. Macey & Geoffrey P. Miller, "Corporate Governance and Commercial Banking: A Comparative Examination of Germany, Japan, and the United States" (1995) 48 Stan. L. Rev. 73 at 101.

24 Richard A. Posner, "Law and the Theory of Finance: Some Intersections" (1986) 54 Geo. Wash. L. Rev. 159 at 166–67.

25 See, for example, Lipton & Rowe, "Pills, Polls and Professors," above note 15 and text accompanying note 67, below in this chapter. For the views of a leading Canadian takeover practitioner, see Gordon Coleman, "Poison Pills in Canada" (1989) 15 Can. Bus. L.J. 1.

loss of employment,[26] loss of innovation,[27] and even a general erosion of trust.[28] In any event, as a recent survey of the academic literature puts it, "although the empirical evidence on the profitability of takeovers is extensive, the conclusions do not entirely converge as to whether takeovers create or destroy company value."[29] However equivocal the empirical evidence may be, there have long been significant popular suspicions about the merits of hostile bids. These have been alluded to earlier in this book. Hostile bidders and their financial advisors have often been painted in the popular media as "raiders," "looters," and "bust-up artists"—terms not usually associated with business leaders who command widespread public affection and approval. In Canada, foreign bidders have been eyed with particular suspicion by finger-wagging nationalists warning about the dire consequences of an imminent "hollowing out" of Canadian business—a "danger," it is supposed, that patriotic Canadian directors could and would prevent if only given the tools needed to fend off foreign raiders. (Why it is only *hostile* for-

---

26   See, for example, M.J. Conyon *et al.*, "Do Hostile Mergers Destroy Jobs?"(2002) 45 Journal of Economic Behavior and Organization 427. Conyon *et al.*'s paper looked at the U.K. market. Later work by Gugler *et al.* suggested that negative effects on employment were not observed in the U.S. market. See Klaus Gugler & Burcin Yurtoglu, "The Effects of Mergers on Company Employment in the USA and Europe" (2004) 22 International Journal of Industrial Organization 481. Alan E. Garfield has argued that job dislocation associated with takeovers is not conceptually different from job dislocations that arise from other causes. ' Accordingly, in his view, it is not coherent as a matter of public policy to seek to prevent takeovers, rather than to identify and address the causes of job dislocation generally. (One might add that it is thus tempting to conclude that the focus on employment is merely a political ploy to gain popular support for rules restricting takeovers for the benefit of incumbent managers or directors.) See Alan E. Garfield, "Helping the Casualties of Creative Destruction: Corporate Takeovers and the Politics of Worker Dislocation" (1991) 16 Journal of Corporation Law 249.

27   See, for example, Michael A. Hitt *et al.*, "Are Acquisitions a Poison Pill for Innovation?" (1991) 5 Academy of Management Executive 22; Michael A. Hitt *et al.*, "The Market for Corporate Control and Firm Innovation" (1996) 39 The Academy of Management Journal 1084. More recently, however, Sapra *et al.* have argued that hostile bids enhance innovation. See Haresh Sapra, Ajay Subramanian, & Krishnamurthy Subramanian, "Corporate Governance and Innovation: Theory and Evidence" (2011) Chicago Booth Research Paper No. 08-05.

28   See Andrei Schleifer & Lawrence H. Summers, "Breach of Trust in Hostile Takeovers" in Alan J. Auerbach, ed., *Corporate Takeovers: Causes and Consequences* (Chicago: University of Chicago Press, 1988) 33.

29   Marina Martynova & Luc Renneboog, "A Century of Corporate Takeovers: What Have We Learned and Where Do We Stand?" (2008) 32 Journal of Banking and Finance 2148.

eign bidders who must be restrained in the interests of deterring such "hollowing out," and not the many foreign buyers to whom Canadian managers may voluntarily choose to sell in friendly transactions remains a mystery; one hopes that the ardent opponents of "hollowing out" are not simply advocating policies that favour the vested interests of specific groups—such as incumbent managers and directors—at the expense of consumers and the Canadian economy as a whole.)

Although the empirical research on the question is complex, the essential policy issue is not: If takeover bids are (generally) good for the economy, they should be facilitated, not impeded by target company managers, whose predictable desire to preserve their lucrative positions will tempt them (consciously or unconsciously) to keep attractive share offers away from their shareholders. If, on the other hand, hostile takeover bids are more likely than not to be launched by heartless, opportunistic, value-destroying "raiders," then the law should empower target directors to resist (or at least to delay) such raids. Resistance in such cases is not futile, but necessary to protect uninformed or unduly "coerced" shareholders from yielding to the unfair pressure of "structurally coercive"[30] hostile bids, or the superficial but mistaken attraction of "substantively coercive"[31] hostile bids, and too readily tendering their shares at an undervalue. So it is, as the following discussion will show, that much of the law of *hostile* bids centres upon the legal duties and obligations of the directors and managers of target companies.

C. STRUCTURE OF HOSTILE BIDS

When a transaction is hostile the bidder does not have the luxury of negotiating with the target to craft a deal structure that best accommodates both parties. There is really only one option: the hostile acquiror must, as it were, go over the heads of the target company's board of directors and make its purchase offer directly to the target company's shareholders. Of course, if the prospective "bidder" is content to secure

---

30   For a discussion of the concept of "structural coercion," see Ronald J. Gilson & Reinier Kraakman, "Delaware's Intermediate Standard for Defensive Tactics: Is There Substance to Proportionality Review?" (1989) 44 Bus. Law. 247.

31   The term "substantive coercion" was coined in 1989 by Ronald Gilson and Reinier Kraakman, *ibid.*, then subsequently invoked by the Delaware Supreme Court, albeit in a context which, as Gilson and Kraakman themselves later remarked, "[changed] utterly the meaning" of their term. See Ronald J. Gilson & Reinier Kraakman, "Takeovers in the Boardroom: Burke Versus Schumpeter" (2005) 60 Bus. Law. 1419 at 1420, n3.

managerial control over the target, without obtaining the formal voting and cash flow rights that accompany the holding of a majority equity position, then the bidder might pursue an alternative strategy. Instead of launching a bid, the would-be acquiror could engage in a proxy contest to replace some or all of the target company's board of directors, as discussed in Chapter 9. But if the goal is to acquire the *shares* of the target company—together with the voting and cash flow interests that come with share ownership—against the wishes of the target board, the purchase must take the form of a takeover bid.

The directors of a company that is the target of a takeover bid—whether hostile or friendly—are subject to a specific array of securities law requirements, as outlined in Chapter 5. In particular, the directors are required to produce an information document (a directors' circular) in response to a takeover bid.[32] In that circular, they are required to provide a recommendation to their shareholders as to whether to accept or reject the bid or, if they are unable to provide any recommendation, to set out the reasons for providing no recommendation, or indicate that they are considering whether to make a recommendation and so advising securityholders not to deposit their securities to the bid until they have received a further communication.[33] Securities legislation also provides for individual officers or directors to make their own recommendations if they are contained in an individual officer's or director's circular.[34]

But the obligations mandated by provincial securities laws by no means fully encompass the responsibilities of the directors and officers of a corporation that is the subject of a hostile takeover bid. There are also a host of more complex, yet somewhat less precisely defined, responsibilities that flow from the overarching corporate law duty of directors and officers to act honestly and in good faith with a view to the best interests of the corporation.

---

32   See, for example, *Securities Act* (Ontario), s. 95(1); Multilateral Instrument 62-104 [MI 62-104], s. 2.17(1).

33   *Securities Act* (Ontario), s. 95(2); MI 62-104, s. 2.17(2).

34   *Securities Act* (Ontario), s. 96; MI 62-104, s. 2.20.

D. ROLE OF THE SECURITIES COMMISSIONS AND THE COURTS IN CONTESTED CONTROL TRANSACTIONS

The complex interplay of securities and corporate law in the hostile takeover bid context, combined with the necessarily adversarial atmosphere of such deals, means that both the courts and provincial securities commissions are frequently called upon to resolve disputes that arise in the course of such transactions. Indeed, on several occasions, the commission and the courts have been asked to resolve specific contentious issues arising from the same takeover bid.

The fact that Canadian takeover battles may be waged in these two different arenas is not simply a matter of procedural interest. The approach of courts and commissions have been markedly different, with commissions tending to prefer shareholder choice, and courts tending to more readily defer to the decisions of target corporate boards of directors. For those who believe directors alone are best positioned to make fundamental decisions about a corporation's future—including decisions concerning the ownership of the corporation—the willingness of provincial securities commissions to compel directors to allow shareholders to decide for themselves whether or not to sell to a hostile bidder is especially irksome. Some director-friendly forces have even tried to buttress their "directors know best" argument with a healthy dose of populist xenophobia—warning that hostile bidders frequently come from foreign lands, and by facilitating their bids, securities commissions may be unwittingly contributing to the "hollowing out" of corporate Canada.[35]

---

35   See, for example, Competition Policy Review Panel, *Compete to Win: Final Report* (Ottawa: Competition Policy Review Panel, 2008) at 77. The Panel suggested that Canadian firms were at risk of foreign takeover because of the "limited tools" they possessed to fend off bidders, compared to their U.S. counterparts. The Panel did not explain why providing the directors with greater powers to prevent hostile acquisition would, in any way, curb the ability or willingness of directors to enter into friendly deals with foreign acquirors. Evidently, "hollowing out" somehow does not have adverse consequences for Canada as long as it is the result of negotiation. In this way, the Panel's recommendation suffers from the same key flaw that has been identified in proposals to provide corporate directors with greater latitude to consider the interests of employees and other non-shareholder constituencies when resisting a takeover bid, namely, if the interests of such non-shareholder constituencies are deserving of protection, surely they are deserving of that protection whether or not a corporation is under threat of takeover. Yet, proponents of increased directorial power to resist takeovers rarely suggest that directors should, for example, not be permitted to lay off their own employees

Court intervention in hostile bids may come about in either one of two ways. First, provincial securities legislation typically provides that an interested person may apply to the court for an order where a person or company has not complied with the takeover bid rules.[36] More often, however, in a number of high profile Canadian hostile takeover bids, bidders have sought to use corporate law provisions, especially the oppression remedy, as a means of seeking the court's assistance in dismantling defensive tactics employed by target directors[37] or in otherwise facilitating the making of a bid. Moreover, certain disputes that arise within the context of a hostile takeover bid may not be wholly or even partly anchored in securities legislation. Such disputes, accordingly, will certainly need to be resolved by the courts.

The authors of the 1983 Practitioners Report envisioned an "enlarged role"[38] for the courts in dealing with legal issues arising from takeover bids. In particular, they were concerned that "the determination of questions of law is the proper function of the courts and not the Commission."[39] Certainly, the statutory language found in section 105 of the Ontario *Securities Act* grants to the court broad powers. It provides that an interested person may apply to the court for an order. Where a court is satisfied that the takeover bid provisions have not been complied with, the court may make *any order* it thinks fit, including (among others) a compensation award, an order rescinding a transaction, an order requiring disposition of securities acquired pursuant to a bid, and an order forbidding a holder from exercising voting rights attached to securities.[40]

---

when no takeover bid is pending. The Panel proposed that Canadian directors ought to be placed on an equal footing with their Delaware counterparts, a goal that would be achieved, in their view, by repealing National Policy 62-202 [NP 62-202], and by having securities commissions cease the regulation of takeover bids. The fact that the Delaware approach in the takeover context has, itself, been the subject of harsh criticism, and that the Canadian approach, in many respects, conforms with what many commentators see as a far superior model of hostile bid regulation, is not mentioned by the Panel.

36 See, for example, *Securities Act* (Ontario), s. 105.
37 See, for example, *347883 Alberta Ltd. v. Producers Pipeline Inc.* (1991), 92 Sask. R. 81 (C.A.); *Rogers Communications Inc. v. MacLean Hunter Ltd.* (1994), 2 C.C.L.S. 233 (Ont. Ct. Gen. Div.); *CW Shareholdings Inc. v. WIC Western International Communications Ltd.* (1998), 39 O.R. (3d) 755 (Gen. Div.) [*CW Shareholdings*]; *Maple Leaf Foods Inc. v. Schneider Corp.* (1998), 42 O.R. (3d) 177 (C.A.).
38 Gordon Coleman, Garfield Emerson, & David Jackson, *Report of the Committee to Review the Provisions of the* Securities Act *(Ontario) Relating to Takeover Bids and Issuer Bids* (Toronto: Ontario Securities Commission, 1983) at para. 2.09.
39 *Ibid.*
40 *Securities Act* (Ontario), s. 105(2).

As a general matter, the distinctly different role of the securities commission in the takeover context is twofold. First, the commission has authority to grant exemptions from the takeover bid rules or to vary otherwise applicable time periods. Exemption or variation orders may be granted following an application by an interested person, and provided that granting such an order would not be prejudicial to the public interest.[41] Second, provincial securities legislation typically provides explicitly that interested persons may apply to the commission for a remedy when it appears that someone is not complying with the takeover bid rules.[42] Nor should it be thought that it is invariably hostile *bidders* that seek a remedy; directors of target companies may also take action against hostile bidders, arguing, for example, that the disclosure in the offeror's circular that has been delivered to target company shareholders is inadequate or misleading.

Because the commission is an administrative tribunal, not a court, its authority when such an application has been made is fairly narrow, yet has proved remarkably effective. Where appropriate, it may make orders to:

- restrain the distribution of documents used in connection with the bid;
- require amendments or variations to such documents, and to have those amended documents distributed to the relevant parties; and
- require compliance with the takeover bid rules.[43]

The Securities Commission does have broader general authority (in addition to its specific powers in the takeover bid context) to make orders in the public interest.[44] The commission's power to make orders in the public interest specifically includes the power to order that a takeover bid circular be provided, amended, or not provided to a party.[45] Moreover, the commission is empowered to make other orders pursuant to its public interest power that could certainly be used to prevent or restrain activities in the takeover bid context that were adjudged not to be in the public interest.[46]

---

41   See, for example, *Securities Act* (Ontario), s. 104(2)(b) & (c); MI 62-104, s. 6.1.
42   See, for example, *Securities Act* (Ontario), s. 104.
43   *Ibid.*, s. 104(1).
44   See, for example, *ibid.*, s. 127.
45   *Ibid.*, s. 127(1)5.
46   For example, *ibid.*, s. 127(1) 2 (cease-trade order); s. 127(1)2.1 (order that acquisition of securities is prohibited); s. 127(1) 3 (order that exemptions in Ontario securities law do not apply to a particular person or company); s. 127(1) 9 (order requiring a person or company who has not complied with Ontario securities law to pay an administrative penalty of up to $1 million).

A series of Ontario takeover decisions in the 1990s made clear that the jurisdiction of Canadian securities regulators is grounded in a broad statutory mandate to protect the public interest, rather than simply a narrow power to enforce technical compliance with securities laws. One of the earliest of these decisions was *Re Canadian Tire Corporation Ltd. et al.*,[47] in which the Divisional Court dismissed an appeal[48] from a decision of the Ontario Securities Commission to issue a cease-trade order in connection with a takeover bid that it found to be contrary to the public interest, notwithstanding that the impugned transaction appeared to involve no actual breach of the *Securities Act*, the regulations, or even commission policy statements. The commission's jurisdiction to make orders in the public interest, even in the absence of a specific breach of Ontario securities law, was reiterated in *Re Mithras Management Ltd. et al.*[49] in which the commission noted that "where the policy objectives of Part XIX [now Part XX] are not carried out, then this Commission will not hesitate to intervene in a bid *even if the strict terms of an exemption have been met.*"[50]

At the same time, the commission's public interest powers are not unlimited. As the Supreme Court of Canada has confirmed (endorsing the language of Laskin J.A. of the Ontario Court of Appeal): "The purpose of the Commission's public interest jurisdiction is neither remedial nor punitive; it is protective and preventive, intended to be exercised to prevent likely future harm to Ontario's capital markets."[51] Thus, in the case that led to this Supreme Court appeal, the Ontario Securities Commission had declined to use its public interest power to sanction the actions of the Quebec government in connection with its acquisition of control of a public company *despite* a finding that those actions were "abusive of the minority shareholders . . . and were manifestly unfair to them."[52]

Provincial securities commissions, accordingly, have broad public interest powers with which to deal with takeover bids that they find

---

47   (1987), 10 OSCB 857.
48   See *Re C.T.C. Dealer Holdings Ltd. et al. and Ontario Securities Commission et al.* (1987), 59 O.R. (2d) 79 (Div. Ct.). Final decisions of the Ontario Securities Commission, other than exemption orders, may be appealed to the Divisional Court pursuant to s. 9 of the *Securities Act* (Ontario).
49   (1990), 123 OSCB 1600.
50   *Ibid.* at 1618 [emphasis added].
51   *Committee for the Equal Treatment of Asbestos Minority Shareholders v. Ontario (Securities Commission)*, 2001 SCC 37 at para. 42 [*Equal Treatment*], quoting Laskin J.A. (1999), 43 O.R. (3d) 257 at 272 (C.A.).
52   *Ibid.* at para. 59 (S.C.C.), quoting Ontario Securities Commission in *Asbestos Corp. (Re)* (1994), 4 C.C.L.S. 233 at para. 71.

to be contrary to the public interest; but those broad powers must be exercised with a view to the twin purposes of securities legislation (investor protection and "fostering fair and efficient capital markets and confidence in capital markets.")[53] Moreover, orders issued by the commission pursuant to the broad public interest powers must be protective and preventive, not remedial or punitive.[54]

Perhaps the most critical, and most frequently litigated, source of dispute (whether before securities commissions or the courts) arises from attempts by directors and officers of companies that are targets of hostile takeover bids to implement defensive tactics to defeat or delay hostile bids, or to adopt "deal protection measures" in agreements with favoured friendly bidders, that are claimed, by hostile bidders, to unfairly interfere with a takeover auction. The following section briefly canvasses some of the legal issues that these measures raise.

E. DEFENDING AGAINST HOSTILE BIDS: GOALS AND TACTICS

1) Introduction

When a public corporation is the target of a hostile (or unsolicited) takeover bid, it is not unusual for the managers and directors of the target company to seek to resist that bid by employing defensive tactics. Since a hostile takeover bid is an offer to purchase shares made to a target corporation's *shareholders* and not to the target corporation itself, the directors and managers of the target corporation do not have control over the timing or terms of such an offer. Defensive tactics, properly used, are designed to enhance the strategic and negotiating position of target directors, typically by delaying or otherwise impeding the hostile bid in one or more of the following ways:

- *"White knights" and deal protection measures:* Finding a preferred alternative buyer (or merger partner), sometimes colourfully referred to as a "white knight," and seeking to ensure the deal with this preferred party is completed instead of the hostile bid. Special provisions are frequently included in friendly merger agreements

---

53   *Securities Act* (Ontario), s. 1.1. See also *Equal Treatment, ibid.* at para. 41.

54   Note, however, that the Supreme Court of Canada has also confirmed that considering the likely general deterrent effects of an administrative penalty is perfectly appropriate for the commission, since general deterrence relates to prevention of future harm. See *Re Cartaway Resources Inc.*, [2004] 1 S.C.R. 672.

in an effort to make it difficult for rival (hostile) bidders to trump the friendly transactions. These provisions are referred to as "deal protection measures." Common deal protection measures, discussed later in this chapter, include "break-up fees," "no shop/no talk clauses," stock options, and lock-ups.

- *Hostile bid defences aimed at making the target less attractive:* If a prospective target corporation has identified specific features about its business that are especially attractive to a hostile bidder, it may attempt to alter those features in some way so that a prospective hostile bidder will no longer wish to pursue the acquisition. Two examples of such defensive strategies are the so-called crown jewel and scorched earth defences. The crown jewel strategy refers to the sale by the prospective takeover target of a strategically important asset to a third party; the more extreme, and more controversial, scorched earth defence involves taking some action that would be potentially ruinous, such as committing the company to make large cash payments (perhaps as dividends, or as payments on restructured debts), or otherwise placing important fetters on the business that would deprive a potential acquiror of opportunities to unlock value or take advantage of operational flexibilities if its bid were to succeed. So, for example, it was reported in April 2006 that Luxembourg-based steel company Arcelor, in an effort to ward off an unwanted bid by Mittal Steel, had transferred an 81% interest in its Canadian subsidiary Dofasco to a special Netherlands entity (referred to as a "stitching"), on terms that would make sale of the unit impossible for at least five years.[55] Of course, in taking these actions the directors of the corporation are always subject to their overriding duty to act honestly, in good faith, with a view to the best interests of the corporation.

---

[55]   See Heather Timmons, "Arcelor Decides on 'Scorched Earth' Plan" *International Herald Tribune* (5 April 2006), online: www.iht.com/articles/2006/04/04/business/steel.php. The stitching strategy apparently works by placing the decision as to whether or not to sell in the hands of the board of the Netherlands stitching, a "foundation-like" entity that is reportedly unique to the law of the Netherlands. It was subsequently reported in January 2007 that Arcelor Mittal would not take legal action to try to force the Dofasco sale, stating, "Arcelor Mittal indicated that the boards of directors reached this decision based on opinions from legal experts that the prospects for success of any such litigation against the stitching are remote." See "Arcelor Mittal Won't Launch Suit to Force Sale of Dofasco" *Globe and Mail* (11 January 2007) B11. More recently, it was reported that Arcelor Mittal would not be compelled by U.S. competition authorities to divest its interest in Dofasco. See Greg Keenan, "Arcelor Mittal Needn't Divest Dofasco" *Globe and Mail* (21 February 2007) B1.

- *Hostile bid defences aimed at stalling the hostile bid—the "poison pill":*
  Where the managers and directors of a target company seek more time
  to find alternatives to a hostile bid that their shareholders might well
  prefer (or at least to gain leverage in negotiations with the original hostile bidder), they may choose to implement defences aimed at delaying
  or impeding the hostile bidder in some way. The most important defence of this sort is the implementation of a "shareholder rights plan"
  (known colloquially as a "poison pill," a device discussed at greater
  length later in this chapter). Other methods used to delay hostile bids
  include launching legal proceedings against the hostile bidder and alleging violations of securities or other laws. Techniques designed to
  make success of a hostile bid impossible or impractical include what
  is sometimes called a "white squire defence," a technique that involves
  ensuring a block of shares substantial enough to make it impossible for
  the hostile bidder to acquire control of the corporation finds its way into
  the hands of parties friendly to the target corporation's management.

  It must be emphasized that all of these techniques are only properly available to a target company if they are implemented by the target company board acting honestly, and in good faith, with a view to
  the best interests of the corporation. Overly aggressive use of such
  tactics—and certainly use of these tactics to entrench existing managers and directors—can run afoul of directors' and officers' corporate
  law duties, as discussed in greater length later in this chapter.

- *Dual class voting structures:* There are other structural devices that
  may operate to deter or prevent the success of hostile takeover bids.
  For example, many Canadian public corporations have dual class
  share structures, which provide enhanced voting rights to the holders
  of one class of shares (often those held by the corporation's original
  founders or members of the founder's family). Although the purpose
  of such dual class structures is primarily related to maintaining ongoing voting control, an ancillary effect of such dual class share structures is that they impede hostile bids, since any potential bidder would
  typically need to acquire the special voting shares in order to obtain
  control. Since the directors of the target corporation would have been
  elected by the holders of these special voting shares, it would be unusual (though certainly not impossible) for a bid opposed by the directors to be accepted by the very shareholders who elected them.[56]

---

56   Interesting cases have arisen in the contrary situation, that is, where the directors of a
     corporation with a controlling shareholder seek to pursue a sale with a party against
     the wishes of the controlling shareholder, or where a controlling shareholder seeks to
     conclude a sale of his or her shares against the wishes of the board of directors.

*   *Staggered or "classified boards" (U.S.):* In the United States, another key takeover bid defence is the "staggered" or "classified" board of directors. With a classified board, the directors of the corporation are divided into two or more classes, and the members of each class are elected for staggered terms. Under certain U.S. corporate statutes—including, crucially, Delaware's *General Corporation Law*—when a board has been classified in this way, directors can only be removed from office before the expiry of their terms, for cause (unless the certificate of incorporation provides otherwise).[57] The practical effect of this is that, even if a hostile bidder acquires voting control of the corporation, it will not be able to replace the existing directors for a year or more. The staggered (or classified board) defence has frequently been used in conjunction with a poison pill (discussed further below.) Hostile bidders, accordingly, will often mount a proxy battle, as discussed in Chapter 8, in tandem with a hostile tender offer, with a view to electing directors to the board of the target who may then take steps to remove the poison pill obstacle. Again, a staggered board structure is an effective defence to this two-pronged attack, because—even if the target company shareholders overwhelmingly support the hostile bidder and its director nominees—it will not be possible to gain control of the board at a single annual meeting. In 2006, it was reported that about 53 percent of publicly traded corporations in the United States had staggered or classified boards.[58]

    In Canada, the use of staggered boards is not a defensive tactic that is typically available to the directors of target corporations because Canadian corporate statutes generally permit shareholders to remove the directors at any time by ordinary resolution (that is, by a simple majority vote),[59] and do not provide exceptions to this power for classified boards similar to those found in Delaware's corporate

---

57   See *General Corporation Law* (Delaware), Delaware Code, Title 8, Chapter 1, ss. 141(d) & (k)(1). Bebchuk, Coates, & Subramanian noted in 2001 that over 70 percent of companies that went public in the 1990s had a staggered board, a development, in their view, that had important implications for the market for corporate control since, as their research indicated, staggered boards represent "a serious impediment to a hostile bidder seeking to gain control over the incumbents' objections." See Bebchuk, Coates, & Subramanian, "The Powerful Antitakeover Force," above note 15 at 887.

58   Committee on Capital Markets Regulation (Hubbard and Thornton, Chairs), *Interim Report of the Committee on Capital Markets Regulation* (30 November 2006) at 95, online: www.capmktsreg.org.

59   See, for example, CBCA, s. 109(1).

statute.[60] (The use of staggered boards in Canada could, nevertheless, raise general corporate governance issues because not every member of the board would be required to seek re-election at the annual meeting of shareholders. Accordingly, on September 9, 2011, the Toronto Stock Exchange issued for comment proposed amendments to the TSX Company Manual which would, if implemented, require annual election of directors for all listed companies.[61])

2) Advantages (for the Target) in Delaying a Hostile Bid

Takeover defence tactics are typically used by target company boards to delay a hostile bid for one of three purposes:

- to provide the target board with additional time to find a competing bidder, and therefore create an "auction";
- to provide the target board with additional time to generate some other alternative to the hostile bid; or
- to compel the hostile bidder to negotiate with the target board with a view to securing a better price for the target company shareholders.

---

60 The CBCA provision allowing directors to be removed by ordinary resolution does include a very limited exception that would apply only in cases where the corporation's articles of incorporation provide for cumulative voting. (See CBCA, s. 107(g).) However, the sole purpose of this exception is to preserve the integrity of the cumulative voting provisions themselves. Without this limited exception, a simple majority of the shareholders could immediately undo the election of directors conducted using cumulative voting procedures. But this exception is quite different, both in scope and application, from the classified board exception provided for under Delaware law. Indeed, the *General Corporation Law* (Delaware), above note 57, s. 141(k)(2) contains its own exception for removal of directors in cases where the corporation's articles provide for cumulative voting that is substantially similar to the exception in CBCA. s. 107(g). Morck and Yeung asserted in 2006 that poison pills and staggered boards had been "proliferating" in Canada, but did not provide specific examples to explain how the apparent bar to establishing effective staggered boards in most Canadian corporate statutes had been effectively circumvented. See Randall Morck & Bernard Yeung, "Some Obstacles to Good Corporate Governance in Canada and How to Overcome Them," Research Study Prepared for the Task Force to Modernize Securities Legislation in Canada, *Canada Steps Up*, vol. 4 (October 2006) 279 at 335. It is possible that a proliferation of staggered boards in Canada could be related less to attempts to block hostile bids and more to the general corporate governance concerns referred to below; see text accompanying note 61 below.

61 See "Request for Comments, Amendments to Part IV of the Toronto Stock Exchange ("TSX") Company Manual ("The Manual"), 9 September 2011, online: http://tmx.complinet.com/en/display/display_main.html?rbid=2072&element_id=791.

At one time, it was also suggested that delaying a bid could assist target company shareholders to make a more informed response to a hostile bid by providing them with sufficient time to consider the terms and seek counsel if they wished. However, it is unlikely that this rationale for takeover defences is usually credible in the Canadian legal environment. As discussed in Chapter 5, Canadian securities laws define takeover bid broadly enough to sweep in all major share acquisitions. With limited exceptions, all bids must remain open for thirty-five days. Accordingly, it seems doubtful that any additional time for reflection created by a takeover bid defence is of significant value to Canadian target company shareholders.

Some boards of U.S. companies have occasionally asserted the right to use takeover defences not merely for the purpose of securing a better deal for target company shareholders, whether from the original hostile bidder or otherwise, but rather for the purpose of altogether preventing a hostile bidder from ever making its bid to the target company's shareholders, a tactic sometimes referred to as a "Just Say No" defence.[62] The legality of defensive tactics for this purpose does not appear to have been accepted in Canada, and even in the United States is highly controversial because of the obvious concern that managers who pursue such strategies may be motivated (consciously or unconsciously) by the desire to entrench themselves rather than by the disinterested pursuit of the best interests of the corporation and the corporation's shareholders.[63]

The fact that directors of U.S. corporations—in particular Delaware corporations—enjoy greater latitude than directors of Canadian corporations to resist hostile takeover bids is a frequent subject of commentary. The Canadian/Delaware divide has recently been the subject of renewed interest following a remarkable 2011 decision of the Dela-

---

62   The "Just Say No" defence is also sometimes facetiously referred to as the "Nancy Reagan Defence." As First Lady in the 1980s, Nancy Reagan led a campaign against the use of illegal drugs. She famously suggested that one solution to the proliferation of illicit drugs was to counsel young people who were offered unlawful substances to "Just Say No," and her anti-drug campaign became identified with that slogan. The "Just Say No" defence has been strongly criticized by some commentators as an inappropriate use by corporate directors and officers of their position to deprive shareholders of their ultimate right to decide whether or not to sell their shares. See, for example, Ronald J. Gilson, "Just Say No to Whom?" (1990) 25 Wake Forest L. Rev. 121.

63   Practitioners Lipton and Rowe, however, have argued that a director-centred takeover bid regime is both appropriate and the long-standing norm (at least in Delaware). Accordingly, it would seem that, for them, in appropriate circumstances it is neither legally impermissible, nor controversial, for target company directors to "just say no" to a hostile bid. See Lipton & Rowe, "Pills, Polls and Professors," above note 15.

ware Court of Chancery, *Air Products and Chemicals, Inc. v. Airgas, Inc.*[64] and a series of decisions by Canadian securities commissions that seemed, at least for a time, to suggest that the traditional Canadian approach to the poison pill might be subject to change. Those developments are discussed further later in this chapter.

3) The Role of the Directors of a Company Subject to a Hostile Takeover Bid

a) Introduction

If directors of a target company consider the terms of a hostile takeover bid to be inadequate or otherwise inappropriate, should they be obliged, or even permitted, to vigorously resist the bid? In one sense, the target company is a stranger to the proposed transaction. The hostile bidder's offer is made to the shareholders, not to the company itself. While directors of the target company clearly have the right to speak for the target company, is it equally clear that they may effectively act as bargaining agents for the shareholders in a "negotiation" for the sale of the shareholders'—*not the corporation's*—assets?

The debate over the extent to which directors should or should not resist a hostile takeover bid, and the jurisprudence that has developed around this issue is part of a broader inquiry surrounding the interpretation of directors' and officers' fiduciary duties.

It is trite to observe that a corporation's directors and officers must, at all times, discharge their duty to act "honestly and in good faith with a view to the best interests of the corporation." This very language is found in many Canadian corporate law statutes,[65] and the essential principle existed at common law as well. There is little doubt, then, in the abstract, about the duties of corporate officers and directors. At the same time, however, directors and officers may find themselves in a position of irreconcilable conflict when their corporation is the target of a hostile bid, since they are well aware that, following a successful hostile takeover bid, they will almost certainly be replaced by nominees or appointees of the bidder. In the case of those inside directors, who are also senior managers, their (often-considerable) incomes are at risk. But even in the case of independent directors, a hostile bid may represent a threat to prestige and perquisites.

In the United States, economic and legal scholars have recognized the very real possibility that in large corporations where ownership has

---

64   16 A.3d 48 (Del. Ch. 2011) [*Airgas*].
65   See, for example, CBCA, s. 122(1)(a).

become separated from control, directors of a corporation may be tempted to use defensive techniques to ward off a hostile acquiror in order to protect their own positions (to "entrench" themselves). Accordingly, as economist Jean Tirole has written: "It is not clear why managers should have a say in such decisions. They face an obvious conflict of interest: a successful takeover is likely to result in the loss of employment and the control of their rents. . . . [I]t would be hard to make a case in favor of any *formal* right held by management in this area!"[66]

The risk of "management entrenchment" is surely real; yet, it also cannot be denied that directors of a target corporation are generally in a much better position than the shareholders themselves, both to assess the adequacy of a proposed takeover bid and to negotiate effectively with a bidder so as to ensure shareholders receive the highest possible price for their shares. Accordingly, many practising lawyers, in particular, have expressed strong support for giving target directors' wide latitude, confident in the integrity and judgment of corporate managers (people wise enough, after all, to hire good lawyers) and doubtful of the research upon which the "academic" theories about the value of the "market for corporate control" supposedly rests. So, for example, Martin Lipton, the prominent New York lawyer credited with inventing the so-called poison pill takeover bid defence, has long been an ardent and articulate advocate for the right, and responsibility, of target directors to oppose hostile bids. As he has recently said, "I have been and continue to be skeptical about the love affair by academics of the Chicago school with the so-called 'market for corporate control.' In particular, I do not accept the efficient capital market and agency theories advanced by academics to justify hostile takeover bids."[67]

In sum, at the risk of oversimplification, there are, broadly speaking, three competing views on the appropriate role of the directors (and managers) of corporations that are subject to a hostile takeover bid:

- The *"managerial passivity"*[68] *view:* Shareholders, and only shareholders, should be concerned about how to respond to hostile takeover

---

66   Jean Tirole, *The Theory of Corporate Finance* (Princeton: Princeton University Press, 2006) at 441.

67   Martin Lipton, "Merger Waves in the 19th, 20th and 21st Centuries," The Davies Lecture, presented at Osgoode Hall Law School, York University, Toronto, 14 September 2006, online: http://osgoode.yorku.ca. For a similar view recently expressed by two Canadian practitioners, see Sean Vanderpol & Ed Waitzer, "Mediating Rights and Responsibilities in Control Transactions" (2010) 48 Osgoode Hall L.J. 639.

68   See, for example, Frank H. Easterbrook & Daniel R. Fischel, *The Economic Structure of Corporate Law* (Cambridge, MA: Harvard University Press, 1991) at

bidders. Directors and officers have no valuable or indeed valid role to play.

- The "managerialist," director-centred or strong representative corporate democracy view:[69] Shareholders' principal right is to elect the board of directors. Once elected, it is the directors (and the managers who report to them) who make managerial decisions. A takeover bid is economically similar to other major corporate decisions, such as amalgamations. Although such transactions require shareholder approval, they cannot be effected—or indeed initiated—without the support of the board of directors. Accordingly, directors should be given the power to block hostile takeover bids that they have determined are not in the best interests of the corporation. Among at least some Canadian legal practitioners, there is, in fact, a view that Canadian law may not arm directors of target companies adequately, particularly when compared with the apparently more pro-manager approach of the U.S. courts, especially in the crucial state of Delaware.[70]

- Ultimate "shareholder choice" view: This view, which steers a middle ground between the "managerialist" and "managerial passivity" approaches referred to above, supports a significant role for the directors of target companies in attempting to secure the greatest value for their shareholders, but with a clear recognition that it is the shareholders, and not the directors, who must ultimately decide whether or not a takeover bid should succeed or fail. Holders of this view reject the managerial passivity view as unrealistic and inappropriate for at least two reasons. First, there may well be information known

---

174: "Managers should leave to shareholders and rival bidders the task of 'responding' to offers. Managerial passivity is best, ex ante, both privately and socially."

69   Lipton & Rowe, "Pills, Polls and Professors," above note 15 at 28, have argued: "[T]he Delaware legislature has decided that Delaware corporations should be representative democracies. Corporate decisions are made by the corporate governors (the board), and in certain cases need to be ratified by the electorate (the shareholders). The statute does not contemplate that 'fundamental' corporate decisions be made by the corporate equivalent of a voter initiative or a plebiscite." See also TW Services, Inc. v. SWT Acquisition Corp., 1989 Del. Ch. LEXIS 19 at 29 (Mar. 2, 1989), n14: "'Shareholder democracy' is an appealing phrase, and the notion of shareholders as the ultimate voting constituency of the board has obvious pertinence, but that phrase would not constitute the only element in a well articulated model. While corporate democracy is a pertinent concept, a corporation is not a New England town meeting; directors, not shareholders, have responsibilities to manage the business and affairs of the corporation, subject however to a fiduciary obligation." (This footnote was quoted in 2011 by Chancellor Chandler in Airgas, above note 64 at 102).

70   See, for example, above note 35.

to managers that would assist shareholders in fairly assessing the value of the company. Nor is this an affront to "efficient market theory," since it has never been suggested that real-world markets are "strong form efficient."[71] And certainly astute managers are in a better position than dispersed shareholders, structurally and institutionally, to press a bidder to raise its offer. On the other hand, the "shareholder choice" view also questions the logic of the managerialist argument. True, directors and senior managers of large corporations are entrusted with authority to make all other major decisions concerning a corporation's operations—including decisions that have consequences for their shareholders' wealth that are arguably every bit as material as a proposed bid to acquire the corporation's outstanding shares. But the question is not, as some managerialists would have it, "Why do the motives of otherwise trusted managers become suspect once a bidder has undertaken to purchase the company's shares?" Hostile takeovers as Ronald Gilson has suggested, are not about the power of directors to *manage* the corporation at all; they are about who is to *control* the corporation.[72] It would appear that many (even, perhaps, most) legal academics would support some version of this ultimate shareholder power approach; and, in Canada, this view seems to underlie most decisions of securities regulators on directors' defensive tactics.

There have been efforts to determine, empirically, whether takeover defences are primarily used as bargaining tactics that ultimately serve the interests of target company shareholders, or are more likely to constitute management entrenchment devices that have an adverse effect on shareholder wealth. By way of example, a few of these studies are, very briefly, mentioned below.

---

71   See Ronald J. Gilson, "Lipton and Rowe's Apologia for Delaware: A Short Reply" (2002) 27 Del. J. Corp. L. 37 at 42: "Management may have nonpublic information concerning the value of the corporation that convinces them that the tender offer price is too low. Nothing in efficient market theory is inconsistent with this circumstance. The shareholder choice position does not depend on the stock market being *strong* form efficient, i.e., that share prices reflect information that only management knows." The three forms of market efficiency that have been identified, originally, for empirical testing purposes are: strong form (all information—public and private—is impounded into share prices); semi-strong form (all publicly available information is impounded in stock prices); and weak form (historical price information is reflected in current stock prices). According to Fama, this classification was pioneered by Harry Roberts. See Eugene F. Fama, "Efficient Capital Markets: A Review of Theory and Empirical Work" (1970) 25 J.F. 383n.

72   Gilson, "A Structural Approach," above note 22.

b) The Developing Canadian Law of the Duty of Directors of Target Companies

i) Overview

In Canada, it is generally understood that directors of a target corporation, in fulfilling their duties to act in the best interests of the corporation, may appropriately use "poison pills" and other defensive measures to resist hostile takeover bids with a view to gaining more time within which to develop other options for maximizing shareholder value. Provincial securities commissions, however, have generally made it clear—subject to two recent anomalous decisions discussed further below—that the ability of directors to impede a hostile bid is carefully circumscribed.

The law surrounding the duties of target company directors continues to develop in Canada. It is a development that has been complicated by the influence of varied English and American jurisprudence and an evolving notion of the nature of corporate directors' and officers' fiduciary duties. Because of the important role played by Canadian securities regulators in the regulation of takeover bids, a number of leading hostile takeover bid decisions—particularly in the area of shareholder rights plans or poison pills—have been rendered by securities commissions rather than by the courts. Many of those decisions are discussed later in this section. But it is the role of the courts, and not securities regulators, to define and interpret the scope of directors' and officers' fiduciary duties in the context of a hostile bid. Accordingly, it is useful to briefly consider how the law in this area has evolved in Canada.

ii) Directors Permitted to Defend

In a widely cited 1972 decision, *Teck v. Millar*,[73] the British Columbia Supreme Court held that directors of a company were permitted to issue shares where that share issuance had the effect of defeating the controlling interest of the (previous) majority shareholder, provided that the directors were acting in good faith in what they believed to be the best interests of the company, and provided, further, that there were reasonable grounds for their belief. *Teck v. Millar* is regarded as a seminal case in the area of directors' duties generally, particularly following the recent Supreme Court of Canada endorsement of a particular passage from the *Teck v. Millar* judgment.[74]

---

73   *Teck Corporation Ltd. v. Millar et al.* (1972), 33 D.L.R. (3d) 288 (B.C.S.C.) [*Teck v. Millar*].

74   See *Peoples Department Stores Inc. v. Wise*, 2004 SCC 68 at para. 42.

Teck v. Millar is not, strictly speaking, a "takeover defence" case at all; the actions of the directors being challenged in that case occurred *after* the plaintiff corporation had already acquired a majority of the target company's outstanding shares. In other words, the directors of the target company were not simply attempting to prevent an unwanted suitor from *gaining* control; their actions were aimed at *depriving* a party that had already gained legal control of its voting majority. It is precisely this aspect of the case that makes *Teck v. Millar* such a strong authority in support of the proposition that directors may vigorously defend against unsolicited bids. Surely if directors are permitted to snatch control away from a shareholder who has actually acquired a majority voting stake, they must also be permitted to take actions to prevent an unwanted buyer from *seeking* such voting control in the first place.

The *Teck v. Millar* case involved a junior mining company, Afton Mines Ltd., whose shares traded on the Vancouver Stock Exchange. Afton had a copper property near Kamloops, B.C., that was of considerable interest to at least two major mining companies: Placer Developments Ltd. and the plaintiff, Teck Corporation Limited; eventually, a third, Cominco,[75] also participated in negotiations with Afton. After trying, unsuccessfully, to negotiate a deal to purchase a number of shares in Afton from several large shareholders (including those of Afton's President, Millar), Teck began acquiring Afton shares in the market. Within a few weeks, Teck had acquired just over 50 percent of all of the outstanding and issued Teck shares.[76] Once in control, and aware that Afton's officers were in negotiations with rivals to develop the Kamloops property, Teck requisitioned an Afton shareholders' meeting. Through its solicitors, Teck sought to direct Afton not to issue any

---

75 In 2001, Teck and Cominco, in fact, merged, by way of plan of arrangement. Indeed, by that time, Teck had ultimately consolidated with Afton Mines Ltd. as well in 1981. See Teck Cominco Limited, 2005 Annual Information Form (1 March 2006) at 1, online: www.sedar.com.

76 This acquisition would, today, constitute a takeover bid, and would have subjected Teck to the formal bid requirements that have been outlined earlier in this chapter. However, it appears that the B.C. securities legislation at that time worked differently. Although this is not discussed in the decision, one notes that the applicable legislation—the *Securities Act, 1967*, S.B.C. 1967, c. 45—exempted from the takeover bid rules any "offer to purchase securities effected through the facilities of a stock exchange or in the over-the-counter market." *Ibid.*, s. 78(b), definition of exempt offer. Until recently, Canadian securities statutes provided an exemption from the formal takeover bid rules where a bid was undertaken through the facilities of a recognized stock exchange and in accordance with that exchange's own bid rules. However, that exception has since been repealed, as explained in Chapter 6, Section G.

further shares or take any steps out of the ordinary course of business until the requisitioned shareholders' meeting had taken place. Despite the fact that Teck was now Afton's controlling shareholder, and despite the warnings of legal action Afton had received, the senior officers of Afton signed a deal with Placer, a competitor of Teck, to develop the Kamloops property. A critical part of the Placer deal provided that, if Placer elected to develop the property, Afton would issue to Placer shares equal to 30 percent of Afton's issued and outstanding shares. A share issuance of that size would dilute Teck's controlling interest.

The *Teck v. Millar* case is regarded as an important part of the Canadian corporate law canon because of its explication of the nature and scope of directors' duties and in particular because of its contribution to the Canadian jurisprudence surrounding the perplexing "proper purpose" doctrine.[77] But the case is also a convenient starting point from which to examine the development of the law in Canada relating to the role of the directors of a company that is the subject of a hostile takeover bid because the *Teck v. Millar* judgment is consistently cast in terms of the rights and duties of corporate directors faced with the prospect of a group "*seeking* to obtain control."[78]

The court makes clear that there is nothing wrong with the directors of a corporation taking action when confronted by a potential takeover that they honestly believe is not in the corporation's best interests. Again, it should be emphasized that this conclusion, though reasonable, was by no means inevitable. The shift in control of a corporation occurs, as it were, over the heads of the directors; it is not a matter of the corporation's "business" at all though as a technical matter, it may well be considered to fall within the meaning of a corporation's "affairs."[79] Accordingly, it is not impossible to imagine that the court might have concluded that the directors ought not to have much to say about *who* should be their ultimate constituents. But the court finds instead that "the directors ought to be allowed to consider who is seeking control and why. If they believe that there will be substantial damage to the company's interests if the company is taken over, then the exercise of their powers to defeat those seeking a majority will not necessarily be categorized as improper."[80]

---

77 For a discussion of this aspect of *Teck v. Millar*, see Nicholls, *Corporate Law*, above note 18 at 310–11.

78 *Teck v. Millar*, above note 73 at 314.

79 See, for example, CBCA, s. 1(1), in which "affairs" is defined to mean "the relationships among a corporation, its affiliates, *and the shareholders*, directors and officers of such bodies corporate . . . ." [emphasis added].

80 *Teck v. Millar*, above note 73 at 315.

Note that the emphasis here is upon the *permissibility* of defensive measures, and that it is expressed in very cautious terms ("directors ought to be *allowed* [not, for example, obliged] to consider who is seeking control"; taking defensive measures is "not necessarily . . . improper").

The court in *Teck v. Millar* ultimately determined that the Afton directors did, indeed, honestly believe the takeover by Teck would not be in the interests of Afton and that they had reasonable grounds for such a belief, thus justifying the controversial share issuance that was the subject of the dispute. The outcome of the *Teck v. Millar* case, insofar as it related to the rights of majority shareholders to preserve their controlling position, caused some consternation. As a later court would put it, referring to a statement in an Australian case denying that majority shareholders had property rights that could not be disturbed by a unilateral decision by corporate directors to allot shares to others: "That rather bold statement, if left unqualified would undoubtedly cause majority shareholders many sleepless nights."[81] The same court essentially dismissed *Teck v. Millar* as a case that could only be understood in the unique context of the Canadian mining industry.[82]

As to the specific issue of the use of the power to issue shares to defeat the interest of an existing majority shareholder, no more will be said here. What is critical to recognize at this point is that *Teck v. Millar* offers relatively early Canadian authority for the proposition that the directors of a target company need not be passive bystanders when an unwelcome attempt is made to acquire voting control of that company.

The view expressed in *Teck v. Millar* that it was permissible for directors of a target company to take active steps to resist a hostile bid for control soon became well-established and uncontroversial. But it is interesting to observe that early articulations of this principle stress the notion that resistance by directors is *not prohibited*. The question of whether directors actually have a positive duty to resist (or to take other actions) was somewhat less clear in the earlier cases. So, for example, in *Re Royal Trustco*,[83] Eberle J. commented: "I do not think that the present state of our law prevents the directors of a target company . . . from actively resisting a takeover bid . . . . The search for a 'white

---

81   *Exco Corp. Ltd. v. Nova Scotia Savings & Loan Co.* (1987), 35 B.L.R. 149 at 261 (N.S.S.C.T.D.).

82   *Ibid.* at 259: "On a careful review of the facts it appears to me that what was under consideration there was a very unusual set of facts which must be somewhat unique to the mining industry."

83   (1981), 14 B.L.R. 307 (Ont. H.C.J.).

knight' is a common enough response to a takeover bid . . . . No crys-
tallized law in this country *prohibits* active opposition of this nature."[84]

In an article published in 1981,[85] then dean (later Supreme Court of
Canada judge) Frank Iacobucci considered the legal duties of directors
of a company that was the subject of a hostile bid. Iacobucci recognized
that there were competing views on the matter, but expressed a preference for what has been dubbed by American commentators the "shareholder choice" position: "Shareholders should enjoy the fundamental
rights of disposing of their shares and of deciding who shall run the
affairs of the corporation, free from director interference."[86]

Much of Iacobucci's analysis of the then current state of the law,
emphasizes the importance of analyzing the propriety of any defensive
actions of directors through the prism of their abiding duty to act in the
best interests of the corporation, a duty which, in the takeover context,
Iacobucci argues, gives "considerable, if not paramount, recognition to
the interests of the offeree shareholders of target corporations."[87] But the
directorial duties upon which Iacobucci focuses are duties "to advise
the offeree shareholders regarding a takeover bid"[88] and to *refrain* from
taking defensive actions aimed solely at defeating a bid. Apart from a
general duty to act in the best interests of the corporation and its shareholders, he does not seem to suggest that there is any specific positive duty upon directors of a company that is the target of a hostile bid
to seek alternatives with a view to maximizing short-term shareholder
value. Perhaps, as the Competition Policy Review Panel suggested in
2008, the Canadian corporate governance and capital market environment was very different in years gone by. Those were the days, after
all, when "there were no hedge funds and institutional shareholders
were by and large passive investors."[89] It was also a world, the Panel
suggested, where governance practices were different, a world that has
changed (for the better, in their view) now that "standards of corporate
governance have improved in response to investor activism and the 'Enron affair.'"[90] The implication, in the Panel's view, appears to be that the
management and boards of the modern Canadian corporation are now
paragons of integrity and ability; the suggestion that the shareholders of

---

84   *Ibid.* at para. 12 [emphasis added].
85   Iacobucci, "Planning and Implementing Defences," above note 13.
86   *Ibid.* at 165.
87   *Ibid.* at 167.
88   *Ibid.* at 168.
89   Above note 35 at 77.
90   *Ibid.*

target companies should have the final word in a hostile takeover battle is old-fashioned and uninformed.

iii) Directors' Duty to Defend against Hostile Bids

The idea that directors were *permitted* to resist a hostile bid that they reasonably believed was not in the best interests of the corporation, was based upon fundamental principles of directorial responsibility. It was, accordingly, a short leap for the courts to acknowledge that, in fulfilling their duties, directors were not only permitted, but at times were positively obligated to resist potentially harmful hostile bids.[91]

But what was to be understood as the ultimate goal of directorial or managerial resistance to a hostile bid? The court in *Teck v. Millar* had declared (in *obiter*) that it might well be proper for directors to consider the interests of certain non-shareholder constituents—specifically, employees and "the community,"[92] a sentiment the Supreme Court of Canada would later endorse (and indeed expand) albeit not in the hostile takeover context.[93] However, a careful reading of the *Teck v. Millar* decision makes clear that none of these non-shareholder interests was relevant to the Afton board. Rather, as the plaintiff's counsel evidently acknowledged, the actions of Afton's board were motivated entirely by a desire to secure the most profitable deal for Afton, believing "that the value of Afton's shares, including their own, would decline, under

---

91   See, for example, *First City Financial Corp. v. Genstar Corp. et al.* (1981), 125 D.L.R. (3d) 303 at 319 (Ont. H.C.J.): "The right *and indeed the obligation* of directors to take steps that they honestly and reasonably believe are in the interests of the company and its shareholders in a take-over contest or in respect of a take-over bid, is perfectly clear and unchallenged" [emphasis added]. See also *Re Olympia & York Enterprises Ltd. and Hiram Walker Resources Ltd. et al.* (1986), 59 O.R. (2d) 254 at para. 63 (Div. Ct.) [*Olympia & York*]: "[The directors] found that while the market was trading at $28 a share and Gulf was offering $32, the real value of the shares was between $40 and $43 a share. What options did the directors have? *If they did nothing it would be a breach of duty to shareholders*" [emphasis added]. See also *Rogers Communications Inc. v. MacLean Hunter Ltd.*, above note 37 at para. 19 (Ont. Ct. Gen. Div.): "It is reasonable that a target board not roll over and play dead. If it were completely passive, *it would be soundly criticized for not doing anything to maximize the situation for the target organization*" [emphasis added].

92   Above note 73 at 412–13.

93   *Peoples Department Stores Inc. v. Wise*, above note 74 at para. 42: "[I]n determining whether they are acting with a view to the best interests of the corporation, it may be legitimate, given all the circumstances of a given case, for the board of directors to consider, *inter alia*, the interests of shareholders, employees, suppliers, creditors, consumers, governments and the environment." See also *BCE Inc. v. 1976 Debentureholders*, 2008 SCC 69 at paras. 39–40 [*BCE*].

Teck's management."[94] In other words, despite the *obiter* nod to non-shareholder constituents, *Teck v. Millar* seemed to be a case in which the directors resisted a hostile bid in order to maximize the corporation's share price, and in which the court supported the directors' actions.

Teck v. Millar also reflected a relatively early use (if not quite adoption) of leading Delaware case authority. At the time of the *Teck v. Millar* decision, two of the leading Delaware cases (both of which were cited by the court in *Teck v. Millar*) were *Kors v. Carey*[95] and *Cheff v. Mathes.*[96] Those decisions established that defensive measures might be permitted, where the target managers determined, based upon a reasonable investigation, that a hostile bid posed a threat to the continued existence of the corporation or, as the court in *Cheff* put it, "at least existence in its present form."[97] Confronted by such a potential threat to a corporation's policy or existence, target directors were permitted to resist the bid provided their primary purpose in doing so was to serve the corporate interest, and not simply to maintain control. Note how closely this formulation maps onto the "proper purpose" framework used by the court in *Teck v. Millar* to analyze, and ultimately endorse, the target directors' and officers' actions. The problem with the *Cheff* test, however, as commentators such as Ronald Gilson have noted, was that "since management can almost always find a conflict over policy between itself and an insurgent, the motive analysis collapses into the business judgment standard."[98]

iv) The Takeover Wave Begins—Delaware Courts Respond

Following *Teck v. Millar*, the Canadian answer to the proper goal to be pursued by directors of a target company subject to a hostile bid was formulated against the background of increasing hostile takeover activity and a corresponding proliferation of U.S. (particularly Delaware) precedent.

Teck v. Millar was decided two years before the watershed 1974 takeover by Inco of ESB Inc., the transaction that, in the view of some, heralded the beginning of a hostile tender offer wave in America.[99] Financing techniques—in particular the junk-bond-financed leveraged buyout—would open the door in the United States to hostile acquisitions of the largest of American public companies. The political shock-

---

94   *Teck v. Millar*, above note 73 at 409. For a more detailed discussion of this point, see Nicholls, *Corporate Law*, above note 18 at 278–80.
95   158 A.2d 136 (Del. Ch. 1960).
96   199 A.2d 548 (Del. Sup. Ct. 1964) [*Cheff*].
97   *Ibid.* at 556.
98   Gilson, "Structural Approach," above note 22 at 829.
99   See above note 15 and accompanying text.

waves created by large hostile acquisitions led to the proliferation in many U.S. states of anti-takeover laws,[100] a development for which there does not appear to have been a Canadian parallel, perhaps, because, among other things, the larger number of corporations with controlling shareholders in Canada (positions often maintained through dual class voting shares) made hostile bids of the sort that had become more common in the United States less prevalent, and perhaps because Canadian securities laws (as discussed in Chapter 5) regulated takeover bids more comprehensively than U.S. federal tender offer rules.

Courts, too, were called upon with increasing frequency to consider the nature and scope of target company directors' duties. And so, as disputes arose between bidders and target boards and between rival bidders, the law surrounding target directors' rights and responsibilities increasingly began to take shape.[101]

The development of the law was especially significant in Delaware. Canada's public corporations are markedly different from the large, widely held companies that are such a significant part of the Delaware corporate landscape. Nevertheless, the salience of the Delaware jurisprudence among Canadian corporate practitioners, and the relative dearth of home-grown precedent, meant that Delaware law had an important (though by no means determinative) influence on the shaping of Canadian judicial views on hostile bids. In some respects, Delaware takeover law became virtually synonymous with U.S. takeover law when Canadian courts sought the guidance of U.S. precedent. And U.S. precedent in the area was assuming special prominence. As one Canadian court put it: "It is clear that the regulatory climate of takeovers is more closely controlled in Canada and the United States than it is in England. For that reason American cases appear to me to be of greater assistance."[102]

By the mid-1980s there had been (among others) three particularly important judicial developments in Delaware touching significantly upon the role and responsibility of target company directors:

---

100 For a detailed discussion of the development of U.S. state-level anti-takeover laws, including the leading cases considering the constitutionality of iterations of such laws, see Ronald J. Gilson & Bernard S. Black, *The Law and Finance of Corporate Acquisitions*, 2d ed. (Westbury, NY: The Foundation Press, 1995) c. 23.

101 Roberta Romano has suggested that the rise of hostile takeover bids in this period sparked a demand for new corporate law scholarship as "lawyers and courts needed new ways to talk and think about, and respond to, these novel transactions": Roberta Romano, "After the Revolution in Corporate Law" (2005) 55 J. Legal Educ. 342 at 348.

102 *Olympia & York*, above note 91 at para. 36.

- *Unocal v. Mesa Petroleum:*[103] The Delaware Supreme Court, recognizing "the omnipresent specter that a board may be acting primarily in its own interests, rather than those of the corporation and its shareholders,"[104] held that defensive measures taken by the board of a company that was the target of a hostile bid did not automatically enjoy the protections of the traditional, deferential Delaware business judgment rule. Rather, these decisions were subject to "enhanced scrutiny." Specifically, the directors were obliged to demonstrate that they had "reasonable grounds for believing that a danger to corporate policy and effectiveness existed,"[105] a burden that required a showing of good faith and the conduct of a reasonable investigation. Then, any defensive actions taken must be proportionate to the threat posed, a test that was significantly narrowed in a later case, *Unitrin, Inc. v. American General Corp.*,[106] to a determination that the defensive actions not be "draconian (preclusive or coercive) and . . . within a 'range of reasonableness.'"[107] (In particular, the robustness of the poison pill defence in Delaware, as discussed below, led prospective hostile acquirors to launch proxy contests in conjunction with hostile bids. In determining whether defensive measures were preclusive, Delaware courts began to focus on the effect such measures would have on such proxy contests. Thus, measures would be said to be preclusive if they would have the effect of rendering the success of a hostile bidder's proxy contest, "either . . . mathematically impossible or realistically unattainable"[108]).
- *Moran v. Household International Inc.:*[109] The Delaware Supreme Court held that the deferential business judgment rule applied to the decision of a target company to adopt a poison pill (or shareholder

---

103   493 A.2d 946 (Del. 1985) [*Unocal*].

104   *Ibid.* at 954.

105   *Ibid.* at 955.

106   651 A.2d 1361 (Del. Sup. 1995).

107   *Ibid.* at 1388.

108   *Ibid.* at 1389. In a recent Delaware Court of Chancery decision (*Airgas*, above note 64) Chancellor Chandler suggested that the Delaware law on shareholder rights plans, as developed by the Delaware Supreme Court, may have effectively left hostile bidders in that jurisdiction—when confronted by a shareholder rights plan adopted by a target company with a staggered board of directors—with no practical alternative other than to launch a proxy contest. See note 270, below in this chapter. For an interesting recent Canadian case involving steps undertaken by the board of a company while under "threat" of a proxy contest by a firm controlled by prominent activist shareholder Carl Icahn, see *Icahn Partners LP v. Lions Gate Entertainment Corp.*, 2011 BCCA 228 [*Icahn Partners v. Lions Gate*].

109   500 A.2d 1346 (Del. 1985).

rights) plan. The *Moran* decision, praised by managerialists, has been criticized by those who believe that hostile takeovers benefit target shareholders and the economy generally. Financial economist Michael Jensen, for example, declared bluntly: "Rights issues like Household's . . . harm shareholders. They will fundamentally impair the efficiency of corporations that adopt them."[110]

- *Revlon Inc. v. MacAndrews & Forbes Holdings Inc.*:[111] In *Revlon*, the Delaware Supreme Court held that once the sale of a target company was inevitable, "[t]he duty of the board . . . changed from the preservation of [the company] as a corporate entity to the maximization of the company's value at a sale for the stockholders' benefit . . . . The whole question of defensive measures became moot. The directors' role changed from defenders of the corporate bastion to auctioneers charged with getting the best price for the stockholders at a sale of the company."[112] In subsequent cases (often referred to by Delaware courts and commentators as *Revlon's* "progeny"), the duty of directors who were in the "*Revlon* zone" or "*Revlon* mode" was refined and clarified. *Revlon* duties would not be triggered when directors of a corporation agreed to a share-exchange bid, for example, provided that, both before and after the proposed deal, the shares of the company would be widely dispersed, with no controlling shareholder.[113] Nor was an auction necessarily the only way in which directors subject to a *Revlon* duty could properly discharge their responsibilities. Circumstances might dictate other ways to maximize shareholder value; there was "no single blueprint."[114] In its most recent discussion of the *Revlon* duty, in *Lyondell Chemical Company v. Ryan*,[115] the Delaware Supreme Court held that the board of a company in the

---

110 Michael Jensen, "The Takeover Controversy: Analysis and Evidence" in Donald H. Chew, Jr., *The New Corporate Finance: Where Theory Meets Practice* (New York: McGraw-Hill, Inc., 1993) 465 at 485.

111 506 A.2d 173 (Del. 1986).

112 *Ibid.* at 182.

113 *Paramount Communications Inc. v. Time Inc.*, 571 A.2d 1140 at 1150 (Del. 1989), citing Chancellor Allen's judgment in the Delaware Court of Chancery. Although the Supreme Court in *Time* chose to base its decision on other grounds, subsequently in *Paramount Communications Inc. v. QVC Network*, 637 A.2d 34 at 46–47 (Del. 1993), the Delaware Supreme Court endorsed the reasoning used by Chancellor Allen in the *Time* decision that there "was no change of control in the original stock-for-stock merger between Time and Warner because Time would be owned by a fluid aggregation of unaffiliated stockholders both before and after the merger."

114 *Barkan v. Amsted Industries*, 567 A.2d 1279 at 1286–87 (Del. Supr. 1989).

115 970 A.2d 235 (Del. 2009).

Revlon zone was under an obligation to obtain the highest possible price for shareholders, but "no court can tell directors exactly how to accomplish that goal."[116] Further, the Supreme Court held that the directors (found to be disinterested, independent, and acting with expert advice) could only be found to have violated their duty of good faith[117] if there had been an intentional failure to act "in the face of a known duty to act, demonstrating a conscious disregard for [their] duties."[118] Only if they had "knowingly and completely failed to undertake their responsibilities"[119] could they be found in breach of their duty of good faith.

v) Duty to Maximize Shareholder Value

Although the *Revlon* duty, at least by that name, was not formally adopted by Canadian courts (and indeed, was expressly rejected at one point by the Ontario Court of Appeal),[120] a very similar type of duty seemed to emerge in Canadian jurisprudence, namely, a duty on the part of the directors of a company to maximize shareholder value when the company was "in play."[121]

It is possible that Canadian legal advisors were advising directors of target companies to treat a hostile bid as a trigger for initiating steps to maximize shareholder value even before Canadian law on this

---

116 *Ibid.* at 242.

117 The plaintiffs were required to establish that the directors were in breach of their duty of good faith, and not merely in breach of their duty of care, because the target company's charter included a provision, permitted by Delaware law and commonly adopted by Delaware corporations, exempting the directors from liability for breaches of the duty of care. Such charter clauses, which would be unlawful under typical Canadian corporate statutes, are permitted under Delaware's *General Corporation Law*, s. 102(b)(7). This section was introduced into Delaware's statute following, and essentially in response to, the 1985 Delaware Supreme Court decision in *Smith v. Van Gorkom*, 488 A.2d 858.

118 Above note 115 at 243.

119 *Ibid.* at 243–44.

120 *Maple Leaf Foods Inc. v. Schneider Corp.*, above note 37 at 199: "*Revlon* is not the law in Ontario." The court simply appeared to mean that directors of target companies were not exclusively under an obligation to conduct an auction for the company, a narrower reading of the *Revlon* duty than had evolved in the Delaware jurisprudence. See discussion accompanying notes 131–33, below in this chapter.

121 Writing in 2008, the Competition Policy Review Panel asserted that "Once a company is 'in play' directors on both sides of the border have an obligation to maximize the value of the company." (Above note 35 at 76.) This was an inaccurate statement of Delaware law: the *Revlon* duty, as explained below, was not triggered simply because a company was "in play." However, it did reflect a commonly held view of the state of Canadian law at the time.

point was entirely settled. It is not inconceivable, that in the absence of significant Canadian jurisprudence, Canadian lawyers had reasonably looked, at least in part, to the emerging Delaware law (including *Revlon* and its progeny) for guidance on such issues. Thus, for example, although one certainly finds some early judicial support for the notion that, when faced with a hostile bid, target directors should (or at least *may* properly) take steps to maximize shareholder value,[122] Halperin and Vaux have suggested that prior to two key Ontario decisions in 1998 (*CW Shareholdings v. WIC Western International Communications Ltd.*[123] and *Pente Investment Management Ltd. v. Schneider Corp.*),[124] "it was unclear whether a Canadian board was subject to a [*Revlon*] duty and, if so, what was required of the board to discharge the duty to maximize shareholder value."[125] Yet, despite the comparative uncertainty of the legal position prior to 1998, it seems apparent that many Canadian directors of target companies *believed* they were under a duty, when faced with a hostile bid, to maximize shareholder value. One notes, for example, that the board of directors of the target company in the *CW Shareholdings* case, "[a]nnounced its stated intention in the circumstances was to maximize near term value for the shareholders, *and that they considered themselves to be under a legal duty to do so.*"[126]

If Halperin and Vaux are correct that it was unclear in Canadian law, prior to the *CW Shareholdings* case itself, that directors were under such a duty, then one wonders if established Delaware precedent was having an impact—perhaps an exaggerated impact—prior to *CW Shareholdings* on the perceived legal duties of Canadian directors. There is no question that Delaware authority was being closely monitored by lead-

---

122 See, for example, *Olympia & York*, above note 91 at para. 62: "It was a legitimate objective for the directors to ensure that as much as possible of all economic value go to all shareholders"; at para. 67: "it is the directors' duty to take all reasonable steps to maximize value for all shareholders." *Benson v. Third Canadian General Investment Trust Ltd.* (1993), 14 O.R. (3d) 493 at 500 (Gen. Div.) [*Benson*]: "I would also observe that the 'in play' concept only becomes relevant in the aspect of concentrating on maximizing shareholder value when a corporation is *truly* in play"; *Armstrong World Industries Inc. v. Arcand*, [1997] O.J. No 4620 at para. 29 (Gen. Div.) [*Armstrong World Industries*]: "As far as the Directors were concerned, the company was not truly 'in play' and therefore they did not have to concentrate on maximizing shareholder value."
123 *CW Shareholdings*, above note 37.
124 Above note 37 (indexed as *Maple Leaf Foods Inc. et al. v. Schneider Corp.*).
125 Stephen H. Halperin & Robert A. Vaux, "The Role of the Target's Directors in Unsolicited Control Transactions" in *Critical Issues in Mergers and Acquisitions-Domestic and International Views, Papers Presented at the 6th Queen's Annual Business Law Symposium* (Kingston, ON: Queen's University, 2000) 109 at 114.
126 *CW Shareholdings*, above note 37 at 764.

ing Canadian practitioners. As I have noted elsewhere,[127] one leading Canadian firm, in a business law guide on mergers and acquisitions in Canada produced in August 1996, included a slightly-flawed quotation from the Delaware Supreme Court's judgment in *Unocal*,[128] in which, as the firm publication put it, the court warned of "the omnipresent spectre [*sic*] that a board may be acting primarily in its own interest rather than those of the corporation." The law firm guide indicated only that this statement had come from "one court," giving no hint that the "court" in question was, in fact, a U.S., not a Canadian court. In fact, one notes that in the quoted passage as it appeared in the law firm publication, the spelling of the word *specter*—which had appeared in the original judgment—was Canadianized to read *spectre*, so that one obvious clue to the American origin of the passage was (no doubt inadvertently)[129] obscured.

Whatever the state of law had been prior to 1998, the Court in *CW Shareholdings* confidently declared:

> In the context of a hostile takeover bid situation where the corporation is "in play" (*i.e.*, where it is apparent that there will be a sale of equity and/or voting control) the duty is to act in the best interests of the shareholders as a whole and to take active and reasonable steps to maximize shareholder value by conducting an auction . . . . In the American authorities this shareholder maximization-through-auction duty is known as the "Revlon Duty."[130]

However, this express adoption of what the court characterized as the *Revlon* duty was, only months later, rejected by the Ontario Court of Appeal in *Maple Leaf Foods Inc. v. Schneider Corp.*[131] Yet, despite this apparently definitive statement, the question of whether a *Revlon*-type duty existed in Ontario was far from settled. Ambiguity lingered because, while the Court of Appeal purported to reject invocation of the *Revlon* case itself, the language of the Court of Appeal's judgment indicated that it was only one narrow aspect of *Revlon* to which it objected—namely, the suggestion that directors of a corporation in the "*Revlon* zone" must conduct an auction. Of course, no such specific

---

127   Christopher Nicholls, *Corporate Finance and Canadian Law* (Toronto: Carswell, 2000) at 342.

128   Above note 103 at 954.

129   The quotation contained two other small errors which suggest mere inadvertence: the word *interest* was used, rather than *interests* and the comma before the word *rather* was omitted.

130   *CW Shareholdings*, above note 37 at 768.

131   Above note 37.

requirement has been considered part of *Revlon* duties in Delaware for years, as the Delaware Supreme Court's 2009 opinion in *Lyondell Chemical Company v. Ryan* makes abundantly clear.[132] With respect to the general *Revlon* principle, that when the sale of a company is inevitable the directors must take *appropriate steps* to maximize shareholder value, the Court of Appeal actually seemed supportive: an auction if necessary, then, but not necessarily an auction. The Court of Appeal says, for example:

> When it becomes clear that a company is for sale and there are several bidders, an auction is an appropriate mechanism to ensure that the board of a target company acts in a neutral manner to achieve the best value reasonably available to shareholders. When the board has received a single offer and has no reliable grounds upon which to judge its adequacy, a canvass of the market to determine if higher bids may be elicited is appropriate, and may be necessary.[133]

In other words, there is a strong suggestion that the Court of Appeal actually supported in principle what the Delaware courts had come to conceive as the *Revlon* duty, as developed in those cases collectively referred to in Delaware as "*Revlon* and its progeny." The narrow version of *Revlon* expressly rejected by the Court of Appeal as "not the law in Ontario" had simply not been the law in Delaware either for many years.

Canadian law surrounding the duties of directors of a hostile bid continued to evolve over the following decade through a series of judicial decisions. Before the Supreme Court of Canada's eagerly awaited 2008 judgment in *BCE Inc. v. 1976 Debentureholders*,[134] those decisions, when read in tandem with more voluminous provincial securities commission decisions concerning takeover defences, appeared to support the following propositions:

- Once a company was "in play," directors were generally obliged to take steps to maximize shareholder value.[135]
- Where directors have a *bona fide* belief, based on reasonable grounds, that a hostile takeover is not in a corporation's best interests, the

---

132 See text accompanying note 116, above in this chapter.

133 Above note 120 at 200.

134 Above note 93.

135 *Casurina Limited Partnership v. Rio Algom Ltd.*, [2004] O.J. No. 177 at para. 27 (C.A.): "Once Rio Algom was 'in play,' its legal obligation was to try to maximize value for shareholders." Leave to appeal to S.C.C. refused, [2004] S.C.C.A. No. 105. See also Halperin & Vaux, above note 125 at 115–16.

board may take defensive steps.[136] Canadian directors could employ defensive tactics in order to secure more time to generate alternatives, but they could not indefinitely stand in the way of a hostile bid being made to their shareholders. There was, in other words, no "Just Say No" defence in Canada—a proposition firmly established by provincial securities commissions, though never definitively addressed in Canadian courts. (Of course, it might well be possible for directors in certain cases to persuade their shareholders to reject an offer that the directors believed to be inadequate. Some Canadian practitioners came to refer to such a strategy of argument and persuasion as a "Just Say No" defence. So, for example, two failed hostile bid attempts in 2005 and 2006 were often said to be examples of such a "Just Say No" strategy.[137] But in the American M & A lexicon, where

136 See, for example, *Icahn Partners v. Lions Gate*, above note 108 at para. 76: "In Canada, it has been clear since *Teck* that where directors have carried out reasonable enquiries to inform themselves as to where their company's best interests lie and are *bona fide* of the belief, based on reasonable grounds, that a proposed takeover will run contrary to those interests, they are entitled to use their power to take defensive measures." In *Icahn* the board of directors of the target company, Lions Gate, had implemented a "deleveraging" transaction, the effect of which was to reduce the corporation's outstanding debt by more than $100 million. This deleveraging transaction involved exchanging outstanding convertible notes for new notes that could be converted into common shares of the corporation on terms that were more attractive economically than the old notes. The new notes were acquired by an investor of which one of the target company directors was a principal. When the notes were converted into equity, the interests of the other shareholders of the corporation (including the hostile bidder) were diluted. The hostile bidder's ability to win a planned proxy contest was therefore compromised. The court was satisfied, however, that the deleveraging transaction was undertaken by the board acting in the best interests of the corporation and, although the board understood that a collateral effect of the transaction would be to weaken the position of the hostile bidder—an outcome that the board also considered to be in the corporation's best interests—nevertheless, the defeat of the hostile bidder was neither the sole nor the primary goal for undertaking the transaction.

137 The two bids referred to here are the 2005 bid by Constellation Brands, Inc. for the shares of Vincor International Inc. and the 2006 bid by Barrick Gold Corporation for NovaGold Resources Inc. Vincor did have a shareholder rights plan (or poison pill) in effect, but chose to effectively withdraw its application to the hostile bidder after discussions with major shareholders indicated that they were likely to reject the bid in any event. See Vincor News Release, "Board Believes Shareholders Will Reject Constellation's Inadequate $31 Offer" (22 November 2005), online: www.sedar.com. The bidder's final bid subsequently failed. In the 2006 bid by Barrick Gold Corporation for NovaGold Resources Inc., as in the case of the Vincor bid, NovaGold did initially have a shareholder rights plan in place. NovaGold chose to waive application of the plan to the Barrick

the facetious phrase originated, "Just Say No" usually refers to the more controversial use by directors of measures aimed at preventing a hostile bid from ever reaching shareholders in the first place.[138] As then Vice-Chancellor (now Chancellor) Strine of the Delaware Court of Chancery once articulated the question: "Can control of the corporation be sold over the objections of a disinterested board that believes in good faith that the sale is inadvisable?"[139]) More recently, as discussed below, the contours of the Delaware "Just Say No" defence have been refined, and those refinements have brought with them their own tongue-in-cheek monikers including "Just Say Never" and "Just Say Wait."

It is curious that this difference between Canadian and Delaware law has arisen.[140] That Delaware directors should enjoy greater latitude to resist hostile bidders might imply that shareholder/director agency concerns are less acute in Delaware corporations than in Canadian corporations. That seems surprising since, generally speaking, Canadian corporations are less likely to be widely held than U.S. corporations. One might, accordingly, have thought that shareholder/director

---

bid (thus allowing the bid to be made to the shareholders) following discussions with major shareholders indicating that they did not intend to tender their shares to the bid. See NovaGold News Release, "NovaGold Waives Shareholder Rights Plan for Barrick's Inadequate Hostile Bid" (25 September 2006), online: www.sedar.com. Following certain amendments to and extensions of the bid, it was announced in November 2006 that the bid had failed. See News Release, "NovaGold Shareholders Overwhelmingly Reject Barrick Hostile Takeover Bid" (8 November 2006), online: www.sedar.com.

138 See, for example, Ronald J. Gilson, "Just Say No to Whom?" above at note 62.

139 Leo E. Strine, Jr., "The Professorial Bear Hug: The ESB Proposal as a Conscious Effort to Make the Delaware Courts Confront the Basic 'Just Say No' Question" (2002) 55 Stan. L. Rev. 863 at 863.

140 Although it should, perhaps, be noted that some U.S. commentators argue that there is some uncertainty as to whether a "Just Say No" defence is, unambiguously, permitted by Delaware law in any event. See, for example, Lucian Ayre Bebchuk & Allen Ferrell, "Federalism and Corporate Law: The Race to Protect Managers from Takeovers" (1999) 99 Colum. L. Rev. 1168 at 1191: "The pro-uncertainty tilt of Delaware's takeover law is as apparent as it is in other areas. Delaware could have given managers a great deal of power to 'just say no' while circumscribing very clearly the boundaries of what managers can and cannot do. But Delaware has chosen to do it in a way that leaves a fair amount of uncertainty as to where exactly the line is drawn." See also Vice Chancellor Strine, ibid. at 863, characterizing an academic paper by Bebchuk, Coates and Subramanian as a clever attempt to "force the hand of the Delaware courts to decide, once and for all, that impartial and well-intentioned directors do not have the fiduciary authority to 'just say no' for an indefinite—even perpetual—period to a noncoercive tender offer made to their company's shareholders."

agency issues would be more prevalent in Delaware than in Canada. On the other hand, companies with controlling shareholders are less likely to be the target of hostile bids in the first place. Further, since Canadian courts, as discussed below, typically find that when control block shareholders are unwilling to sell their shares, the corporation is not in play, perhaps the Canadian aversion to the "Just Say No" defence simply represents the most prudent judicial response to hostile bids for those (relatively fewer) Canadian public corporations that do have widely dispersed shareholders.

a.   "In Play"
In interpreting their duty to "act honestly in good faith with a view to the best interests of the corporation," are directors under a particular obligation to take steps to maximize shareholder value when their company is "in play"? If they are, when, precisely, may a company be said to be "in play"? These two questions are critically interrelated, since the legal significance of determining whether or not a company is "in play" depends entirely on the legal obligations that flow from such a determination.

i. *When Is a Company "In Play"?*
A number of Canadian courts have concluded, based on the specific facts before them, that a corporation is in play. But this conclusion is rarely accompanied by comprehensive analysis that would make it possible to determine what specific factor, or factors, have led the court to reach this conclusion.

Indeed, the structure chosen for friendly transactions may well be influenced by the concern that once a deal is announced, a company may be said to be in play. So, for example, in *McEwen v. Goldcorp Inc.*,[141] a friendly transaction was structured in a way that would not require the approval of the shareholders of one of the parties to the transaction, a decision taken, at least in part, to enhance deal certainty given that the other party "would effectively put itself in play once it entered this Agreement and publicly announced the transaction."[142]

Certainly, as noted above in *CW Shareholdings*, Blair J. did equate "in play" to a *Revlon*-type notion, but the threshold test he articulated seems considerably lower than the Delaware court had suggested in *Revlon*. One notes, after all, that Blair J. glosses the phrase "in play" to mean "where it is *apparent* there will be a sale of equity and/or voting control"[143]—not, as in *Revlon*, where such a sale is *inevitable*. In other

---

141   *McEwen v. Goldcorp Inc.*, 2006 CanLII 35985 (Ont. S.C.J.).
142   *Ibid.* at para. 17.
143   Above note 37 at 768 [emphasis added].

instances, the court's determination that a corporation is in play is announced rather summarily.[144] In 2006, the OSC suggested that once a purchaser had acquired a 19.8 percent stake in a company (Falconbridge) and so became Falconbridge's largest single shareholder, even though the purchaser had not yet announced its intention to acquire any additional shares, nevertheless "there should have been no doubt that Falconbridge was 'in play'—it was apparent that there would be a sale of equity and/or voting control."[145]

More recently, in *BCE Inc. v. 1976 Debentureholders*, the Supreme Court of Canada stated that a company (BCE) was put "in play" when one of its shareholders filed a Schedule 13D report with the U.S. Securities and Exchange Commission indicating "a change from a passive to an active holding of BCE shares."[146] This latter finding is particularly interesting when viewed in light of a statement of the Delaware Supreme Court on exactly the same issue and around the same time. In *Lyondell Chemical Company v. Ryan*[147] a hostile bidder also filed a Schedule 13D report which the directors of the target company acknowledged had put the company "in play." However, as the Delaware Supreme Court made clear, the mere fact that a company is "in play" does *not* place the directors under a *Revlon* duty and thus oblige them to take steps to maximize shareholder value. The Delaware Supreme Court was explicit and unequivocal on this point: ". . . *Revlon* duties do not arise simply because a company is 'in play.'"[148]

It is reasonably clear that a company with a controlling shareholder cannot be said to be in play if there is some legal bar (such as a statutory provision) that makes it impossible for a single shareholder to obtain control,[149] or if the controlling shareholder is not prepared to

---

144 See, for example, *Rogers Communications Inc. v. MacLean Hunter Ltd.*, above note 37 at para. 8: "I think it disingenuous not to think that MHL (or its constituent parts) was not in play both in respect of its shares and assets." *Golden Star Resources Ltd. v. IAMGold Corp.*, [2004] O.J. No. 2869 at para. 37 (S.C.J.) [*Golden Star*]: "It seems to me that IAMGold became in play as a result of the GSR Proposal."

145 *In the Matter of Falconbridge Limited* (2006), 29 OSCB 6784.

146 *BCE*, above note 93 at paras. 12–13.

147 Above note 115.

148 *Ibid.* at 242.

149 See, for example, *Airline Industry Revitalization Co. v. Air Canada* (1999), 45 O.R. (3d) 370 at 383 (S.C.J.): "Air Canada argues that it is protected from being the target of a takeover bid by an Act of Parliament which remains in full force and effect and which means that Air Canada is simply not 'in play'—to use the jargon of takeover practitioners." Note that, on the facts of the case, the court did not need to, and did not, make a determination on this argument.

sell its controlling interest.[150] Conversely, it appears that a proposed transaction that will effect a change in *board* control but leave the target company a widely held corporation, with no controlling shareholder, may also *not* put the target in play.[151] And it seems equally clear that where the directors of a corporation determine that a sale of the company is inevitable, the company is certainly in play.[152]

But what of the situation where a publicly-traded company does not have a controlling shareholder? Can it truly be said that *every* hostile bid for the shares of that company immediately places the company in play and so places directors under a duty to maximize shareholder value in the short term? Such a proposition seems rather surprising. Certainly it goes well beyond the duty imposed on directors of Delaware corporations by *Revlon* and its "progeny," as the Delaware Supreme Court has recently made clear in *Lyondell Chemical Company v. Ryan*.[153]

It is at this point, then, that the two questions posed above begin to converge. It is only critical to determine what it means for a Canadian company to be "in play" if, as some courts and commentators have suggested, the directors of a company that is truly "in play" must thereafter take steps to maximize shareholder (short-term) value. If no such

---

150 *Benson*, above note 122 at 500: "I would also observe that the 'in play' concept only becomes relevant in the aspect of concentrating on maximizing shareholder value when a corporation is truly in play. If there is a veto block of shareholders who are entitled to ignore, disregard and/or reject an offer, then if that be the circumstances under the prevailing law, how can one say that the corporation is in play?" *Maple Leaf Foods Inc. v. Schneider Corp.*, above note 37; *Armstrong World Industries*, above note 122 at para. 23: "I have concluded that Domco has never really been 'in play' since Sommer refused to sell its control block of Domco to Armstrong."

151 See *Golden Star*, above note 144 at para. 16: "[B]ecause IAMGold will continue to be broadly held after closing the transaction does not effect a change in voting control of IAMGold . . . . I note that the fact that I have concluded that the Wheaton transaction has the effect of changing control of the board of IAMGold does not in my view mean that, as a result IAMGold is, in the words of the various parties to this application, 'in play.'" The suggestion that no change of control of a public corporation occurs when, following a proposed transaction involving two public companies, control will remain "in a large, fluid, changeable and changing market" is found in the Court of Chancery decision in *Paramount Communications Inc. v. Time Inc.*, 1989 WL 79880; this analysis was subsequently endorsed and applied by the Delaware Supreme Court in *Paramount Communications Inc. v. QVC Network*, above note 113 at 47.

152 *CW Shareholdings*, above note 37 at 768. Halperin & Vaux, above note 125 at 155 note that, "[o]ne of the most critical issues that will need to be addressed is the circumstances in which a company is actually 'in play.'"

153 Above note 115.

obligation is triggered when a company is "in play," then the "in play" question is one of academic or metaphysical interest only.

Let us begin, then, with the most simple, extreme case: a bid made at a price significantly below the current market price of a corporation's shares surely does not force the directors and officers to abandon their current course, and turn their attention to maximizing short-term shareholder value. Of course, a formal bid—even a wholly inadequate one—will always trigger directors' obligations under securities laws to prepare a directors' circular.[154] But beyond mandatory securities law requirements, surely a board's time and attention cannot be peremptorily hijacked by the commencement of a clearly below-market bid. The launch of a bid that manifestly undervalues the company and is surely doomed to fail can hardly be said to create a situation where a "sale of equity and/or voting control" is "apparent," let alone "inevitable." So the directors may, presumably, conclude that the company is not "in play" and continue to implement their current long-term strategy without compunction. To be sure, it is often suggested that some large shareholders of public corporations have launched bids for those corporations, not necessarily with a genuine desire to seek control for themselves, but rather for the very purpose of putting the corporation "in play," and so stimulating an auction that will drive up the price of the corporation's shares and allow the original bidder to sell his or her holdings at a quick profit.

Yet, if the law permits directors to safely dismiss obviously inadequate bids, at what point may it properly be concluded that a bid price is so low that it has not effectively placed a company "in play"? After all, one notes that it has become rather routine for directors of target companies to immediately and publicly condemn hostile bids as "inadequate," "opportunistic," or even "insulting." Yet, these knee-jerk (or perhaps well-rehearsed) outbursts of righteous indignation are often coupled with a solemn commitment on the part of the board to "seek alternatives to maximize shareholder value." That seems rather puzzling. If the directors genuinely considered such bids unambiguously (even preposterously) "inadequate," why then would they consider themselves to be under any duty whatsoever to seek alternative transactions? Obviously, the rote condemnation of hostile bids as inadequate and opportunistic may merely constitute so much chest-beating bluster and posturing. But this fact makes it all the more critical that the legal duties of target company directors be clarified; if directors need not, as a matter of law, be deflected from their current course of action by the mere fact that someone has launched a wholly inadequate bid—or for that

---

154 See *Securities Act* (Ontario), s. 95; MI 62-104, s. 2.17.

matter, as the Delaware Court of Chancery has recently stated, by the mere fact that a bidder has launched a *premium bid*[155]—then might they actually be *faulted* for choosing to maximize short-term shareholder value in response to such a bid? That is, could it be a breach of directors' duties to inappropriately set long-term plans on hold to focus on short-term value maximization when the company is *not*, in fact, "in play"?

Alternatively, could the fact that directors or senior officers acknowledge that they are under a duty to maximize shareholder value be taken as presumptive proof that, regardless of how noisily and indignantly they may complain publicly about the value of a particular bid, in fact, behind closed doors they have come to the quiet realization that it is a fair and adequate offer that will almost certainly begin a process that will result in a sale of the company, either to the original bidder or to someone else? Yet, if that is the conclusion they have reached, what are we to make of the public denunciations? Are these misrepresentations—even, might one suggest, actionable misrepresentations, depending on the nature of the public statements or disclosures?[156]

ii.   The Duty of Directors When a Company Is "In Play"

If there is some uncertainty surrounding when a company may be said to be "in play," the precise implications that flow from a determination that a company is "in play" are even more perplexing, notwithstanding the occasionally bold statements that have been made on this topic.[157]

Where a company is, unequivocally, "in play," is it clear that the directors must focus from that point forward upon short-term shareholder value maximization? This question raises two distinct issues. First, does the fact that a company is "in play" necessarily imply that directors' duties are materially affected in *any* particular way? In other words, to borrow from the language of the Delaware courts, is a company's board subject to *Revlon* (or Canadian *Revlon*-like) duties when a company is "in play" at all? Second, if it is conceded that directors' dut-

---

155   See *Airgas*, above note 64 at 129: "At the same time, a board cannot be forced into *Revlon* mode any time a hostile bidder makes a tender offer that is at a premium to market value."

156   See, for example, *Securities Act* (Ontario), s. 138.3.

157   For example, as indicated at note 121, above in this chapter, the Competition Policy Panel, in 2008, confidently asserted that "once a company is 'in play' directors on both sides of the border have an obligation to maximize the value of the company." This statement reflected a widely held view of Canadian law at the time, but must be revisited in light of recent developments, including, most importantly, the Supreme Court of Canada's decision in *BCE*, above note 93.

ies are (at least presumptively) affected in some important way when the company is put "in play," how precisely are directors to interpret their duties at that point? Must the directors, for example, single-mindedly focus from that point forward on shareholder value maximization, recognizing, as the Delaware courts have, that when the company is to be sold there is no "long-term" for the current shareholders? Might they not also consider the implications of a proposed bid for other non-shareholder stakeholders such as employees, suppliers, customers, or the community in which the corporation operates?

It is perhaps worth noting at the outset that the "shareholder maximization" duty often associated by Canadian lawyers and judges with U.S. law in general, and Delaware law in particular, has also been addressed by courts in the United Kingdom.[158] And the particular issue of the extent to which directors may contractually constrain themselves from entertaining potentially higher bids has also been contested in U.K. courts. As Gower and Davies explain:

> . . . the initial bidder may wish to secure from the directors of the target company a legally binding undertaking to recommend the bid to the shareholders of the target in any event and not to seek, encourage or co-operate with any 'white knight.' Such an agreement with the directors is not necessarily against the interests of the target's shareholders, for the initial bidder may not be willing to make a bid at all for the target unless such undertakings are forthcoming. *The courts, however, have been unwilling to give full effect to such·agreements, especially the commitment always to recommend the initial offer, even if a better one emerges, whilst offering a variety of rationales for their reluctance.*[159]

Prior to the 2008 Supreme Court of Canada decision in *BCE Inc. v. 1976 Debentureholders*, there seemed to be scarce judicial support in Canada for the proposition that, when a corporation is truly "in play," any interests other than the financial interests of shareholders should be considered by the directors. Though a number of U.S. states have enacted so-called "stakeholder constituency" statutes expressly permitting (though not, typically, mandating) target company directors to consider non-shareholder interests, no Canadian corporate law statute

---

158   See, for example, *Heron International Ltd v. Lord Grade*, [1983] BCLC 244 at 265 (CA): "Where directors have decided that it is in the best interests of a company that the company should be taken over, and where there are two or more bidders, the only duty of the directors . . . is to obtain the best price."

159   Paul L. Davies, *Gower and Davies' Principles of Modern Company Law*, 8th ed. (London: Sweet & Maxwell, 2008) at 1011.

includes such provisions. For that matter, no such provision is found in the Delaware corporate statute under which more than half of America's largest public corporations are incorporated.

In Delaware, it has been suggested that some judicial comments support the view that in certain circumstances, the directors of a target company, in defending against a hostile bid, may take into account the interests of non-shareholder interests.[160] However, it is important to recall that in those Delaware cases where such non-shareholder interests were apparently vindicated, the corporation had not entered the all-important *Revlon* zone, discussed above. That is, although the target companies in those cases might well have been "in play," they had not reached the crucial point at which a sale or change of control transaction had become inevitable. Moreover, the extent to which defensive measures may be taken by a Delaware corporation to protect non-shareholder interests (such as corporate culture) was carefully circumscribed in the recent, remarkable decision of the Delaware Court of Chancery in *eBay Domestic Holdings, Inc. v. Newmark*.[161] There, the directors of craigslist, Inc. sought to defend their actions, in part, on the basis that they wished to protect the unique corporate culture of craigslist—indeed they sought to prevent their shares from falling into the wrong hands even after their deaths. Chancellor Chandler rejected the notion that preservation of corporate culture was a robust feature of Delaware law:

> It is true that on the unique facts of a particular case—*Paramount Communications, Inc. v. Time Inc.*—this Court and the Delaware Supreme Court accepted defensive action by the directors of a Delaware corporation as a good faith effort to protect a specific corporate culture. It was a muted embrace. Chancellor Allen wrote only that that he was "not persuaded that there may not be instances in which the

---

160   See, for example, Bebchuk & Ferrell, above note 140 at 1180, citing *Paramount Communications Inc. v. Time*, above note 113 (1989) and *Unocal*, above note 103 at 955.

161   16 A.3d 1 (Del Ch. 2010). This decision involved a dispute between eBay, in its capacity as a minority shareholder of the corporation that operates craigslist, and the directors and majority shareholders of craigslist. The case was unusual because, among other things, craigslist, Inc. was a privately held company with just three shareholders. As Chancellor Chandler noted: "To my knowledge, no decision under Delaware law has addressed a challenge to a rights plan adopted by a privately held company with so few stockholders. The ample case law addressing rights plans almost invariably involves publicly traded corporations with a widely dispersed, potentially disempowered, and arguably vulnerable stockholder base." *Ibid.* at 30–31.

law might recognize as valid a perceived threat to a 'corporate culture' that is shown to be palpable (for lack of a better word), distinctive and advantageous." This conditional, limited, and double-negative-laden comment was offered in a case that involved the journalistic independence of an iconic American institution. Even in that fact-specific context, the acceptance of the amorphous purpose of "cultural protection" as a justification for defensive action did not escape criticism.

More importantly, *Time* did not hold that corporate culture, standing alone, is worthy of protection as an end in itself. Promoting, protecting, or pursuing non-stockholder considerations must lead at some point to value for stockholders.[162]

In any event, Chancellor Chandler regarded the putative craigslist "culture" as little more than a "sales tactic":

Having heard the evidence and judged witness credibility at trial, I find that there is nothing about craigslist's corporate culture that *Time* or *Unocal* protects. The existence of a distinctive craigslist "culture" was not proven at trial. It is a fiction, invoked almost talismanically for purposes of this trial in order to find deference under *Time*'s dicta.[163]

Chancellor Chandler also reiterated the importance of recognizing that the decision to organize as a *business* corporation necessarily means that philanthropic goals—no matter how laudable in the abstract—cannot be pursued to the detriment of other shareholders:

The corporate form in which craigslist operates, however, is not an appropriate vehicle for purely philanthropic ends, at least not when there are other stockholders interested in realizing a return on their investment. Jim and Craig opted to form craigslist, Inc. as a *for-profit Delaware corporation* and voluntarily accepted millions of dollars from eBay as part of a transaction whereby eBay became a stockholder. Having chosen a for-profit corporate form, the craigslist directors are bound by the fiduciary duties and standards that accompany that form. Those standards include acting to promote the value of the corporation for the benefit of its stockholders.[164]

---

162 *Ibid.* at 32–33 [footnotes omitted].
163 *Ibid.* at 33.
164 *Ibid.* at 34.

In a leading Canadian takeover bid case, *Maple Leaf Foods Inc. v. Schneider Corp.*,[165] the Ontario Court of Appeal referred to a well-known Delaware case on this point, noting, "[w]hile *Paramount* . . . indicates that non-financial considerations have a role to play in determining the best transaction available in the circumstances, *here it was conceded that the court should only have regard to financial considerations.*"[166] Of course, Berger J. did suggest in *Teck v. Millar*[167] that directors could properly consider the interests of the corporation's employees or the community; however, these remarks were clearly *obiter* and, in any event, could be read as referring to the non-controversial proposition that considering such interests is not inconsistent with acting in the best interests of the shareholders.[168]

Prior to 2008, proponents of the stakeholder constituency view could, no doubt, point to apparently helpful language in the 2004 Supreme Court of Canada decision in *Peoples Department Stores Inc. (Trustee of) v. Wise.*[169] The Supreme Court there declared "that in determining whether they are acting with a view to the best interests of the corporation it may be legitimate, given all the circumstances of a given case, for the board of directors to consider, *inter alia*, the interests of shareholders, employees, suppliers, creditors, consumers, governments and the environment."[170] But *Peoples v. Wise* did not involve a takeover; and, of course, the fundamental point of the *Revlon* or "in play" cases is precisely that the way in which directors are to operationalize their fiduciary duties may be fundamentally altered when a company is undergoing a change in control. Accordingly, even leaving aside the many troubling features of the *Peoples v. Wise* case,[171] it really offered no guidance on this issue in the takeover context.

---

165 Above note 120.
166 *Ibid.* at 194 [emphasis added].
167 Above note 73.
168 Note, for example, Berger's language to the effect that if directors were to consider certain non-shareholder interests, ". . . it could not be said that they had not considered bona fide *the interests of the shareholders.*" *Ibid.* at 314 [emphasis added].
169 [2004] 3 S.C.R. 461.
170 *Ibid.* at para. 42.
171 Among other things, the Supreme Court of Canada in *Peoples Department Stores*, after citing the language from *Teck v. Millar* referred to above, states that "[the case of *Re Olympia & York Enterprises Ltd. and Hiram Walker Resources Ltd.* . . . approved, at p. 271, the decision in *Teck, supra.*" Yet, in fact, *Olympia & York*, above note 91, approved *Teck v. Millar*, above note 73, only for the limited proposition that the primary purpose of the directors was to serve the interests of the company and not to retain control of the company. Second, immediately after quoting with approval certain language from *Teck v. Millar*, the Divisional

The Ontario Court of Appeal, in 2007, appeared to consider it a matter of settled law that directors of a company that is the target of a takeover are under a duty to maximize shareholder value, albeit in the context of a sale of assets subject to shareholder approval, rather than a takeover bid. In *Ventas, Inc. v. Sunrise Senior Living Real Estate Investment Trust*,[172] the Ontario Court of Appeal noted in its reasons:

> There is no doubt that the directors of a corporation that is the target of a takeover bid—or, in this case, the Trustees—have a fiduciary obligation to take steps to maximize shareholder (or unitholder) value in the process . . . .[173]

The Court of Appeal thus seemed to confirm that a *Revlon*-type duty was, indeed, part of the law of Ontario. In fact, the court's statement seemed to suggest that Ontario directors would be more readily subject to an obligation to maximize shareholder value than their Delaware counterparts, since it is clear that Delaware directors do not become subject to *Revlon* duties simply because their corporation has become subject to a takeover bid. Something more is required—namely, that a sale or change of control has become "inevitable."

But there are several more layers to the *Ventas* case. To begin, *Ventas* did not arise in the context of a takeover bid—hostile or otherwise. The case instead concerned the interpretation of an asset purchase agreement entered into between a publicly traded real estate investment trust (as vendor) and Ventas, Inc. (as purchaser). The agreement had been signed following an auction undertaken by the trust for the sale of substantially all of its assets. Ventas, Inc. had emerged as the winning bidder in the auction. In fact, it was the only bidder to submit a final bid. The other prospective bidder, HCPI, had withdrawn from the auction process after being unable to reach an agreement with the third party manager of the properties being sold.

Then, shortly after the trust publicly announced its deal with Ventas, HCPI announced its proposal to "top" the Ventas deal, that is, to offer a price materially higher than the price that the trust's unitholders would receive if the Ventas transaction, which required the approval of the trust's unitholders, were completed. However, HCPI, as part of the earlier auction process, had signed a confidentiality agreement which

---

Court in *Olympia & York* states explicitly at 211: "It is the directors' duty to take all reasonable steps to maximize value for all shareholders." And later this principle is reiterated at 212: "Is it a proper objective for the directors to attempt to maximize the value to all shareholders? The answer is obvious."

172   2007 ONCA 205 [*Ventas*].

173   *Ibid.* at para. 53.

included a "standstill" provision—that is, a covenant not to make an offer to purchase the trust's assets without the trust's consent. The purchase agreement between Ventas and the trust included a provision requiring the trust to enforce all standstill agreements it had entered into. The purchase agreement also, however, included a "fiduciary out," that is, a clause that would allow the trust to consider an unsolicited "superior proposal" from another party.

Accordingly, the issue before the Ontario courts, simply put, was whether or not the trust's "fiduciary out" clause would permit it to consider the HCPI proposal or whether, instead, it would be required to enforce its standstill agreement with HCPI and therefore refuse to permit HCPI to proceed with such a proposal, pending a unitholder vote on the Ventas offer. The Superior Court ruled that the trust was, indeed, obliged to enforce the terms of its standstill agreement against HCPI. The Court of Appeal upheld the trial court's decision. In so doing, the Court of Appeal also suggested that, despite the directors' "fiduciary obligation to take steps to maximize shareholder (or unitholder value)" when subject to a takeover bid, that obligation would not prohibit trustees (and directors) from placing themselves under reasonable contractual constraints, as part of the sale process, even where these constraints might prove to prevent them from being able to accept the highest possible price for their securityholders. On this issue, the court considered that Ontario law might depart from the law of Delaware:

> It is not necessary—nor would it be wise, in my view—to go as far as HCPI suggests this court might go, and adopt the principle gleaned from some American authorities, that the target vendor can place no limits on the directors' right to consider superior offers and that any provision to the contrary is invalid and unenforceable: see *Paramount Communications, Inc. v. QVC Network Inc.*, 637 A. 2d 34 (Del. 1994), and *ACE Ltd. v. Capital Re Corp.*, 747 A. 2d 95 at 105 (Del. Ch. 1999). That is not what happened in this case.[174]

It is beyond the scope of this chapter to provide a detailed analysis of this intriguing case.[175] Suffice it to say, however, that the judgment left a number of issues concerning target company directors' fiduciary

---

174 *Ibid.* at para. 54.

175 It is noted that, following the Canadian dispute, Ventas, Inc. subsequently brought an action against HCP, Inc. in the United States alleging tortious interference in connection with the Canadian acquisition. The claim succeeded, and the judgment was recently upheld on appeal. See *Ventas, Inc. v. HCP, Inc.*, 647 F. 3d 291 (6th Cir. 2011).

duties to be resolved in future cases. For example, the Court of Appeal rejected only the absolute proposition that the "target vendor can place *no limits* on the directors' right to consider superior offers." [Emphasis added.] Although Delaware courts certainly are wary of limits placed by directors on their ability to consider superior offers, it is not at all clear that even Delaware law goes so far as to forbid any limits of any kind under any circumstances whatsoever.[176] The critical legal issue, therefore, is not whether it is impossible to place any limits whatsoever on directors' right to consider superior offers, but rather at what point are such limits considered excessive, inappropriate, and therefore subject to legal challenge. By rejecting only the most extreme position, the proposition that no limits of any kind should ever be permitted, the Court of Appeal left for another day the more subtle—and frankly more significant—question of precisely which limits should be permitted, and which rejected as void or unenforceable.

When the *BCE Inc. v. 1976 Debentureholders* case came before the Supreme Court of Canada in 2008, there had been some speculation that the Supreme Court might finally clarify the extent to which *Revlon* (or some Canadian version of *Revlon*) was, or was not, the law of Canada. The trial judge in *BCE*, for example, had expressly invoked *Revlon*:

> . . . the Court finds that the ruling in *Peoples* is not necessarily incompatible with the application of the *Revlon* duty by the BCE Board . . . .[177]

Moreover, the *BCE* case clearly involved a company that was not merely "in play" but which had, in Delaware terms, unmistakably entered the *Revlon* zone: the directors of BCE had made a decision to sell the company. However, the issues in dispute in the *BCE* litigation were rather different from the issues typically raised in Delaware *Revlon*-type cases. It was not alleged, for example, that the BCE directors had improperly favoured one (lower) bidder over another; nor was there any suggestion that the BCE directors had not worked hard enough to secure the highest possible sale price. Instead, the dispute revolved around the issue of whether the proposed terms of sale—no matter

---

176   The Delaware Supreme Court decision that, perhaps, comes closest to suggesting that directors can place no limitations on their ability to consider superior offers was *Omnicare, Inc. v. NCS Healthcare Inc.*, 818 A.2d (Del. S.C. 2003) [*Omnicare*]. That case, however, represented an unusual "split" decision, with a vigorous dissenting opinion by two judges of the Delaware Supreme Court, including then Chief Justice Veasey.

177   *BCE Inc. (Arrangement relatif à)*, 2008 QCCS 905 at para. 162, adopting by reference para. 203 of the court's judgment in a related proceeding, referred to by the court as the "1976/1996 Oppression Remedy" decision.

how generous they might be from the perspective of shareholders—were unfair to one particular non-shareholder constituency, holders of debentures issued by BCE's subsidiary Bell Canada. Accordingly, American lawyers might well have seen the *BCE* case as more akin to *Metropolitan Life Insurance Company v. RJR Nabisco, Inc.*,[178] a case that, like *BCE*, involved a leveraged buyout that triggered a credit ratings downgrade on outstanding debentures.

The Supreme Court of Canada, however, did refer to *Revlon*, using language that might fairly be characterized as constructively ambiguous. The Court's discussion, unfortunately, faltered a little out of the gate: the Court suggested, for example, that one of the two "most important" of the "*Revlon* line" of cases in Delaware was *Unocal Corp. v. Mesa Petroleum Co.*, a case which is not a *Revlon* case at all.[179] After this small misstep, the Court went on to make the following observation about the Delaware *Revlon* duty:

> What is clear is that the *Revlon* line of cases has not displaced the fundamental rule that the duty of the directors cannot be confined to particular priority rules, but is rather a function of business judgment of what is in the best interests of the corporation, in the particular situation it faces.[180]

To the extent that this statement is taken to mean that the *Revlon* cases are not understood in Delaware to create new fiduciary duties, it is accurate.[181] However, to suggest that the *Revlon* duty does not call for directors to pursue a very specific short-term objective (pursuant to their fiduciary obligations when the company is in *Revlon* mode) is problematic. Indeed, the Supreme Court went on to cite a passage from an article co-authored by former Delaware Chief Justice Norman Veasey in apparent support of the proposition that directors must at all times focus upon the best interests of the corporation, without narrowly focusing on any particular corporate interest. However, that very quotation includes the following sentence (upon which the Supreme Court offered no comment or qualification): "There are times, of course, when the

---

178 716 F. Supp. 1504 (S.D.N.Y. 1989).
179 *BCE*, above note 93 at para. 86. While it is incorrect to describe *Unocal*, above note 103, as a *Revlon* case, it is, however, accurate to characterize *Revlon* as a special case of the *Unocal* "enhanced scrutiny" standard.
180 *BCE*, *ibid.* at para. 87.
181 See, for example, *Lyondell*, above note 115 at 239: "As the trial court correctly noted, *Revlon* did not create any new fiduciary duties. It simply held that the 'board must perform its fiduciary duties in the service of a specific objective: maximizing the sale price of the enterprise.'"

focus is directly on the interests of stockholders [i.e., as in *Revlon*]."[182] For the reasons indicated above, BCE was by no means a typical *Revlon*-type case, in any event. However, the Supreme Court did not appear to accept that directors of Canadian corporations would be required to focus on short-term shareholder wealth maximization, even when a sale or change of control was inevitable. Instead, their duty is, and under all circumstances continues to be, to act honestly and in good faith with a view to the best interests of the corporation. In discharging that duty, the directors could properly consider the interests of many different constituents, and, provided their decisions were within a range of reasonableness, the courts will accord considerable deference to their business judgment. Thus, for example, the Court explains:

> In considering what is in the best interests of the corporation, directors may look to the interests of, *inter alia*, shareholders, employees, creditors, consumers, governments and the environment to inform their decisions. Courts should give appropriate deference to the business judgment of directors who take into account these ancillary interests, as reflected by the business judgment rule. The "business judgment rule" accords deference to a business decision, so long as it lies within a range of reasonable alternatives: see *Maple Leaf Foods Inc. v. Schneider Corp.* (1998), 42 O.R. (3d) 177 (C.A.); *Kerr v. Danier Leather Inc.*, [2007] 3 S.C.R. 331, 2007 SCC 44. It reflects the reality that directors, who are mandated under s. 102(1) of the *CBCA* to manage the corporation's business and affairs, are often better suited to determine what is in the best interests of the corporation. This applies to decisions on stakeholders' interests, as much as other directorial decisions.[183]

A corporation, then, may certainly maximize profit and shareholder value, subject to the caveat that they must not do so "by treating individual stakeholders unfairly."[184] *Revlon*, then, does not appear to be part of Canadian corporate law. However, directors, in the exercise of their fiduciary duties, may well determine that they ought to take steps to maximize shareholder value in a change of control situation, subject to fairly considering non-shareholder interests. Indeed, that is

---

182   Norman Veasey with Christine T. Di Guglielmo, "What Happened in Delaware Corporate Law and Governance from 1992–2004? A Retrospective on Some Key Developments" (2005) 153 U. Pa. L. Rev. 1399 at 1431, cited in *BCE*, above note 93 at para. 87.

183   *BCE, ibid.* at para. 40.

184   *Ibid.* at para. 64.

precisely what the Supreme Court conceived that the directors in *BCE* had done.[185]

b. Mitigating Directors' Conflict: Special Committees and Independent Advisors

The central agency problem identified in the hostile takeover bid context is the potential conflict of interest with which directors and officers of the target corporation are faced. On the one hand, it is their clear duty to act in the best interests of the target corporation in assessing a bid. Yet, because the directors and officers are aware that, if a hostile bid succeeds, they will likely be replaced, their personal interests conflict with their corporate duty. To address this potential conflict, it has become standard practice for directors of a corporation that is the target of a hostile bid to appoint a special committee of independent directors to assess the bid, and to manage the process generally with a view to making a recommendation to the board as a whole as to how to proceed. These directors must be independent of management of the corporation and of its major shareholders. To further enhance its independence and credibility, the special committee will typically have the power to appoint legal and financial advisors. The use of independent committees is regarded favourably by the courts, although there is an obvious practical problem with the creation and operation of such committees: those people with the best knowledge and experience concerning the target—the target's senior managers—are the very people who must be excluded from the committee charged with managing perhaps the most important transaction in the corporation's history.

Confronted by this challenge, corporations have occasionally stumbled. In *CW Shareholdings*, for example, the board chose to include the target company's chief executive officer on the special committee. The court declared that his presence on the committee was a mistake,[186] but ultimately concluded that, despite this "flaw in the composition of the Special Committee,"[187] the conclusions of the committee were, nevertheless, not undermined. This conclusion, it should be emphasized, was highly fact-specific.

---

185 It might be noted that, despite the decision of the Supreme Court of Canada to uphold the proposed BCE arrangement, the transaction was, in fact, subsequently aborted. See BCE News Release, "BCE Privatization Transaction Will Not Proceed" (11 December 2008), online: www.sedar.com/GetFile.do ?lang=EN&docClass=8&issuerNo=00000326&fileName=/csfsprod/data94/ filings/01356604/00000001/x%3A%5CASedar%5C2008%5CBCE%5CPress%5C PR_11dec08En.pdf.

186 *CW Shareholdings*, above note 37 at 779.

187 *Ibid.* at 780.

In *Maple Leaf Foods Inc. v. Schneider Corp.*,[188] the board of Schneider Corporation, the target company, sought to take advantage of the expertise of their chief executive officer without actually including him on the Special Committee by deputizing him to deal extensively with the bidders, an approach that, on the specific facts of the case, the court did not find inappropriate. The Court of Appeal quoted, with apparent approval, the comments of the trial judge, Farley J., who noted that "[p]otentially there could be conflict, but that must be balanced against the reasonable benefits to be obtained."[189] The expertise of the officers who participated in the negotiations, the fact that the independent committee retained the ultimate decision-making power, and the fact that any potential conflict was mitigated by "bail out packages" that had been granted to the senior officers (meaning that they would receive significant compensation even if they were to lose their positions following a takeover) were among the key factors noted by Farley J. in support of his conclusion that the participation of the senior officers in the negotiations did not taint the process.

In the U.S., where the standard of review applied by courts to directors' decisions can determine which party to a litigation proceeding will bear the onus of proof, the creation of an independent committee can have major procedural implications. In Canada, where "business judgment" cases are not characterized by the same level of formalism, the question of shifting onus is considerably less clear. However, one does note that in *Maple Leaf v. Schneider*, Weiler J.A. made the following comment concerning the burden of proof issue:

> . . . it may be that the burden of proof may not always rest on the same party when a change of control transaction is challenged. The real question is whether the directors of the target company successfully took steps to avoid a conflict of interest. If so, the rationale for shifting the burden of proof to the directors may not exist. If a board of directors has acted on the advice of a committee composed of persons having no conflict of interest, and that committee has acted independently, in good faith, and made an informed recommendation as to the best available transaction for the shareholders in the circumstances, the business judgment rule applies. The burden of proof is not an issue in such circumstances.[190]

---

188 Above note 120.
189 *Ibid.* at 196.
190 *Ibid.* at 193.

vi) Defensive Tactics

a. Justification of Defensive Tactics: Coercive Bids

It is often argued that the directors of companies that are the targets of hostile takeover bids must have adequate tools with which to resist such bids so that they may protect their shareholders from being subtly (or not so subtly) coerced into tendering their shares at an undervalue. Indeed, the notion that at least some bids are coercive is key to the arguments of proponents of takeover defences.

There are two ways in which a bid may be said to be coercive. First, it may be structurally coercive,[191] that is, strategically designed in such a way that shareholders of the target company feel pressured to tender their shares in spite of the fact that they genuinely and reasonably believe the bid price is too low. The classic example of a structurally coercive bid is a two-tier, "front-end loaded" bid in which target shareholders who tender to the bid can expect to receive a higher price for their shares than non-tendering shareholders who are later "squeezed out" in a post-bid going-private transaction of the sort discussed in Chapter 8. Partial bids (that is, bids for anything less than 100 percent of the shares of the target company) may also be coercive. If a partial takeover bid is successful, those shareholders who did not tender will be left as minority shareholders in a company that is no longer widely held. The post-bid market for their shares will be less liquid, and so the market price of those shares may fall well below the bid price. Thus, even if shareholders genuinely believe the bid price is inadequate, they may still feel compelled to tender to the bid.

Structural coercion has been widely recognized as unfair or even abusive, and many of the features of Canadian takeover bid law canvassed in Chapter 5 were intended to prevent the use of various structurally coercive devices. More controversially, a bid may be coercive in a different way. To borrow the phrase coined by Gilson and Kraakman, a bid may be "substantively coercive."[192] Substantive coercion, as Gilson and Kraakman emphasized in the 1989 paper that introduced the term, is a controversial—indeed a "slippery"[193]—concept. In the hands of the courts, it also proved to be an elusive idea. As Gilson and Kraakman observed in 2005, although the Delaware Supreme Court had

---

191 The concept of "structural coercion", was articulated by Gilson & Kraakman in "Delaware's Intermediate Standard," above note 30. A structurally coercive bid is one in which there is "risk that disparate treatment of non-tendering shareholders might distort shareholders' tender decisions." *Ibid.* at 258.

192 *Ibid.* at 248.

193 *Ibid.* at 274.

invoked the term (and cited their 1989 paper as its source), in doing so, the court "[changed] utterly"[194] Gilson and Kraakman's meaning.

For a hostile bid to be considered substantively coercive, in Gilson and Kraakman's view, two conditions would need to prevail. First, the price offered would, in fact, have to undervalue the target corporation shares. This factor alone, however, would not be enough, since directors of a company subject to such a bid would, presumably, make efforts to explain to their shareholders why the bid price was inadequate and so persuade them not to tender. Accordingly, a bid could not be substantively coercive unless, for some reason, target shareholders were not prepared to believe the (accurate) view of the company directors that the bid undervalued the target. Only if both of these conditions were present could a bid be characterized as substantively coercive, and thus might result in shareholders mistakenly tendering their shares to an inadequate bid.

But although, as Gilson and Kraakman pointed out, one may acknowledge in the abstract the possibility that a bid might be substantively coercive, the likelihood that both of their identified conditions would exist in a real world bid should be very low indeed. Such an abstract possibility, in their view, "cannot be a basis for rubber-stamping management's *pro forma* claims in the face of market skepticism and the enormous opportunity losses that threaten target shareholders when hostile offers are defeated."[195]

b. Methods of Defending against Hostile Bids

Thus far, we have focused upon the overall *goal* of target company resistance to hostile takeover bids, the inherent conflict faced by target company management, and the process of managing that conflict to pursue appropriate corporate goals. Now we turn to consider some of the key *methods* used to achieve those target company goals. In particular, this section will focus on two types of measures frequently used by target boards to defend against hostile bids or to insulate friendly transactions from hostile interference: the shareholder rights plan (or poison pill) and deal protection measures. It should not be forgotten in the discussion that follows that an issue of considerable interest to shareholders and practitioners alike is the question of whether defensive tactics do, in fact, provide directors with bargaining leverage that

---

194 Gilson & Kraakman, "Takeovers in the Boardroom," above note 31 at 1420, n3.
195 Gilson & Kraakman, "Delaware's Intermediate Standard," above note 30 at 274.

ultimately benefits target shareholders, or whether, instead, they merely operate to inhibit bids and perhaps entrench directors and officers.[196]

i.   *"Shareholder Rights Plans" ("Poison Pills")*[197]
The proliferation of hostile bids in the United States in the 1980s, the
perceived unfairness (or coerciveness) of many of those bids, and the
apparent vulnerability of target company directors and managers created
the impetus for the design of effective takeover bid defences, of which the
shareholder rights plan or poison pill was to become the most famous.

The earliest version of the poison pill, according to its universally
acknowledged creator, Martin Lipton, was first crafted in 1982.[198] The
crucial 1985 Delaware Supreme Court decision, *Moran v. Household
International Inc.*,[199] established the basic legality of the poison pill
defence in Delaware, although the validity of certain aggressive variants of the poison pill (such as "dead hand"[200] plans) was subsequently
called into question.[201]

Poison pill plans proved to be a popular takeover defence, and
were widely adopted by both U.S. and Canadian public companies,[202]
although the law governing the use of such plans did not evolve in
the same way on both sides of the border. Stock exchanges also took
an interest in such plans. The Toronto Stock Exchange, for example,

---

196 For a recent article concluding that the "bargaining power hypothesis is only
true in a subset of all deals, contrary to the claims of defence proponents that
the hypothesis applies to all negotiated acquisitions," see Guhan Subramanian,
"Bargaining in the Shadow of Takeover Defences" (2003) 113 Yale L.J. 1.

197 According to Lipton and Rowe, the facetious term *poison pill* was coined in 1983 as
a result of a glib response by an investment banker to a *Wall Street Journal* reporter
who had asked him to identify a security issued by Lenox, Inc., on Mr. Lipton's
advice. See Lipton & Rowe, "Pills, Polls and Professors," above note 15 at 10, n30.

198 *Ibid.* at 9.

199 Above note 109.

200 Under "dead hand" plans, only directors in office at the time the rights plan was
adopted had authority to redeem the rights before expiration. In other words,
a hostile bidder could not undo the effect of the rights plan by launching a
successful proxy contest with a view to replacing the board of directors with
directors who would redeem the rights.

201 See *Carmody v. Toll Bros. Inc.*, 723 A.2d 1180 (Del. Ch. 1998).

202 Inco Limited was the first Canadian company to adopt a poison pill, in October
1988. See Jeffrey G. MacIntosh, "The Poison Pill: A Noxious Nostrum for Canadian Shareholders" (1989) 15 Can. Bus. L.J. 276. In 2001, over 2,200 corporations in the United States had poison pills in place, although the popularity of
the poison pill declined significantly over the following ten years such that, by
2011, fewer than 900 companies had such plans in place. See Andrew L. Bab &
Sean P. Neenan, "Poison Pills in 2011" in The Conference Board, *Directors Notes*
(March 2011) at 2.

includes provisions dealing with poison pills (or "securityholder rights plans") in the *TSX Company Manual*.[203] Briefly, those provisions emphasize a preference for shareholder approval of a poison pill within six months of its adoption except in the case of a "tactical pill" (that is, a poison pill put into place in response to a current hostile bid), in which case the TSX has indicated that it will normally defer to actions by securities regulators.

The structure of poison pill plans has developed significantly since the 1980s. Modern poison pill plans adopted by Canadian corporations typically work in this way. The "plan" takes the form of a rights agreement entered into between the corporation and a "rights agent" (typically, a trust company). Pursuant to this agreement, share purchase "rights" are created and attached to all outstanding common shares. Each right entitles the holder to purchase one additional common share at a price (the "exercise price") which is originally set significantly above the market price for the common shares.[204] In other words, when the rights are first created they have no intrinsic value at all. No shareholder would exercise the rights at this point, even if he or she were permitted to do so. The agreement will frequently provide, in any event however, that the rights are not exercisable until the "separation time," as described below. Moreover, the rights when first created are attached to the shares themselves, and cannot be traded apart from the shares.

The key to the operation of a poison pill plan is that the number of shares which a rights holder is entitled to purchase upon payment of the exercise price is subject to adjustment.[205] Specifically, in the event that any person (an "acquiring person") acquires some specified percentage of the company's outstanding voting shares (often 20 percent),[206] each

---

203 See *TSX Company Manual*, ss. 634–37.

204 U.S. shareholder rights plans often provide for the issue of rights that entitle shareholders to purchase a small number of shares of another class, such as preference shares structured to facilitate operation of the plan.

205 Of course, the exercise price may also be subject to adjustment from time to time on the basis of the usual "anti-dilution" clauses typically found in instruments creating convertible securities and warrants of all kinds. See, for example, Nicholls, *Corporate Finance and Canadian Law*, above note 127 at 46.

206 This event is typically referred to in poison pill plans as a "flip-in" event. This peculiar term arose because of the path of development of poison pill plans in the United States. Originally, poison pills were not triggered by the initial acquisition of a major share interest, but rather by any subsequent post-bid attempt to squeeze out minority shareholders. Such an attempted squeeze-out was referred to in early rights plans as a "flip-over" event because, theoretically, if triggered, the rights of the target company shareholders would flip over to become rights

right typically entitles a holder to purchase from the corporation, for the exercise price, the number of shares having a market price equal to *double* the exercise price.[207] This remarkable "two for one" deal would result in massive dilution that would, for all practical purposes, make it impossible for the acquiring person to complete a successful bid for the company.

Of course, it is crucial to the effectiveness of a poison pill plan that these special purchase rights not be available to the acquiring person (despite the fact that the acquiring person is also a shareholder). Accordingly, poison pill plans provide that, upon the occurrence of the triggering (or "flip-in") event, any rights held by an acquiring person become void. Because this particular feature of poison pill plans seems to involve treating holders of the same class of shares differently, it has sometimes been suggested that it may run afoul of the basic corporate law principle of equal treatment of shareholders.[208] This issue has not yet been considered squarely in Canada, although at least one Canadian court has expressed some support for U.S. decisions upholding the legality of this aspect of poison pill plans.[209] In the U.S. context, Wachtell, Lipton, Rosen & Katz have noted that although in some U.S. jurisdictions the discriminatory features of the typical shareholders rights plan were initially found to violate corporate law, the corporate law in those very jurisdictions was subsequently amended to specifically establish the legality of rights plans.[210]

---

to acquire shares in the new, merged entity. Because a flip-over plan does not protect a target company from a hostile bid launched by a bidder that chooses not to undertake a second-stage freeze-out or squeeze-out transaction, a modified version of the poison pill was developed in which the triggering event was the initial acquisition of a major share interest. This new triggering event was dubbed a flip-in event, in contrast to the traditional flip-over triggering event.

207 Though the rights are to be adjusted in this way once a "flip-in" event has occurred, they are typically not exercisable until the "separation time." The "separation time" typically begins following a specified number of trading days (often ten) after the date on which there is a public announcement indicating that an acquiring person has obtained the specified (for example, 20 percent) share interest. But the separation time can also occur under other circumstances, including within a specified number of trading days following the launch, or public announcement, of a takeover bid for the company other than a "permitted bid" as defined in the plan.

208 See, for example, Stephen Wishart, "Are Poison Pills Illegal?" (1992) 30 Can. Bus. L.J. 105. On the general issue of equal treatment of shareholders, see Nicholls, *Corporate Law*, above note 18 at 370–72.

209 *Primewest Energy Trust v. Orion Energy Trust* (1999), 1 B.L.R. (3d) 294 (Alta. Q.B.).

210 Wachtell, Lipton, Rosen, & Katz, "The Share Purchase Rights Plan" (1996), quoted in Ronald J. Gilson & Bernard S. Black, *The Law and Finance of Corpo-*

Modern Canadian poison pill plans also typically include a "permitted bid" provision.[211] Where a bid is a permitted bid, it will not trigger the poison pill rights.[212] A permitted bid is a takeover bid that complies with certain provisions intended to ensure that all shareholders are treated alike, have adequate time, and are not otherwise "coerced" into accepting the offer. So, for example, a permitted bid must be left open for a certain minimum period of time, say sixty days (well beyond the thirty-five-day statutory minimum mandated by provincial securities laws). A permitted bid must typically be made for all outstanding voting shares of the corporation, and must provide that the bidder will not take up and pay for shares unless more than 50 percent of the outstanding shares—excluding those held by the bidder, its affiliates, associates, or joint actors—have been tendered. Where that condition is satisfied, typical permitted bid provisions will require that the bidder make a public announcement to that effect and then leave the bid open for deposit of shares for some additional minimum period (perhaps ten business days) to ensure that shareholders have an opportunity to tender after learning that a majority of their fellow shareholders have, in fact, accepted the bid.

There are many reasons that a prospective hostile bidder will find it impractical or undesirable to structure a bid that satisfies the typical "permitted bid" exception. There may, in fact, be some legal impediment to doing so.[213] Or a bidder may not be prepared to give up the flexibility of being entitled to waive any minimum tender conditions. Thus, hostile bidders may find the existence of a shareholder rights (or

---

rate Acquisitions, 2d ed., 2003–2004 Supplement (New York: Foundation Press, 2003) at 59.

211 Shareholder rights plans with "permitted bid" provisions are often facetiously dubbed "chewable pills." See, for example, Andrew R. Brownstein & Igor Kirman, "Can a Board Say No When Shareholders Say Yes? Responding to Majority Vote Resolutions" (2004) 60 Bus. Law. 23 at 70.

212 As a technical matter, this result is achieved in typical Canadian poison pill plans in this way: a person who acquires shares in the target pursuant to a "permitted bid" is excluded from the definition of "acquiring person" in the plan; accordingly, because the definition of "flip-in event" typically is tied to a transaction by which a person becomes an "acquiring person," a permitted bid will not constitute a "flip-in event."

213 In the recent *Inco/Teck Cominco* matter, Teck's bid for Inco complied in most respects with the "permitted bid" conditions in Inco's shareholders' rights plan, except that it did not provide that Teck would take up additional shares after the initial take-up, evidently because of concerns that, in a cash and share bid, U.S. securities laws prohibit multiple take-ups, absent an exemption order. See *In the Matter of Inco Limited and Teck Cominco Limited* (2006), 29 OSCB 7078.

poison pill) plan a formidable obstacle, despite the permitted bid provisions and so may seek to attack the plan as illegitimate.

In Canada, the principal goals of a poison pill plan are (a) to provide the directors of the target company with additional time to respond to a hostile bid (either by entering into a friendly transaction with another party, or generating some other alternative); and (b) to encourage the hostile bidder to negotiate with the directors of the target company, with a view to arriving at better terms for target company shareholders.

In Canada, most cases in which hostile bidders have sought to attack a target company's use of a poison pill have come before provincial securities commissions rather than the courts. Indeed, a key distinction between the U.S. and Canadian takeover environment generally has been the more significant role played by Canadian securities regulators in arbitrating contested takeover disputes.[214] This is important because the jurisdiction of the securities commissions is delimited by the securities statutes. They do not have the authority to make authoritative determinations of corporate law, including determinations as to whether or not directors have acted in accordance with their fiduciary obligations. On the other hand, the critical role envisioned by securities legislation for the securities commissions in dealing with takeover bid issues has occasionally made the courts reluctant to take bold steps in the takeover bid context. As one court put it: "Considering the regulatory atmosphere of takeovers and the role of the Ontario Securities Commission, courts should be reluctant to interfere except in the clearest of cases."[215]

Neither corporate statutes nor securities legislation in Canada deal specifically with the use of poison pills or other defensive tactics by target directors. However, the Canadian Securities Administrators have promulgated a national policy statement, National Policy 62-202 (NP 62-202), expressing their views on defensive tactics. This policy statement indicates the view of regulators that "unrestricted auctions produce the most desirable results in takeover bids," and further warns that regulators "will take appropriate action if they become aware of defensive tactics that will likely result in shareholders being deprived of the

---

214 This feature of the Canadian takeover bid environment has attracted some recent criticism. See, for example, Competition Policy Review Panel, above note 35; Vanderpol & Waitzer, above note 67.

215 *Re Olympia & York Enterprises Ltd. and Hiram Walker Resources* (1986), 59 O.R. (2d) 254 at 278 (H.C.J.), Montgomery J. This judgment was appealed to the Divisional Court. The Divisional Court's judgment was reported in the Ontario Reports immediately following Montgomery J.'s judgment.

ability to respond to a takeover bid or to a competing bid."[216] Although the policy statement does not have the force of law, it is nevertheless an important guide to the manner in which securities regulators are likely to exercise their public interest discretion.

The approach to poison pills that has been taken by Canadian securities regulators since about 1992 (apart from a few ostensibly anomalous recent decisions discussed below) reflects an attitude toward such plans very similar to the views articulated in a 1988 decision of the influential Delaware Court of Chancery. In Delaware, however, that approach had already been rejected by the Delaware Supreme Court by 1990.

The 1988 case was *City Capital Associates v. Interco Inc.*[217] There, Chancellor Allen of the Delaware Court of Chancery ruled that the directors of a target company were required to redeem the rights originally issued under a poison pill to permit a clearly non-coercive bid from a hostile bidder to proceed. He noted that the question came before the court "at what I will call the end-stage of this takeover contest. That is, the negotiating leverage that a poison pill confers upon this company's board will, it is clear, not be further utilized by the board to increase the options available to shareholders or to improve the terms of those options."[218] Later in the judgment, appears the following sentence: "[I]n the setting of a noncoercive offer, absent unusual facts, there may come a time when a board's fiduciary duty will require it to redeem the rights and to permit the shareholders to choose."[219]

Interco's endorsement of "ultimate shareholder choice" was echoed by the Ontario Securities Commission several years later in *Re Canadian Jorex*,[220] in which the Ontario Securities Commission cease traded a poison pill that no longer appeared to be needed to provide the target company board with additional time to generate alternatives for the shareholders, declaring that "the time had . . . come when 'the pill has got to go.'"[221] The "ultimate shareholder choice" approach to poison pills suggested by Chancellor Allen in *Interco* proved to be relatively short-lived in Delaware, however. In *Paramount Communications Inc. v. Time Inc.*,[222] the Delaware Supreme Court rejected the notion that, in

216 NP 62-202 (1997), 20 OSCB 3525.
217 551 A.2d 787 (Del. Ch. 1988) [*Interco*].
218 *Ibid.* at 790.
219 *Ibid.* at 798.
220 (1992), 15 OSCB 257.
221 *Ibid.* at 265.
222 Above note 113.

the case of an all-shares, all-cash bid, the only "threat" posed was one of inadequate value. This position, said the court:

> represents a fundamental misconception of our standard of review under *Unocal* principally because it would involve the court in substituting its judgment for what is a "better" deal for that of a corporation's board of directors. To the extent that the Court of Chancery has recently done so in certain of its opinions, we hereby reject such an approach as not in keeping with a proper *Unocal* analysis. See e.g., *Interco* . . . and its progeny.[223]

However, the *Jorex* approach prevailed in Canada and was applied in a number of subsequent securities commissions' decisions.[224] In its most recent statement on the subject, the OSC explains the general principle animating securities commissions' poison pill decisions:

> In our view, it is generally time for a shareholder rights plan "to go" when the rights plan has served its purpose by facilitating an auction, encouraging competing bids or otherwise maximizing shareholder value. A rights plan will be cease traded where it is unlikely to achieve any further benefits for shareholders.[225]

This general approach underlies a detailed list of factors or guidelines that may be considered by regulators in determining whether or not a rights plan should, or should not, be cease traded that was offered by the Securities Commission in the *Royal Host*[226] decision. These *Royal Host* guidelines, still the most specific set of factors that have been offered by the commission, include the following:

- whether shareholder approval of the rights plan was obtained;
- when the plan was adopted;
- whether there is broad shareholder support for the continued operation of the plan;
- the size and complexity of the target company;

---

223 *Ibid.* at 1153.
224 See, especially, *Re Lac Minerals Ltd.* (1994), 17 OSCB 4963; *Re MDC Corp.* (1994), 17 OSCB 4971; *Re BGC Acquisition Inc. and Argentia Gold Corp.*, [1999] 6 B.C.S.C. Weekly Summary 23; *Re Ivanhoe III Inc.* (1999), 22 OSCB 1327 [*Ivanhoe*]; *Re Royal Host Real Estate Investment Trust* (1999), 22 OSCB 7819 [*Royal Host*]; *Re Consolidated Properties* (2000), 23 OSCB 7981; *Re Chapters Inc. and Trilogy Retail Enterprises L.P.* (2001), 24 OSCB 1663; *Re Cara Operations Limited and Second Cup* (2002), 25 OSCB 7997 [*Cara Operations*].
225 *Baffinland Iron Mines Corp. (Re)* (2010), 33 OSCB 11385 at para. 26 [*Baffinland*].
226 *Royal Host*, above note 224.

- the other defensive tactics, if any, implemented by the target company;
- the number of potential, viable offerors;
- the steps taken by the target company to find an alternative bid or transaction that would be better for the shareholders;
- the likelihood that, if given further time, the target company will be able to find a better bid or transaction;
- the nature of the bid, including whether it is coercive or unfair to the shareholders of the target company;
- the length of time since the bid was announced and made; and
- the likelihood that the bid will not be extended if the rights plan is not terminated.[227]

These factors have been regularly referred to by provincial securities commissions since 1999, and were reiterated by the OSC in its most recent shareholder rights plan decision in 2010.[228] Although rather less specific, a helpfully illuminating set of "guiding considerations" was also set out in *Cara Operations*.[229] There, the commission explained:

> [52] Rights plans may perform a useful function in limited cases, but are rightly scrutinized with suspicion.

> [53] While it may be important for shareholders to receive advice and recommendations from the directors of the target company as to the wisdom of accepting or rejecting a bid, and for directors to be satisfied that a particular bid is the best likely bid under the circumstances, in the last analysis the decision to accept or reject a bid should be made by the shareholders, and not by the directors or others.

> [54] The Commission's role in determining whether a rights plan is in the best interest of shareholders is to be an impartial referee in the takeover bid process, not to be drawn into the game tactically to the advantage of one or more of the interest groups involved in a struggle for control.

> [55] The paramount consideration in deciding whether a rights plan should be allowed to stand in the way of a takeover bid is the best interest of the shareholders generally.

---

227 *Ibid.*
228 *Baffinland*, above note 225 at para. 30.
229 Above note 224.

[56] What is in the best interests of the shareholders cannot be determined in the abstract, but must be ascertained in the context of our existing legal and business environment as reflected in the rules and policies for takeover bids under the Act and as reflected in the various cases.

[57] At least two underlying principles emerge from the rules, policies and cases.

[58] First, there is the principle of procedural fairness for all: bidders, potential bidders, existing shareholders, management, and those whose business fortune is tied to any one of these groups. The rules of the game should be clear and consistently applied to encourage bidders to come forward. And the game must be played in an acceptable timeframe.

[59] A fair process with clear rules and timelines for takeover bids is in the best interest of shareholders generally: it encourages bidders to come forward and gives shareholders opportunities to realize upon their investment at optimum values.

[60] The longest period following the announcement of a bid that a rights plan was permitted to operate in the cases referred to us was the period of 108 days in *Ivanhoe*. That would have been an inordinate period of time, except for the special circumstances of that case. While absolute numbers of days, on their own, should not be the deciding factor in determining whether a rights plan no longer serves the interest of shareholders, the longer the period the higher the onus is on those alleging that the rights plan still serves the interest of shareholders.

[61] Secondly, there is the principle of the fiduciary duty of directors, members of a special committee of directors, and their advisors. Adherence to this principle should be reflected in conduct and recommendations that are based upon the best interest of the shareholders generally and not those of any group of shareholders, bidders, potential bidders or others.

[62] Certain guideposts or indicia have been outlined in *Royal Host* and other cases to help determine whether a rights plan in a given case is in the best interest of the shareholders.

[63] Tactical rights plans generally will not be found to be in the best interest of the shareholders.

[64] If a plan is not put in place before a particular bid becomes evident, it very likely will be that the plan is tactical and directed at the particular bid.

[65] If a plan does not have shareholder approval, it generally will be suspect as not being in the best interest of the shareholders; however, shareholder approval of itself will not establish that a plan is in the best interest of the shareholders.

[66] If, in the face of a takeover bid, a director, a special committee member, or an advisor acts in a manner that raises serious questions as to whether such person is acting solely in the best interest of the shareholders, then the onus of establishing that the rights plan is in the best interest of the shareholders may be significantly increased.

[67] Where a rights plan has delayed significantly a takeover bid and no competing bid obviously superior to the bid has actually emerged, the rights plan will almost certainly be considered to no longer be in the best interest of the shareholders, even if it once had been in their interest.[230]

Shareholder rights plans, then, would generally be permitted to stay in place only so long as there appears to be a "real and substantial possibility"[231] (or perhaps a "reasonable possibility"[232]) that, "given a reasonable period of further time, the board of the target corporation can increase shareholder choice and maximize shareholder value."[233] Once a plan has achieved that objective, the time will come when the "pill has got to go," and shareholders of the target corporation must be permitted to decide for themselves whether or not they wish to accept a bid.

Although Canadian securities commission poison pill decisions appeared to be following a straight and reasonably predictable path for many years following *Jorex*, there have been a few recent curves. The August 2006 OSC decision, *In the Matter of Falconbridge Limited*,[234] for example, seemed to allow a poison pill to remain in place for a much longer period than had been regarded as reasonable in the past. *Fal-*

---

230 *Ibid.*

231 See, for example, *Re MDC Corp.*, above note 224 at 4979.

232 See *Consolidated Properties*, above note 224 at 7984: "[In view of cases decided following *Regal Greetings*] 'reasonable possibility' would appear to us to be a more appropriate description than 'real and substantial possibility,' although both may in practice amount to the same thing."

233 *Re MDC Corp.*, above note 224 at 4979.

234 Above note 145.

conbridge involved a takeover contest for control of Falconbridge Limited. The two competing bidders were Inco Limited, which had made a friendly bid, and Xstrata, a 19.8 percent shareholder of Falconbridge which had launched a hostile bid.

The Falconbridge board adopted a shareholder rights plan, without shareholder approval, on 22 September 2005. The plan provided that it was to expire in six months unless it had received shareholder approval by that time. Yet one day before this six-month period ended, instead of seeking shareholder approval, the Falconbridge board executed a "Replacement Rights Plan" substantially similar to the original plan and, again, adopted without shareholder approval.

Inco's formal (friendly) offer was launched on 10 October 2005. The offer was extended three times, with the last expiration date set at 30 June 2006. The frequent extensions were implemented to give the parties more time to secure regulatory approvals, especially European Union competition approvals. On 18 May 2006, Xstrata made its competing hostile offer for Falconbridge's shares. The Xstrata bid was an all cash bid for all of Falconbridge's shares. It contained a minimum tender condition—namely that Xstrata would not be obliged to complete the bid unless it acquired at least 66 $^2/_3$ percent of the Falconbridge shares. That condition was waivable at the option of Xstrata. While it was not unusual for such a condition to be waivable at the option of the bidder, on the particular facts of this case Falconbridge and Inco viewed the right to waive with concern. Their concern was that Xstrata—already a holder of 19.8 percent of the shares—might be able to acquire just enough additional shares to effectively block the Inco bid.

Xstrata applied to the Ontario Securities Commission to have the Falconbridge Replacement Rights Plan cease traded. Despite the fact that the plan was a tactical plan that had not been approved by Falconbridge's shareholders and had been in place for a period (including the time during which the substantially similar First Rights Plan was in effect) of over nine months by the time of the hearing, the commission held that "it would be in the public interest for the Replacement Rights Plan to continue to operate for a brief period."[235] That "brief period" however, was an additional month—a period of time almost equal to the full thirty-five-day minimum statutory bid period.

To put the *Falconbridge* time lines into perspective, in a previous 2002 ruling (*Cara Operations*),[236] the commission had characterized the 108-day period during which the poison pill in another earlier case

---

235   *Ibid.* at para. 64.
236   Above note 224.

(*Ivanhoe*[237]) had been allowed to remain in place as "an inordinate period of time, except for the special circumstances of that case."[238] In light of such earlier commission precedent, permitting the Falconbridge plan to remain in place for more than double that length of time must be regarded as somewhat remarkable.

Three subsequent securities commission decisions—two in Alberta and one in Ontario—seemed to represent a significant refinement on commission shareholder rights plans jurisprudence, a refinement more supportive of board decisions to resist a hostile bid, at least in cases involving partial bids, and in which the impugned rights plan had received recent shareholder approval.

The first of the three cases was *Re Pulse Data Inc. (Pulse Data)*,[239] a 2007 decision of the Alberta Securities Commission. In *Pulse Data* the commission appeared to accept the target company's argument that, at least in some cases, a poison pill could remain in place to prevent a potentially "abusive" form of takeover acquisition—even where the target board was taking no steps to develop an alternative to the hostile bid.

The target company in *Pulse Data* argued that its poison pill plan was necessary not to provide it with more time to create value for shareholders, but rather to prevent a "creeping takeover" by a hostile bidder. Under the poison pill plan, a bid would be permitted only if it included an irrevocable minimum tender condition. Without such a condition, the target argued, a hostile bidder could launch a takeover bid under which the bidder's obligation to take up and pay for shares tendered to the bid was subject to the condition that a certain minimum number of shares were tendered (for example, 50 percent or perhaps 66 2/3 percent); later, however, if an insufficient number of shares were tendered, the bidder could choose to waive that condition and take up whatever shares had been tendered. Now, the purpose of a minimum tender condition has traditionally been understood as a feature of a bid designed to protect the interests of the bidder. A bidder launching a bid to acquire control of a corporation would not want to find itself legally obliged to buy shares if not enough shares could be purchased to obtain control. But the target in *Pulse Data* argued that a hostile bidder might well want to waive the condition and purchase a relatively small number of shares under the right circumstances. Even if a bidder lacked sufficient shares to have legal control of the corporation (that is, at least 50 percent of the voting shares plus one), if it held a large enough non-

---

237 *Ibid.*
238 *Ibid.* at para. 60.
239 2007 ABASC 895.

controlling block of shares, it could effectively discourage future bidders from acquiring control of the corporation, and so deprive shareholders of a full premium in a later change-of-control transaction.

Despite the fact that there was no reasonable possibility of a superior offer emerging if the Pulse Data poison pill remained in place, the Alberta Securities Commission decided *not* to immediately cease trade the pill. In making this decision, the commission was primarily influenced by the fact that the shareholders of the target company, just six days before the commission hearing, had approved the rights plan by a significant majority, and had done so, as the commission found, with the benefit of complete disclosure. Accordingly, the commission was persuaded that this recent, informed shareholder vote "demonstrated that the continuation of the Rights Plan as at 27 September 2007 was in the *bona fide* interests of Pulse Shareholders."[240]

The *Pulse Data* case was followed by *Neo Materials Technologies (Re)*,[241] a 2009 decision of the Ontario Securities Commission. *Neo Materials* involved a partial bid, for a maximum of 20 percent of the shares of the target company not already owned by the bidder. In fact, the bidder subsequently amended its offer to reduce the maximum number of shares it was prepared to purchase to about 9.5 percent. The bidder already held just over 20 percent of the target company's shares. The target company adopted a poison pill that would require any permitted bid to have an irrevocable minimum tender condition, then subsequently adopted a second rights plan (or poison pill), after the hostile partial bid was launched. That second plan would require any permitted bid to be made to all shareholders for all of their shares. This second plan was ultimately approved by a very significant majority of the target company's shareholders under circumstances that, in the view of the commission, indicated that the shareholders knew, "or ought reasonably to have known, that they were voting against the Pala Offer and we have not been presented with any evidence to suggest otherwise."[242]

The Ontario Securities Commission dealt squarely with the proposition, argued on behalf of the hostile bidder, that the only legitimate use of a shareholder rights plan was to provide the directors of the target company with adequate time to find alternative bidders. The panel rejected this narrow proposition, stating

> Consistent with the Supreme Court's statements in *BCE* and the established body of corporate case law it is our view that, shareholder

---

240 *Ibid.* at para. 102.
241 (2009), 32 OSCB 6941 [*Neo Materials*].
242 *Ibid.* at para. 72.

rights plans *may* be adopted for the broader purpose of protecting the long-term interests of the shareholders, where, in the directors' reasonable business judgment, the implementation of a rights plan would be in the best interests of the corporation.[243]

The panel agreed that the central issue for the commission in reviewing a shareholder rights plan was whether or not the time had come for the pill to go, but endorsed a broad view of how to evaluate whether or not a plan had outlived its usefulness. That view was based upon enabling directors to fulfill their fiduciary duties (language that had been found in the earlier *Regal* decision), but did not attempt to link the fulfillment of fiduciary duties to specific actions (such as steps to conduct an auction or otherwise maximize shareholder value):

> We echo the statements of the Commission in *Regal*, in finding that so long as the rights plan continues to allow the target's management and board the opportunity to fulfill their fiduciary duties, the plan continues to serve a purpose.[244]

Earlier poison pill decisions by Canadian securities regulators, such as those referred to above, evaluated poison pills on the basis of whether they had achieved the objective of providing directors of a target company with sufficient time to generate a value-maximizing alternative. Did these three decisions signal a shift in regulatory policy or attitudes? Or were they to be seen as highly fact specific?

Two days after the final written reasons[245] in *Neo Materials* were issued, the Alberta Securities Commission issued its final written decision[246] in *1478860 Alberta Ltd (Re)*,[247] (*Canadian Hydro Developers*). *Canadian Hydro Developers* involved a takeover bid for Canadian Hydro Developers, Inc. by a wholly owned subsidiary of TransAlta Corporation. The board of Canadian Hydro Developers had adopted a shareholder rights plan in February 2008, which was then submitted to the shareholders for approval at a meeting in April of that year. The shareholders approved the plan. In July of the following year, following an unsuccessful attempt to negotiate a friendly acquisition, TransAlta launched a takeover bid for the outstanding shares of Canadian Hydro

---

243 *Ibid.* at para. 112.
244 *Ibid.* at para. 144.
245 Owing to the urgency of the matter, the OSC had issued its decision several months earlier, indicating that full reasons were to follow.
246 The Alberta Securities Commission had also issued a brief oral decision nine days earlier.
247 2009 ABASC 448.

Developers. TransAlta applied to the Alberta Securities Commission seeking an order to prevent the shareholder rights plan from standing in the way of its bid. TransAlta argued, among other things, that in deciding whether or not the directors of Canadian Hydro Developers had been afforded sufficient time to generate an alternative to the TransAlta bid, the commission should look not simply to the period of time since the formal bid had been launched, but should also consider the time that had elapsed since TransAlta had initiated discussions with Canadian Hydro Developers concerning a possible acquisition.

The commission concluded that Canadian Hydro Developers had successfully discharged the initial burden of establishing that there was a "real and substantial probability" that if the plan were maintained there would be a superior result for Canadian Hydro Developers shareholders. In deciding not to intervene, the Alberta Securities Commission placed particular emphasis on the fact that the rights plan had been approved by the shareholders of the corporation well in advance of the hostile bid's launch.[248] As the commission Panel put it:

> We concluded that this was not a case warranting our intervention at the time of the hearing, as that would undermine the Hydro shareholders' earlier decision of what would serve their interests.[249]

Although the Panel was not prepared to intervene at the time of the hearing, they indicated that they "foresaw that time could arrive—and quite soon—when the Plan ought to go . . . ."[250]

The reasoning in *Canadian Hydro Developers* was consistent with the long post-*Jorex* line of authority: the time will come when the pill has to go; that moment had not, however, yet been reached.

In 2010, the British Columbia Securities Commission dipped its oar into the rights plan waters. In *Icahn Partners LP (Re)*[251] investment vehicles controlled by well-known shareholder activist Carl Icahn launched a takeover bid on 1 March 2010 for the shares of entertainment company Lions Gate Entertainment Corp. In response to the bid, the board of Lions Gate adopted a shareholder rights plan, but otherwise took no steps to seek an alternative transaction. Icahn applied to the British Columbia Securities Commission for an order cease trading the rights plan. In reviewing the principles applicable to securities commissions' poison pill decision, the B.C. Securities Commission contended that the "reluctance" of regulators to interfere with

---

248 *Ibid.* at para. 60.
249 *Ibid.* at para. 69.
250 *Ibid.* at para. 70.
251 2010 BCSECCOM 432.

target directors' exercise of their fiduciary duties was premised on "the practice of target company boards of making efforts to maximize shareholder value (whether through enhancements to the bid, competing bids, or alternative transactions) in discharging their fiduciary duty"[252] as well as a recognition "that the shareholders ultimately have the opportunity to decide whether or not to tender into the bid."[253]

In this case, the directors of Lions Gate had chosen not to take such value-maximizing steps, and urged the commission to adopt the approach taken in *Pulse Data* and in *Neo Materials*, where shareholder rights plans were not cease traded despite the fact that the target board was not actively seeking alternative transactions. The majority was unequivocal in its views: "[I]n the absence of any attempts by the target company board to take any steps to increase shareholder value through an improvement of the bid or the presentation of alternative transactions, there is no basis for allowing [a shareholder rights plan] to continue."[254]

What then of *Pulse Data* and *Neo Materials*? The majority rejected the proposition that *Pulse Data* and *Neo Materials* could be interpreted as authority for the proposition that directors could "just say no" to a hostile bid. Such an interpretation, they said, "would mean that the *Pulse* and *Neo* panels intended to reverse the long-standing policy of Canadian securities regulators that [shareholder rights plans], if they are to continue, can be allowed [to]do so only for a temporary period, at the end of which shareholders must be given the opportunity to decide whether to tender to the bid."[255] Noting that the long-standing principles underlying Canadian securities commissions' approach to poison pills were affirmed in both *Pulse Data* and *Neo Materials*, the B.C. Securities Commission maintained that these two ostensibly anomalous decisions did not, in fact, represent ". . . any significant change to the Canadian securities regulators' public interest policy principles governing [shareholder rights plans]."[256] Certainly, the fact that, in each of those cases, shareholders of the target companies had endorsed the poison pills was highly significant; moreover, the B.C. Securities Commission noted, both decisions alluded to the fact that, if circumstances changed, the rights plans might well be cease traded in the future. However, the failure of either *Pulse Data* or *Neo Materials* to articulate precisely what changes would lead to this outcome, in the view of the B.C. Securities

---

252 *Ibid.* at para. 53.
253 *Ibid.*
254 *Ibid.* at para. 68.
255 *Ibid.* at para. 83.
256 *Ibid.* at para. 86.

Commission, "limits their usefulness as authorities."[257] Accordingly, the B.C. Securities Commission cease traded the Lions Gate shareholder rights plan, reiterating that to do otherwise in a case where there was "no expectation that the target company will seek alternatives . . . would be a dramatic and, in our view, unwelcome change in the public interest policy principles governing the use of [shareholder rights plans] in takeover bids in Canada."[258] The decision of the B.C. Securities Commission was subsequently upheld by the British Columbia Court of Appeal.[259]

The Ontario Securities Commission subsequently had the opportunity to clarify the significance of *Neo Materials* in its 2010 decision *Baffinland Iron Mines Corp. (Re)*.[260] The *Baffinland* case did not involve a situation where the board of directors of the target company had decided not to take steps to maximize shareholder value in the face of a hostile bid. Rather, following the launch of a hostile bid, the target company had entered into a friendly deal with another party; but because the hostile bid had been commenced earlier, the hostile bidder's bid enjoyed a timing advantage. The OSC, noting that the support agreement entered into with the friendly bidder included a "no shop" or "no solicitation" clause, concluded that the target board was no longer at liberty to seek other offers. The poison pill had served its purpose. It had helped facilitate an auction. But it was now time for the pill to go.

The target company, however, urged the OSC to consider the traditional *Royal Host* factors "'through the lens of deference to the reasonable business judgment of the target company's directors' as con-

---

257 *Ibid.* at para. 87.
258 *Ibid* at para. 89.
259 *Lions Gate Entertainment Corp. v. Icahn Partners LP*, 2010 BCCA 231. Later that year, a second hearing before the B.C. Securities Commission was convened to consider whether or not a second shareholder rights plan adopted by the Lions Gate board in July 2010 should be cease traded. The B.C. Securities Commission ordered this plan to be cease traded as well: *Icahn Partners LP (Re)*, 2010 BCSECCOM 629. After Icahn's first takeover bid expired, and just before the launch of its second takeover bid, the board of Lions Gate undertook a deleveraging transaction, the effect of which was to reduce the corporation's outstanding debt by over $100 million through the issue of new equity to the holders of convertible debt. This deleveraging transaction had the effect of diluting Icahn's ownership interest. Icahn, accordingly, launched a corporate law oppression action. The action was dismissed by the British Columbia Supreme Court in 2010, and an appeal to the British Columbia Court of Appeal was dismissed in 2011. See above note 108.
260 Above note 225.

templated in *Re Neo Material Technologies . . . .*"[261] The commission thus had the opportunity to explicate its earlier *Neo Materials* decision.

The commission emphasized that *Neo Materials* did "not stand for the proposition that the commission will defer to the business judgment of a board of directors in considering whether to cease trade a rights plan, or that a board of directors in the exercise of its fiduciary duties may 'just say no' to a take-over bid."[262] Such an outcome, they noted, would, of course, have run contrary to the long line of regulatory decisions concerning poison pills, and contrary to the policy objectives articulated in NP 62-202.[263] Rather, the key to the *Neo Materials* decision was that the commission deferred "to the wishes of the shareholders,"[264] as expressed in their strong approval of the rights plan, in the face of the very bid that was the subject of the hearing, and at a meeting held just two weeks before the *Neo Materials* hearing. NP 62-202 specifically referred to the cleansing effect of prior shareholder approval, the commission noted, and the *Neo Materials* case must be viewed in that light.

Thus, the commission has forcefully reiterated its commitment to the approach of *Jorex* and its progeny in assessing the propriety of shareholder rights plans.

In addition to the attention poison pills have attracted amongst practitioners and regulators, they have generated considerable academic interest as well. The basic question that studies of poison pills have sought to answer is simple enough: Are poison pills good or bad for shareholders of companies that adopt them? There is a wealth of empirical evidence on this question,[265] too voluminous to be discussed in detail here.

Two specific issues concerning poison pills that have been dealt with recently by the courts also merit brief mention. First, in Canada,

---

261 *Ibid.* at para. 47.
262 *Ibid.* at para. 51.
263 *Ibid.*
264 *Ibid.* at para. 48.
265 See, for example, Paul H. Malatesta & Ralph A. Walking, "Poison Pill Securities: Stockholder Wealth, Profitability and Ownership Structure" (1980) 20 J.F. Econ. 347; Michael Ryngaert, "The Effect of Poison Pill Securities on Shareholder Wealth" (1988) 20 J.F. Econ. 377; Robert Comment & William G. Schwert, "Poison or Placebo? Evidence on the Deterrence and Wealth Effects of Modern Antitakeover Measures" (1995) 39 J.F. Econ. 3; John S. Strong & John R. Meyer, "An Analysis of Shareholder Rights Plans" (1990) 11 Managerial and Decision Economics 73; John C. Coates IV, "Takeover Defences in the Shadow of the Pill: A Critique of the Scientific Evidence" (2000) 79 Tex. L. Rev. 271.

where a considerable number of public issuers have been trusts[266] rather than corporations, inevitably acquisitions, including hostile acquisitions, have frequently come to involve trusts. Trusts, of course, are governed by the trust documents under which they are created, rather than corporate legislation. Accordingly, although basic principles of corporate law can often be applied to analyze takeover bid defences in the trust context,[267] ultimately specific terms of a trust document may make it impossible for trustees to lawfully adopt shareholder rights plans in the absence of the approval of trust unitholders.[268]

Further, while the issue does not appear to have been dealt with squarely by a Canadian court, the Delaware Court of Chancery has recently held that a poison pill plan triggered by a tender offer, not for the adopting company itself, but for the adopting company's *parent company* was an acceptable use of the device.[269]

Two recent Delaware Court of Chancery decisions and a Delaware Supreme Court decision have highlighted the apparent latitude directors of Delaware corporations enjoy in the creation and use of shareholder rights plans.[270] It is beyond the scope of this chapter to discuss these important and illuminating American decisions here.

---

266 As noted in Chapter One, the future of the income trust sector in Canada is uncertain in light of the 31 October 2006 announcement by the federal Minister of Finance of proposals to amend Canadian tax legislation to end the tax advantages previously enjoyed by trusts.

267 See, for example, *Primewest Energy Trust*, above note 209.

268 See, for example, *Rio Tinto Canadian Investments Ltd. v. Labrador Iron Ore Royalty Income Fund*, [2001] O.J. No. 2440 (S.C.J.), aff'd [2001] O.J. No. 3499 (C.A.).

269 *Hollinger International Inc. v. Black*, 844 A.2d 1022 (Del. Ch. 2004).

270 See *Yucaipa American Alliance Fund II, L.P. v. Riggio*, 1 A.3d 310 (Del. Ch. 2010); *Versata Enterprises, Inc. v. Selectica, Inc.*, 5 A.3d 586 (Del. S. Ct. 2010); *Airgas*, above note 64. The *Airgas* case is of special interest because, it appears to vindicate the use of a poison pill to defend against an all-cash, all-shares structurally non-coercive bid. (As Chancellor Chandler puts it: "In short, if there were an antonym in the dictionary for 'structural coercion,' Air Products' offer might be it." *Ibid.* at 107.) Yet, the Court of Chancery—apparently considering itself constrained by Delaware Supreme Court authority—held that the poison pill in this case could not be considered preclusive, even when considered in combination with the target company's staggered board, since the hostile acquiror would merely be *delayed* by these devices from acquiring control, and not precluded. The opinion did reveal an apparent tension between the Delaware Court of Chancery and the Delaware Supreme Court on the point. For example, early on in the opinion, Chancellor Chandler expresses his "personal view" that "Airgas's poison pill has served its legitimate purpose . . . . It has given Airgas *more time than any litigated poison pill in Delaware history* . . . ." Nevertheless, he concludes, "as I understand binding Delaware precedent, I may not substitute my business judgment for that of the Airgas board." (*Ibid.* at 57.) Later in

Two American developments in 2006, however, do merit mention because they highlight the extent to which the poison pill has become a critical issue for those concerned with the governance of U.S. public companies. In November, 2006, the Committee on Capital Markets Regulation, an independent committee of leading capital market experts co-chaired by Glenn Hubbard and John L. Thornton, released its *Interim Report of the Committee on Capital Markets Regulation*.[271] The purpose of the report was to examine and make recommendations to maintain and enhance the competitiveness of U.S. capital markets. On the subject of poison pills (adopted by companies with staggered or classified boards) the report recommends that companies not be permitted to adopt such plans without prior shareholder approval unless the company is a takeover target. Even where the company is a target, if a classified board adopts a poison pill, the committee recommends that such a pill must be ratified by the shareholders within three months, failing which it should be automatically redeemed.[272]

Earlier that year, Harvard Law School corporate law professor Lucian Bebchuk proposed by-law amendments at several leading corporations that, if enacted, would have required any proposed shareholder rights plan to be unanimously approved by the board of directors, and that would expire within one year of adoption, unless, in either case, the plan were approved by the shareholders.[273]

---

the opinion, Chancellor Chandler states that "while I agree theoretically with former-Chancellor Allen's and Vice-Chancellor Strine's conception of substantive coercion and its appropriate application, the Supreme Court's dictum in *Paramount* (which explicitly disapproves of *Interco*) suggests that unless and until the Supreme Court rules otherwise, that is not the current state of our law." (*Ibid.* at 101.) Finally, Chancellor Chandler suggests in a note that "our law would be more credible if the Supreme Court acknowledged that its later rulings have modified *Moran* and have allowed a board acting in good faith (and with a reasonable basis for believing that a tender offer is inadequate) to remit the bidder to the election process as its only recourse. The tender offer is in fact precluded and the only bypass of the pill is electing a new board. If that is the law, it would be best to be honest and abandon the pretense that preclusive action is *per se* unreasonable." (*Ibid.* at 122, n480.)

271 Above note 58.

272 *Ibid.* at 102. For a discussion of the concept of classified or staggered boards, see text accompanying notes 57–61, above in this chapter.

273 See Mark Maremont & Erin White, "Stock Activism's Latest Weapon" *The Wall Street Journal* (4 April 2006); See also Professor Bebchuk's website, www.law.harvard.edu/faculty/bebchuck/policy.htm, which includes not only details of Professor Bebchuk's proposals, but also a sharp criticism of his efforts by lawyers Martin Lipton & Mark Gordon, entitled, "Deconstructing American Business" (10 April 2006), online: www.harvard.edu/faculty/bebchuk/Policy/deconstructing.pdf.

Finally, it is important to recall that the issue of hostile takeovers and defensive measures is not a uniquely North American phenomenon. Regulators and legislators in many jurisdictions have directed their attention to these issues. For example, the issue of measures that might be taken by directors of a target corporation to frustrate an offer or prevent shareholders from having the opportunity to consider an offer on its merits is also dealt with in the European Takeover Directive[274] and the U.K. Takeover Code.[275]

ii.   *"Deal Protection Measures"*

When a corporation enters into a friendly, or negotiated merger transaction both parties to the agreement will typically be eager to take steps to ensure that their deal is not derailed by a hostile bidder. In many cases, the prospect of third-party interference will not be merely speculative, since striking a friendly bargain with a favoured "white knight" is a common target company response to a hostile takeover bid.

At first, it might seem odd that any special measures to "protect" a deal would be necessary. After all, isn't the very purpose of a contract to ensure that mutual promises will be legally enforceable? How can actions of a third party displace existing contractual relations, unless one of the parties to the original contract voluntarily chooses to breach, exposing itself to a lawsuit and possible damages?

However, merger agreements are unlike ordinary commercial arrangements. Because corporate directors are bound by fiduciary duties to act in the best interests of the corporation, they are obliged to remain open to the possibility that a superior proposal might emerge after they have entered into a merger agreement. As one American court has put it, "to the extent that a contract, or a provision thereof, purports to require a board to act or not to act in such a fashion as to limit the exercise of fiduciary duties, it is invalid and unenforceable."[276]

But no one wants to be a "stalking horse"—that is, a bidder lured to the negotiating table solely for the purpose of inducing a different party to make, or raise, a bid. It is costly to prepare an offer, both in terms

---

274   Directive 2004/25/EC of the European Parliament and of the Council of 21 April 2004 on Takeover Bids, Article 3 1(c), Article 9(2)–(4), online: http://eur-lex.europa.eu/LexUriServ/LexUriServ.do?uri=OJ:L:2004:142:0012:0012:EN:PDF.

275   The U.K. Takeover Code, Rule 21, online: www.thetakeoverpanel.org.uk/wp-content/uploads/2009/01/Code_190911.pdf. The Takeover Code was formerly a non-statutory instrument. However, the Takeover Panel now has express statutory authority pursuant to the *Companies Act 2006* (U.K.) c. 45, Part 28.

276   *Paramount Communications Inc. v. QVC Network*, above note 113 at 51 (1993). This issue was adverted to *Ventas*, above note 172.

of time spent investigating and analyzing a prospective merger partner, and in terms of out of pocket costs for professional advisors and so on. So before they commit to expend such resources, prospective corporate suitors, understandably, demand assurances that any deal they ultimately reach is likely to close.

Deal protection measures, then, can be generally understood as provisions included in friendly merger agreements, intended to accomplish one or more of the following purposes:

- to prevent the target company from simply "shopping" a bid in order to obtain a higher price from another buyer;
- to bond the target company—financially—to completing the bid or, at least, to ensure significant compensation for the bidder in the event that the target, ultimately, is sold to another party; and
- to induce a friendly bidder to make a bid and, directly or indirectly, to deter other bidders from attempting to undertake a rival bid for the same target.

Four common deal protection measures are:

- *"No solicitation" (or "no shop") clauses:* A no solicitation or no shop clause prohibits the target company from soliciting takeover proposals from any third party, or providing information to a third party that might be used to make a proposal. However, such provisions will typically include a "fiduciary out," permitting the directors, to the extent required by their fiduciary obligations, to negotiate with a third-party offeror if the directors of the target, in good faith and with the assistance of counsel, determine that the third-party offer constitutes a superior proposal. (For greater certainty, the term *superior proposal* is typically defined in the merger agreement.) "Matching rights" may also be extended, permitting the original offeror the opportunity to match any such superior proposal. (Parenthetically, "matching rights"—essentially rights of first refusal to purchase a corporation's shares in the event that an offer to purchase is received from a third party—have also been used from time to time in the U.S. as a kind of proactive protection against a corporation's change of control.)[277] The inclusion of such a fiduciary out has become standard practice in merger agreements, since the courts have made it clear that, even in the absence of such a clause, directors' fiduciary obligations would typically prevent them from

---

277 For a useful discussion of matching rights (or rights of first refusal), see David I. Walker, "Rethinking Rights of First Refusal" (1999) 5 Stanford J.L. Bus. & Fin. 1.

blindly ignoring an unsolicited superior proposal in any event.[278]

A more recent relaxing of "no shop" provisions has led to the inclusion of so-called "go shop" provisions—that is, clauses that specifically *permit* a company to "shop" a deal within a specified time frame. One of the most well-publicized uses of a "go shop" clause was included in the 2007 merger agreement between Topps Company, Inc. and a group led by Michael Eisner, a clause that Vice-Chancellor (now Chancellor) Strine of the Delaware Chancery Court colourfully explained, meant that "[f]or 40 days the Topps board could shop like Paris Hilton."[279]

- *"Break, " "break-up, " or "termination" fees:* A break-up fee is a substantial cash payment that the target company agrees, as a term of a merger agreement, to make to the (proposed) acquiring company in the event that the deal is not completed, in particular if the reason for non-completion is that the target company accepts a superior proposal from another party. (In "mergers of equals" transactions, where it is not clear that one party is the acquiror and the other party the target, each party may agree to pay the other such a fee in the event that the paying party ultimately completes an alternative deal with a third party.) The break-up fee is typically a lump sum payment that represents some percentage of the value of the acquisition price. In the 1998 Ontario decision, *CW Shareholdings*, the court commented that a break-up fee representing 2.6 percent of the bid price was "by all accounts . . . well within the normal parameters for such inducements in the industry."[280] Elsewhere, the judgment included extracts of board of directors meeting minutes suggesting that the board's financial advisors had suggested that there were

---

278 See, for example, *ibid.* at 51. There are few Canadian cases considering no shop or no talk clauses in detail. The Delaware law on this topic is complex and cannot be discussed in detail here. Some of the leading Delaware authorities include *Ace Ltd. v. Capital Re Corp.*, 747 A.2d 95 (Del. Ch. 1999); *Phelps Dodge Corp. v. Cyprus Amax Minerals Co.*, 1999 Del. Ch. Lexis 202; *In Re IXC Communications, Inc. v. Cincinnati Bell, Inc.*, 1999 WL 1009174 (Del. Ch.). For an interesting perspective from a leading Delaware jurist, see Leo E. Strine, "Categorical Confusion: Deal Protection Measures in Stock-for-Stock Merger Agreements" (2001) 56 Bus. Law. 919. Recent research by FactSet suggests a growing use of go-shop clauses in U.S.-friendly tender offers. Of the fourteen announced friendly tender offers as of April 2011, six (or about 43 percent) reportedly included go-shop clauses. See Michael Benkert, "The Increasing Occurrence of Go-Shop Provisions Used in Agreed Tender Offers," online: www.factset-mergers.com/marequest?an=dt.getPage&st=1&pg=/pub/rs_20110413.html&go_shop_provisions_in_agreed_tender_offers&rnd=253052.

279 *In re Topps Co. Shareholders Litigation*, 926 A.2d 58 at 86 (Del Ch. 2007).

280 Above note 37 at 790.

"numerous precedents" for break-up fees in the range of 2.5 percent to 5 percent.[281] In Delaware, a recent practitioner's paper has suggested that break-up fees "typically [range] up to 4% of the transaction value on a capitalization basis."[282] Some recent Delaware cases have mooted the question of whether, in judging the acceptability of the size of a break fee, the break fee amount should be evaluated as a percentage of the target firm's equity value, or, instead, its enterprise value—that is, equity value plus the value of the firm's debt, minus the amount of cash on a company's balance sheet. Obviously, if a company is highly leveraged and does not have significant cash, enterprise value will be a higher number than equity value, and so a break fee will represent a smaller percentage of enterprise value. Conversely, if a company has a substantial amount of cash, enterprise value may be lower than equity value and so an agreed break fee will represent a higher percentage of equity value. Although the Delaware Court of Chancery did assess the propriety of a break fee by assessing it as a percentage of enterprise value in *In Re Lear Corporation Shareholder Litigation*,[283] subsequent cases appear to have established that "Delaware's case law, however, teaches that such termination fees are generally measured according to a Company's equity value."[284] It might also be noted that in the U.K., the Takeover Panel has indicated, in its notes to Rule 21.2 of the U.K. Takeover Code, that a break fee (or an "inducement fee," as it is called) will not normally be permitted if it is more than 1 percent of the value of the offeree company.[285] The overarching legal principle in determining whether the amount of break-up fees is acceptable is that such fees are permissible to the extent that they entice a bidder to the table (and therefore help create an auction that will benefit target shareholders); but they must not be so high that they have the effect of deterring any other bidder from making a competing bid.[286] (Because a break-up fee would become a liability of the target company, any rival bidder would be aware that, if its bid were to succeed, the company

---

281 *Ibid.* at 785.
282 See Steven A. Rosenblum, "Takeover Law and Practice 2011" in *43rd Annual Institute on Securities Regulation*, Vol. 2 (New York: Practising Law Institute, 2011) 21 at 83.
283 967 A.2d 640 at 643 (Del. Ch. 2008).
284 *In re Orchid Cellmark Inc. Shareholder Litigation*, 2011 Del. Ch. Lexis 75 at *21; *In re Cogent, Inc. Shareholder Litigation*, 7 A.3d 487 at 503–4 (Del. Ch. 2010), appeal denied, 30 A.3d 782 (Del S.C. 2010).
285 See *The Takeover Code*, Rule 21.2, Notes, online: www.thetakeoverpanel.org.uk/wp-content/uploads/2008/11/code.pdf.
286 See *CW Shareholdings*, above note 37.

it was buying would immediately become subject to this liability.)

One also should note here the more recent technique of providing for "reverse break fees" intended to protect *selling* firms from closing risk. Reverse break fees were discussed in Chapter 2. The only additional point to be mentioned here is that, during the recent financial crisis, it was not uncommon for buyers, and their financiers, to become eager to explore ways of extricating themselves from deals that had become unattractive. One issue that occasionally arose was the question of whether or not a would-be buyer could walk away from a deal with no financial obligation to the seller that would find itself left at the proverbial altar beyond the obligation to pay the amount of the previously negotiated reverse break fee. In effect, buyers in such circumstances sought to treat the merger agreement as tantamount to a call option, with the reverse break fee functionally equivalent to the premium or price to be paid for enjoying that option. So, for example, in *United Rentals, Inc. v. RAM Holdings, Inc.,*[287] United Rentals brought an action in Delaware seeking specific performance of a merger agreement. The agreement included provision for the payment of a $100 million reverse break-up fee if RAM did not complete the transaction. The case was factually complex, and the language of the contract somewhat ambiguous. The Delaware Court of Chancery ultimately ruled that the plaintiff failed to satisfy the burden of proof that the contract between the parties entitled the plaintiff to specific performance. Accordingly, the plaintiff was limited to the $100 million reverse break-up fee.

- *Stock options:* A target company might offer share purchase options as an inducement to a prospective bidder. In some respects, such stock options could function economically as a form of break-up fee. If a friendly bidder to whom options have been granted ultimately loses the bidding contest to a rival, then, *ex hypothesi,* the price to be paid for the target's shares would be higher than the price offered by the first bidder, who now holds stock options. Accordingly, the options could be exercised at a profit, and that profit would compensate the unsuccessful bidder for the time spent in preparing and pursuing its failed bid.

It is also not uncommon for bidders to seek "lock-up" or "support" agreements from major shareholders of the target company, a practice that, in Canada, has raised certain issues with respect to post-bid squeeze-out transactions, as discussed in Chapter 8, and proxy solicitation rules, as discussed in Chapter 9. In Delaware, a much-publicized

---

287 937 A.2d 810 (Del. Ch. 2007).

and controversial decision of the Delaware Supreme Court in 2003 cast doubt on the ability of a bidder to lock-up a deal with complete certainty through the use of agreements with major shareholders combined with a so-called force the vote provision—a feature of Delaware corporate law that permits directors to convene a shareholders' meeting to vote on a resolution, notwithstanding that the directors are no longer prepared to recommend acceptance of that resolution.[288]

- *Matching Rights:* Even though a target company will typically include a "fiduciary out" in a fiendly merger agreement, allowing it to entertain a potentially "superior proposal," the original friendly bidder may still be granted "matching rights," that is, the right to match the rival "superior proposal" and so complete its acquisition.

Finally, it should be remembered that the propriety of deal protection measures requires courts or securities regulators not only to scrutinize each individual measure, but also to consider carefully the cumulative effect of all measures employed. The general principle applied by securities commissions and the courts in assessing deal protection measures is simple to state, though often challenging to apply. Deal protection measures are acceptable to the extent that they help facilitate an auction, chiefly by inducing a perhaps reticent bidder to make an offer in the first place. However, to the extent that such measures are auction-inhibiting, or preclusive, they may be seen as unduly favouring one prospective bidder over others, adverse to the interests of a target corporation's shareholders, and so impermissible. But where does one draw the proverbial line? As a recent Delaware court has aptly put it:

> Deal protection measures evolve. Not surprisingly, we do not have a bright line test to help us all understand when too much is recognized as too much. Moreover, it is not merely a matter of measuring one deal protection device; one must address the sum of all devices. Because of that, one of these days some judge is going to say "no more" and, when the drafting lawyer looks back, she will be challenged to figure out how or why the incremental enhancement mattered. It will be yet another instance of the straw and the poor camel's back. At some point, aggressive deal protection devices—amalgamated as they are—run the risk of being deemed so burdensome and costly as to render the "fiduciary out" illusory."[289]

---

288 *Omnicare*, above note 176.
289 *In re Orchid Cellmark Inc. Shareholder Litigation*, above note 284 at *23.

c. The Role of Institutional Investors and Arbitrageurs

Before leaving the topic of the directors' duties in the face of a hostile takeover bid, it is important to note briefly an important aspect of capital markets and the takeover bid regime. When much of the law concerning hostile takeover bids first developed, it was implicitly assumed that shareholders of a corporation were traditional investors, perhaps of limited sophistication, and who had originally acquired their shares in the target company with a view to holding those shares for some significant length of time. It is now well-understood that institutional and other sophisticated investors play a critical role in Canadian capital markets generally, and certainly once a hostile takeover bid has been announced, the profile of a target company's shareholders can change rather dramatically. Sophisticated players, including hedge funds, commonly engage in "merger arbitrage" or "risk arbitrage." When a hostile takeover bid is announced, such firms (sometimes referred to as "arbs") will often purchase large blocks of shares in the target company, and sell (or short) shares in the bidding company.[290] What this means is that shortly after a bid is announced, regardless of what the shareholder profile of the target company may have been prior to the announcement, it will often be the case that the shareholders who will ultimately be asked to tender to the bid are short-term financial buyers. This fact was specifically alluded to in evidence given by a director of Goldcorp Inc. quoted by the court in *McEwen v. Goldcorp Inc.*:[291]

> One of the things we have realized in recent history is that in the context of an M & A transaction, your shareholder body shifts. It changes. And the long-term holders who are interested in the long-term viability and health of the company realize upon their investment, and they are replaced by short-term investors. And in this context, in the context of an M & A transaction, I believe the Board is the ideal body to make the decision as to the long-term health of the company.

It must be remembered, of course, that those supposedly "long-term" investors have chosen to sell their shares, suggesting that their primary interest was, after all, not the "long-term health" of the company, but rather the desire to gain a profit, at lower risk than those prepared to buy the shares while the possibility still remained that the proposed acquisition transaction might not be consummated. Then Chancellor Chandler of the Delaware Court of Chancery made pointed

---

290 See, for example, Sam Kirschner, Eldon Mayer, & Lee Kessler, *The Investor's Guide to Hedge Funds* (Hoboken: John Wiley & Sons, Inc., 2006) c. 5.
291 Above note 141 at para. 18.

reference to this important, but frequently (sometimes conveniently) overlooked fact, in a recent decision:

> The defendants do not appear to have come to grips with the fact that the arbs bought their shares from long-term stockholders who viewed the increased market price generated by Air Products' offer as a good time to sell.[292]

Further, to the extent that shares of any particular corporation are considered to be interchangeable with the shares of any other corporation with the same (market) risk/return profile, it is not entirely clear how much economic significance ought to be attached to the presumed distinction between "genuine" long-term investors, and opportunistic short-term investors. Nevertheless, it may very well be that this distinction may strike a responsive chord with some courts and so may come to have an influence on future legal developments in this area.[293]

F. HOSTILE BIDS AND *COMPETITION ACT* PRE-MERGER REVIEW

As discussed in Chapter 2, large acquisitions in Canada are subject to pre-merger review under the federal *Competition Act*. This pre-merger review requirement poses a number of particular logistical and strategic challenges in the case of hostile takeover bids. To assess the competitive impacts of any proposed acquisition, the Competition Bureau

---

292 *Airgas*, above note 64 at 109.
293 One notes that the Competition Policy Review Panel, above note 35, referred to the role of arbitrageurs in its 2008 report. The Panel's report recognized that "every share that moves into the hands of these arbitrageurs is a vote for the proposal and increases the likelihood that the target company will be sold." *Ibid.* at 78. Yet, the Panel, nevertheless, went on to suggest (somewhat remarkably) that this fact somehow supported (rather than undermined) their case for strengthening the role of the directors of target corporations. Perhaps, the Panel's curious reasoning is an example of the cognitive bias that behavioural psychologists have labelled "cognitive conservatism," the tendency for one's pre-existing views to persist despite evidence to the contrary and, in fact, for the rigidity of one's pre-existing views actually to *increase* when confronted with evidence to the contrary. As Lord, Ross, and Lepper famously argued, "completely inconsistent or even random data—when 'processed' in a suitably biased fashion—can maintain or even reinforce one's preconceptions." See Charles G. Lord, Lee Ross, & Mark R. Lepper, "Biased Assimilation and Attitude Polarization: the Effects of Prior Theories on Subsequently Considered Evidence" (1979) 37 Journal of Personality and Social Psychology 2098 at 2099.

requires significant amounts of information from both parties to the acquisition. But of course, in the context of a hostile bid, the target corporation does not have the same incentive to expedite this process as do the parties to a friendly merger. In 2011, the Commissioner of Competition released two interpretation guidelines dealing with issues that arise in the context of pre-merger review of hostile acquisitions. The effect of these guidelines was canvassed briefly in Chapter 2.[294]

G. POST-BID COMPULSORY ACQUISITIONS/ GOING-PRIVATE OR SQUEEZE-OUT (BUSINESS COMBINATION) TRANSACTIONS

Frequently, most, but not all, shareholders of a target corporation will tender their shares to a takeover bid. The bidder may, therefore, find itself holding something less than 100 percent of the shares of the target corporation. This is particularly problematic in the case of a public corporation because the enduring interest of a small number of minority shareholders would compel the corporation to continue to comply with the various expensive continuous disclosure, reporting, and annual meeting requirements mandated by provincial securities laws. The *Canada Business Corporations Act*, and most other Canadian corporate statutes,[295] explicitly permit bidders that have acquired, generally within 120 days of the date of a takeover bid, at least 90 percent of the shares of a public corporation (not including the shares the bidder owned before launching the bid) to acquire the remaining shares as well, whether or not the remaining securityholders wish to sell their interest, upon compliance with a specific statutory acquisition procedure.[296] Some Canadian corporate statutes also provide a reciprocal right to minority shareholders to compel a successful bidder to subsequently

---

294 See Chapter 2, text accompanying notes 72 and 73.
295 See, for example, Alberta *Business Corporations Act*, s. 195(2); British Columbia *Business Corporations Act*, s. 300; New Brunswick *Business Corporations Act*, s. 133(2); Newfoundland and Labrador *Corporations Act*, s. 317; Nova Scotia *Companies Act*, s. 132(1) [NSCA] (The NSCA provision differs from the CBCA regime in a few respects. Among other things, it is triggered by a "scheme or contract involving the transfer of shares" rather than a takeover bid.); Ontario *Business Corporations Act*, s. 188(1) [OBCA]; Quebec *Business Corporations Act*, s. 398; Saskatchewan *Business Corporations Act*, s. 188; Northwest Territories *Business Corporations Act*, s. 197(2); Nunavut *Business Corporations Act*, s. 197(2) Yukon *Business Corporations Act*, s. 197(2).
296 See CBCA, Part XVII.

acquire their shares so that they are not left with an illiquid minority interest following a takeover bid.[297]

Where a bidder has acquired less than 90 percent of the shares of the target corporation, corporate law does not expressly provide a mechanism by which the remaining minority shares may be squeezed in. However, a well-known technique has developed for accomplishing this objective, often referred to as a post-bid "amalgamation squeeze." The subject of such "going-private transactions" is of crucial importance both in the hostile and friendly takeover bid context, and is so dealt with in considerable detail in Chapter 8.

H. CONCLUSION

Although hostile takeover bids still represent a relatively small percentage of all Canadian M & A activity, there are reasons to believe that hostile takeover activity could become increasingly important in the near term. Directors and senior officers of companies that are the targets of such bids face a formidable challenge as they seek to carry out their duties faithfully in an environment in which conflict of interest— real or perceived—is unavoidable. As the pressures for consolidation and vertical integration, on the one hand, and the continued interest of financial buyers, on the other, favour large and sometimes aggressive takeovers, Canadian legal practitioners, securities regulators, and the courts will be called upon to develop practices and principles that will balance conflicting business interests and safeguard the integrity of the Canadian capital markets. In the meantime, the vested interests of those who serve as managers and directors of Canadian corporations and other non-shareholder corporate "constituents," coupled with real or feigned concerns for Canadian economic sovereignty and the protection of non-shareholder interests, may spur lobbying efforts aimed at tilting the balance in hostile takeover disputes away from shareholders and in favour of target company managers. Any such development should be approached cautiously and with a careful and disinterested consideration of the impact of such developments on the vigour and integrity of our capital markets and the long-term health of the Canadian economy.

---

297 See, for example, CBCA, s. 206.1; OBCA, s. 189.

CHAPTER 8

INSIDER BIDS, GOING-PRIVATE TRANSACTIONS, AND OTHER BUSINESS COMBINATIONS

A. INTRODUCTION

Special rules apply when corporate transactions have been initiated by persons likely to have inside knowledge or special influence or control over publicly traded corporations. Regulatory concern about the potential abuse of minority shareholders in such related-party transactions might be expected to be a more pressing issue in Canada than in the United States because of the ownership structure characteristic of many Canadian public corporations. In the United States, most of the largest publicly traded corporations have widely dispersed share ownership. Controlling shareholders of large corporations are relatively rare. Accordingly, the principal agency concern arises from the possibility of unconstrained managerial opportunism, since effective monitoring of corporate managers by shareholders is lacking, and collective action problems make it difficult for shareholders to act to replace underperforming managers.

However, in Canada, although there certainly are a number of large corporations with widely dispersed shareholdings, the relative significance of such corporations is different. So it is, as Daniels and Morck have argued, that the prevalence of controlling shareholders in Canadian public corporations, means that "dealing with controlling share-holders is . . . the central issue in Canadian corporate governance."[1]

Following a lengthy evolutionary process, Canadian securities regulators have developed regulatory instruments aimed at addressing the principal issues raised by major corporate transactions involving insiders or other persons related to the corporation. The most important of these today is Multilateral Instrument 61-101,[2] which was adopted in Ontario and Quebec in 2008. This Multilateral Instrument supersedes Ontario Securities Commission (OSC) Rule 61-501, and, in Quebec, Autorité des marchés financiers ("AMF") Regulation Q-27 (formerly Policy Q-27). There are four basic categories of transactions for which special rules are thought necessary to protect minority shareholders:

- insider bids;
- issuer bids;
- related party transactions; and
- going-private transactions and other "business combinations."

Although related party transactions can certainly include sales or purchases of major business assets, the other three forms of transaction are more central to the conduct of mergers and acquisitions in Canada, and so are the focus of the remainder of this chapter.

B. ISSUER BIDS AND INSIDER BIDS

Canadian securities regulators have long been aware of the need to scrutinize corporate transactions in which there may be significant information or power imbalances. In 1976, the Ontario Securities Commission became concerned that there were no specific rules (other than under the *Canada Business Corporations Act*) dealing with the purchase by a corporation of its own shares (popularly known as a share buy-back, or more formally in Canada as an "issuer bid," or in the U.S. as an "issuer self tender offer"). To address these concerns, the OSC formulated a policy statement dealing specifically with such purchases, OSC Policy 3-37.[3] Policy 3-37 required an issuer intending to purchase its own securities to prepare an information circular containing dis-

---

1   Ronald J. Daniels & Randall Morck, *Canadian Corporate Governance Policy Options*, Discussion Paper No. 3 (Ottawa: Industry Canada, March 1996) at 28, online: http://corporationscanada.ic.gc.ca.
2   (2008), 31 OSCB 1321 [MI 61-101].
3   Ontario Policy No. 3-37, [1977] OSCB 253.

closures prescribed in Appendix B of the policy statement. This information circular was then to be filed with the OSC and mailed to the holders of securities subject to the bid. In addition, the policy stated that issuer bids were to be made in compliance with a number of the takeover bid rules in the *Securities Act*.

One of the items in Appendix B required disclosure of "any appraisal or valuation known to the directors or officers of the issuer, regarding the issuer, its material assets or securities within the two years preceding the date of the bid." Policy 3-37 would later mark an important step in the development of the regulatory approach to "going-private transactions" as discussed in some detail later in this chapter. However, with respect to issuer bids themselves, no more will be said here. An issuer bid, after all, is not an acquisition transaction in the sense that it represents a change in corporate control, although it has occasionally been suggested that an issuer bid can be used to effectively place control of a corporation in the hands of its incumbent managers.

One special category of acquisition transaction that does merit particular mention here, however, is the "insider bid." An insider bid is not typically defined in provincial securities statutes, but is defined in Multilateral Instrument 61-101 to mean:

a take-over bid made by

(a) an issuer insider of the offeree issuer,
(b) an associated or affiliated entity of an issuer insider of the offeree issuer,
(c) an associated or affiliated entity of the offeree issuer,
(d) a person or company described in paragraph (a), (b) or (c) at any time within 12 months preceding the commencement of the bid, or
(e) a joint actor with a person referred to in paragraph (a), (b), (c) or (d);[4]

Insider bids raise special concerns. Since insiders, by virtue of their positions, have access to information about the corporation that is not generally available to the corporation's shareholders, the insiders are in a far better position than ordinary shareholders to assess the corporation's future prospects and determine the value of the corporation's assets and business. Of course, we should expect that a corporation's public shareholders are also well aware of this information asymmetry, and so will greet with appropriate caution any offer to purchase their shares they may receive from information-privileged insiders. But this

---

4   MI 61-101, s. 1.1. Needless to say, a number of the terms found within this definition are also specifically defined in MI 61-101, including *issuer insider, affiliated entity, associated entity,* and *joint actors.*

awareness is not enough. Shareholders may, in general terms, recognize the advantage enjoyed by insiders and even, somehow, (perhaps inefficiently or at great cost) factor this knowledge into an assessment of the adequacy of a takeover bid launched by insiders. Yet the central problem remains: shareholders do not have (or at the very least may not perceive that they have) the full benefit of disinterested, informed advice from company insiders to assist them in assessing—with precision—the adequacy and fairness of a proposed insider bid.

To address this informational gap, Multilateral Instrument 61-101 sets out a series of rules and processes to be followed in the case of formal takeover bids (that is, takeover bids that are not exempt from the formal bid requirements set out in Part 2 of Multilateral Instrument 62-104 and sections 100 to 100.6 of the Ontario *Securities Act*) that are insider bids.[5] The principal protections that Multilateral Instrument 61-101 offers to shareholders are:

- *Disclosure of prior valuations:* In addition to a general obligation to give shareholders adequate disclosure, the offeror is required to disclose details of any prior valuation of the issuer, its securities, or its material assets made within the twenty-four months prior to the date of the insider bid, "the existence of which is known, after reasonable inquiry, to the offeror or any director or senior officer of the offeror."[6] The directors of the target company, in their directors' circular, must also disclose details of any formal valuation made within the twenty-four months before the date of the insider bid known, after reasonable inquiry, to the target company or any director or senior officer.[7]

- *Preparation of a valuation:* The offeror must (subject to certain exemptions) obtain a formal valuation at its own expense. The valuator must be chosen not by the offeror, but by an independent committee of the board of directors of the target company, and that independent committee must also supervise the preparation of the valuation.[8] The exemptions from the formal valuation requirement relate to situations where (a) the apparent insider in fact has had neither board nor management representation in respect of the target company for the previous 12 months nor access to material undisclosed information about the target company,[9] (b) specific circumstances exist that provide objective evidence that the offered price is reasonable (or at

---

5   MI 61-101, ss. 2.1 and 1.1 (definition of "bid").
6   *Ibid.*, s. 2.2 (1)(b).
7   *Ibid.*, s. 2.2(2)(a).
8   *Ibid.*, s. 2.3.
9   *Ibid.*, s. 2.4(1)(a).

least could be fairly assessed against objective benchmarks by target shareholders),[10] or (c) the regulator (the AMF in Quebec, the OSC in Ontario) is satisfied that it is appropriate to grant a discretionary exemption.[11]

Insider bids raise many additional legal and practical questions, but a full treatment of this complex topic is beyond the scope of this book. The remainder of this chapter will focus on the last type of transaction regulated by Multilateral Instrument 61-101 that is a common feature of many traditional takeover bids in Canada: second-stage business combinations or going-private transactions. Closely related to the type of business combination regulated by Multilateral Instrument 61-101 are the compulsory and compelled acquisitions undertaken pursuant to provisions contained in many Canadian corporate statutes. Accordingly, those provisions are also outlined briefly in the following section.

C. POST-BID SQUEEZE-OUT TRANSACTIONS: COMPULSORY AND COMPELLED ACQUISITIONS AND GOING-PRIVATE TRANSACTIONS (BUSINESS COMBINATIONS)

1) "Taking a Company Private"

When one corporation (the "bidder") completes a successful takeover bid for another publicly traded corporation (the "target"), the bidder may well own enough shares of the target to ensure complete control over every subsequent meeting of the target's shareholders, including, among other things, control over the election of directors to the target's board. Indeed, unless a corporation's articles provide for cumulative voting, or has dual-class voting shares,[12] a shareholder holding 50 percent + 1 of the voting shares will normally be able to elect all of the

---

10   Ibid., ss. 2.4(1)(b) ("previous arm's-length negotiations") & (c) ("auction").
11   Ibid., s 9.1.
12   Dual-class shares refer to shares that entitle their holders to differing numbers of votes and, in particular, that entitle the holders of one class of shares a disproportionately large number of votes, relative to their entitlement to distributions of dividends or other cash flow rights. Such shares are often issued to enable a corporation's founders or their families to control a majority of votes at a shareholders' meeting with a relatively small investment of capital. For a discussion of the historical use of dual-class shares in Canada, see Stephanie

members of the board of directors. A shareholder holding 66 ²/₃ percent of voting shares will be able to authorize any fundamental change such as an amendment to the corporation's articles, an amalgamation, a continuance, or a sale of all or substantially all of its assets that requires approval by special resolution of shareholders.[13]

If a bidder has acquired 50 percent + 1 or perhaps 66 ²/₃ percent of the target shares and is satisfied with the considerable control conferred by such a block of shares, then the bidder may be content for the target's shares to continue to trade publicly. But often successful bidders have other plans. They may be keen to free the publicly traded cor-, porations they control from the expensive and burdensome obligations to which "reporting issuers"[14] in Canada are subject. In such circumstances, the bidder may well wish to "take the company private"—that is, to transform it from a company whose shares are traded on public markets, to a private, "non-distributing"[15] or "non-offering"[16] corporation. In particular, shortly after the introduction of increased regulatory burdens placed upon public companies in the United States with the passage of the *Sarbanes-Oxley Act of 2002*[17] (SOX) and in Canada by a series of SOX-copycat initiatives,[18] it was argued that the prospect of withdrawing from the rather expensive rigours of public company

---

Ben-Ishai & Poonam Puri, "Dual Class Shares in Canada: An Historical Analysis" (2006) 29 Dal. L.J. 117.

13   See, for example, *Canada Business Corporations Act*, ss. 173, 174, 184, 188, and 189(3) [CBCA].

14   "Reporting issuer" is the term used in Canadian securities laws to refer to an issuer of securities that has filed a prospectus and so become subject to the periodic and timely disclosure requirements of Canadian securities statutes, regulations, and instruments.

15   The CBCA uses the term *distributing corporations* to refer to those corporations that would colloquially be described as public companies. See CBCA, s. 2(1); *Canada Business Corporations Regulations, 2001*, s. 2(1). The same term is also used in the Alberta *Business Corporations Act*, s. 1(p), *The Business Corporations Act* (Saskatchewan), s. 2(1)(o), and the Newfoundland and Labrador *Corporations Act*, s. 2(m). Variants of the term are found in several other Canadian corporate statutes. See Christopher C. Nicholls, *Corporate Law* (Toronto: Emond-Montgomery, 2005) at 98.

16   The Ontario *Business Corporations Act* [OBCA] uses the term *offering corporation* to refer to those corporations that would colloquially be described as public companies. See OBCA, ss. 1(1) & (6).

17   United States, PL 107-204, 116 Stat 745 (2002).

18   See Nicholls, *Corporate Law*, above note 15 at 311–12.

regulation (if even temporarily) had become an attractive option for some entities.[19]

Gilson and Black have questioned, in the U.S. context, whether the advantages gained by controlling shareholders of public corporations when they eliminate the shareholding interests of minority shareholders are enough to outweigh the disadvantages. They have gone so far as to speculate that the *perceived* advantages of going private may arise from the overly conservative advice of risk-averse lawyers.[20]

Certainly it cannot be universally true that it is undesirable to be a controlling shareholder of a public corporation with minority shareholders since this is a structure that is commonplace among Canadian public companies. However, it is no doubt true that in many cases, it will be seen as important and beneficial, from the perspective of a successful takeover bidder, to take steps, after the bid is complete, to secure 100 percent control of the takeover target and it is in those situations that the legal rules surrounding "going-private" transactions become critical.

Now if the takeover bid by which the bidder gained control of the target's shares had been a bid for all of the outstanding shares and, indeed, had been accepted by each and every one of the target's shareholders, then it would be a very simple matter to have the target's status as a "reporting issuer" changed. It would not, perhaps surprisingly, happen automatically. An application would have to be made to the securities regulatory authorities for an order deeming that the target had ceased to be a reporting issuer.[21]

As a practical matter, however, it is highly unlikely that a takeover bid for the shares of a publicly traded company would ever result in the tender of 100 percent of the target shares. No matter how generous the offer, there may well be some small number of shareholders who, perhaps for non-financial reasons, are unwilling to part with their shares at any price. Moreover, some small shareholders—who might well have been *willing* to tender their shares—may simply have neglected to do so through inadvertence, absence or lack of interest.

---

19 Marc Morgenstern & Peter Nealis, "Going Private: A Reasoned Response to *Sarbanes-Oxley*?", online: www.sec.gov/info/smallbus/pnealis.pdf. See also Hal S. Scott, "U.S. Capital Markets Need an Overhaul" *Wall Street Journal* (20 April 2011). Not all commentators agree that *Sarbanes-Oxley* has had this effect. See, for example, Robert P. Bartlett III, "Going Private but Staying Public: Reexamining the Effect of *Sarbanes-Oxley* on Firms' Going-Private Decisions" (2009) 76 U. Chi. L. Rev. 7.

20 See Ronald J. Gilson & Bernard S. Black, *The Law and Finance of Corporate Acquisitions*, 2d ed. (Westbury, NY: The Foundation Press, 1995) at 1249–52.

21 See, for example, *Securities Act* (Ontario), s. 1.2(10)(b).

If the law provided no practical way for successful bidders who obtain anything less than 100 percent of the shares of target corporations to take those corporations private, at least two problems could arise. First, potential bidders might be dissuaded from launching takeover bids in the first place, to the general disadvantage of shareholders of potential target corporations. Second, small shareholders of target corporations would have an incentive to behave opportunistically. Knowing that a bidding corporation would later have to acquire their shares in order to avoid the ongoing costs of being a reporting issuer, such opportunistic shareholders might refuse to tender their shares to a generous bid, planning, instead, to later "hold up" the bidder for a disproportionately large post-bid payment. Worse still, since it would be especially advantageous financially for a shareholder to hold out in this way, many—even most—shareholders might be expected to employ this strategy and refrain from tendering to a fairly priced bid, leading, in the worst case, to its failure.

2) Corporate Law Compulsory and Compelled Acquisition Provisions

a) Introduction
Corporate statutes, accordingly, frequently include special rules that permit bidders whose bids have been accepted by an overwhelmingly high percentage of target company shareholders (typically at least 90 percent) to forcibly acquire the shares of those few remaining stragglers that were not originally tendered to the bid. Section 206 of the *Canada Business Corporations Act* ("CBCA") is an example of such a provision.

b) History of Compulsory Acquisition Provisions
Provisions like this are not new. For example, section 128 of the old federal *Companies Act*[22] (the federal statute that preceded the CBCA) contained a compulsory acquisition provision. Where a transfer of shares of any company had been approved by nine-tenths of the shareholders of that company within a specified period of time, the acquiring company could give notice to dissenting shareholders of its desire to acquire the dissidents' shares. Unless the dissenting shareholders obtained a court order to the contrary, the acquiring company would be permitted (and indeed required) to acquire the dissenting share-

---

22   R.S.C. 1952, c. 53. An equivalent provision survives today in at least one Canadian corporate statute. See the *Companies Act* (Nova Scotia) [NSCA], s. 132.

holders' shares under the terms of the original transfer. The legislation did allow for dissenting shareholders to seek a court order to stop the transfer. However, it seemed clear that dissenters pursuing such an order faced a formidable challenge. The burden would be on the dissenters to establish the *unfairness* of the proposed transaction, since the very fact that an overwhelming majority of the corporation's shareholders had given their assent provided a strong *prima facie* indication that the terms of the deal were objectively fair to the shareholders.

Section 128 was not an invention of the drafters of the Canadian statute. It was based upon an earlier section of the English *Companies Act* and had been part of the English legislation since 1929. It had been introduced into the English statute following a recommendation of the 1926 Greene Report. The Greene Report indicated that its recommendation on this point was based upon representations made to the committee

> that holders of a small number of shares of the company which is being taken over (either from a desire to extract better terms than their fellow shareholders are content to accept or from lack of real interest in the matter) frequently fail to come into an arrangement which commends itself to the vast majority of their fellow shareholders, with the result that the transaction fails to materialise.[23]

It is of some significance that the 90 percent compulsory acquisition provision in Canadian corporate statutes is of English, not American, origin. Indeed, such provisions are not typically found in U.S. corporate statutes, where second-step going-private transactions (that is, going-private transactions undertaken after a largely successful takeover bid—or "tender offer") are typically accomplished by way of freeze-out merger.[24] It is evident, however, that Canadian legislators adopted the English compulsory acquisition measures without detailed analysis of whether distinctive characteristics of Canada's markets might make such a measure less useful in Canada than in England. So, for example, Elliott Weiss, in considering whether a 90 percent compulsory acquisition provision ought to be added to U.S. corporate law statutes, cautioned:

> Controlled but not wholly owned subsidiaries are relatively uncommon in England, and it is not clear whether a market-based approach will work as effectively with regard to a bid to acquire a minority

---

23   Great Britain Board of Trade Company Law Amendment Committee, *Report* (1925-26) Cmd. 2657 (London: H.M. Stationery Office, 1926) at 43–44.

24   There are some exceptions. See, for example, *New Jersey Business Corporation Act*, New Jersey Statutes, Title 14A, s. 10-9(3).

interest in a controlled subsidiary as it would with regard to an offer
for more than a majority of a company's shares.[25]

In Canada today controlled subsidiaries are not uncommon, and
so the cautionary note raised by Weiss is also of relevance here. The
Dickerson Committee's recommendation with respect to including
compulsory acquisition provisions in the CBCA does not appear to
have been influenced by this consideration, however. Perhaps the advantages of a compulsory acquisition provision in Canada outweigh
the disadvantages, even in the case of transactions involving controlled
subsidiaries, because the Canadian corporate oppression remedy may
serve to provide minority shareholders with adequate protection.

In any event, the compulsory acquisition provision first entered
the Canadian federal corporate statute in 1934, essentially adopted
verbatim from the then current English statute.[26] The operation of an
early version of the Canadian provision was considered by the Supreme
Court of Canada in *Rathie v. Montreal Trust Co.*[27] The judgment of the
majority in *Rathie* turned on a technical timing issue: the initial offer
to purchase shares from dissidents had been open for acceptance for
just two weeks rather than for the four-month period that the language
of the Act required, in the majority's opinion. This somewhat technical misstep was fatal, in the majority's view, because "[i]n a matter involving what amounts to a forced sale of the shares of the dissentients,
there must clearly be strict compliance with the terms of the section."[28]

The minority opinion of Rand J. (with whom Taschereau concurred)
revealed an especially wary judicial attitude toward the compulsory acquisition mechanism. Rand J. characterized the statutory provision in
question as one "by which a majority may *coerce* a minority."[29] He later
described the power granted by the compulsory acquisition provision
in these terms: "a more complete negation of the terms upon which
originally, at least, individuals entered into the association of company
membership can hardly be imagined."[30] Finally, one notes that, at least
in the view of Rand and Taschereau JJ., the possibility that this power
could be used "for a purely arbitrary acquisition of shares of a small

---

25   Elliott J. Weiss, "The Law of Take Out Mergers: A Historical Perspective" (1981)
     56 N.Y.U.L. Rev. 624.
26   In *Rathie v. Montreal Trust Co.*, [1953] 2 S.C.R. 204 at 209, the Supreme Court
     discussed the history of the section, including its English origins.
27   *Ibid.*
28   *Ibid.* at 209.
29   *Ibid.* at 213 [emphasis added].
30   *Ibid.* at 215.

interest by a larger one" was a purpose for which "I cannot think the provision was introduced."[31]

Some years later, the Supreme Court of Canada had occasion to consider the 90 percent compulsory acquisition rules again in *Esso Standard (Inter-America) Inc. v. J.W. Enterprises Inc.*[32] *Esso Standard* involved an offer to purchase the shares of International Petroleum launched by Esso Standard at a time when an affiliate of Esso Standard, Standard Oil Company, already owned more than 90 percent of International Petroleum's shares. In other words, it was a foregone conclusion that Esso's offer to purchase would be successful. It was equally certain that, since holders of more than 90 percent of International Petroleum's shares would approve the offer, the shares of the remaining shareholders could be compulsorily acquired under section 128 (unless the court were to order otherwise).

In fact, of the shares held by shareholders unaffiliated with Esso Standard, far less than 90 percent had approved the transfer. In other words, the *Esso Standard* case compelled the court to face squarely the question of whether it should matter that the shares to be counted in determining whether or not the 90 percent approval threshold had been satisfied were held by parties that were not independent of the acquiring corporation. The Supreme Court of Canada rejected the suggestion that the section was intended to be used in cases where the shareholders approving the transaction were not independent of the acquiror. Judson J. for the court held, "the section contemplates the acquisition of 90 per cent of the total issued shares of the class affected and *that this 90 per cent must be independently held*."[33]

c)   CBCA, Section 206

It is a specific precondition of the compulsory acquisition provisions in the CBCA today that a bidder obtain 90 percent of the *independently held* shares. The provision is found in section 206 of the CBCA. Section 206 is a lengthy provision, dealing in some detail with a process for determining the fair value of dissenters' shares similar to the dissent and appraisal procedure detailed in section 190. At the core of section 206, however, is section 206(2), which reads as follows:

(2) If within one hundred and twenty days after the date of a take-over bid the bid is accepted by the holders of not less than ninety

---

31   *Ibid.* at 213.
32   [1963] S.C.R. 144.
33   *Ibid.* at 151 [emphasis added]. The court relied on this point on the judgment of the English Court of Appeal in *Re Bugle Press Limited*, [1961] 1 Ch. 270 (C.A.).

per cent of the shares of any class of shares to which the take-over bid relates, other than shares held at the date of the take-over bid by or on behalf of the offeror or an affiliate or associate of the offeror, the offeror is entitled, on complying with this section, to acquire the shares held by the dissenting offerees

If a successful bidder chooses to exercise this right, it must deliver a notice to that effect to each dissenting shareholder. Dissenting shareholders then may elect to receive for their shares either (a) the same consideration paid to those shareholders who tendered to the bid (the Act actually uses the phrase *on the terms on which the offeror acquired the shares of the offerees who accepted the take-over bid*);[34] or (b) *fair value*[35] (the determination of which is made in accordance with a process detailed in the section.)

i)   Same Terms as Original Takeover Bid

When the takeover bid that preceded the compulsory acquisition was a cash bid, determining the amount to be paid to each dissenting shareholder who does not elect to receive "fair value" is straightforward. But the matter can become considerably more complicated when the takeover bid includes a "paper" component (that is, where the bidder is paying for the target's shares by issuing shares or other securities of its own). This complication was highlighted in a 1998 decision of the Ontario Court of Appeal, *Shoom v. Great-West Lifeco Inc.*[36]

Shoom arose out of the acquisition by Great-West Lifeco Inc. ("Great-West") of the shares of London Insurance Group ("LIG"). In its takeover bid for LIG, Great-West had offered LIG shareholders several options. They could elect to receive cash for their shares or, if they preferred, they could elect one of three other options each of which included a Great-West share component. Under one of those three options in particular, a LIG shareholder could elect to receive a specified number of common shares of Great-West in exchange for their LIG shares. This share option, however, was subject to an overall cap, or maximum, stipulated by Great-West so that it would not be required to issue more shares in total than it thought appropriate. The cap would apply if the number of LIG shareholders electing to receive shares of Great-West, rather than cash, was so great that the number of Great-West shares needed to meet the demand would exceed the cap set by Great-West. If that were to happen, then Great-West would issue shares

---

34   CBCA, s. 206 (3)(c)(i).
35   *Ibid.*, s. 206(3).
36   (1998), 40 O.R. (3d) 672 (Gen. Div.), aff'd (1998), 42 O.R. (3d) 732 (C.A.).

only up to the capped number. Those rationed shares would then be pro-rated amongst the LIG shareholders who had chosen this share exchange option. The remainder of the purchase price for their LIG shares would be paid in cash, despite the fact that they had elected to receive payment in Great-West shares.

In fact, most LIG shareholders did tender to the bid. Many elected the Great-West common share option—so many, in fact, that the cap imposed by Great-West was indeed reached. The tendering shareholders accordingly had to accept a portion of their consideration in cash. Great-West came to hold over 99 percent of LIG's outstanding shares, and sought to take advantage of section 206 of the CBCA to acquire the remaining shares. All the shares Great-West had intended to make available for the share exchange option had been exhausted in the takeover bid. Thus, Great-West proposed to offer only cash to those shareholders whose shares were being compulsorily acquired pursuant to section 206.

Shoom, a dissenting shareholder, insisted that Great-West also make available to those remaining hold-out shareholders, a share exchange option on the same terms as had been available to shareholders who had tendered to the bid. The court agreed and ordered that the shareholder was entitled to transfer his LIG shares on the same basis as those shareholders who had originally accepted the Great-West offer. (This was very favourable to the dissenting shareholder, because the Great-West shares had risen significantly in value.) The motions judge recognized that this interpretation of section 206 was especially generous to the dissenting shareholder in this particular case, but reasoned that the purpose of section 206 was not merely to protect dissenting shareholders from prejudice. If that were the sole goal of section 206, the argument ran, it would be enough to provide that dissenters were entitled to receive fair value for their shares.[37]

The Ontario Court of Appeal upheld the lower court's judgment, emphasizing that the purpose of section 206 would not be achieved unless it was clear that "a dissenting shareholder cannot be penalized as a result of his failure to tender his shares to a bid."[38] In other words, if it were possible to structure a bid such that shareholders who chose to tender were assured of receiving at least some shares, while shareholders who chose not to tender might not be able to obtain any shares at all in a subsequent compulsory acquisition, shareholders could be unfairly pressured into tendering in the first place even, perhaps, if they doubted the adequacy of the bid. They might fear that, if they failed to

---

37   *Ibid.* at 680 (Gen. Div.).
38   *Ibid.* at 736 (C.A.).

tender, they could ultimately end up forced to accept something less for their shares than those who tendered in the first place. Such a bid would, thus, be tantamount to a coercive two-tier, front-end loaded bid.

Of course the risk of an overly generous interpretation of section 206 is that one of the fundamental purposes of the section may be undermined: if dissenting shareholders are placed in a *more* advantageous position by refusing to tender to an otherwise fair bid, the "hold-up" problems that section 206 sought to address would be exacerbated rather than relieved. Lederman J., the motions judge in *Shoom*, recognized this theoretical possibility but considered that the incentive of some minority shareholders to speculate in this way would be tempered by the possible downside risk. (In other words, by purchasing and holding shares in a target company for the purpose of benefiting from the terms of a subsequent compulsory acquisition, the speculator would run the risk that the bid might fail altogether, and the price of the shares he or she had purchased would subsequently fall.) Philip Anisman, writing shortly after the *Shoom* case had been decided, indicated that, as a result of *Shoom*, takeover bidders that wished to offer target shareholders alternative forms of consideration (subject to a predetermined maximum, as in *Shoom*) had adopted the practice of prorating based on the proportion of each form of consideration elected by shareholders at each take-up of shares.[39] Anisman was critical of the unequal treatment of shareholders that resulted from this practice.[40]

ii) Compelled Acquisitions

It is not only successful bidders that may wish to eliminate a small residual minority shareholder interest after the conclusion of the bid. Often those few remaining shareholders may themselves prefer to have their shares acquired rather than be left holding an insignificant interest in a public company that is now dominated by a controlling shareholder. Once a public company is in the hands of a shareholder holding more than 90 percent of the voting shares, minority shareholders have no effective voting power and face an illiquid market for their shares.

Many Canadian corporate statutes contain provisions designed to relieve minority shareholders from the marked disadvantages of holding such a minority interest in cases where a successful takeover bidder is eligible to acquire the remaining shares under the compulsory acquisition rules, but has chosen not to do so. These provisions are

---

39 Philip Anisman, "Squeezing Out Minority Shareholders: A Comment" in *Critical Issues in Mergers and Acquisitions*, Queen's Annual Business Law Symposium, 1999 (Kingston: Queen's University, 2000) 229 at 239.
40 *Ibid.*

sometimes referred to as "compelled acquisition" provisions.[41] So, for example, section 206.1 of the CBCA states that, in cases where a bidder was permitted to purchase dissenting shareholders' shares under section 206, but has not offered to do so, the dissenting shareholders may require the bidder to acquire their shares on the same terms as those offered to holders who tendered to the bid.

Other Canadian corporate statutes provide a similar right to shareholders, although the method for determining the price of the dissenting shareholders' shares is not identical in every case. For example, under the Ontario *Business Corporations Act*,[42] the obligation to purchase the dissenting shareholders' shares falls upon the target corporation itself, rather than the bidder, and the price is to be either a price offered by the corporation or "fair value." Under the New Brunswick *Business Corporations Act*,[43] the terms are to be essentially the same as those that apply when the bidder is exercising its compulsory acquisition rights, that is, the dissenting shareholder is permitted to choose to receive from the bidder the same consideration as shareholders who tendered to the bid, or "fair value."

iii) Conclusion

The statutory compromise between the proprietary right of shareholders and the need to avoid "hold-up" problems that could discourage bids seems reasonable and necessary. And the high threshold of shareholder acceptance ensures sound, objective evidence that only fair and reasonable bids will trigger the otherwise extraordinary expropriation rights that the compulsory acquisition rules provide. However, over time alternative methods of squeezing out minority shareholders have been devised—methods that did not reflect such an explicit legislative compromise. It is to these alternative "going-private" methods that we now turn.

---

41   See, for example, Uniform Law Conference of Canada, Civil Law Section, Report of the Uniform Income Trusts Act Working Group, *The Uniform Income Trusts Act*: Closing the Gap Between Traditional Trust Law and Current Governance Expectations (Edmonton: ULCC, 2006) at para. 155. See also the title of Part XVII of the CBCA, "Compulsory and Compelled Acquisitions."

42   OBCA, s. 189(4).

43   *Business Corporations Act* (New Brunswick), s. 133(17).

3) Post-Bid "Going-Private" or "Squeeze-Out Transactions"

a) Alternative Methods of Squeezing Out Minority Shareholders

We have seen that when a takeover bidder acquires at least 90 percent of the shares of an offeree (that is, target) corporation that the bidder did not already own, many Canadian corporate statutes provide that the bidder may, if it wishes, acquire the remaining shares of any shareholders who did not choose to accept the bid price.

But alternative methods for eliminating the interests of minority shareholders *without first acquiring 90 percent of the independently held shares* have also been developed in Canada. The legality and propriety of these methods have been scrutinized and discussed by courts and regulators for a number of years. There are several methods by which the interests of minority shareholders may be so eliminated, but perhaps the two most frequently used are share consolidations (sometimes in the United States referred to as "reverse stock splits") and amalgamation squeeze-outs.[44]

i) Consolidation

The consolidation technique works this way. A corporation seeking to eliminate the interests of its smallest shareholders would propose a "consolidation" of the corporation's shares, that is, a transaction by which all of the outstanding shares of the corporation would be converted into a smaller number of shares. The corporation might, for example, propose that the outstanding shares would be consolidated on a 1 for 100 basis. Every outstanding block of 100 shares of the corporation would, following the date of the consolidation, be transformed into just a single share. Needless to say, a share consolidation of this sort is an economic non-event (just as its polar opposite—a share split—is). The value of the corporation is not changed by this sort of change to its shares, any more than the value of 100 pennies is changed when those pennies are swapped for a single one-dollar coin. If, for example, each share of a publicly traded corporation were worth $10 before this consolidation, then a pre-consolidation block of 100 shares would be worth $1,000. A person holding 100 shares before the consolidation would hold just a single share after the consolidation. But that single post-consolidation share would now be worth $1,000—exactly what the holder's pre-consolidation shares would be worth in total.

---

44 Other methods include statutory plans of arrangement, discussed in Chapter 4, and capital reorganizations.

Why, then, would a corporation choose to undertake such an economically meaningless action? Outside of the squeeze-out context, a corporation might undertake a share consolidation so that its stock price would meet minimum requirements imposed by stock exchanges and so avoid being de-listed. For our purposes here, however, the answer lies in the treatment of the holdings of any small shareholders owning fewer than 100 shares.[45] Consider, for example, a small shareholder who owned just fifty shares of this hypothetical corporation. After a one for 100 consolidation, this shareholder would hold just half a share. Any share interest that constitutes less than one full share is known as a "fractional" share, and fractional-share interests are administratively cumbersome for corporations and of minimal use to investors. (One cannot, for example, cast half a vote.) Accordingly, it is not unusual for corporations to eliminate fractional shares by making a cash payment to their holders, and that is precisely the next step taken by a corporation using the consolidation technique as a squeeze-out method.

The consolidation technique has been considered in several Canadian cases, including *P.L. Robertson Manufacturing Co.*,[46] *Re Ripley International Ltd.*,[47] and *Grouse Mountain Resorts Ltd. v. Angeli.*[48]

ii) Amalgamation Squeeze-Out

Perhaps a more common method of effecting a going-private transaction, in cases where the corporate law compulsory acquisition rules are not available, is an amalgamation squeeze-out. An amalgamation squeeze takes advantage of the broad wording of corporate amalgamation provisions discussed in Chapter 4. Briefly, the technique works this way. Imagine a publicly traded corporation (ABC Limited) incorporated under the CBCA, with a controlling shareholder (Controllco) who owns 67,000 of ABC's 100,000 outstanding shares. Controllco wishes to take ABC private and begins by launching a takeover bid for the shares of ABC that Controllco does not already own. The bid is fairly successful; Controllco acquires an additional 20,000 of ABC's shares. But about 13,000 ABC shares are not tendered to Controllco's bid and so remain in the hands of ABC's public shareholders.

---

45   A holding of at least one hundred shares of an equity security trading at $1.00 or more per unit constitutes a "standard trading unit" (what was once known as a "board lot") as defined in the Universal Market Integrity Rules. See Universal Market Integrity Rules, s. 11, definition of "standard trading unit," online: www.iiroc.ca/English/Documents/Rulebook/UMIR_en.pdf.

46   (1974), 7 O.R. (2d) 98 (H.C.J.).

47   (1977), 1 B.L.R. 269 (Ont. H.C.J.).

48   (1989), 42 B.L.R. 219 (B.C.C.A.).

Of course, if 90 percent of the minority shares had been acquired in the bid (that is 90 percent of the 33,000 shares Controllco did not already own, or 29,700 in total), then Controllco would have been able to take advantage of the compulsory acquisition rules in section 206 of the CBCA. Because the section 206 technique is not available, Controllco decides to attempt an amalgamation squeeze. Controllco first incorporates a new wholly owned subsidiary (XYZ Limited), to which Controllco transfers Controllco's 87,000 shares of ABC Limited. Next, Controllco proposes an amalgamation between ABC Limited and XYZ Limited.

It will be recalled from Chapter 4 that an amalgamation of two CBCA corporations must first be approved by the shareholders of each of those corporations, and that approval must be by way of a special resolution (that is, the affirmative vote of two-thirds of the shareholders who vote on the resolution.)[49] Since Controllco holds 100 percent of the shares of XYZ Limited and 87 percent of the shares of ABC Limited, in the absence of any other protections, approval of the amalgamation— by both amalgamating corporations—would be a foregone conclusion.

Section 182(1)(d) of the CBCA anticipates that when two corporations are amalgamated, some shareholders of the predecessor corporations may receive money or securities other than securities of the amalgamated corporation in exchange for their shares. Accordingly, the ABC/XYZ amalgamation agreement would be drafted to provide that, upon amalgamation, (a) shareholders of XYZ Limited (that is, Controllco) would receive common shares in the new amalgamated corporation; and (b) shareholders of ABC Limited, in exchange for their shares, would receive either cash or (more commonly) redeemable preferred shares in the new amalgamated corporation which would promptly be redeemed for cash following the amalgamation. Thus, when the transaction is completed, all of the shares of the minority shareholders will have been redeemed for cash. Their share interests in ABC will be eliminated.

Were the amalgamation provisions of the CBCA (and those Canadian provincial corporate statutes that followed the CBCA model) intended to facilitate squeeze-out amalgamations? Or was the development of the amalgamation squeeze technique an unintended consequence of features of corporate law amalgamation rules crafted for other, perhaps more benign, purposes? Gilson and Black have noted, in the U.S. context, that one of the key U.S. statutory developments that facilitated the use of mergers[50] to freeze out minority shareholders was

---

49   CBCA, s. 183(5).

50   The term *merger* is a U.S. corporate law concept that is similar, but not identical, to the Canadian corporate law concept of "amalgamation." The principal difference between a merger of two corporations under, for example, Delaware

the provision in U.S. corporate statutes, beginning with Florida's legislation in 1925, for the distribution of cash to some shareholders of merging corporations in exchange for their shares, instead of a requirement that all shareholders receive new shares in the merged corporation.[51] In Canada, the federal corporate statute in effect prior to 1975 did *not* provide for distribution of cash upon amalgamation, requiring instead that the articles of amalgamation include details concerning "the manner of converting the authorized and issued capital of each of the companies into that of the amalgamated company."[52] The Dickerson Committee's 1971 draft for a new proposed federal corporate statute included a provision allowing for the payment of cash to shareholders of amalgamating corporations in lieu of or in addition to converting their shares into securities of the amalgamated corporation.[53] The Dickerson Committee made no comment on this specific proposed change in their commentary, saying only, as a general matter:

> Sections 14.08 to 14.13 deal with corporate amalgamations. Although influenced by both the substantive and administrative provisions of the New York and Delaware Laws, these sections continue substantially the policy of s. 128A of the present Canada Corporations Act, modified in respect of formalities and in respect of amalgamations of or with subsidiary corporations.[54]

Apart from explanatory comment on subsection (2) (which is not relevant to the squeeze-out technique), the committee considered the rest of the amalgamation provisions they had proposed to be "self-

---

corporate law and an amalgamation of two corporations under, for example, the CBCA, is that in a Delaware merger one of the constituent corporations disappears upon the merger, and the other corporation continues. In other words, one corporation is merged into the second. See *General Corporation Law* (Delaware), Delaware Code, Title 8, Chapter 1, s. 251(a). In a Canadian amalgamation, as discussed in Chapter 4, both amalgamating corporations are said to somehow continue to exist albeit only through the new amalgamated corporation. The Delaware concept of "consolidation" appears to be closer, conceptually, to the Canadian notion of amalgamation. See *General Corporation Law* (Delaware), s. 251(a).

51   Gilson & Black, *Law and Finance*, above note 20 at 1253–54.

52   Canada *Companies Act*, as amended by S.C. 1964, c. 52, s. 41, s. 128A(2)(h). Section 128A was subsequently renumbered at the time of the 1970 federal statute consolidation. See *Canada Corporations Act*, s. 137(3)(h).

53   See Robert W.V. Dickerson, John L. Howard, & Leon Getz, *Proposals for a New Business Corporations Law for Canada*, vol. 2 (Ottawa: Information Canada, 1971) at 114 (s. 14.09(1)(d)) [Dickerson Committee].

54   *Ibid.*, vol. 1, para. 361.

explanatory."[55] The new provision was enacted into law,[56] and remains part of the CBCA amalgamation provisions today.[57]

In the broadest sense, the new amalgamation provisions fit within the Dickerson Committee's recommendations concerning fundamental corporate changes. Referring generally to the approval and implementation of fundamental changes, the Dickerson Committee noted a key shift that had occurred in the philosophical underpinning of corporate law. At common law, they noted, changes to a corporation's charter required the unanimous consent of all the corporation's shareholders, a situation reflecting the "vested rights" doctrine.[58] The inflexibility of the vested rights doctrine, they noted, had gradually given way to a more flexible approach. In this newer era, it was recognized that minority shareholders could, effectively, be bound by the will of the majority, that this principle extended to amendments—even fundamental amendments—to the corporation's charter, and that the fact that such amendments could be made to the corporate "contract" even against the fervent wishes of some dissenting shareholders was not seen as improper, since everyone who chose to acquire shares of a corporation did so with full knowledge that the terms of his or her share ownership might well be altered in the future by a majority vote.

Yet, it seems clear that the Dickerson Committee's expressed support for majority corporate rule (coupled with dissent and appraisal rights for minority shareholders) would not have extended to endorsement of the amalgamation squeeze technique. Elliott J. Weiss,[59] analyzing the development of cash merger statutes in the United States, has argued that these provisions were *not* originally intended by the legislators to facilitate going-private transactions, but were in fact enacted to deal with other issues.[60] However, as Weiss notes: "[S]tate legislators often are inclined to adopt statutory language developed in other states . . . without fully analysing all the consequences of such action."[61]

At the time of the Dickerson Committee's report, the use of the freeze-out merger technique in the United States had become well-known, and the law surrounding the technique was continuing to evolve. Thus, the Dickerson Committee referred to the use of short-

---

55   *Ibid.*, para. 362.
56   *Canada Business Corporations Act*, S.C. 1974–75–76, c. 33, s. 176(1)(d) [CBCA].
57   CBCA, s. 182(1)(d).
58   Dickerson Committee, above note 53, vol. 1 at para. 344.
59   Weiss, "Law of Take Out Mergers," above note 25.
60   Specifically, Weiss suggests that allowing cash mergers addressed "artificial barriers" (*ibid.* at 638) to certain complex merger transactions. *Ibid.* at 637*ff.*
61   *Ibid.* at 633, n52.

form mergers in the United States to freeze out minority shareholders, noting that "federal law, in particular Rule 10b-5 under the *Securities Exchange Act, 1934*, has been successfully invoked to prevent such squeeze-outs."[62] The fact that the Dickerson Committee proposed amalgamation provisions modelled on New York and Delaware law, without significant comment, coupled with concern expressed elsewhere in the Dickerson Committee report about the importance of *not* permitting the short form amalgamation procedures to be used in the way they had been used in U.S. jurisdictions to squeeze out minority shareholders, strongly suggests that the Dickerson Committee did not intend, or envision, that the changes they proposed to the federal corporate statute's long-form amalgamation rules would give controlling shareholders greater power to eliminate minority shareholders' interests.

However, neither the pivotal U.S. Supreme Court case, *Santa Fe Industries v. Green*,[63] nor the watershed Delaware Supreme Court decision in *Singer v. Magnavox Co.*[64] had yet been decided at the time of the Dickerson Committee Report. It was not, therefore, until some time after the new CBCA came into force that squeeze-out transactions became the focus of heightened legal and regulatory scrutiny.

Though going-private transactions are now undertaken in Canada almost routinely, they raise important shareholder protection concerns. Those concerns are addressed at two levels. First, securities regulators have implemented a specific regulatory regime in the case of going-private transactions. Second, when going-private transactions are effected through corporate transactions such as amalgamations, corporate law dissent and appraisal rights are triggered, and the corporate law oppression remedy may also in some cases be invoked by aggrieved minority shareholders.

b) OSC Regulation of "Business Combinations/Going-Private Transactions"

i) A Brief History of "Going-Private Transactions"
In 1976 the Ontario Securities Commission issued a rather brief policy statement, OSC Policy 3-37, dealing with disclosure requirements the commission considered appropriate in the case of issuer bids.

In a December 1977 notice, the OSC indicated that certain of the disclosure requirements in Policy 3-37 would also apply in respect of an

---

62 Dickerson Committee, above note 53, vol. 1, para. 364.
63 430 U.S. 462 (1977).
64 380 A.2d 969 (Del. 1977) [*Singer v. Magnavox*].

information circular prepared in connection with "a proposed change in the corporate structure of an issuer . . . which has or is intended to have the effect of compelling any shareholder of the issuer to terminate his interest in the issuer"[65] (in other words, in the case of a "going-private transaction").

OSC Policy 3-37 was adopted, of course, many years before the decision in *Ainsley Financial Corp. v. Ontario (Securities Commission)*[66] challenged the propriety of OSC policy statements that included mandatory, "legislation-like" provisions.

There had been a proliferation of going-private transactions in the United States in the early 1970s for a variety of reasons,[67] and transactions of this sort, accordingly, began to prompt more litigation and more regulatory attention. In fact, Hadden, Forbes, and Simmonds have suggested that initially in Canada, going-private transactions had generally been regarded as relatively benign (provided they were not carried out at a price that was "completely unfair to the minority"[68]). However, they suggest that Canadian judges began to become wary of these transactions in the late 1970s, a change they suggest that seems "to have emanated largely from developments in the United States."[69]

In *Re Cablecasting*,[70] the OSC had occasion to consider the application of the then current legislation and policy statements to a going-private transaction. The proposed going-private transaction involved a class of non-voting equity shares of Cablecasting Limited. The corporation's voting shares were held by a group of three shareholders. An application was made to the OSC seeking a cease-trade order under what was then section 144 of the *Securities Act*. Section 144 was an early "ancestor" of section 127 of the current Ontario *Securities Act*—the provision that empowers the OSC to make a number of specified orders if it considers it "in the public interest" to do so. However, at the time of the *Re Cablecasting* decision, the OSC's powers were considerably more circumscribed than they are today under section 127.

Counsel for the minority shareholders of Cablecasting Limited argued, among other things, "there is a fiduciary element present in such situations" and, accordingly, no such transaction should be allowed

---

65   [1977] OSCB 253 at 273–74 (2 December 1977).
66   (1993), 14 O.R. (3d) 280 (Gen. Div.), aff'd (1994), 21 O.R. (3d) 104 (C.A.).
67   See Weiss, "Law of Take Out Mergers," above note 25 at 654.
68   Tom Hadden, Robert E. Forbes, & Ralph L. Simmonds, *Canadian Business Organizations Law* (Toronto: Butterworths, 1984) at 608.
69   *Ibid.* at 611.
70   [1978] OSCB 37.

unless there was a "valid business purpose."[71] Although the OSC declined to issue a cease-trading order in the case, it did indicate "that it would review Policy 3-37 and its other policy statements in light of the submissions [of the minority shareholders' counsel and the OSC Director]."[72] Specific reference was made to consideration of the Delaware Supreme Court's decision in *Singer v. Magnavox*[73] in the course of such a policy review. Finally, although there was no mandated requirement for

---

71   *Ibid.* at 41.

72   *Ibid.* at 48.

73   *Singer v. Magnavox*, above note 64. In *Singer v. Magnavox*, the Delaware Supreme Court held that a merger "made for the sole purpose of freezing out minority shareholders, is an abuse of the corporate process." *Ibid.* at 980. The *Singer v. Magnavox* case was regarded as especially significant by U.S. commentators because it came close on the heels of the U.S. Supreme Court's decision in *Santa Fe Industries, Inc. v. Green*, above note 63, a case that helped establish the scope of s. 10(b) of the *Securities Exchange Act of 1934* and Rule 10b-5 promulgated thereunder in actions by minority shareholders opposed to attempted freeze-out transactions. See, for example, Robert C. Clark, *Corporate Law* (Aspen, CO: Aspen Law & Business, 1986) at 518*ff.* The specific dynamic revealed by the *Santa Fe/Singer* decisions is uniquely American. U.S. corporate law is legislated at the state level. Defenders of the American corporate law system argue that it has led to a healthy competition between states, which has served the interests of American shareholders well. (See, for example, Roberta Romano, *The Genius of American Corporate Law* (Washington: AEI Press, 1993). Others argue that that very competition between states has led to the proliferation of "lax" management-friendly state corporate laws, and that the only antidote to such declining corporate law standards may be an increased role for the federal government in the regulation of publicly traded corporations. (For further details of this "race to the bottom"/"race to the top" debate, see Nicholls, *Corporate Law*, above note 15 at 32*ff.*) In Canada, provinces do not enjoy exclusive legislative authority with respect to the incorporation of business corporations, there is no apparent significant competition amongst incorporating jurisdictions to attract corporate charters, and there is no federal body comparable to the U.S. Securities and Exchange Commission, because securities regulation has, thus far, been legislated exclusively at the provincial level. The federal government recently proposed the enactment of a federal securities act and the creation of a national Canadian securities regulator. However, the Supreme Court of Canada ruled in December 2011 that this proposed legislation is not valid under the so-called "general" branch of the federal trade and commerce power in s. 91(2) of the *Constitution Act, 1867* (U.K.), 30 & 31 Vict., c. 3, reprinted in R.S.C. 1985, App. II, No. 5. See *Reference re Securities Act*, 2011 SCC 66. Accordingly, the sophisticated interplay between federal and state (or provincial) interests that underlies the development of the "squeeze out" (or "freeze out") jurisprudence in the U.S. simply does not exist. Instead, the key elements in the Canadian debate on this issue seem to be centred on the conceptual nature of share ownership, the meaning and nature of corporate democracy, and the extent to which minority shareholders are vulnerable to actions taken by majority shareholders.

a "majority of the minority vote" to approve the proposed transaction, Cablecasting, through its counsel, committed to obtain such approval as a pre-condition to completing the going-private transaction.

The Re Cablecasting matter thus spurred the OSC to reconsider its approach to going-private transactions. The Director of the OSC produced a memorandum on this topic in May 1978, and the OSC convened a public meeting in June of that year to discuss this memorandum.[74] One of the key facts that emerged from this process was that market participants believed that going-private transactions deserved special attention in Canada because of particular features of the Canadian capital markets.

A submission to the OSC specifically linked the need to scrutinize going-private transactions to "imperfections in the Canadian securities markets."[75] The nature of those supposed "imperfections" evidently related to the fact that there were "very few Canadian corporations that have a large enough float of securities in the hands of enough public shareholders to support a true market."[76] Many Canadian public companies then (as now) were, in fact, controlled by major shareholders. This differs from the situation in the United States where shareholdings of the largest public corporations tend to be widely dispersed. The presence of controlling shareholders in so many Canadian public companies meant, according to the same submission, that "minority shareholders in public companies may need some of the same protection afforded shareholders in private companies by means of shareholders' agreements."[77]

It is useful to recall that, at that time, the Ontario Business Corporations Act contained no oppression remedy[78] (although the CBCA did).

---

74   [1978] OSCB 214.

75   Ibid. at 217.

76   Ibid.

77   Ibid. at 218.

78   The current version of the OBCA does, of course, include an oppression remedy, indeed one of the broadest in Canada. However, historically there had been resistance to adopting such a remedy in Ontario. The Lawrence Committee, in 1967, had specifically considered and roundly rejected introducing such a remedy into the Ontario corporate statute, saying that such a remedy, "raises as many problems as it lays to rest and, more importantly, is objectionable on the ground that it is a complete dereliction of the established principle of judicial non-interference in the management of companies." Interim Report of the Select Committee on Company Law (Toronto: Queen's Printer, 1967) at para. 7.3.12 (Chair: Allan F. Lawrence).

Moreover, the dissent and appraisal remedy under the Ontario statute was only available to shareholders of private corporations.[79]

In response to the concerns raised about "going-private transactions," the OSC introduced "Appendix 1" as a supplement to OSC Policy 3-37. Appendix 1 was quite short, and made no attempt to specifically define "going-private" or "squeeze-out" transactions. However, the supplement did introduce two additional requirements for the completion of going-private transactions that continue to form the cornerstone of going-private regulation:

- *An independent valuation requirement:* A valuation of the corporation was to be obtained so that securityholders whose interests were being eliminated would be able to assess fairly the amount of any consideration being offered to them in exchange for their securities.
- A *"majority of the minority" voting requirement:* Before a squeeze-out transaction could be completed, holders of a majority of the corporation's shares—excluding shares held by the controlling shareholders—were required to approve the transaction. In the case of a "two-stage transaction" (that is, a going-private transaction undertaken following an offer to the minority shareholders to purchase their shares), the shares of those who accepted the offer in the first stage could be included in the calculation of the majority for purposes of approval in the second stage provided adequate disclosure of the intention to undertake a second stage transaction and a full valuation were provided to shareholders at the first stage of the transaction. Special rules also applied where the tax consequences for shareholders differed depending on whether or not their shares were tendered at the first stage.[80]

The procedures followed by corporations undertaking going-private transactions were also tested in the courts. Shortly after the Re Cablecasting decision, and before the OSC introduced its supplement to Policy 3-37, the British Columbia Supreme Court rendered its decision in *Neonex International Ltd. v. Kolasa*.[81] *Neonex* was an appraisal case concerning a CBCA corporation that had undertaken an amalgamation. The terms of the amalgamation agreement provided that shareholders of one of the amalgamating corporations could elect to receive, in exchange for their shares, either cash or non-voting preference shares in the amalgamated corporation. Some shareholders were opposed to

---

79   *Business Corporations Act* (Ontario), R.S.O. 1970, c. 53, s. 100.
80   [1978] OSCB 224.
81   (1978), 84 D.L.R. (3d) 446 (B.C.S.C.) [*Neonex*].

the amalgamation. They exercised their dissent and appraisal rights. The amalgamation was nevertheless approved by special resolution of the shareholders of the amalgamating corporations. Following the amalgamation, the amalgamated corporation applied for an order to fix the fair value of the shares to be paid to the dissenting shareholders. Bouck J. noted that the then new CBCA did not afford minority shareholders opposed to an amalgamation the same right to undo such a transaction that had been available under prior federal corporate law. Once a certificate of amalgamation had been granted under the CBCA, the amalgamation could not be undone; dissenting shareholders were limited to seeking monetary value for their shares. It was evident that the court did not entirely approve of the flexibility the new amalgamation rules provided to majority shareholders. As Bouck J. put it:

> Parliament decided to grant a controlling shareholder an easier way to force out the minority than was previously the case . . . . The legality of the amalgamation is not in question. Its morality is for others to assess . . . .[82] The reason for these new provisions is not clear because it would seem the 90 percent forcing-out method is redundant.[83]

Nor was there any doubt that Bouck J. regarded the use of the amalgamation technique as a tool of expropriation rather than a manifestation of corporate majority rule.[84] However, *Neonex* did not involve a decision on the merits. It had come before the court as a petition by Neonex seeking an order fixing fair value of the dissenters' shares, and the court's order was that the petition be converted into an action. Nevertheless, it was clear that the opportunities to squeeze out minority shareholders by use of the CBCA amalgamation provisions had been recognized by the business community. The uncertain interplay between the flexible squeeze-out technique and the formal, protective rules of the explicit 90 percent compulsory acquisition provisions had been identified and would, perhaps in later cases, need to be more definitively clarified.

About eight months later, the Ontario High Court released its decision in *Carlton Realty Company v. Maple Leaf Mills Limited*.[85] *Maple Leaf Mills* involved a publicly traded corporation of which about 73 percent

---

82   *Ibid.* at 451.

83   *Ibid.* at 452.

84   See, for example, *ibid.* at 452: "If a shareholder wants to acquire all the other shares in the company by using the amalgamation sections rather than the forcing-out provisions then the law will be particularly concerned over the rights of the dissenters. Their property is being expropriated."

85   (1978), 22 O.R. (2d) 198 at 205 (H.C.J.).

of the shares had been owned by a single company (Norin). Norin had launched a takeover bid, through a subsidiary, for the shares of the target company it did not already own. With the shares acquired in the bid, as well as shares acquired later through market purchases, Norin's stake in the target company constituted more than 94 percent of the company's equity. The target company was incorporated under Ontario's *Business Corporations Act*, a statute which, at that time, contained no compulsory acquisition provision similar to section 206 of the CBCA.

Norin sought to eliminate the interest of the few remaining public shareholders by way of an amalgamation squeeze, similar to the structure described earlier in this section. Some minority shareholders sought an injunction to prevent the holding of the shareholders' meeting called to approve that amalgamation. Steele J. granted this injunction. Since this matter came before the court as an injunction application, and was not preceded by a trial on the merits, Steele J. refrained from making definitive comments on the legality of the proposed amalgamation. At the same time, he did note that there was "no clear right under the Act to permit the taking of the applicants' common shares by the means proposed,"[86] and further wondered whether this amalgamation was an attempt to do indirectly what could not be done directly.[87] Steele J. might well have been influenced by the fact that the Ontario statute, at that time, not only contained no compulsory acquisition provision, but also did not extend dissent and appraisal rights in the case of amalgamation and other fundamental changes to shareholders of offering corporations.

Less than a month after Steele J.'s decision in *Maple Leaf Mills*, the issue of the legality of squeeze-out amalgamations came before the Ontario courts again in *Alexander et al. v. Westeel-Rosco et al.*[88] *Westeel-Rosco*, significantly, involved a corporation governed by the CBCA.[89] A takeover bid had been launched for the shares of Westeel-Rosco. The bidder had indicated that, if it were to acquire 90 percent of the shares of Westeel-Rosco through this bid, it intended to use the CBCA's compulsory acquisition provisions to acquire the remaining minority shareholders' interests. However, the bidder did not acquire 90 percent of the shares. Accordingly, the compulsory acquisition provisions were not

86   *Ibid.* at 317.
87   *Ibid.*
88   (1978), 22 O.R. (2d) 211 (H.C.J.) [*Westeel-Rosco*].
89   The corporation Westeel-Rosco Limited had originally been incorporated under the federal *Canada Corporations Act*, but as part of the transition to the then new CBCA, Westeel-Rosco had been continued under the CBCA.

available. Undeterred, the bidder proposed to eliminate the interests of the minority shareholders through an amalgamation squeeze.

The matter, as in *Maple Leaf Mills*, came before the court as an application for an interim injunction to restrain the holding of a shareholders' meeting to approve the amalgamation. The court distinguished the earlier *Neonex* case on the basis that in *Neonex* the impugned amalgamation had already been completed (and could not be undone) and further on the basis that, in *Westeel-Rosco*, the matter came before the court under the broad CBCA oppression remedy provisions. Montgomery J. noted, among other things, that "[i]t appears on the facts before me that the minority are being treated as second-class citizens."[90] Indeed, in his view, "the conduct of the directors is discriminatory."[91] To end, Montgomery J. granted the injunction sought by the minority shareholders.

Sometime later, a strong condemnation of the amalgamation squeeze technique was delivered by the Quebec Superior Court in *Burdon v. Zeller's Ltd.*[92] In the *Zeller's* case the Quebec Superior Court enjoined a proposal to effect an amalgamation squeeze proposed following the Hudson's Bay Company's takeover bid for Zeller's Limited, ruling that the CBCA's compulsory acquisition provision was the only method by which minority shareholders could be squeezed out.

It is clear, however, that squeeze-out transactions continued through the 1980s, although the explicit question of their legality was not much litigated. At least two frequently cited cases, *Jepson v. Canadian Salt Co.*[93] and *Domglass Inc. v. Jarislowsky, Fraser,*[94] clearly involved squeeze-out transactions, but the court decisions focused on questions of valuation of the dissenting shareholders' interests, and did not suggest that the squeeze-out transactions themselves were unlawful. Similarly, in *LoCicero v. BACM Industries Ltd.,*[95] a case involving an amalgamation squeeze under the Manitoba *Corporations Act*, the court did not suggest that an amalgamation squeeze was, in and of itself, illegal.[96]

---

90   Above note 88 at 219.
91   *Ibid.* at 221.
92   (1981), 16 B.L.R. 59 (Que. Sup. Ct.).
93   [1979] 4 W.W.R. 35 (Alta. S.C.).
94   (1982), 138 D.L.R. (3d) 521 (Que. C.A.), aff'g (1980), 13 B.L.R. 135 (Que. Sup. Ct.).
95   (1988), 49 D.L.R. (4th) 159 (S.C.C.), rev'g (1985), 25 D.L.R. (4th) 269 (Man. C.A.), rev'g (1984), 31 Man R. (2d) 208 (Q.B.).
96   Of course, squeeze-out transactions were also undertaken pursuant to the arrangement provisions of Canadian corporate statutes, such as s. 192 of the CBCA or s. 182 of the OBCA. In the context of such an arrangement in a 1993 decision, Farley J. of the Ontario Court (Gen. Div.) rejected the argument of dissenting shareholders for a "forcing out premium" saying that "the OBCA

It may be useful to note the developments that were taking place in Delaware law during this same period. Recall that the Delaware experience was of considerable interest to Canadian regulators and policymakers: the OSC Panel in the *Cablecasting* decision had specifically referred to the Delaware Supreme Court's decision in *Singer v. Magnavox* in the context of matters that ought to be considered in the review of what was then OSC Policy 3-37. The *Singer v. Magnavox* case had involved a "freeze-out merger" undertaken at the initiative of the controlling shareholder of a public company, solely for the purpose of eliminating the minority shareholders of that company. The Delaware Supreme Court made three critical findings. First, the minority shareholders who objected to the merger were not limited to pursuing an appraisal remedy as their exclusive remedy (unless the transaction were found to be entirely fair, as described below). Second, "a . . . merger, made for the sole purpose of freezing out minority stockholders, is an abuse of the corporate process."[97] Third, even where the majority shareholder is able to demonstrate some corporate purpose for the freeze-out merger beyond merely freezing out the minority, the transaction must, nevertheless, satisfy the test of "entire fairness."

It is clear that the Delaware Supreme Court's decision in *Singer* was based upon the premise that the majority owes a fiduciary duty to the minority shareholders under Delaware law, a proposition that does not appear to form part of Canadian law.[98] However, despite the lack of a similar legal underpinning in Canada, Canadian policymakers have found it useful to consider the protective mechanisms that have been sanctioned by the Delaware courts. The *Singer* decision itself, however, was modified by subsequent Delaware cases. The so-called business purpose test, for example, following some judicial elaboration in *Tanzer v. International General Industries*[99] and *Roland International Corp. v. Najjar*,[100] was ultimately overruled in the 1983 decision, *Weinberger v. UOP Inc.*,[101] a case that also importantly refined the meaning of "entire fairness" as including both procedural ("fair dealing") and substantive

---

provides that a minority may be 'squeezed or forced out' in return for fair value." See *New Quebec Raglan Mines Ltd. v. Blok-Anderson*, [1993] O.J. No. 727 (Gen. Div.).

97   *Singer v. Magnavox*, above note 64 at 980; see also at 982 (McNeill J., concurring).

98   See, for example, *Brant Investments Ltd. v. Keeprite Inc.* (1991), 3 O.R. (3d) 289 (C.A.).

99   379 A.2d 1121 (Del. 1977).

100   407 A.2d 1032 (Del. 1979).

101   457 A.2d 701 (Del. 1983) [*Weinberger*].

("fair price") elements, and endorsed the use of modern valuation techniques "in appraisal and other stock valuation cases."[102]

By the time of the *Weinberger* decision, the "business purpose" test had already been so diminished in practical importance in Delaware that its wholesale elimination was, as two American commentators have put it, "one of the great anticlimaxes in corporate law history."[103] However, *Weinberger* was instructive on the issue of procedural fairness. The court placed particular emphasis on the need, in cases like this (involving a controlling shareholder and its subsidiary) of establishing a structure between parent and subsidiary that would mimic arm's-length negotiation. Specifically, the court expressed support for the establishment of a special committee of the independent directors of the subsidiary (that is, directors who were neither officers nor employees of the subsidiary itself or of the controlling shareholder). Indeed, the court went so far as to suggest:

> Although perfection is not possible, or expected, the result here could have been entirely different if [the subsidiary] had appointed an independent negotiating committee of its outside directors to deal with [the parent company that was pursuing the freeze out merger] at arm's length . . . . Since fairness in this context can be equated to conduct by a theoretical, wholly independent, board of directors acting upon the matter before them, it is unfortunate that this course apparently was neither considered nor pursued . . . . Particularly in a parent-subsidiary context, a showing that the action taken was as though each of the contending parties had in fact exerted its bargaining

---

102 One might wonder why so much significance was attached to determining the circumstances under which a minority shareholder would be limited, in the event of a freeze-out merger that he or she opposed, to pursuing an appraisal remedy rather than an action based on the lack of "entire fairness." After all, under the appraisal remedy a dissenting shareholder is entitled to be paid "fair value" for his or her shares. (See *General Corporation Law* (Delaware), s. 262; for a comparable Canadian provision, see, for example, CBCA, s. 190.) Would one not expect that "fair value" would also be the measure of compensation even if appraisal were *not* the exclusive remedy available to the aggrieved shareholder? In fact, however, the Delaware courts have made clear that when a minority shareholder who has been frozen out is not limited to an appraisal remedy, the remedy to which he or she is entitled may well differ from the "fair value" of his or her shares as that value would have been determined for purposes of an appraisal remedy. See, for example, *Cede & Co. v. Technicolor*, 634 A.2d 345 (Del. 1993).

103 Gilson & Black, *Law and Finance*, above note 20 at 1286.

power against the other at arm's length is strong evidence that the transaction meets the test of fairness.[104]

Moreover, a second practice had already been developed to protect minority shareholders in freeze-out mergers: a "majority of the minority vote." Thus, in *Weinberger*, the proposed merger had been structured such that success of the transaction was dependent upon receiving an approval vote from holders of a majority of the shares of the subsidiary corporation, *other than those shares held by the parent company that had initiated the freeze-out*. (On the particular facts of *Weinberger*, however, the court held that the effect of this majority of the minority vote was vitiated by the fact that certain "critical information"[105] had not been disclosed to the minority shareholders prior to the vote.) Around that same time there had even been commentary arguing that requiring a majority of the minority vote as a precondition to completing a freeze-out merger offered better protection to minority shareholders than "objective indicators of intrinsic value."[106]

Weinberger had been long-settled law in Delaware by the time the Director under the CBCA entered the debate.[107] In November 1989, the Director issued a policy statement concerning "going-private transactions," essentially denouncing such transactions as impermissible under the CBCA.[108] In the meantime, the Ontario Securities Commis-

---

104 *Weinberger*, above note 101 at 709–10, n7.

105 *Ibid.* at 712.

106 See Kent T. van den Berg, "Approval of Take-Out Mergers by Minority Shareholders: From Substantive to Procedural Fairness" (1984) 93 Yale L.J. 1113 at 1115. Robert Clark, citing van den Berg's note, described the proposal that freeze-out mergers be approved by a majority of the minority vote, as "one of the most appealing ideas" for dealing with going-private transactions. See Clark, *Corporate Law*, above note 73 at 517–18.

107 The Delaware law of going-private transactions has had less impact on the Canadian regime since *Weinberger*, but it has by no means stood still. See, for example, *Re Siliconix Inc. Shareholders Litigation*, [2001] WL 716787 (Del. Ch.); *Re Pure Resources Shareholders Litigation*, 808 A.2d 421 (Del. Ch. 2002); *Glassman v. Unocal Exploration*, 777 A.2d 242 (Del. Sup. Ct. 2001); *Next Level Communications Inc. v. Motorola Inc.*, 834 A.2d 828 (Del. Ch. 2003); *Omnicare, Inc. v. NCS Healthcare, Inc.*, 818 A.2d 914 (Del. Sup. Ct. 2003); Bradley R. Aronstam, R. Franklin Balotti, & Timo Rehbock, "Delaware's Going-Private Dilemma: Fostering Protections for Minority Shareholders in the Wake of *Siliconix* and *Unocal Exploration*" (2003) 58 Bus. Law. 519; Jon E. Abramczyk, Jason A. Cincilla, & James D. Honaker, "Going-Private 'Dilemma'?—Not in Delaware" (2003) 58 Bus. Law. 1351; Michael J. McGuinness & Timo Rehbock, "Going-Private Transactions: A Practitioner's Guide" (2005) 30 Del. J. Corp. L. 437.

108 Policy Statement of CBCA Director (9 November 1989), reproduced in "Going-Private Transactions under the CBCA Discussion Paper" (1989) 24:4 Canada

sion had reworked Policy 3-37, which by 1982, had become OSC Policy 9.1,[109] although this original version of Policy 9.1 was still, prior to significant revisions in 1990 to 1992, quite modest in scope.

The CBCA Director's objections seemed to lag behind market opinion and market practice. Gradually, it became clear that going-private transactions were to be permitted in Canada, provided they were completed under circumstances that provided certain safeguards for minority shareholders. In 1994, the CBCA Director repealed the 1989 Policy Statement on Going-Private Transactions, in favour of a statement much more favourable to such transactions. The 1994 policy statement stated that going-private transactions would, indeed, be permitted under the CBCA subject to certain considerations. In the case of public corporations, the policy statement provided that

> compliance with established regulatory indicia of fairness will, as a general rule, be viewed by the Director as sufficient. For example, compliance with the requirements set forth in Ontario Securities Commission Policy 9.1 or Quebec Securities Commission Policy Q-27 will usually suffice for these purposes.[110]

In 1995, Industry Canada released a discussion paper on going-private transactions, reviewing the law, and canvassing possible options for legislative reform. But by this point it was evident that provincial securities commissions, notably the Ontario Securities Commission and the Quebec Securities Commission, were firmly taking the lead on the regulation of such transactions, a role that was significantly enhanced by the grant to such regulators of "rule-making power."

ii)   OSC Rule 61-501

By 1995, the OSC had received such rule-making power,[111] and so began the process of "reformulating" its existing policies. The reformulation project was complex. It required the commission to isolate the mandatory or quasi-legislative provisions of existing policies from the non-legislative provisions. The former were then reformulated into rules, the latter into new policy statements. But this reformulation pro-

---

Corporations Bulletin 106 at 111.

109   (1982), 4 OSCB 538e.

110   "Notice of Revised Policy on Going-Private Transactions" (22 September 1994) 24:10 Canada Corporations Bulletin 58.

111   For a discussion of the significance of rule-making power for Canadian securities commissions, and the developments that led legislatures to grant such powers to securities regulators, see Jeffrey G. MacIntosh & Christopher C. Nicholls, *Securities Law* (Toronto: Irwin, 2002) at 80–83.

cess, complicated enough in itself, had to be undertaken in a dynamic environment in which the commission also needed to direct resources toward the framing of altogether new rules and policies.

OSC Policy 9.1 was one of the most far-reaching of the existing OSC policies, and its reformulation was of profound interest to the securities industry and the practising bar. The reformulation of Policy 9.1 was, accordingly, an especially challenging project and the launch of the rule that eventually replaced Policy 9.1—OSC Commission Rule 61-501— could not be criticized as overly rushed.

Because Ontario is the financial centre of Canada, as a practical matter, the OSC's rule came to apply to transactions involving the largest of Canada's public corporations. Rule 61-501 was, of course, an instrument of securities regulation, not corporate law. However, courts could allude to corporations' compliance with Rule 61-501 in assessing the performance by officers and directors of their corporate duties.

The OSC expressly acknowledged that it did "not consider that the types of transactions covered by Rule 61-501 [including going-private transactions] are inherently unfair. The commission recognizes, however, that these transactions are capable of being abusive and unfair."[112] Accordingly, Rule 61-501 prescribed a series of procedures intended to safeguard against such potential abuses. These safeguards included, in appropriate cases:

- special disclosure requirements;
- requirements to obtain independent valuations; and
- requirements for minority shareholder ("majority of the minority") voting approval

iii) Multilateral Instrument 61-101

a. Introduction

In August 2006, the CSA released for comment proposed Multilateral Instrument 61-101.[113] The purpose of this proposed multilateral instrument would be to replace OSC Rule 61-501 in Ontario and Regulation Q-27 in Quebec, with a view to harmonizing the Ontario and Quebec regimes, and to introduce minor amendments and integrate the instrument within the harmonized Canadian takeover bid regime embodied in Multilateral Instrument 62-104 and corresponding changes to the Ontario *Securities Act* and rules. The final version of Multilateral In-

---

112 Companion Policy 61-501CP (2004), OSCB 6011 at 6012, s. 1.1, revoked (2008), 31 OSCB 1230.

113 (2006), 29 OSCB 6813 [Proposed MI 61-101].

strument 61-101 was published in December 2007,[114] and came into force on 1 February 2008.[115] OSC Rule 61-501 and Quebec Regulation Q-27 were repealed,[116] and the companion policies to those earlier instruments revoked.

b.   "Business Combination" vs. "Going-Private Transaction"

Multilateral Instrument 61-101 applies to several different types of transactions including, for example, insider bids, issuer bids, and related-party transactions. But discussion here is confined to those aspects of Multilateral Instrument 61-101 that relate to "business combinations." The term *business combination*, which is defined in section 1.1 of Multilateral Instrument 61-101, was also found in OSC Rule 61-501. There, it had replaced the term *going-private transaction*, which had appeared in earlier versions of the rule.

When the OSC first proposed this change in definition, it explained that the definition of the term *going-private transaction* that appeared in Rule 61-501 differed in some respects from conventional understanding of that term, and in fact differed from the definition that had appeared in former OSC Policy 9.1, which Rule 61-501 had originally been created to replace. Among other things, the Rule 61-501 definition of going-private transaction could apply to certain transactions in which minority shareholders received, in exchange for the shares they originally held, new *participating* securities. (Under the traditional definition, a transaction would be considered a going-private transaction, only in cases where shareholders did *not* receive participating securities.) Accordingly, the OSC suggested:

> The changes in the definition that were brought about by the Rule have given rise to some confusion among market participants and their advisers as to the definition's application. One of the reasons for this confusion is that the definition is somewhat counter-intuitive, in that it does not match the normal English meaning of the defined term . . . . As a result, there have been instances in which issuers have not realized that their transactions were "going private transactions" within the Rule's definition.[117]

---

114   (2007), 30 OSCB, Supp-6, 45.

115   (2008), 31 OSCB 1230. The text of the instrument as of 1 February 2008 is at (2008), 31 OSCB 1321.

116   OSC Rule 61-801 (2008), 31 OSCB 1365; "Regulation to repeal Regulation Q-27 respecting protection of minority security holders in the course of certain transactions," G.O.Q. 2008.II.53.

117   Notice of Proposed Amendments to Rule 61-501 (2003), 26 OSCB 1822.

Thus, the broader phrase *business combination* was introduced into the rule, although it is still perhaps simpler to refer to the specific type of business combination being discussed here as a going-private transaction. One notes that the Ontario *Business Corporations Act* still refers to going-private transactions,[118] and purports to impose certain obligations on parties undertaking such transactions. However, as a practical matter, those OBCA provisions have been rendered inoperative by Multilateral Instrument 61-101. Specifically, section 4.7 of Multilateral Instrument 61-101 states that, if a transaction is not a business combination as defined in Multilateral Instrument 61-101 (and therefore not subject to the business combination procedures in Multilateral Instrument 61-101) or is exempt from Multilateral Instrument 61-101 by virtue of section 4.1 or an exemption in Part 4, such a transaction is also automatically exempt from the going-private rules in the OBCA. Furthermore, if a proposed transaction *is* a business combination, then compliance with Multilateral Instrument 61-101 will result, again, in automatic exemption from the OBCA's rules.

Under the CBCA, corporations that comply with applicable provincial securities laws—which would include Multilateral Instrument 61-101—are also expressly authorized to undertake going-private transactions.[119]

c. Requirements for Business Combinations (Squeeze-Outs and Other Going-Private Transactions)

Although Multilateral Instrument 61-101 applies to a wide range of business combinations, we are concerned here only with one particular aspect of the rule: the requirements that must be satisfied when a reporting issuer seeks to complete a post-takeover bid amalgamation squeeze. Such a transaction is referred to in the rule as a "second step business combination."[120]

The key requirement to completing a second-step business combination (or going-private transaction) is that the issuer must normally obtain "minority approval."[121] The other major requirement that applies to business combinations—the requirement to obtain a valua-

---

118 OBCA, s. 190.
119 CBCA, s. 193. A "going-private" transaction for purposes of the CBCA is defined in CBCA, s. 2(1) and *Canada Business Corporations Regulations, 2001*, s. 3(1).
120 See, for example, MI 61-101, s. 4.4(1)(d).
121 *Ibid.*, s. 4.5. There is an exception in certain cases where the interested party owns 90 percent of the securities, and the minority shareholders have, or are given, an effective appraisal remedy. *Ibid.*, s. 4.6. An exemption is also available in cases where the transaction will have no adverse effect on the corporation or the minority shareholders. *Ibid.*, ss. 4.6(1)(b) and 4.4(1). Discretionary exemp-

tion—will normally not apply in the case of a second-step going-private transaction, provided: (a) the transaction is completed by the bidder (or an affiliate) within 120 days after the expiry of the original takeover bid and for securities of the same class as those subject to the bid; (b) the consideration to be received by the minority shareholders is at least equal (and in the same form) as the consideration offered to security-holders who tendered to the bid; and (c) the takeover bid circular used for the bid disclosed the bidder's intention to undertake a second-step going-private transaction, and provided certain disclosure that would permit shareholders to make an informed decision about the tax con-sequences of tendering to the bid, on the one hand, or, on the other hand, of having their shares acquired as part of a proposed subsequent going-private transaction.[122]

Obtaining "minority approval" (or, as it is often called by practi-tioners, "majority of the minority approval") involves the calling of a shareholders' meeting, with the corresponding obligation to provide an information circular and forms of proxy, as discussed further in Chapter 9.

The critical inquiry, however, for purposes of a post-bid amalgama-tion squeeze is who may be counted as the "minority" for purposes of the minority approval vote?

Recall that, as a matter of strict corporate law, in order to complete an amalgamation between two corporations (other than a so-called short-form amalgamation as discussed in Chapter 4), the sharehold-ers of each amalgamating corporation must approve the transaction by special resolution, that is, by a two-thirds vote. Needless to say, this certainly does not mean that two-thirds of all of the shareholders of each corporation must approve. Rather, provided the shareholders' meetings are properly constituted (that is, the notice and quorum re-quirements are satisfied), a special resolution will pass if two-thirds of those shareholders *who actually voted* vote in favour. If, following the completion of a takeover bid, the bidder holds at least two-thirds of the outstanding shares, then *as a matter of corporate law only*, approval of an amalgamation aimed at squeezing out the remaining minority shareholders would be assured. But Multilateral Instrument 61-101 im-poses an additional "minority approval" hurdle. And in determining whether minority approval has been obtained, certain votes must be excluded, including the votes of any shares held by the issuer or an

---

tions from regulatory authorities may also, of course, be granted in appropriate cases. *Ibid.*, s. 9.1.

122 *Ibid.*, s. 4.4(1)(d).

"interested party" (namely, the bidder) or any "joint actor" with, or "related party" (with some exceptions) to, the bidder.

The minority approval requirement is subject to a special qualification, however, in the case of second-step going-private transactions. Shares that were tendered to the bidder's takeover bid may actually be counted as part of the minority, provided the selling shareholders were not "joint actors" with the bidder or otherwise parties to a connected transaction and did not receive any different consideration or collateral benefit for their securities, the second-step transaction is effected within 120 days after the expiry of the bid by the bidder, the consideration to be received by shareholders in the second-step transaction is at least equal in value (and in the same form) as the consideration received by tendering shareholders, and certain disclosure obligations were satisfied in the original takeover bid circular.[123]

At first, this qualification may seem to undermine the very purpose of requiring minority approval. After all, by definition, the shares that were tendered to the bidder will be owned (and voted) by the *majority* shareholder, not the minority shareholders. The underlying rationale that is often offered for permitting the votes attached to these shares to be counted in the minority approval vote is this: by tendering their shares, shareholders have, as it were, signalled their approval of the transaction. If the same deal had been structured as a single-step transaction rather than as a takeover bid followed by an amalgamation, those tendering shareholders, presumably, would have voted in favour of the deal. Accordingly, the argument runs, it would be anomalous not to count the votes attached to shares held by those who clearly favoured the transaction, simply because it was structured in one way (that is, takeover bid followed by a going-private transaction) rather than another (for example, a one-step amalgamation or arrangement).

While this explanation enjoys widespread support, it has also attracted some criticism. Philip Anisman, for example, has argued that it is inaccurate to equate tendering shares to a bid with voting those shares at a shareholders' meeting. He notes:

> A shareholder who accepts a takeover bid . . . is not voting shares, but selling them. Once the bid is completed, that person is no longer a shareholder . . . . Characterizing selling shareholders as being disenfranchised is a fiction created to justify a result.[124]

---

123 *Ibid.*, s. 8.2.
124 Anisman, "Squeezing Out Minority Shareholders: A Comment," above note 39 at 235–36.

There is a more pragmatic explanation for permitting the shares of tendering shareholders to be voted in cases where the minority will receive no less than the original bid price, an explanation that does not need to invoke the "fictitious" concept of disenfranchisement. It is simply this: permitting tendered shares to be voted encourages bidders to make fairly priced bids in the first place, confident that, if a substantial majority of shareholders accept the bid—thus providing objective evidence of its fairness—it will not be possible for an obstinate or unreasonable minority to hold up the bidder in an attempt to extract unreasonably high payment for his or her shares or prevent the bidder from taking the target company private, and thereby saving ongoing public reporting and related costs.[125]

Whatever the preferred rationale for permitting shares tendered to a bid to be counted as part of the "majority of the minority" vote to approve a second-step going-private transaction, one principle is certain. Such shares can only properly be included in the minority if they were tendered by shareholders who were not "joint actors" with the bidder. Accordingly, questions are frequently raised concerning who ought to be considered a "joint actor" in this context.

It is common, for example, for bidders to enter into pre-bid agreements with major shareholders of a target corporation pursuant to which those security holders bind themselves contractually to tender to the bid ("lock-up agreements"), or to vote in favour of a going-private transaction ("support agreements"). Should shareholders who have entered into such pre-bid agreements be considered "joint actors" with the bidder? Although Ontario regulators had come to the view that such agreements should not necessarily mean that shareholders who had signed them should be treated as joint actors with bidders, a B.C. decision in 2000, *Re Sepp's Gourmet Foods Ltd.*,[126]suggested otherwise. In response to this decision, the OSC amended the definition of "joint actors" in Rule 61-501 to make clear that a person would *not* be considered a joint actor, merely because he or she had entered into a support or lock-up agreement with the bidder.[127] That clarification is now found in the definition of "joint actors" in section 1.1 of Multilateral Instrument 61-101.

---

125 See James C. Baillie, Alfred Avanessy, & Peter Johnson, "'Acting Jointly or in Concert' in Corporate Law: *Re Sepp's Gourmet Foods Ltd.*" (2002) 37 Can. Bus. L.J. 281 at 282.

126 (2000), 211 D.L.R. (4th) 542 (B.C.C.A.).

127 Rule 61-501, s. 1.1, definition of joint actors. See "Notice of Proposed Amendments to Rule 61-501" (2003), 26 OSCB 1822 at 1823.

Not all support agreements, however, involve a simple promise on the part of a shareholder to tender his or her shares to a bid. Where agreements are more extensive, they may transgress the proverbial line and so constitute the parties to the agreement "joint actors." For example, in *Re Sterling Centrecorp Inc.*,[128] the Ontario Securities Commission was asked to consider whether or not shareholders of a target corporation might be considered "joint actors" with the acquiror where those shareholders had signed very broad support agreements committing the shareholders, among other things, not only to vote in support of the transaction proposed by the acquiror, but to oppose any other transaction initiated by a third party unless the acquiror itself was prepared to accept such an alternative deal. *Sterling Centrecorp* involved a going-private transaction, not to be undertaken following a takeover bid, but rather to be completed as a one-step transaction under the Ontario *Business Corporations Act's* arrangement provisions.[129]

A rival bidder applied to the OSC for an order preventing the going-private transaction pending revision of the disclosure in the information circular provided to target company shareholders indicating, among other things, that shares voted by signatories to the support agreements could not be counted for purposes of the "minority approval" vote required under OSC Rule 61-501 (the predecessor to Multilateral Instrument 61-101) as those signatories should be regarded as "joint actors" with the acquiror.

The Commission Panel found that only one of the shareholders in question was a joint actor and, although his share interest was significant, exclusion of his votes did not alter the outcome of the shareholders' meeting (which had already been held by the time of the OSC's hearing.) Accordingly, the arrangement was approved by the target company's shareholders; the arrangement was, subsequently, approved by the court[130] as required by the *Business Corporations Act*.

The Panel rejected the argument that a shareholder who had entered into a support agreement with an acquiror would necessarily be considered a joint actor if that agreement dealt with any matters "beyond provisions solely regarding voting in relation to the Going Private Transaction."[131] Rather, the determination calls for a more nuanced examination of the facts and circumstances. While the Ontario *Securi-*

---

128   (2007), 30 OSCB 6683 [*Sterling OSC*].
129   OBCA, s. 182. The use of the statutory arrangement as an acquisition technique is discussed in Chapter 4.
130   See *Re Sterling Centrecorp. Inc.*, [2007] O.J. No. 3072 (S.C.J.).
131   *Sterling OSC*, above note 128 at para. 113.

ties Act[132] (and, one might add today, Multilateral Instrument 62-104)[133] creates a rebuttable presumption that parties that have entered into agreements with the acquiror are "joint actors," the language referring to support agreements in the definition of "joint actors" then found in Rule 61-501 (and today found in Multilateral Instrument 61-101) overrides that presumption in the case of support agreements, and so calls for an examination of all the facts, "not just the existence or the provisions of the agreement."[134] Moreover, the Panel found, the fact that the obligations in the agreement may "go beyond merely tendering to the bid or voting in favour of the transaction,"[135] while relevant to the "joint actor" issue, are not determinative. Joint actors, the Panel noted, "are intimately involved in structuring, planning and promoting the Going Private Transaction and not solely signatories to a support agreement."[136]

d.   Excluding Shares Other Than Those of "Joint Actors" for Purposes of "Minority Approval"

A number of recent cases reveal additional complexities surrounding which shares may be counted in determining whether or not "minority approval" has been obtained in a vote to approve a second-stage going-private transaction. In *Re Financial Models*[137] a publicly traded corporation had three major shareholders who collectively held more than 80 percent of the corporation's shares. The largest single shareholder was Katotakis, who held about 40 percent of the outstanding shares. The three shareholders had entered into a shareholders' agreement that included, among other things, a "right of first offer" provision. Under this provision, a shareholder was not permitted to sell his or its shares to a third party without first offering those shares to the other parties to the agreement. Aware that a third party was prepared to make a takeover

---

132 See *Securities Act* (Ontario), s. 91(1)(b)(i).

133 MI 62-104, s. 1.9(1)(b)(i).

134 *Sterling* OSC, above note 128 at para. 119.

135 *Ibid.*

136 *Ibid.* at para. 183.

137 (2005), 28 OSCB 2184 [*Re Financial Models*]. Another aspect of this same matter came before the Ontario courts as well. See *BNY Capital Corp. v. Katotakis* (2005), 1 B.L.R. (4th) 168 (Ont. C.A.), aff'g (2005), 2 B.L.R. (4th) 171 (Ont. S.C.J.). The court hearing concerned (a) the scope of the bid financing rules in s. 96 of the *Securities Act* (discussed in Chapter 6); and (b) the question of whether or not parties to a shareholders agreement which contained rights of first offer could, effectively, include "superior proposal" outs in selling notices delivered to a fellow shareholder pursuant to those contractual rights of first offer. For a detailed discussion of the *Katotakis* decision, see Christopher C. Nicholls, "Lock-Ups, Squeeze-Outs, and Canadian Takeover Bid Law: A Curious Interplay of Public and Private Interests" (2006) 51 McGill L.J. 407.

bid for the shares of the company, the major shareholders other than Katotakis delivered selling notices to Katotakis pursuant to the right of first offer in the shareholders' agreement. In these selling notices, the shareholders offered to sell their shares to Katotakis at a price of $12.20 per share, subject to certain terms and conditions contained in a *draft* acquisition agreement between the target company and the third-party prospective bidder. Katotakis accepted these selling notices, agreeing to buy the shares at this price. He then proposed to launch a takeover bid for all of the remaining shares—at the same price—with the intention of completing a subsequent amalgamation squeeze to acquire the shares of any shareholders who chose not to tender to his bid. In order to approve that subsequent going-private transaction, he intended to vote all of the shares acquired pursuant to the rights of first offer, thus guaranteeing that the post-bid squeeze would be effective.

But there was a twist in the case. Between the day the other shareholders had delivered their selling notices and the day Katotakis had accepted them, the third-party bidder had actually launched its bid—at a *higher* price per share than specified in the draft agreement (and, therefore, at a higher price than the shareholders had originally specified in the selling notices that had previously been delivered to, and accepted by, Katotakis). Thus, if Katotakis were permitted to acquire the shares of the other parties to the shareholders' agreement at the lower price, and then allowed to have the votes attached to those shares counted as "minority" shares for purposes of approving the second-step going-private transaction, the dissenting shareholders would have no choice but to accept the initial lower price for their shares, notwithstanding the existence of a current, rival takeover bid by a third party for a higher price.

The special committee of the board of the target company tried to find a way to make it possible for the shareholders to tender to the higher bid. They applied to the OSC seeking an order that would prevent the Katotakis bid from proceeding. The OSC refused to grant such relief. The panel found that Katotakis's offer complied with Rule 61-501. The rights of first offer in the shareholders' agreement, in the panel's view, were "tantamount or functionally equivalent to a 'hard' lock-up agreement"; and the expectations of the public minority shareholders of the target company could hardly be said to have been defeated, since the existence of these (publicly-disclosed) contractual rights amongst the controlling shareholders ensured that the target company "was never in 'play' for an auction."[138] In other words, Katotakis would, indeed, be permitted to complete his bid as planned, and, in the post-bid minority approval vote,

---

138 See *Re Financial Models, ibid.* at 2190.

all of the shares he had acquired pursuant to the right of first offer in the shareholders' agreement could be counted as "minority" shares. The success of the second step squeeze-out was thus assured. (In fact, the Katotakis bid did not proceed because another outside bidder emerged willing to pay an even higher price, and all of the major shareholders— including Katotakis—chose to tender their shares to this higher bid.)

The OSC dealt with the minority approval question again in the *Sears Canada*[139] case. The facts in the *Sears Canada* case have been dealt with at some length in Chapter 5 and will not be repeated here. It will only be noted that the OSC concluded in that case that shares that had been acquired by the bidder from a party found by the OSC to have received a collateral benefit (in the form of the Release discussed in Chapter 5) were not to be included in calculating the majority of the minority for purposes of determining shareholder approval thresholds for a second-step acquisition transaction. Moreover, the shares of the target held by certain banks that had entered into support agreements with the bidder were also to be excluded from the calculation of the majority of the minority again on the basis that the banks had received collateral benefits (as discussed in Chapter 5). Those benefits gave rise, in the OSC Panel's view, to at least a perceived conflict of interest that made it inappropriate to permit their votes to be potentially determinative in eliminating the minority shareholders' interests.

In *Re HudBay Minerals Inc.*[140] the Ontario Securities Commission expressed its views on the propriety of an acquiror in a merger transaction voting shares in the target it acquired by way of a private placement prior to the merger transaction at a meeting of the target convened to approve the transaction. *Hudbay* did not involve a second-step going-private transaction; rather, the key issue in the case turned on whether or not shareholders of an acquiring corporation ought to be permitted to vote on a deal that would involve a significant issue of shares, and therefore a massive dilution of their interest. However, the OSC's comment on shares received by way of private placement were subsequently scrutinized by the Alberta Securities Commission in *Re ARC Equity Management (Fund 4) Ltd.*[141]

There, the Alberta Securities Commission considered whether shares of the target company obtained by the bidder from the target through a private placement of special warrants negotiated as part of

---

139 *Sears Canada Inc. (Re)* (2006), 22 B.L.R. (4th) 267 (O.S.C.), aff'd (*sub nom. Sears Holdings Corporation v. Ontario Securities Commission*), 2006 CanLII 34453 (Ont. Div. Ct.) [*Sears Canada*]. See Chapter 5, text accompanying notes 97–111.

140 (2009), 32 OSCB 3733.

141 2009 ABASC 390.

the takeover bid transaction could be voted by the bidder at the meeting to approve the second-step going-private transaction.

The bidder and the target company had negotiated a friendly takeover bid. However, a major shareholder of the target (ARC) opposed this bid. Because ARC held about 31 percent of the target company's shares, the bidder faced a formidable challenge. For the bidder to obtain enough shares to ensure the success of a post-bid going-private transaction (namely, 66 2/3 percent of all outstanding shares) almost all of the target company shares—other than those held by ARC—would have to be tendered to the bid. But the bidder's chances of gaining control were significantly enhanced when the target agreed to sell, by way of a private placement, special warrants that, upon exercise, would entitle the bidder to acquire 19.9 percent of the target company's outstanding shares. The terms of this private placement were complex; among other things, the price to be paid by the bidder to the issuer was attractive and the agreement was negotiated at a time when the target company was looking for financing in a challenging environment. In other words, there was evidence before the Alberta Securities Commission, which the commission accepted, that this private placement agreement was entered into not merely for tactical purposes to ensure that the bidder's bid would succeed, but also to meet genuine and important financing needs.

The effect of the private placement arrangement on the eventual success of the bidder's takeover bid was significant. Although shares representing less than 60 percent of the outstanding voting shares were tendered to the bid (an amount well below the 66 2/3 percent the bidder would need to complete a post-bid amalgamation squeeze), the additional shares acquired through the private placement gave the bidder more than enough shares to ensure the going-private transaction would succeed.

ARC applied to the Alberta Securities Commission (ASC) for an order that would have the effect of preventing the bidder from voting those shares that it had acquired through the private placement, citing, among other things, the Ontario Securities Commission's statement in *Re Hudbay Minerals Inc.* that

> . . . an acquirer should not generally be entitled, through a subscription for shares carried out in anticipation of a merger transaction, to significantly influence or affect the outcome of the vote on that transaction.[142]

---

142 *Ibid.* at para. 41, quoting above note 140 at para. 266.

The ASC dismissed ARC's application, and so permitted the bidder to vote the shares it had acquired in the private placement to approve a second-step going-private transaction. The ASC noted that the OSC's statement from *Hudbay* was, as the OSC itself made clear, *obiter dicta*. It did not represent, in the ASC's view, "anything amounting to an invariable principle binding participants in the Canadian capital market."[143] Finding then that on the particular facts before it, there was "not a clear case of abuse warranting the exercise of our public interest jurisdiction,"[144] the ASC did, nevertheless, caution that "depending on the circumstances, a future effort to follow [the bidder's] approach might encounter not just serious challenge, but possibly also a different outcome."[145]

e. Other Constraints on a Second-Step Going-Private Transaction

One of the most intriguing analyses of the going-private rules occurred in *Re Patheon Inc.*,[146] a case in which the Ontario Securities Commission considered and perhaps refined the contours of the takeover bid regime's "equal treatment" principles. The facts of *Re Patheon* were briefly reviewed in Chapter 5 and will not be repeated here. The key points raised in the case for purposes of Multilateral Instrument 61-101's going-private rules are these:

- Can a second-step going-private transaction be undertaken at a price *higher* than the price offered in the preceding takeover bid?
- Can a bidder enter into an agreement with a shareholder of the target *after* the bid is complete, under which the shareholder agrees to support the bidder's post-bid going-private transaction (or Subsequent Acquisition Transaction)?

With respect to the first issue, the commission noted that subparagraph (e) of section 8.2 of Multilateral Instrument 61-101 states that, in a second-step transaction, the consideration received by shareholders must be "at least equal in value" to the consideration received by shareholders who tendered to the bid. This language would seem to imply that there is no objection to undertaking a post-bid transaction in which shareholders who did not tender to the original bid receive a higher price for their shares than the bid price. However, the commission was not persuaded that this provision could be interpreted as authority for the proposition that consideration offered to shareholders in

---

143 *Ibid.* at para.76.
144 *Ibid.* at para. 116.
145 *Ibid.*
146 (2009), 32 OSCB 6445.

a second-stage transaction could exceed the price paid in the original bid. First, the Panel observed that section 8.2 was not "a substantive provision imposing legal obligations or restrictions."[147] The Panel recognized that the purpose of section 8.2 was to prevent coercive bids by removing the risk to shareholders of being "squeezed out" at a price lower than the bid price—a risk that would, needless to say, put pressure on the shareholders to tender to the bid in the first place. The Panel also endorsed the notion that the effect of section 8.2 was to treat the original bid and the subsequent going-private transaction "as the equivalent of a single transaction."[148] The Panel declined to rule that section 8.2 would never permit a second-step transaction to be completed at a price higher than the original bid price; although they ruled that in this particular transaction the second step transaction could not be completed at such a higher price.

In some ways, the Panel's characterization of the bid and the second-step transaction as a single transaction leads naturally enough to a conclusion that the going-private transaction cannot be completed at a price higher than the original bid price. Yet, it is worth noting that the effect of such a holding is to increase by almost six-fold[149] the restriction on post-bid acquisitions of shares required by the takeover rules themselves. Of course, it is perfectly appropriate for the commission to vary the takeover bid rules where the public interest requires it; but where there has genuinely been no agreement to acquire a hold-out shareholder's shares within a 20-day period following the bid (which agreement would surely constitute an "offer to acquire" and so would violate the post-bid restriction rules), such an intrusive use of the public interest power would, one hopes, be used very gingerly indeed. The possibility, after all, that a shareholder might be able to command a price higher than the bid price in a post-transaction, it should be recalled, will tend to place more pressure on the bidder, *ex ante*, not the target company shareholders.

A comprehensive treatment of the sensitive and complex topic of squeeze-out transactions would require far more space than is available here. Certainly in the United States, similar issues have gener-

---

147 *Ibid.* at para. 128.

148 *Ibid.* at para. 129.

149 Bidders are prohibited for a period of twenty business days from the expiry of a formal bid from acquiring securities of the same class that was subject to the bid except "by way of a transaction that is generally available" to all holders of the class. There are limited exceptions for normal course market purchases. See MI 62-104, s. 2.5; *Securities Act* (Ontario), s. 93.3.

ated a host of high-profile judicial decisions,[150] and a significant body of academic[151] and professional[152] commentary, much of it focused on the question of determining the appropriate standard of court review for such transactions. The core issue, however, appears to be to what extent are the private property rights of a minority shareholder expected to yield to accommodate broader economic goals (such as the goal of encouraging takeover bids)—subject, of course, to overarching considerations of fairness to individual holders? The question, like so many in the M & A area, depends significantly on one's view of the overall economic value of a robust market for corporate control.

c) Corporate Law Rights and Remedies

When a going-private transaction is undertaken by way of an amalgamation squeeze, dissenting shareholders are typically entitled to exercise dissent and appraisal rights.[153] When a shareholder exercises a right of dissent, the corporation is normally obliged to offer to purchase the shareholder's shares at an amount that the directors consider to be fair value.[154] If the corporation fails to make such an offer, or if dissenting shareholders do not accept the corporation's offer, application may be made to the court to fix a fair value for the shares in question.[155] The calculation of fair value, in the context of a squeeze-out transaction, can be a complex matter indeed, as the recent decision in *Ford Motor Company v. OMERS*[156] illustrates. Further, the broad corporate law oppression remedy may also be invoked by shareholders where a corporate action is taken that is "oppressive, or unfairly prejudicial to or that unfairly disregards the interests of" any shareholder, although it not clear that there is much scope for the application of the oppression remedy in the case of squeeze-out transactions where an appraisal remedy is available, and where no other independent act of oppression, unfair prejudice or unfair disregard exists.[157]

---

150 See cases cited in note 107, above in this chapter.

151 See, for example, Guhan Subramanian, "Fixing Freezeouts" (2005) 115 Yale L.J. 2.

152 See, for example, the papers cited above in note 107, above in this chapter.

153 See, for example, CBCA, s. 190(1)(c).

154 See, for example, *ibid.*, s. 190(12)(a).

155 See, for example, *ibid.*, ss. 190(15) & (16).

156 *Ford Motor Company of Canada, Ltd. v. Ontario Municipal Employees Retirement Board*, 2006 CanLII 15 (Ont. C.A.)

157 For a detailed discussion of the Canadian corporate law oppression remedy, see Christopher C. Nicholls, *Corporate Law*, above note 15 at 419*ff*.

d) "Top-Up Options"

They have recently been described by one Delaware judge as "common-place in two-step tender offer deals"[158] and by another as "ubiquitous in two-step acquisitions."[159] "Top-up options" are stock purchase options provided by a target company to a friendly acquiror in many U.S. friendly tender offers. Top-up options, as the Delaware Court of Chancery has explained, are "designed to allow the holder to increase its stock ownership to at least 90 percent, the threshold needed to effect a short-term merger under section 253 of the Delaware *General Corporation Law*."[160] A top-up option will thus typically be structured such that, provided a majority of the target company's shareholders tender their shares to the offeror's bid, the target company will permit the offeror to purchase sufficient additional shares from the treasury, at the bid price, to bring the offeror's total shareholding in the target up to 90 percent plus one share. Under Delaware law, with a 90 percent ownership interest, a parent company can undertake a freeze-out merger by a simple directors' resolution, saving the considerable time and expense of calling a public meeting of shareholders to vote on a transaction where the outcome is a foregone conclusion in any event. Though the use of top-up options in friendly Delaware tender offers has been common for several years, there was very little judicial consideration of their legality until 2010. Many of the challenges to top-up options focused on the form (and perhaps amount) of the consideration to be paid by the acquiror for the optioned shares. Specifically, the consideration was often in the form, in whole or in part, of a promissory note from the acquiror, a practice that raised a number of issues under Delaware's corporate law. It appears that the law and practice of top-up options has now been well settled in Delaware, and so their widespread use will undoubtedly continue going forward.[161] However, it is important to note that the extensive use of top-up options in Delaware is related to a number of features of Delaware corporate law that differ from Canadian corporate law. First, as discussed in Chapter 4, Canadian corporate statutes typically permit the use of the streamlined "short form" amalgamation technique only in the case of wholly-owned subsidiaries, not subsidiaries in which the holding corporation holds 90 percent of the shares. Second, Canadian corporate law post-bid compulsory acquisitions, as

---

158 *In re Cogent, Inc. Shareholder Litigation*, 7 A.3d 487 at 505 (Del. Ch. 2010).

159 *Olson v. ev3, Inc.*, 2011 Del. Ch. Lexis 34 at *4.

160 *Ibid.* at *2.

161 See, for example, Steven A. Rosenblum, "Takeover Law and Practice 2011" in Practising Law Institute, *43rd Annual Institute on Securities Regulation* (New York: PLI, 2011) 21 at 127–29.

discussed earlier in this chapter, are typically only permitted where the bidder has acquired 90 percent of the outstanding shares of the target company that the bidder did not previously own. Acquiring additional "top up" shares from the target corporation itself after the bid would not help the bidder satisfy this requirement. Third, in most Canadian jurisdictions, it would not be legally permissible to satisfy the purchase price of newly issued shares even partly by way of a promissory note issued by the buyer.[162] Finally, there is a well-established procedure, now set out in Multilateral Instrument 61-101, for undertaking post-bid going-private transactions for which there is no explicit statutory or regulatory equivalent in Delaware. Accordingly, although it is important for Canadian lawyers to be aware of the use of the top-up option has it has evolved in Delaware, the critical differences between Delaware and Canadian corporate law must always be kept in mind.

---

162 See, for example, CBCA, s. 25(5). The current practice in Delaware is, evidently, to provide that an amount equal to the par value of any issued shares will be paid in cash, with any additional amount to be paid by way of promissory note.

CHAPTER 9

PROXY CONTESTS

A. INTRODUCTION

Most of this book has dealt with ways by which ownership of a business changes hands. But there is another way in which a person or company can effectively acquire managerial control of a business without acquiring an ownership interest. When the business is operated by a corporation, those seeking control can mount a proxy contest (also known as a "proxy fight," "proxy battle," or even "proxy war"). A proxy contest is something like a political election campaign. A dissident or insurgent group of shareholders attempts to win the hearts, the minds, and—most of all—the votes of the majority of the corporation's shareholders, so that the dissidents' slate of directors will be elected to the board instead of the candidates nominated by the corporation's incumbent managers.

This method of seeking control of a corporation's board of directors is called a proxy contest because most shareholders of public corporations choose to cast their votes for the election of directors at shareholders' meetings by proxy rather than in person. Accordingly, competing campaigns seek to convince shareholders to cast their votes in a particular way by requesting shareholders to fill out a proxy form (a document appointing a representative to attend the meeting on behalf of the shareholder) in which the signing shareholder directs his or her proxyholder to vote for or against the resolutions that are to come before the meeting.

A basic knowledge of proxy contests is important to a broader under-standing of mergers and acquisitions. In the United States, proxy con-tests have often been launched in connection with hostile takeover bids as hostile bidders sought to gain control of a target board of directors in order to dismantle a particular form of takeover defence—the "poison pill,"[1] since the ability of directors to sustain a poison pill has been con-siderably more robust in certain U.S. jurisdictions, notably Delaware, than in Canada. And indeed it is sometimes suggested that American (especially Delaware) courts' strong emphasis on shareholder elections, as opposed to direct shareholder voice in corporate decision-making, goes some way to explaining U.S. hostile takeover jurisprudence.[2]

In Canada where poison pills cannot as a practical matter be kept in place indefinitely, the strategy of coupling a hostile bid with a proxy battle is of somewhat less importance (see Chapter 7). Proxy contests at Canadian public corporations are in fact unusual, but they are not unheard of. In the case of certain regulated industries, however, where

---

1   For a discussion of the use of a proxy contest for this purpose, see Lucian Ayre Bebchuk, John C. Coates IV, & Guhan Subramanian, "The Powerful Antitakeover Force of Staggered Boards: Theory, Evidence and Policy" (2002) 54 Stan. L. Rev. 887. To prevent hostile bidders from using a proxy contest in this way, many U.S. companies introduced staggered or classified boards. The members of board of directors would be divided into different classes, with different terms of office specified for the members of each class. Thus, even if a hostile bidder were to wage a successful proxy battle in connection with the target's annual meeting, it would not be possible to replace all of the board's directors at that meeting since the terms of one or more classes of directors would not expire until a subsequent annual meeting. This technique generally cannot be used in Canada. Although staggered terms for directors are often permitted under Canadian corporate law (see, for example, *Canada Business Corporations Act*, s. 106(4) [CBCA]), there is typically an overriding power in Canadian corporate statutes that permits shareholders, by ordinary resolution, to remove the directors at any time. (See, for example, CBCA, s. 109(1).)

2   See, for example, Leo E. Strine, Jr., "The Professorial Bear Hug: The ESB Propos-al as a Conscious Effort to Make the Delaware Courts Confront the Basic 'Just Say No' Question" (2002) 55 Stan. L. Rev. 863 at 876: "One of the reasons that the Delaware courts approved the use of the poison pill was that the director election process provided an ultimate escape from the pill . . . This proxy out provided an elegant way for courts in later cases to avoid finding that a board's deployment of a poison pill was preclusive . . . . The defenders [of elections] pre-fer elections not because they enable boards to defeat worthy offers, but because elections are seen as permitting stockholders to exercise an undistorted choice on the worthiness of a bid, divorced from a concern that a failure to tender will relegate a stockholder to the uncertain fate of a back-end merger." See also the recent comments of former Chancellor Chandler of the Delaware Court of Chancery in *Air Products and Chemicals, Inc. v. Airgas, Inc.*, 16 A.3d 48 (Del. Ch. 2011), reproduced in Chapter 7 at note 270.

legislation restricts the percentage of shares that may be owned by any single shareholder, a proxy contest may be the only expedient way for anyone, including a major corporate shareholder, to acquire managerial control over the corporation. On the other hand, it might be noted that a proxy contest in Canada has the potential to be a more robust form of shareholder activism than in Delaware because of the usual Canadian corporate law requirement (absent from Delaware's corporate statute) empowering shareholders to remove directors of a corporation at any time by simply majority vote.[3] As the Ontario Securities Commission has recently stated: "A proxy solicitation in connection with a merger or acquisition transaction raises the same investor protection issues as a take-over bid."[4]

An understanding of basic Canadian proxy rules is also important in the context of negotiated merger transactions. These transactions may be structured as long-form amalgamations (discussed in Chapter 4) or, more frequently, as statutory plans of arrangement (discussed in Chapter 5), and so require shareholder approval. It is not unheard of in Canada for larger shareholders—especially institutional investors such as pension plans—to undertake a proxy context in order to persuade other shareholders to vote against such planned transactions. The purpose of such a campaign is primarily to pressure the parties who have negotiated a friendly acquisition to revisit the terms of the deal, in hopes that the shareholders will receive an improved price.[5] The proxy process has also been the subject of well-publicized legislative and regulatory reform proposals to expand "shareholder access"— including a recent U.S. reform, discussed further in Section C, below in this chapter, that was successfully challenged in federal court.

B. PROXY RULES

1) Meaning of the Word *Proxy*

The word *proxy*, in the corporate context, originally referred to the *person* appointed by a shareholder to act in the shareholder's place. The document that was used to appoint a proxy to act on behalf of the

---

3   See, for example, CBCA, s. 109.
4   *Re VenGrowth Funds* (2011), 34 OSCB 6755 [*VenGrowth*].
5   There have been several examples of such opposition to friendly transactions requiring shareholder approval including the *Re Pacifica* case, below note 59, and the 2005 proposed reorganization of O & Y Real Estate Investment Trust.

absent shareholder was known as the "instrument of proxy."[6] Over time, however, the word *proxy* has come to be used often to refer to the document appointing the shareholder's representative,[7] and the representative of the absent shareholder is now commonly referred to as the "proxyholder."[8]

2) Origin of Proxy Rules

At common law, it was presumed that shareholders of a corporation were not permitted to vote their shares by proxy;[9] if they wished to have their votes counted, they were obliged to attend the shareholders' meeting and cast their vote in person. Otherwise, their right to be heard was lost.

For large corporations, with many shareholders located across the country and even around the world, it is unreasonable to think that all or even most shareholders will be able to attend shareholders' meetings. It would be unfair to deprive shareholders of their right to vote simply because they are unable to travel to a meeting at a cost that might well (in the case of small shareholders) exceed the entire value of their shareholdings. Nor would it be prudent to discourage shareholders from holding modest investments in many different companies. Investors, on the contrary, should strive to hold a diversified portfolio, an insight suggested by common sense, and confirmed by financial economic theory.[10]

Companies could, of course, provide their own tailor-made rules for shareholder voting by proxy, and the best companies would undoubtedly do so, whether compelled by legislation or not. Investors,

---

6   *Report of the Attorney General's Committee on Securities Legislation in Ontario* (Toronto: March, 1965) at para. 6.01 (J.R. Kimber, Chair) [Kimber Report].

7   As Davies and Gower explain, in the U.K. context: "The word 'proxy' is used indiscriminately to describe both the agent and the instrument appointing him." Paul L. Davies, *Gower and Davies' Principles of Modern Company Law*, 7th ed. (London: Sweet & Maxwell, 2003) at 360, n35. In the U.S., the official comment to the *Model Business Corporation Act* [MBCA] refers to this ambiguity as well: "The word 'proxy' is often used ambiguously, sometimes referring to the grant of authority to vote, sometimes to the document granting the authority, and sometimes to the person to whom authority is granted." MBCA, Official Comment on s. 7.22, Committee on Corporate Laws of the Section of Business Law, *Model Business Corporation Act* (Chicago: American Bar Foundation, 1999) at 7–37.e.

8   This is the term used, for example, in the CBCA. See, for example, CBCA, s. 148(1).

9   See, for example, Davies, above note 7 at 360, citing *Harben v. Philips* (1883), 23 Ch. D. 14 (C.A.) and *Woodford v. Smith*, [1970] 1 W.L.R. 806.

10 See Christopher C. Nicholls, *Corporate Finance and Canadian Law* (Toronto: Carswell, 2000) at 101–3.

one might reasonably presume, would insist on being given such a right by every company in which they chose to invest, and companies, seeking to attract those investors, would wisely grant it. But a sensibly uniform set of legislatively mandated proxy voting rules, understood and observed by all publicly traded companies, would be expected to lower costs for companies and investors alike. And, of course, to the extent that the lack of such rules could lead to the disenfranchisement of shareholders by some companies, comprehensive proxy rules also serve an important investor-protection function. Stronger investor-protection laws, it has been argued, improve the competitiveness of a jurisdiction's capital markets,[11] provided that they do not become overly intrusive and expensive for issuers.

A principal source of modern Canadian corporate law proxy rules was the March 1965 Report of the Attorney General's Committee on Securities Legislation in Ontario (the "Kimber Report"). The Kimber Report had been commissioned following a controversial takeover in Canada that had led to allegations of improper trading. But the recommendations of the Kimber Report were not narrowly confined to suggested improvements to insider trading legislation. Its wide-reaching reforms became the basis for the *Securities Act, 1966* (Ontario),[12] a key milestone in the evolution of modern Canadian securities regulation. Among the Kimber Report's many proposed reforms were extensive proposals relating to corporate proxy rules.

The Kimber Report's recommendations addressed various deficiencies in the then current Ontario proxy rules.[13] A number of the Kimber Report's recommendations dealt with technical issues aimed at enhancing the position of shareholders of public companies where the proxy

---

11   See, for example, Rafael La Porta, Florencio Lopez-de-Silanes, Andrei Schleifer, & Robert Vishny, "Legal Determinants of External Finance" (1997) 52 J. of Fin. 1131; "Law and Finance" (1998) 106 J. Pol. Econ. 1113.

12   S.O. 1966, c. 142.

13   In addition to the matters discussed in this chapter, for example, the Kimber Committee recommended: (a) the legislated proxy regime they proposed was to apply to public companies that sold securities in Ontario; (b) shareholders should be given proxy forms that ensured that they had the right to appoint the proxyholders of their choice; (c) that proxy forms allow for "two-way" voting on resolutions (other than those relating to the election of directors or appointment of auditors); (d) that management be required to solicit proxies in connection with shareholder meetings, and that they be required to send to their shareholders an information document (an information circular) to assist them in making an informed vote—a requirement modeled on the proxy statement requirement in Reg. 14 under the U.S. *Securities Exchange Act of 1934*; and (e) that legislation provide certain protections for the beneficial owners of shares registered in the names of others.

solicitation mechanism has long been very much within the control of a corporation's managers.

The Kimber Report influenced Ontario corporate and securities law proxy rules and was also the principal basis for proxy rules introduced into the federal *Canada Corporations Act*[14] in 1970. The *Canada Corporations Act* proxy rules were, in turn, the primary source of the proxy rules in the *Canada Business Corporations Act* ("CBCA").

The four most fundamental aspects of modern Canadian proxy rules are these:

- Solicitation of proxies by management of public corporations is mandatory.
- Whenever proxies are solicited (whether by management or others), an information document—a proxy circular—must be prepared and distributed to the shareholders whose proxies are being solicited. There are limited exceptions to this requirement.
- The word *solicitation* is defined very broadly to ensure that the mandatory disclosure and other rules designed to protect shareholders are not easily avoided.
- Complex rules have been put into place to ensure that all beneficial owners of shares of public companies are able to vote their shares by proxy, even in cases where the shares are registered in the name of depositories, brokers, or others.

3) Management Control of Proxy Process

It is often observed that managers of a publicly traded corporation have significant control over the proxy process. There is nothing very new about this observation. In their classic 1932 work, *The Modern Corporation & Private Property*, Adolf A. Berle and Gardiner C. Means referred to the fact that the proxy mechanism, originally designed "as a convenience to the absent shareholder"[15] had become, instead, "one of the principal instruments not by which a stockholder exercises power over the management of the enterprise, but by which his power is separated from him."[16]

The control managers have over the meeting and proxy process has two major components:

---

14   R.S.C. 1970, c. C-32.
15   Adolf A. Berle & Gardiner C. Means, *The Modern Corporation and Private Property* (London: Transaction Publishers, 1991) [originally published in 1932 by Harcourt, Brace & World Inc.] at 129.
16   *Ibid.*

- significant power to control the timing of shareholders' meetings; and
- the right to use the resources of the corporation itself when soliciting proxies in support of management.

a)   Timing of Shareholders' Meetings

Canadian corporate statutes typically state that it is the directors of the corporation that must call the annual meeting of shareholders, subject to some general time parameters. For example, section 133(1) of the CBCA provides that each annual meeting is to be called not more than fifteen months following the previous annual meeting. Additionally, directors may call a special meeting of shareholders at any time.[17] Although shareholders under certain circumstances do have the right to requisition the directors to call a shareholders' meeting,[18] there are a few constraints on this power imposed by corporate legislation itself[19] and, more significantly, by judicial interpretation of that legislation.

Two Ontario cases from 1999 and a third from 2006 illustrate the extent to which the directors of a corporation can manage the meeting process in the face of a shareholder-requisitioned meeting. *RioCan Real Estate Investment Trust v. RealFund*[20] involved a trust (RealFund) rather than a corporation. However, the declaration of trust contained provisions dealing with meeting requisitions by trust unitholders analogous to corporate-law shareholder-meeting requisition requirements, a fact that was expressly acknowledged by the court.[21] Unitholders associated with a second trust (RioCan), which was seeking to acquire or merge with RealFund, requisitioned the trustees of RealFund to call a meeting of unitholders to consider RioCan's proposed offer.

The requisition was made on 23 March 1999, and the RioCan offer was set to expire on 21 May 1999. The RealFund trustees responded to the requisition by calling for a meeting to be held on 29 June 1999, that is, after the offer to be considered at the meeting would already have expired. RioCan, accordingly, applied to the court arguing, as Blair J. put it, that "although the Declaration of Trust is silent as to the timing of a special meeting held in accordance with [a unitholder] requisition, there is inherent in the Unitholders' right ... a right to have the meeting

---

17   See, for example, CBCA, s. 133(2).

18   See, for example, *ibid.*, s. 143(1), which provides that "the holders of not less than five per cent of the issued shares of a corporation that carry the right to vote at a meeting sought to be held may requisition the directors to call a meeting of shareholders for the purposes stated in the requisition."

19   See, for example, *ibid.*, s. 143(3).

20   [1999] O.J. No. 1349 (S.C.J.).

21   *Ibid.* at para. 15.

held within a certain outside date which does not render the calling of the meeting useless."[22] Blair J. found that the trustees were, in fact, under an obligation to call the meeting for a date prior to the expiry of the offer proposed for consideration at the meeting.

Within a few months of the *RealFund* decision, Blair J. ruled on a shareholders' meeting requisition in *Airline Industry Revitalization Co. v. Air Canada*.[23] The *Air Canada* case arose during an especially difficult time for the Canadian airline industry. Canadian Airlines, at that time Canada's second national airline, was in the midst of a financial restructuring. Onex Corporation had proposed to acquire Canadian Airlines and to merge it with Air Canada. A conventional "hostile" takeover bid for Air Canada was not possible, however, because a federal statute—the *Air Canada Public Participation Act*[24]—made it unlawful for any single shareholder of Air Canada to hold more than 10 percent of its voting shares. Accordingly, Onex proposed to have a meeting of Air Canada shareholders called, with a view to passing a resolution to amend Air Canada's articles in a way that would make it possible for a bid to be launched pending amendment by Parliament of the restrictive provisions of the *Air Canada Public Participation Act*.[25]

On 31 August 1999, the Air Canada board announced that it would hold a special meeting to consider various proposals, including the Onex proposal, on 7 January 2000. Later on the same day as the August announcement, the Onex acquisition entity, with the co-operation of other shareholders who, in the aggregate, held more than 5 percent of Air Canada's shares, requisitioned the directors of Air Canada to call a special meeting of shareholders much earlier: between 4 November 1999 and 8 November 1999. These earlier dates were significant for two reasons. First, the Onex offer was set to expire on November 9th. Thus, unless the offer were extended, by 7 January 2000 there would be no Onex proposal for Air Canada shareholders to consider. Second, a special order that had been issued by the federal cabinet under the *Canada Transportation Act* was set to expire on 10 November 1999. That order

---

22 *Ibid.* at para. 6.
23 (1999), 45 O.R. (3d) 370 (S.C.J.).
24 R.S.C. 1985, c. 35 (4th Supp.).
25 The details of the proposed amendment to Air Canada's articles are not relevant to this discussion. However, briefly put, the proposal involved creating a new class of Class B Air Canada shares with restricted voting rights (such that a single shareholder would be permitted to hold more than 10 percent of the class). Any common shares tendered to the Onex bid would be converted into such Class B shares. If and when Parliament removed the 10 percent voting restriction, these Class B shares would then be converted back into common shares.

made it possible to negotiate a possible merger of Canada's two major airlines without a merger review by the Competition Bureau of Canada.

Accordingly, the shareholders applied to the court for an order compelling the directors of Air Canada to comply with their meeting requisition and so hold the shareholders' meeting at an earlier date than the directors themselves had proposed.

Justice Blair held that, as the directors of Air Canada had not called the meeting as properly requisitioned by the shareholders, the shareholders themselves were permitted to call a meeting pursuant to section 143(4) of the CBCA. Blair J. explicitly rejected the directors' argument that the shareholders' application must fail, based on the provision in section 143(3)(a) stating that directors are not obliged to call a meeting in response to a shareholder requisition where the directors have already set a record date for a meeting. The court's reasoning was that in order to rely on the section 143(3)(a) exemption, the meeting called by the directors must be a meeting that will deal with the same business as that proposed by the shareholders' requisition. Blair J. was not satisfied, based on the material before the court, that the proposed January 7th meeting would, in fact, involve consideration of the business referred to in the shareholder meeting requisition.

In a more provocative interpretation of section 143, Blair J. went on to conclude that even if the directors had validly relied on the section 143(3)(a) exemption in refusing to call the shareholders' meeting within the time frame requested, it would still be open to the requisitioning shareholders to call a meeting of their own. Blair J. reached this conclusion by noting that section 143(4) of the CBCA simply stated that if the directors, within twenty-one days of receiving the requisition, had not called a meeting, any shareholder who had signed the requisition was permitted to call a meeting. The provision did *not* say that this right was triggered only in those cases where the directors' refusal was improper. (Blair J. noted that in the Ontario *Business Corporations Act* ("OBCA") provision equivalent to section 143(4),[26] there was express language indicating that the shareholders' rights were "subject to subsection (3)." In his view, this meant that shareholders of OBCA corporations could only call a meeting if the directors had *improperly* refused to call a meeting, whereas no such limitation applied under the CBCA.)

In *Paulson & Co. v. Algoma Steel Inc.*,[27] the largest single shareholder of a publicly traded corporation (Algoma) requisitioned the directors

---

26   See *Business Corporations Act* (Ontario), R.S.O. 1990, c. B.16, s. 105(4) [OBCA].
27   [2006] O.J. No. 36 (S.C.J.).

of the corporation (pursuant to section 105 of the OBCA)[28] to call a special meeting of shareholders to consider various resolutions, including resolutions to remove five of Algoma's directors and to consider a capital reorganization that would involve a substantial cash distribution to shareholders. The requisition was delivered to the directors on 1 November 2005, and the meeting was requested to be held before 31 December 2005. The directors of Algoma responded to the requisition by issuing a press release on November 21st announcing that a shareholders' meeting had been scheduled for 22 March 2006. The requisitioning shareholder applied to the court for a declaration that the directors of Algoma had not complied with section 105 (thereby entitling the shareholder to call an (earlier) meeting of its own) or, alternatively, that the date chosen by the directors was unreasonable and so should be changed to an earlier date by the court.

Justice Cumming dismissed the application, ruling that the directors' November 21st announcement (an announcement made within twenty-one days of the shareholder requisition) satisfied the statutory requirement that the directors "call a meeting" within twenty-one days after receiving the requisition. In other words to "*call* a meeting" did not require the directors actually to have *delivered notice* of such a meeting. Rather, Cumming J. held: "[T]o 'call a meeting' as stipulated by s. 105(3), means establishing by resolution and announcing publicly the date on which the requisitioned meeting is to be held."[29] Cumming J. went on to find that the scheduling of such a meeting "is left to the business judgment of the directors"[30] and noted that the court must defer to the directors' judgment as long as their decisions fall "within a range of reasonableness."[31]

The ability to control the timing of a shareholders' meeting can also prevent a surprise proxy attack. In *Ewart v. Higson-Smith*,[32] dissident shareholders, taking advantage of exemptions from the proxy solicitation rules available where the proxies of no more than fifteen shareholders are solicited,[33] quietly garnered support for a rival slate of directors to replace management nominees at the annual sharehold-

---

28   OBCA, s. 105 is substantially similar to s. 143 of the CBCA.

29   Above note 27 at para. 35. To like effect is *1184760 Alberta Ltd. v. Falconbridge Ltd.*, 2006 CanLII 23948 (Ont. S.C.J.).

30   *Ibid.* at para. 42.

31   *Ibid.* at para. 43, citing *Kerr v. Danier Leather Inc.*, [2005] O.J. No. 5388 at para. 157 (C.A.), in turn quoting with approval *Maple Leaf Foods Inc. v. Schneider Corp.* (1998), 42 O.R. (3d) 177 at paras. 64–67 (C.A.).

32   (2009), 61 B.L.R. (4th) 228 (Ont. S.C.J.).

33   OBCA, s. 112(1.1).

ers' meeting. The dissident proxies were delivered shortly before the deadline for the deposit of proxies. No such proxy battle had been anticipated by the corporation's management (or, presumably, by most other shareholders.) Thus, until the dissident proxies were delivered, it was widely expected that the annual meeting would be the usual— rather uneventful—occasion. Accordingly, as is generally the case for run-of-the mill annual meetings, a relatively small percentage of the corporation's other shareholders had delivered proxies. When the corporation's managers realized that the management slate of directors would be contested, the corporation promptly announced an adjournment of the meeting to provide all shareholders with additional time to deposit proxies of their own, now with full knowledge that the directors' election was to be hotly contested. The dissidents protested this managerial tactic, arguing that such a tactic defeated their reasonable expectation that the shareholders' meeting would be convened as scheduled and that the election of directors would take place at that time. Cumming J. dismissed the dissidents' application, holding that "the special circumstances in the instant situation warranted the unusual step of exercising judgment such as adjourn the shareholders' meeting for a brief period of time."[34]

It would be misleading, however, to suggest that managers invariably enjoy the upper hand in the conduct of contentious meetings. One tactic that dissenting shareholders have occasionally used with some success is to take advantage of meeting quorum requirements to prevent the holding of a shareholders' meeting through the simple expedient of refusing to attend. Canadian corporate statutes typically provide that, in the absence of any provision in a corporation's by-laws to the contrary, the necessary quorum for a valid meeting of shareholders is a majority of shareholders present in person or by proxy.[35] Of course corporations can (and frequently do) choose to set their own quorum requirements. It is not unusual, for example, for public corporations to set lower quorum requirements—such as two or more shareholders holding 25 percent or more of the corporation's voting shares. The advantage of less stringent quorum requirements is that the validity of a shareholders' meeting is less likely to be placed in jeopardy if a majority of the corporation's shareholders, whether through inattention, lack of interest, or otherwise, choose neither to attend nor to submit a valid proxy.

---

34   Above note 32 at para. 18.
35   See, for example, CBCA, s. 139(1).

A recent Ontario Superior Court decision illustrates how the quorum requirement can become a factor in a proxy contest. *Wells v. Melnyk*[36] involved a proxy contest between management of Biovail Corporation[37] and a major shareholder. Under Biovail's by-laws, a quorum for a meeting of shareholders was 51 percent of the corporation's outstanding shares represented in person or by proxy. Just before the date of the meeting, the major shareholder revoked the proxies for the shares held or controlled by him. The effect of this revocation was that the number of shares represented in person or by proxy at the meeting was less than 51 percent. In an effort to hold a valid meeting, despite this proxy revocation, the directors of the corporation, on the very morning of the scheduled shareholders' meeting, purported to amend the corporation's by-laws to reduce the quorum requirement. Under applicable corporate law, directors are permitted to amend the corporation's by-laws, with immediate effect, provided the amendment is submitted to the shareholders at the next shareholders' meeting for confirmation.[38] The directors could not validly place the proposed by-law amendment before the shareholders' meeting to be held later that day because such a proposal would require adequate notice. At the meeting, management's slate of directors was elected; however, the Ontario Superior Court subsequently held that the shareholder's revocation of his proxies was valid, the necessary quorum was not obtained, and so the election of the directors that had taken place at the meeting was invalid. The court ordered that the meeting be reconvened at a later date.[39]

In sum, although the power of the directors to determine the timing of shareholders' meetings is not absolute, it is, nevertheless, considerable. But of even greater moment is the advantage managers enjoy

---

36   (2008), 92 O.R. (3d) 121.

37   In 2010, Biovail merged with Valeant Pharmaceuticals International, Inc., and the merged corporation continues under the Valeant name. See online: www. valeant.com/about/merger.jsp.

38   CBCA, s. 103.

39   For a further example of a tactical attempt to modify by-laws to gain the upper hand in a proxy battle in the Delaware "staggered board" context, see *Airgas, Inc. v. Air Products and Chemicals, Inc.*, 8 A.3d 48 (Del. Ch. 2011). There, a hostile bidder attempted to thwart a target company's staggered board structure by proposing a by-law amendment which, if effective, would have accelerated the timing of the company's 2011 annual meeting, such that it would be held just four months after the 2010 annual meeting. The significance of this accelerated timetable was that it would effectively shorten the term of directors of the company who could not be removed until the company's 2011 annual meeting. Although the Delaware Court of Chancery upheld this by-law amendment in Civil Action No. 5817-CC (Oct. 8, 2010), that decision was reversed on appeal to the Delaware Supreme Court.

over dissidents in being able to have proxy solicitation costs covered by the corporation itself. It is to this advantage that we now briefly turn.

b) Proxy Solicitation Expenses

Soliciting proxies is expensive. In most cases, a person soliciting proxies is required to prepare a detailed information document—a "proxy statement" or a "proxy circular." The contents of this document are prescribed by law. Ensuring full compliance with the legal rules will typically require legal advice, and sound legal advice can be costly. There is also a cost to printing proxy materials, as well as mailing costs. Frequently, proxy solicitation firms are retained to contact shareholders to remind or encourage them to send in their completed proxies and those firms must also be compensated. In the case of a proxy solicitation by the managers of a public company, all of these proxy solicitation expenses are borne by the company itself. But when opponents of a corporation's incumbent managers solicit proxies in an effort either to block a management-sponsored transaction or to propose a rival slate of directors, the costs of this solicitation must be paid by these dissident shareholders out of their own pockets. It is for this reason that staging a proxy contest is rarely a feasible option for small shareholders. However, for well-financed entities seeking effective control over a target corporation, or for large institutional shareholders seeking negotiating leverage in the context of a proposed major corporate transaction, launching a proxy context may well prove to be a strategic move worth considering.

4) Proxy Solicitation Rules and the Proxy Contest

a) Source of Proxy Rules

Proxy solicitation rules skirt the boundaries between corporate and securities laws. On the one hand, as Mark Roe puts it: "[C]orporate voting [is] perhaps the core 'internal affair' of a corporation."[40] On the other hand, shareholder voting rights, and the means by which those rights are exercised, form a critical part of investor rights and so, understandably, have attracted the attention of securities regulators as well.

As a result, proxy rules relating to Canadian public companies may be found both in the corporate statutes under which those companies are incorporated and in provincial securities regulation. In fact, when the Kimber Committee originally proposed proxy rules for public companies with securityholders in Ontario, the committee envisioned that these rules would be added to Ontario's corporation statute; public

---

40   Mark J. Roe, "Delaware's Competition" (2003) 117 Harv. L. Rev. 588 at 598.

corporations incorporated under other statutes, under their proposed model, would then undertake to comply with the Ontario proxy rules, an undertaking to be buttressed by Toronto Stock Exchange rules compelling listed companies to adhere to such rules.[41]

This cumbersome procedure is not in fact the way in which Canadian corporate and securities law proxy rules operate today. Instead, Canadian corporate statutes typically contain their own proxy rules, and Canada's securities regulators have also promulgated a national instrument,[42] National Instrument 51-102, which includes proxy rules applicable to public companies (or "reporting issuers," as such companies are called under provincial securities statutes). As the following paragraphs reveal, there is considerable overlap between the provisions of many Canadian corporate law proxy rules and the proxy rules contained in National Instrument 51-102. For the most part, proxy rules contained in Canadian corporate statutes and similar rules in National Instrument 51-102 duplicate rather than contradict one another. However, Part 9 of National Instrument 51-102 specifically provides that a reporting issuer is exempt from the proxy solicitation rules of National Instrument 51-102 if the issuer "complies with the requirements of the laws relating to the solicitation of proxies under which the reporting issuer is incorporated, organized or continued" provided those requirements "are substantially similar to the requirements of this Part."[43]

The corporate law statutes of most Canadian provinces and territories contain broadly similar (although not identical) proxy provisions.

A majority of Canada's largest publicly traded corporations are incorporated under the CBCA, and the proxy rules are primarily of significance in the case of public corporations. Accordingly, the discussion that follows will focus upon the proxy rules in the CBCA as well as National Instrument 51-102.

---

41   Kimber Report, above note 6 at para. 6.27.
42   National instruments refer to legislative instruments adopted by all Canadian securities regulators, and subsequently promulgated as "rules" in those provinces where provincial securities regulators have been granted rule-making power. The promulgation of such rules is subject to a specific process involving specified notice and comment periods, and culminating in delivery of the proposed rule to the appropriate government minister. (See, for example, *Securities Act* (Ontario), s. 143.2.) Once effective, a rule generally "has the same force and effect as a regulation" (*ibid.*, s. 143(13)). For a more detailed discussion of the rule-making authority of Canadian securities regulators and the effect of rules, see Jeffrey G. MacIntosh & Christopher C. Nicholls, *Securities Law* (Toronto: Irwin Law, 2002) at 80*ff*.
43   NI 51-102, s. 9.5.

b)   Corporations Subject to Proxy Solicitation Rules

Complex proxy solicitation legislation is primarily intended to protect the interests of minority shareholders of corporations with publicly traded securities. First, it is in this context that there is the greatest risk of significant "information asymmetries"; that is, minority sharehold-ers will not have access to the same information as insiders about the corporation, and so will be at a disadvantage when trying to assess the desirability of proposals for corporate mergers, restructurings, or other significant matters for which shareholder approval may be required under corporate legislation. Second, it is in the case of large publicly traded corporations with widely dispersed shareholders that there will most frequently be significant numbers of shareholders who will not be able to attend shareholders' meetings in person, and so must rely on a fair and efficient proxy mechanism to ensure that their voices are heard and their votes counted.

Accordingly, one might well have expected that proxy legislation might apply only to such publicly traded corporations. Certainly, Part 9 of National Instrument 51-102 applies only to "reporting issuers" (sub-ject to the exemption discussed above in the case of issuers complying with substantially similar corporate law proxy rules). Canadian corpor-ate law (as opposed to securities law) proxy rules, however, may in cer-tain cases also extend to many privately held corporations. For example, prior to 2001, the CBCA required the management of all CBCA corpora-tions with fifteen or more shareholders to solicit proxies in connection with shareholders' meetings, whether the corporation's securities were publicly traded or not. That requirement was modified in 2001 such that the only non-distributing corporations to which the rules now apply are those with more than fifty shareholders entitled to vote.[44]

c)   Broad Definition and Consequences of "Soliciting" Proxies

The CBCA and National Instrument 51-102 seek to protect sharehold-ers whenever their proxies are "solicited" by management or others. When proxies are solicited, the soliciting party is to provide a proxy circular—a detailed disclosure document intended to provide share-holders with sufficient information to cast an informed vote on the matter at issue. In the case of a proxy solicitation by management of a corporation—which, it will be recalled, is mandatory in the case of all public corporations and even certain private CBCA corporations—that circular is known as a "management proxy circular."[45] The contents

---

44   CBCA, s. 149(2).
45   See, for example, CBCA, s. 150(1)(a).

of a management proxy circular are prescribed, in the case of a CBCA corporation, in Part 7 of the *Canada Business Corporations Regulations, 2001*,[46] and, more generally for reporting issuers, in Form 51-102F5. Similarly, when someone other than management solicits proxies, a "dissident's proxy circular"[47] (to use the language of the CBCA) must be provided, subject to limited exemptions intended to facilitate appropriate shareholder communication.[48] The *Canada Business Corporation Regulations, 2001* also prescribe the content of such dissident proxy circulars.[49]

To ensure that these protections cannot easily be circumvented, the term *solicit* is broadly defined.[50] The definition includes not only explicit requests for a shareholder to deliver a proxy in favour of the soliciting party's position, but also sweeps in requests *not* to execute a rival's form of proxy, and requests to revoke a proxy previously delivered. In fact, any "communication to a securityholder under circumstances that to a reasonable person will likely result in the giving, withholding or revocation of a proxy" will be considered a solicitation.[51]

This expansive definition of solicitation is of little concern in the case of an ordinary annual meeting of shareholders where management, and only management, is soliciting proxies and where there is no "special business" to be transacted at the meeting. Special business would be any business other than the basic matters that are dealt with at each annual shareholders' meeting: the election of directors, the re-appointment of the corporation's incumbent auditors for the ensuing year, and consideration of the corporation's financial statements and auditor's report.[52]

However, the question of whether a particular communication to shareholders constitutes a "solicitation" (and so triggers the requirement to prepare and deliver a proxy circular) becomes critical when a contentious meeting is in the offing. Thus, for example, in *Brown v. Duby*[53] the members of a shareholders' committee of United Canso Oil & Gas Ltd. opposed to the corporation's management distributed two letters to shareholders of United Canso. The first was sent only to

---

46   S.O.R./2001-512.

47   See, for example, CBCA, s. 150(1)(b).

48   See, for example, *ibid.*, ss. 150(1.1) & (1.2).

49   Above note 46, s. 61.

50   See CBCA, s. 147, definition of "solicit" or "solicitation"; NI 51-102, s. 1.1, definition of "solicit."

51   NI 51-102, s. 1.1, definition of "solicit" at para. (c).

52   See, for example, CBCA, s. 135(5).

53   (1980), 28 O.R. (2d) 745 (H.C.J.).

shareholders resident in the United States; the second was sent to all shareholders. The court held that the second letter was not a solicitation of proxies and provided little detail about the content of that letter.

The decision, accordingly, focused on the first letter. That first letter contained a series of statements strongly critical of management. It indicated that the shareholders' committee did "intend to solicit proxies at the next meeting of shareholders" but asserted that "we are not requesting proxies at this time."[54] Indeed, the letter indicated that the committee would not seek proxies until "we have prepared a definitive proxy statement, which cannot be done for the next shareholders' meeting until the incumbents' materials have been sent out." The letter also included a specific request for shareholders "not to sign any proxy for the [management] slate of directors."[55]

The court held that, despite the assertions to the contrary in the letter, the letter did constitute a solicitation of proxies within the meaning of section 141 [now section 147] of the CBCA because it constituted either a "request not to execute a form of proxy" or a "withholding of proxies" from management or both. Because the letter was found to constitute a proxy solicitation, the committee ought to have provided to the shareholders a dissident proxy circular pursuant to what is now section 150(1)(b) of the CBCA. The committee had included a document that briefly described the committee members, but the court noted that this document did not satisfy the requirements of a dissident's proxy circular. The court also held that, although the letter had been sent only to U.S. shareholders (and evidently in compliance with U.S. law), this was no answer to the complaint that the committee had not complied with the CBCA; as the court said: "The status of a corporation is to be determined by the law of the incorporating jurisdiction."[56] And, later, the court stated: "[T]he provisions of the [CBCA] apply to Canso and its shareholders wherever Canso carries on business, even though they are required to comply with the laws of the host jurisdiction."[57]

The court found that the sending of this letter did indeed constitute a solicitation and that the committee, therefore, was in violation of the CBCA for failing to send to shareholders a proxy circular containing the prescribed information. Nevertheless the court declined to grant an interlocutory injunction to restrain the defendants from soliciting proxies. The court noted that there was an active proxy contest underway and, in that context, "ample time remains within which to make full

---

54 Ibid. at 748.
55 Ibid.
56 Ibid. at 750.
57 Ibid. at 751.

presentation of the relevant information and conflicting contentions of both sides, and the shareholders will have the particulars omitted from the March 7th letter. It seems unlikely to this Court that the shareholders will not be fully exposed to the issues involved."[58] The court was also evidently cognizant of the fact, based on certain U.S. authorities, that the granting of an injunction could well be misconstrued by some shareholders as a finding on the merits that would inappropriately affect the outcome of the proxy contest.

The broad definition of solicitation was highlighted in the provocative 2001 British Columbia Court of Appeal judgment in *Re Pacifica Papers Inc.*[59] The case concerned a plan of arrangement under section 192 of the CBCA (such arrangements were discussed in Chapter 4). Two major shareholders of the company involved, Pacifica Papers Inc., opposed the arrangement. The decision raised a number of issues relating to the question of the requirements to be satisfied in approving a statutory plan of arrangement. However, the feature of the judgment relevant to an analysis of Canadian proxy rules related to the support agreements signed by a number of Pacifica's largest shareholders in advance of the shareholder meeting called to approve the transaction. These support agreements consisted of contractual commitments on the part of these larger shareholders to deliver proxies in favour of approving the plan of arrangement. It was argued by the dissenters that, by seeking these agreements, Pacifica was soliciting proxies within the meaning of section 150(1) of the CBCA. Accordingly, they argued, those agreements were made in violation of the CBCA since the CBCA required a proxy circular to be distributed before proxies may lawfully be solicited. No such circular had been distributed to signatories to these agreements.

The dispute turned upon the interpretation of section 150(1) of the CBCA. That section states that "a person shall not solicit proxies unless [in the case of a solicitation by management, a proxy circular] *is sent to the auditor of the corporation, to each shareholder whose proxy is solicited,* [and] *to each director.*"

The section does not specifically say that this proxy circular must be sent *before* the proxy is solicited or even concurrently with the proxy solicitation. Where the proxy solicitation is undertaken by management, section 150(1)(a) only states that the proxy circular must be sent "either as an appendix to or as a separate document accompanying the notice of the meeting." The dissidents argued, however, that a requirement that

---

58   *Ibid.* at 754.

59   *Re Pacifica Papers Inc. (sub nom. Pacifica Papers Inc. v. Johnstone)* (2001), 92 B.C.L.R. (3d) 158 (S.C.), aff'd (2001), 93 B.C.L.R. (3d) 20 (C.A.).

a circular be sent before, or concurrently with, the solicitation was implicit in the section, since the purpose of the proxy circular requirement was to ensure that shareholders had full information before executing a form of proxy. The corporation's view, on the other hand, was that no such additional constraint ought to be added by the court. Provided that the proxy circular is properly provided in advance of the meeting, it argued, the requirements of section 150(1) have been satisfied.

The trial judge interpreted section 150(1) as imposing a condition precedent to the soliciting of proxies and, accordingly, found on these facts that there had indeed been a contravention of section 150(1).[60] Despite this finding, the trial court approved the arrangement. The trial judge held that the votes of shareholders who were parties to the support agreements were not invalid precisely because the support agreements themselves were unenforceable (having been obtained, in the court's view, in violation of section 150(1)). In other words, since the agreements did not bind the signatories, they were free, as a matter of law, to vote as they wished at the ensuing meeting, and they had (freely, the court assumed) voted to support the arrangement. Though the dissidents argued that signatories to the support agreements may well have believed they were, in fact, legally obliged to honour those agreements, the court stated:

> [T]here is no evidence to that effect, and they were in fact under no legal compulsion to do so. Given that the support agreements, as the subject of an unlawful solicitation, were of no force or effect, I consider that the inference, in the absence of any evidence to the contrary, must be that the proxies were given because the shareholders were content to vote for the Arrangement after the information circular was distributed and they had the opportunity to consider it.[61]

Finding that the shareholders were not, in fact, misled or misinformed about the transaction, the court approved the arrangement, despite the breach of section 150(1).

This decision was affirmed on appeal to the British Columbia Court of Appeal, although the Court of Appeal's reasoning on the effect of section 150(1) differed from that of the trial judge. Acknowledging that it was "unnecessary for the disposition of this appeal to express any firm view on the correctness of the judge's interpretation" of section 150, the Court of Appeal went on say that "the learned judge's interpretation, and the position contended for by the appellants, appear to import into

---

60   *Ibid.* at para. 95 (S.C.).
61   *Ibid.* at para. 99.

section 150 a restriction on proxy solicitation that the language, on a plain reading, does not bear."[62] The Court of Appeal also took issue with the trial judge's conclusion that signatories to the support agreements could not be compelled to vote their shares as they had promised on the basis that these support agreements were illegal. Rather, the Court of Appeal suggested that the support agreements could not be considered binding for a different reason: a shareholder's proxy is *always* revocable[63]—even, evidently, when he or she appears to be subject to a contractual commitment to deliver a proxy in support of a proposed transaction.

The ambiguity in the wording of the CBCA provision is unfortunate. It will be recalled that the broad wording of "solicitation" found in the CBCA ultimately derives from U.S. law. As the Dickerson Committee explained: "Subparagraphs (i) to (iii) of this definition are borrowed from Regulation 14a-1 issued by the Securities and Exchange Commission."[64] The SEC's rules, however, leave no doubt that no solicitation may be made "unless each person solicited is *concurrently furnished or has previously been furnished with*" a proxy statement.[65]

The Kimber Report's discussion of the issue that later came to be raised in *Re Pacifica* is illuminating. The report expressed the view that "Ontario should adopt certain statutory requirements comparable to those in Regulation 14 of the *Securities Exchange Act of 1934*."[66] The committee's recommendation was:

> [I]f management solicits proxies for use at any meeting of shareholders, information be furnished to shareholders prior to any such meeting in a document to be known as an "information circular" which should be provided either as an appendix to, or as a separate document accompanying, the notice of the meeting or, in the case of solicitation of proxies by a person or group of persons other than management, as part of the material by which the solicitation is made.[67]

The Kimber Report thus explicitly recommends that, in the case of a solicitation by dissidents, the information circular must accompany the solicitation, whereas in the case of a solicitation by management,

---

62   *Ibid.* at para. 13 (C.A.).

63   See, for example, CBCA, s. 148(4).

64   Robert W.V. Dickerson, John L. Howard, & Leon Getz, *Proposals for a New Business Corporations Law for Canada*, vol. 2 (Ottawa: Information Canada, 1971) at para. 304 [Dickerson Committee].

65   Rule 14a-3(a) [emphasis added].

66   Kimber Report, above note 6 at 6.20.

67   *Ibid.* at 6.21.

the circular must accompany the notice of meeting, leaving open the possibility that a solicitation by management could perhaps occur before notice of the meeting (and therefore the proxy circular) had been delivered. What the Kimber Report did not seem to anticipate was that the solicitation might take the form not of mere communication with shareholders but of actual negotiation of a contractual *commitment* to deliver a proxy.

Moreover, the Court of Appeal's dictum in *Pacifica* reveals an anomaly in the current wording of the legislation. Clearly, shareholders are entitled to enter into binding contracts in which they agree as to how their shares will be voted. Such agreements were permitted at common law, and section 145.1 of the CBCA now expressly sanctions them. Thus, the parties in *Pacifica* might have entered into a shareholders' agreement with, among others, the purported party to the proposed merger to be completed by way of arrangement. That agreement could have provided that the shareholders would vote their shares in favour of the arrangement at the meeting called to consider it. It appears that such an agreement would be valid and enforceable, at least in cases where the merger partner owned at least one share of the corporation.[68] Yet, if, based on the language of the *Pacifica* decision, an agreement provides for votes to be cast by proxy in support of the arrangement, this agreement appears to become a proxy solicitation that will trigger the proxy solicitation rules and thereby potentially become unenforceable for one of two reasons: (a) because a proxy circular was not provided in advance (*per* the trial court's reasoning); or (b) because the shareholders are always entitled to revoke their proxies (*per* the Court of Appeal's reasoning).

Could such a result have been intended by Parliament? If shareholders can lawfully agree in advance as to how they will vote their shares in person at a meeting, they ought also to be permitted to agree as to how they will vote their shares by proxy at the same meeting. Why should such radically different results flow from the shareholders' decision not to attend the meeting in person? One possible explanation is that the proxy solicitation rules did not anticipate the private negotiation of a contract between shareholders in advance of the meeting. Alternatively, it may perhaps have been intended that only in agreements to which shareholders—and only shareholders—were parties could shareholders lawfully fetter their voting rights (unless 100 percent of the shareholders were parties to such an agreement in which

---

68   CBCA, s. 145.1 refers to "a written agreement *between two or more shareholders*." Compare s. 146, which also includes reference to "an otherwise lawful written agreement . . . among all the shareholders *and one or more persons who are not shareholders*" [emphasis added].

case non-shareholders may also be parties without "tainting" the legal effectiveness of the shareholders' voting commitment).[69]

One notes, in this regard, that a "pooling agreement" for purposes of CBCA section 145.1 may only be entered into between shareholders. Thus, on its terms, this provision would not apply in cases where managers of a corporation attempted to enter into contracts with shareholders. If managers were allowed to enter into such agreements, they might effectively avoid what would otherwise be their obligation to deliver a proxy circular before those shareholders had committed themselves to vote in support of a management-sponsored initiative. It is not entirely clear, however, how the proxy rules could be expected to affect the enforceability of a voting agreement in such cases. (Under a voting agreement, shareholders would agree to attend the meeting in person and vote in a particular way, rather than merely promise to deliver proxies directing their representatives to vote their shares for them.) Such a voting agreement, in other words, would not require the signing shareholders to deliver proxies at all. It seems to strain the definition of solicit in section 147 to suggest that the negotiation of a voting agreement could constitute a "communication to a shareholder under circumstances reasonably calculated to result in the . . . withholding . . . of a proxy [for example, opposed to the vote in question]."

Moreover, in many cases, it would not necessarily be the management of a corporation that would seek to obtain support agreements from major shareholders. Rather, it would frequently be an outside third party—such as a party seeking to merge with or acquire the corporation—that would seek such agreements. Negotiation of support agreements of this sort might well be permitted by section 150(1.1) of the CBCA, which expressly allows the solicitation of proxies, without imposing a requirement to produce a proxy circular, where proxies are solicited "other than by or on behalf of the management of the corporation" and where the number of shareholders solicited is not more than fifteen. At the time of the *Pacifica* case, however, the CBCA did not include the section 150(1.1) exemption. Moreover, even had this exemption been in place at the time, it appears that the "solicitation" in the *Pacifica* case also involved management of the corporation.

Even assuming that the negotiation of support agreements of the sort at issue in *Pacifica* ought to trigger the proxy circular requirement, the case revealed a further ambiguity in the CBCA relating to the tim-

---

69   CBCA, s. 146(1) provides that a valid unanimous shareholder agreement may be entered into "among all the shareholders *and one or more persons who are not shareholders*" [emphasis added].

ing of the circular delivery obligation. The CBCA does not explicitly say that a dissident proxy circular must be delivered at the same time as, or before, proxies are solicited. By way of contrast, it is worth noting that Canadian provincial securities rules do expressly provide that a dissident's proxy circular must be delivered before, or at the same time as, the solicitation.[70] U.S. federal securities law proxy rules also require that no solicitation may occur unless "each person solicited is concurrently furnished or has previously been furnished with . . . a publicly-filed preliminary or definitive written proxy statement . . . "[71] In a 1995 Industry Canada discussion paper,[72] the writer interpreted the CBCA provision as imposing a requirement on those soliciting proxies to deliver a proxy circular "concurrently" with the solicitation. An express statement to this effect appears in the discussion paper;[73] moreover, one of the proposals in the paper was for the institution of a "preliminary circular" mechanism, similar to the preliminary prospectus device used in connection with the public offering of securities.[74] Such a preliminary circular, it was envisioned, could permit solicitation to begin, provided no form of proxy was actually delivered until the final circular was available. Needless to say, such a mechanism would only be necessary if it is assumed that proxies could not *otherwise* be lawfully solicited before a circular had been provided.

Regardless of any statutory drafting ambiguities, however, it certainly would be prudent practice to ensure that shareholders have a proxy circular when their proxies are solicited.

A recent decision of the Ontario Securities Commission considered the issue of whether solicitation of support agreements in somewhat unusual circumstances constituted a solicitation of proxies. In *Re Ven-Growth Funds*,[75] a hostile bidder (GrowthWorks) seeking to acquire control of a number of labour-sponsored venture capital mutual funds (the VenGrowth Funds), solicited shareholders of the VenGrowth Funds to enter into support agreements. The support agreements were structured in a novel way, evidently intended to overcome some structural challenges facing a bidder in these circumstances, owing, among other

---

70   See, for example, NI 51-102, s. 9.1(2)(b).

71   *Securities Exchange Act of 1934*, Rule 14a-3(a).

72   *Canada Business Corporations Act* Discussion Paper: Shareholder Communications and Proxy Solicitation Rules (August 1995), online: http://dsp-psd.pwgsc.gc.ca/Collection/C2-280-2-1995E.pdf.

73   *Ibid.* at 35.

74   Such a preliminary/final proxy circular device is found in U.S. federal securities law proxy rules.

75   Above note 4.

things, to the facts that the conventional method for merging Canadian
mutual funds differed from the approach used in a conventional corporate acquisition,[76] and that the shares of the VenGrowth Funds were
not listed on any stock exchange and were not directly transferable.[77]
The support agreements, among other things, purported to grant to
GrowthWorks an irrevocable power of attorney "(i) to requisition meetings of the VenGrowth shareholders, (ii) to vote the VenGrowth shares
that are subject to the Support Agreements . . . in favour of the Growth-
Works Proposal, (iii) to vote the [shares] to elect certain directors of
the VenGrowth Funds and to make certain amendments to the articles
of the VenGrowth Funds, and (iv) to vote against any transaction competing with the GrowthWorks Proposal."[78] The agreements did contain
a provision allowing shareholders to accept a "superior proposal," if
one were to emerge. However, the determination of whether a competing offer did, in fact, constitute such a "superior proposal" was to
be made not by the shareholders themselves but by three individuals
designated by GrowthWorks.

Although GrowthWorks had sent an information circular to the
target shareholders providing "very substantial information,"[79] that
circular evidently did not comply with the dissident proxy circular
requirements. Thus, if these support agreements constituted proxies, GrowthWorks would have been soliciting proxies contrary to the
requirements of securities laws. The Panel concluded that, although
GrowthWorks' solicitation of the support agreements did constitute a
"solicitation" within the meaning of section 84 of the Ontario *Securities
Act*, it nonetheless did *not* constitute a solicitation of *proxies* because, in
the view of the Panel, the support agreements were not proxies.[80] They
were merely documents providing for a power of attorney to execute
proxies. The solicitation of the agreements, therefore, was found not
to violate Ontario securities law. With respect, this conclusion, apparently based on a well-known ambiguity[81] in the drafting of the proxy
solicitation rules common to the *Securities Act* and corporate legislation such as the *Canada Business Corporations Act* is, nevertheless, difficult to reconcile with existing Canadian jurisprudence interpreting the

---

76 See, for example, *ibid.* at para. 17.

77 *Ibid.* at paras. 10, 11, and 39.

78 *Ibid.* at para. 1.

79 *Ibid.* at para. 2.

80 *Ibid.* at para. 52.

81 The ambiguity derives from the fact that the definition of "solicit" in s. 84 does
    not refer to solicitation *of proxies*, though the obligation to deliver an informa-
    tion circular is triggered where a person or company "[solicits proxies]."

proxy solicitation rules. If, as the OSC suggested, a "solicitation" only engaged the information circular rules where a proxy was solicited, it is not entirely clear what purpose the language found in paragraph (b) of the definition of "solicit" and the reference to "or other communication" in paragraph (c) of section 84 of the *Securities Act* fulfills. One recalls, for example, that in *Brown v. Duby*,[82] the court, interpreting substantially similar language in the CBCA, found that dissidents were in violation of their statutory obligation to deliver an information circular under circumstances where there was a "solicitation" (as broadly defined) despite the fact that in no sense was a "proxy" yet being solicited.

The fact that the support agreements, by their terms, were irrevocable was problematic, however. The inability of a shareholder to revoke the power of attorney ran contrary to the protections provided to shareholders of reporting issuers subject to a takeover bid, protections that included the right to withdraw securities tendered to a bid before the securities are taken up, or the right to revoke a proxy prior to a meeting called to approve a transaction. The Panel thus found that the terms of the support agreements "[undermined] one of the animating principles of the Act."[83] Despite this finding, the Panel concluded that the solicitation of the support agreements was *not* abusive of the shareholders or of the capital markets generally,[84] a conclusion that was influenced by the degree of disclosure that GrowthWorks had provided to the solicited shareholders and, perhaps, conditioned by the acknowledgement of GrowthWorks that it would, in fact, undertake a proper solicitation of proxies—complying with all requisite disclosure rules—prior to any meeting convened to consider the GrowthWorks acquisition proposal. One infers that the Panel was not prepared to invalidate the solicitation process in its entirety because it regarded the use of the support agreements to facilitate the requisitioning of VenGrowth shareholders' meeting as appropriate.[85] Thus, without purporting to "blue pencil" the inappropriate aspects of the support agreements—a remedy surely not available to an administrative tribunal—the Panel effectively preserved the acceptable provisions of the support agreements, while clearly signalling to future bidders its concern with those aspects of the agreements that could undermine key shareholder protections.

---

82 Above note 53.
83 *VenGrowth*, above note 4 at para. 59.
84 *Ibid.* at para. 62.
85 *Ibid.* at para. 68.

d) Defective Proxies or Proxy Circulars

Occasionally, proxy circulars or executed forms of proxy will be deficient in some way. Such alleged deficiencies may be attacked before the relevant shareholders' meeting takes place. *Brown v. Duby*, discussed earlier in this chapter, is an example of just such a case. But it will sometimes happen that the alleged deficiencies will not be identified until immediately before a contested shareholders' meeting is held, or indeed until after the meeting has actually begun. When that occurs, the person chairing a contested shareholders' meeting will often be called upon to rule on the validity of the proxies and, accordingly, on the outcome of the vote in respect of which proxies have been delivered. This can place the chair in a difficult position, especially if he or she is also a director seeking election or re-election at the meeting. In *Blair v. Consolidated Enfield Corp.*,[86] the chairman of a shareholders' meeting ruled, based on legal advice received from the corporation's solicitors, that proxy votes cast for the election of a particular individual to the board of directors were invalid. Although the court subsequently held that the chairman's decision was incorrect, the chairman ultimately succeeded in his application for indemnification for costs arising from the original action challenging his ruling. The Supreme Court of Canada found that, in relying on the legal advice he received, the Chairman had fulfilled his fiduciary duty notwithstanding that his decision had proved to be incorrect.

In *Kluwak v. Pasternak*,[87] the chair of a shareholders' meeting ruled, based on submissions made at the meeting by a lawyer representing the corporation's chief executive officer, that a dissident proxy circular contained material misrepresentations. Accordingly, he disallowed the dissident proxy votes, and so declared the management slate of directors elected. Mesbur J., of the Ontario Superior Court, found that the proxy circular was, indeed, misleading. However, the court did not agree with the decision of the chair to invalidate the dissident proxy votes. Rather, the court held that the directors' election was invalidated, and a new shareholders' meeting was to be convened at a date in the future that would allow time for new, corrected, proxy circulars to be distributed to shareholders so that they would be able to cast fully informed votes.

To similar effect was the decision of the British Columbia Supreme Court in *AnorMed Inc. v. Baker Bros. Investments LP.*[88] *AnorMed* involved a dispute that arose following a decision by the majority of the direc-

---

86   [1995] 4 S.C.R. 5.
87   2006 CanLII 41292 (Ont. S.C.J.).
88   2006 BCSC 755.

tors of a corporation to pursue a bought deal financing rather than a rights offering. A member of the board who favoured the rights offering launched a proxy battle with a view to replacing the other members of the board. The dissident proxy circular contained statements that might have led the reader to conclude that the directors, in electing to pursue the bought deal, had not followed the recommendation of its independent financial advisor when, in fact, they had. The court did not accept the argument of the dissidents that, since the financial advisor's full report was available to shareholders from other sources, no correction of the dissident circular was necessary. The court disagreed, stating that "both circulars had to be accurate and not contain untrue statements of a material fact. There is nothing in [section 154 of the CBCA] which would allow me to consider that a lesser degree of truth can be set out in one circular because what is set out in another circular is accurate."[89] Accordingly, the court ordered that the dissident circular be corrected in order to permit shareholders to make an informed decision as to how to cast their votes.

C. PROPOSED SHAREHOLDER ACCESS RULES

Although not directly relevant to the use of proxy contests as a means for gaining corporate control,[90] recent proposals in Canada and the United States for enhanced shareholder proxy access deserve at least brief mention here.

In the wake of the 2007–09 financial crisis, the United States Congress enacted sweeping reforms of U.S. capital market legislation in the *Dodd-Frank Wall Street Reform and Consumer Protection Act*.[91] Section 971 of the *Dodd-Frank Act* included provisions dealing with "proxy access." Specifically, section 971 empowered the U.S. Securities and Exchange Commission (SEC) to "issue rules permitting the use by a shareholder of proxy solicitation materials supplied by an issuer of securities for the purpose of nominating individuals to membership on the board of directors of the issuer . . . ."

The significance of "proxy access" rules is that they are intended to provide shareholders with a right to nominate directors directly—

---

89 *Ibid.* at para. 24.
90 Indeed, the SEC's proposed proxy access rule, discussed below in this chapter, would not be available to any shareholder holding securities with the intent of effecting a change of control of the company. See Rule 14a-11(a)(6), SEC Release No. 33-9136, 34-62766 (10 August, 2010).
91 Pub. L. No. 111-203 [*Dodd-Frank Act*].

without incurring the hurdles and expense of engaging in a proxy contest. Needless to say, expanded proxy access had little to do with the financial crisis; the proxy access provisions of *Dodd-Frank* may be viewed as opportunistic regulatory reform. In fact, the SEC had attempted to introduce proxy access rules several times in the past, beginning in 2003.[92] But there had been nagging concerns, before *Dodd-Frank*, that the regulator may have lacked legislative authority to regulate in this area.[93]

With much fanfare and an unmistakable air of self-congratulation, the SEC adopted its final proxy access rule, Rule 14a-11, on 25 August 2010.[94] The final vote had been close, however, and the dissenting commissioners expressed considerable concern about the new measures.[95]

Alas, the SEC's bold reform suffered a major setback in 2011 when the United States Court of Appeals for the D.C. Circuit ruled that the SEC acted "arbitrarily and capriciously" in promulgating Rule 14a-11 "for having failed once again . . . adequately to assess the economic effects of a new rule" and so vacated the new rule.[96] Criticizing the SEC for, essentially, overemphasizing the presumed benefits of the new rule and downplaying the expected costs—in each case on the basis of slim empirical evidence—the court was unequivocal in its condemnation of the rule.

Of course, it is important to remember that proxy rules have traditionally been a matter of corporate law, and corporate law, in the United States, is legislated at the state level. Accordingly, regardless of whether the SEC has or has not promulgated valid proxy rules, it is certainly possible for the states to introduce such rules into their corporate statutes. Indeed, Delaware, the state in which half of all U.S. publicly traded corporations, including almost two-thirds of all Fortune 500 corporations are incorporated,[97] amended its corporate statute in 2009 to permit corporations to include in their by-laws provisions

---

92   See SEC Release No. 34-48626, online: www.sec.gov/rules/proposed/34-48626. htm.

93   See, for example, Cravath, Swaine & Moore LLP, "SEC Adopts Proxy Access" in *42nd Annual Institute on Securities Regulation*, Vol. 1 883 (New York: Practising Law Institute, 2010).

94   See, for example, Elisse B. Walter, "Opening Statement at the SEC Open Meeting" (25 August 2010), online: www.sec.gov/news/speech/2010/spch082510ebw. htm.

95   See, for example, Troy A. Paredes, "Statement at Open Meeting to Adopt the Final Rule Regarding Facilitating Shareholder Director Nominations," online: www.sec.gov/news/speech/2010/spch082510tap.htm.

96   *Business Roundtable et al. v. Securities and Exchange Commission*, No. 10-1305 (U.S.C.A. D.C. Cir. July 22, 2011).

97   Delaware, Division of Corporations, online: http://corp.delaware.gov.

requiring shareholder nominees to be included in a corporation's proxy solicitation materials.[98] Also, although the SEC's proposed Rule 14a-11 did not survive judicial scrutiny, a concurrent rule change was made to amend Rule 14a-8 to permit shareholders to include in shareholder proposals matters relating to amendments to a corporation's governing documents regarding director nomination procedures or shareholder nominations.[99]

In the meantime, Canadian securities regulators have also been reviewing various issues relating to "shareholder democracy" including matters relating to the proxy process. In January 2011, the Ontario Securities Commission published for comment OSC Staff Notice 54-701.[100] At the date of writing, the comment period for this notice had recently concluded.

D. CONCLUSION

Winning a proxy battle results in no change in the ownership of the shares of a corporation. Yet it may well result in a crucial change of managerial control. To the extent that competing shareholders seek the levers of managerial power, a proxy contest is an important weapon in the M & A arsenal, whether launched on its own, or, as has been common in the U.S., in conjunction with a tender offer (or takeover bid).

---

98   See Delaware General Corporation Law, §112.
99   SEC Release No. 33-9136 at 225*ff.*, online: www.sec.gov/rules/
final/2010/33-9136.pdf.
100 (2011), 34 OSCB 404.

CHAPTER 10

CONCLUSION

One commentator has described mergers and acquisitions as "undoubtedly among the most significant macroeconomic phenomena of the industrialized West during the last twenty years."[1] Those words were written more than ten years ago, before the burst of merger and acquisition activity in Canada and around the world in 2007, and the subsequent international financial system crisis.

The story, nevertheless, has become a familiar one. Businesses have responded to the pressures of competition and globalization. The power of institutional and activist shareholders has grown. And as conditions have coalesced once again to encourage and facilitate business consolidations of ever-increasing size, we have seen the re-emergence of a volatile but growing M & A market.

M & A transforms businesses, impacts the capital markets, tests well-worn legal doctrines and regulatory practices, and creates challenging opportunities for lawyers, regulators, and business leaders. In smaller countries such as Canada, where foreign ownership of leading firms is a perennial political concern, M & A activity raises broader economic and political questions as well.

Investment bankers, fund managers, and other financial players sometimes consider law a tiresome obstacle, and lawyers a form of deadweight loss. (I still recall from a Capital Markets class at the

---

1   Yedidia Z. Stern, "A General Model for Corporate Acquisition Law" (2001) J. Corp. L. 675 at 676.

Harvard Business School many years ago, the professor's frequent references to "the lawyers and other bloodsuckers" who, he maintained, burdened businesses with excessive, if not entirely needless, costs.)

But the law is not simply a necessary evil plaguing creative business leaders. Law is best understood not as the thorn in the lion's paw, but as the sand in the oyster's shell. The form and structure of our laws help to frame and focus business decision-making. A careful weighing of the alternative legal forms of structuring an M & A transaction can generate important insights about the business aspects of a transaction. The law governing hostile takeover bids, going-private transactions, and proxy contests provides the structure within which the market for corporate control can operate, and through which the interests of investors and managers can be balanced and defined.

Both conceptually and practically, the legal rules and principles relating to M & A transactions are complex but important. In many ways, they represent an amalgam of the laws of modern business enterprise, and so merit careful and continuing study.

TABLE OF CASES

INDEX

ABOUT THE AUTHOR

Christopher C. Nicholls holds the Stephen Dattels Chair in Corporate Finance Law at the University of Western Ontario. He is a graduate of the University of Ottawa, Osgoode Hall Law School, and Harvard University.

Before coming to Western in 2006, Professor Nicholls was a member of the Dalhousie University Faculty of Law (now the Schulich School of Law at Dalhousie University) where he was the inaugural holder of the Purdy Crawford Chair in Business Law. Prior to joining the faculty of Dalhousie, he practised corporate and securities law in Toronto and in Hamilton, Bermuda.

Professor Nicholls has been a visiting (adjunct) professor at the University of Toronto Faculty of Law, a visiting professor at Queen's University Faculty of Law, a visiting scholar at the Centre for Corporate and Commercial Law at the University of Cambridge, the Falconbridge Professor of Commercial Law at Osgoode Hall Law School, and a Herbert Smith Visitor to the University of Cambridge Faculty of Law.

He has served as a member (Commissioner) of the Nova Scotia Securities Commission, as associate editor and corporate finance law specialist editor for the *Canadian Business Law Journal*, and as a member of the editorial board of the *Canadian Journal of Law and Technology*. He is the author of numerous articles and monographs, as well as four other books including *Securities Law* (with Jeffrey MacIntosh, Irwin Law, 2002).